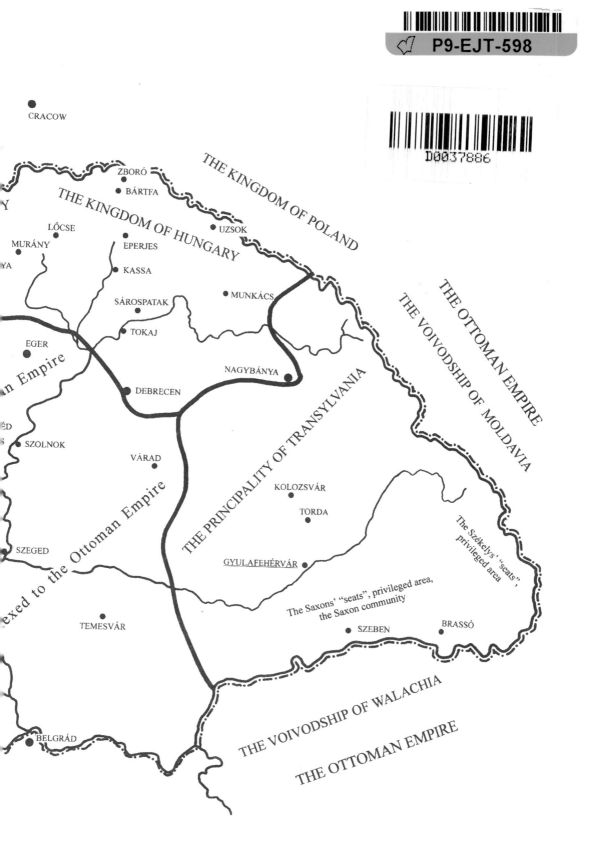

CRACOW

ZBORÓ

BÁRTFA

Y

LŐCSE

THE KINGDOM OF HUNGARY

UZSOK

MURÁNY

EPERJES

YA

KASSA

MUNKÁCS

SÁROSPATAK

TOKAJ

EGER

n Empire

NAGYBÁNYA

DEBRECEN

THE OTTOMAN EMPIRE

THE VOIVODSHIP OF MOLDAVIA

THE PRINCIPALITY OF TRANSYLVANIA

ÉD

S

SZOLNOK

VÁRAD

KOLOZSVÁR

TORDA

exed to the Ottoman Empire

The Székelys' "seats", privileged area

SZEGED

GYULAFEHÉRVÁR

TEMESVÁR

The Saxons' "seats", privileged area, the Saxon community

SZEBEN

BRASSÓ

BELGRÁD

THE VOIVODSHIP OF WALACHIA

THE OTTOMAN EMPIRE

Europica varietas

———

Hungarica varietas

1526–1762

*This book has been published
with support
from the Hungarian Ministry
of Cultural Heritage
and the Frankfurt '99 Kht.
(Budapest)*

ÁGNES R. VÁRKONYI

Europica varietas
Hungarica varietas

1526–1762

SELECTED STUDIES

AKADÉMIAI KIADÓ, BUDAPEST

This book contains selected papers translated from the original Hungarian
Europica varietas – Hungarica varietas, Akadémiai Kiadó, Budapest 1994, and other studies

Translated by

Éva Pálmai
Kálmán Ruttkay
Sándor Simon

Cover. A painting in oil on canvas by an unknown artist from Hungary, 260 × 180 cm in size, in the Roman Catholic parish church of Árpás, a small village in the county of Győr, in North-West Hungary. Standing with his back to the viewer, the Pope receives the Emperor Leopold I clad in armour escorted by temporal and clerical high dignitaries of the Kingdom of Hungary, the Palatine, the Lord Chief Justice, the Ban of Croatia, the Archbishop of Esztergom, other ecclesiastics and captains. In the upper part of the picture the Blessed Virgin Mary appears, in a vision, as it were, to the Head of the Church, destined for rallying the forces of Christendom to fight against the Ottoman power possessing two thirds of Hungary. Above the head of the Madonna two angels hold the Hungarian crown, symbol of the Hungarian state, offered her by István the Saint, King of Hungary and protected by her cloak there is a map of the country with the Hungarian coat of arms. The painter (perhaps two painters?) followed the traditions of Bolognian academicism on the one hand, and a more modern trend on the other, as the recognizable portraits and the map show. The topic can be linked in particular to the anti-Turkish war of 1663–1664, and it may indicate the task of 17th-century Hungarian politics, the idea of restoring the unity of the country and an all-European collaboration. In 1671 several of the temporal dignitaries seen in the painting were charged by the Emperor with conspiracy, and executed. The picture was hidden behind the altarpiece of the parish church of Árpás, to be recovered only as late as the middle of the 20th century.

ISBN 963 05 7627 9

Published by
Akadémiai Kiadó
P.O. Box 245
H-1519 Budapest
http://www.akkrt.hu

Table of Contents

ഇ ൈ

PREFACE / 7

CHARLES V IN HUNGARY / 9

RELIGIOUS TOLERANCE IN THE PRINCIPALITY
OF TRANSYLVANIA / 43

CARDINAL PÉTER PÁZMÁNY THE DIPLOMAT / 55

PRINCE BETHLEN – WESTPHALIA – UTRECHT / 89

ZRÍNYI, "THE HERO UPON WHOM PROVIDENCE HATH
DEVOLVED THE FATE OF EUROPE" / 103

THE RECONQUEST OF BUDA AND PUBLIC OPINION / 149

ALTERNATIVES IN HUNGARY RECAPTURED
FROM THE TURKS / 165

HUNGARIAN INDEPENDENCE AND THE EUROPEAN
BALANCE OF POWER / 175

"AD PACEM UNIVERSALEM". THE INTERNATIONAL ANTECEDENTS
OF THE PEACE OF SZATMÁR / 187

PUBLIC HEALING AND BELIEF IN WITCHCRAFT / 227

THE CHANCES OF CENTRAL EUROPE.
SOME PERTINENT THOUGHTS FROM MÁTYÁS BÉL'S NOTITIA HUNGARIAE NOVAE / 273

AN UNDIVIDED EUROPE? / 285

LIST OF ABBREVIATIONS / 303
BIBLIOGRAPHY / 305
INDEX OF NAMES / 331
INDEX OF PLACE NAMES / 345

5

Preface

Addressing the Imperial Diet of Regensburg in 1541, Ferenc Frangepán, Archbishop of Kalocsa emphasized that if Buda, the capital of the Kingdom of Hungary should be taken by the Turks, this would be a loss to all Christendom. In 1663, Chancellor János Bethlen informed the European public opinion about the political aims of the country organizing a coalition with the League of the Rhine against the Ottoman power, and pointed out that the security of the Principality of Transylvania was closely related to that of all Europe. In 1706 George Stepney, English Ambassador to Vienna declared that the common cause of Europe would suffer a loss, if peace in Hungary could not be secured with international guarantees.

What happened to Hungary for three centuries was the common cause of Europe. The papers collected in Europica Varietas – Hungarica Varietas focus on some of the particularly problematic aspects of a wide range of relevant topics. They are intended to elucidate the coincidence of changes in Europe and in Hungary in the course of the radical transformations taking place in the early modern period. It is examined how, even during the century and a half while the middle part of the country was occupied by a non-European, non-Christian power, the Ottoman Empire, Hungary managed to preserve its statehood coeval with that of Bohemia and Poland and the birth of the community of Europe; how it could be a stabilizing factor in this constantly war-ridden region at a time when the country itself had immense difficulties to face; how and in what universal frame of reference it formulated the terms for its own renewal, i.e. religious toleration, the co-existence of different peoples, social welfare work, a demand for peace with guarantees, all under the conditions of Central European economic and social circumstances and the predominance of the interests of the Habsburg Empire. Further questions discussed are: where did the country take its receptivity from, and how did it appear on the scene offering its experiences at a time when Europe was seeking to establish a balance of power, and what did it receive from the Western world with its well-established or emerging national states, and what did it contribute in its own turn to the preservation of the identity of Europe in a century of crises?

These papers appeared in Hungarian and foreign learned journals, their findings were presented at international conferences and were included in my university lectures and elicited general interest. One reason for publishing them in volume form is that even now, in the last decade of the twentieth century it is invariably valid what Theodore Roosevelt wrote in 1913, one year before the outbreak of World War I: "If the Western world wants to bridge the gulf that separates it from Central and Eastern Europe, it will have to know more of these regions' history, a subject of which the average British and American students is blissfully ignorant."

The bibliographies affixed to the papers have not been updated, except that I have given the publication data of works printed since I first used them in manuscript from. Also, a few titles have been added, indicating essentially new, important contributions to the literature of the topics concerned.

Place names are used in the forms current in the given historical periods, with their modern equivalents included in the Index of Place Names.

July 2000

Ágnes R. Várkonyi

Charles V in Hungary

ᐄ   ᐅ

He had, of course, never been to Hungary. His horse left no hoofprints on Hungarian soil. Even in 1532, he went no farther east than the plains around Wienerneustadt. For all that, he was a living presence in Hungary for a century and a half. People talked about him. Long after his death, they remembered him.

He is the only Habsburg ruler to have had his praises sung by a Hungarian *Meistersinger*. Hungarian deputations had sought him out in Naples, Toledo and Augsburg, to speak of things they dared hardly think of back home. Later, they would cite his name in memoranda, as they implored the courts of Europe to take united action against the Ottoman Turks. He was the example they pointed to as they urged the great powers to rally to the aid of what was left of Hungary, "a country which is more a name than a reality", as Miklós Zrínyi (1620–1664) would ruefully put it. Charles V was the inspiration during the campaign to retake Buda, and he was the only Habsburg to be made the central figure of one of Kelemen Mikes's (1690–1762) poignant anecdotes.

This image of Charles V has totally disappeared from our historical consciousness. Nor can we find any reference to the Hungarian cult of the most powerful sovereign in Christendom in any of the vast international literature dealing with his life.

The evocative portrait of Charles V painted by the historian Gyula Szekfű (1883–1955) at the beginning of the second chapter of his *History of Hungary*, for instance, practically rules out the possibility that there ever could have been some affinity between the emperor and Hungary: "The emperor was a distinguished figure, unapproachable and aloof.... He went about like some Titian painting come to life, the somber splendor of his black horse heightening his aura of distant, superhuman dignity".[1]

"V. Károly Magyarországon". In *Europica varietas – Hungarica varietas*. Akadémiai Kiadó, Budapest, 1994 (Transl. by Éva Pálmai).
[1] Szekfű: 1935a, p. 64.

Reading the works of Miklós Zrínyi, poet, soldier, and Ban of Croatia (1620–1664), however, makes one try to track down Charles's Hungarian policy. For one simply has to find out why, in his *Meditations on the Life of Matthias Corvinus* (1655–1656), Zrínyi draws a parallel between Hungary's great Renaissance king and the first of the country's Habsburg rulers. This is what he writes: "God took his [Matthias'] soul to Himself, though he had been His champion here on earth .... A few days later, Vienna was burned. It was as if the genius of this great king could not bear his death without some reprisal; indeed, from that time on, the country started to suffer many losses, as if all had become superfluous, now that King Matthias (1443–1490) was dead. Carolus Quintus' genius did much the same: as soon as the emperor had disembarked from the ship that had brought him across the ocean for the last time *post regnorum resignationem*, a powerful gale sprang up – so writes Framianus Strada – and overturned the ship, *quasi non vecturam amplius Caesarem*."

An extraordinary parallel indeed. Zrínyi, we find, had spared no effort to study Charles V's career. "Carolus Quintus had exerted himself in vain", he notes in connection with Charles's efforts to take Tunis and Algiers. He also reflects on Charles's doings in his *Discourses* on warfare, in the section discussing generals who had failed to follow up their advantage and strike at the enemy when he was weakened: "Carolus Quintus, for all his skill and wisdom, fell prey to this fault", he notes, for he did not make the most of his victory at Pavia.[2]

In the *Obsidio Sigetiana*, Zrínyi invests the figure of Charles V with symbolic significance. Though Charles had been dead for over eight years in 1566 when Suleiman I set siege to the fortress of Szigetvár, in the first canto of the epic, Zrínyi speaks of him as if alive: Charles calls one council after the other, for he has no "ready troops" to do battle with the Turks in a Europe divided by religious strife. The only resistance that Suleiman in fact encountered in what was to prove his last Hungarian campaign was put up by the commander of Szigetvár, Miklós Zrínyi (1508–1566), the poet's great-great-grandfather. And though the garrison all fell fighting, and the Ottoman attacker ultimately took Szigetvár, Sultan Suleiman, too, died in the siege. The defenders of Szigetvár had been vindicated: the Heavens had looked kindly on their sacrifice. For the poet Miklós Zrínyi writing his epic in 1647–48, and publishing it in Vienna in 1651 as part of a collection of poems entitled *Adriai tengernek Syrenaia* (The Siren of the Adriatic), Charles V was a symbol and an example. In the same way as his epic, and most of the other symbolic poems in the volume, were alle-

---

[2] *Zrínyi könyvtár*: 1985, I, pp. 203–204; 196; 118.

gories for how the challenge of the century – the European expansion of the Ottoman empire – might be met.

Zrínyi also wrote a work entitled "An extract of a treatise on the military, written in the time of Charles V, with reference to every estate". His heroic forefather, the commander of Szigetvár, had fought alongside Charles V in 1529 when the Turks lay siege to Vienna, and had received the treatise from the emperor as a "present". That, at least, was the story.

Zrínyi was not the only Hungarian political thinker to mention Charles V in order to make a point. The emperor is conjured up in two important *Opinio*s drafted by Hungary's leading politicians in the summer of 1660, and in January of 1661. The former had been prepared for the conference in Graz, the latter for a conference to be held in the home of Duke Porcia (1605–1655), the president of the Geheimsrat. Both these documents present Charles V as the paragon of the good ruler, and their drafters echo Zrínyi in expressing their desire to see revived in Leopold I, Holy Roman Emperor and King of Hungary, Charles V's greatness, and greatness of spirit.[3]

The Hungarian political elite, Zrínyi and his circle, were preparing to try to oust the Turks, and seemed, all at once, to attach a great deal of significance to Charles V. The question is, why?

For all that has been written of Charles V and Hungary, we shall find no answer to this question in the literature to date. Indeed, the picture that emerges suggests that, for a variety of reasons, Charles V never had any real interest in Hungary, and failed to provide its king, Ferdinand I (his younger brother), with any substantial help against the Turks.[4] Clearly, the time has come for another look. In what follows, it is the workings of the Respublica Christiana as a complex system that we shall examine in hope of an answer.

ERASMUS'S FOLLOWERS

The developments of the decades after Mohács will never make sense unless we consistently keep our eye on their international context. The humanist sources of the age – tracts, pamphlets, diplomatic addresses, and the international correspondence of the European scholarly community – all make amply clear that everyone understood – and expressly proclaimed

[3] Zrínyi: 1951 (1980): *Obsidio Sigetiana* I/63. – ZK 46 (BZ 201) – 79 (BZ 377) – 80–87 (BZ 49) – 432 Ms (3497)/– 697 (BZ 40) *Zrínyi könyvtár*: 1991, IV. – Klaniczay, T.: 1964, pp. 13, 107, 323, 375. – Opinio Consiliariorum Hungarorum Jan. 15, 1661, Vienna, MOL P 125 91, No. 9321: 24.

[4] Kellenbenz: 1960. – Kohler: 1980, pp. 26–28. – Kellenbenz: 1982, p. 41. – Csáky: 1982,

his conviction – that the collapse of Hungary as a Christian nation would involve all of Europe in incalculable danger.

Just how inseparable the fate of Hungary was from that of the rest of Europe even in times when its borders were sharply drawn by the sword is illustrated by the fortunes of the *Institutio Principis Christiani* (The Education of a Christian Prince), one of the finest of Erasmus's works. Completed in 1516 and dedicated to Charles, the young Habsburg heir to the kingdoms of Castile and Aragon (as the first king of a united Spain, Charles, just sixteen, had inherited the most powerful throne in Europe), the *Institutio* was meant to instruct the young prince in the art of government. A copy of the work is to be found in the episcopal library in Győr.[5] This was the copy that had been used in Buda to tutor the teenage Lajos II (1505–1526), King of Hungary and Bohemia.

Subsequent to the death of the young king in the Battle of Mohács (1526), someone inscribed on its frontispiece: "*Sum Johannis Regis Electi Hungariae*" ("I belong to János, the elected King of Hungary"). Following the demise of King János Szapolyai (1487–1540), his son, János II (1540–1571) inherited the velvet-bound book. It would be in his name that, in 1562, the crown would finally be conferred upon Ferdinand of Habsburg (1503–1564) who, as we know from a letter of his to Erasmus, had likewise pored over the *Institutio* to learn the art of government.

Mohács opened the door to the Ottoman Turks' penetration into the heart of Europe. Left without a ruler, the Hungarian estates had to elect a king; one group chose János Szapolyai, the other opted for Ferdinand of Habsburg. With the country's eastern half under Turkish rule, what had been medieval Hungary effectively fell into three political units.[6] All the while, however, there were those who were doing their utmost to prevent a civil war, and to keep at least the non-occupied central and eastern parts of the country together. In the much-ignored documents pertaining to this unsuccessful attempt, the names of Erasmus and Charles V figure prominently next to those of several Hungarian politicians.

Erasmus taught his pupils principles of government which would enable them to establish a unified Europe. In one pamphlet after another dealing with the situation in Hungary, he emphasized that without the united action of all Christian nations, there would be no holding back the

---

pp. 223–238. – Kohler: 1982, p. 124. – Rabe: 1982, p. 175. – Török: 1930. – Kárpáti: 1941. – Bárdossy: 1943, pp. 64, 176–178, 240. – Gunst: 1976. – Zombori: 1980. – Rázsó: 1986.

 [5] Erasmus: 1516 (1987), pp. 151–152.

 [6] Barta: 1986. – Kosáry: 1978. – Kubinyi: 1986. – Perjés: 1979, pp. 254–257. – Rázsó: 1986. – Rúzsás: 1976.

spread of the Ottoman Empire in Europe. And while the Ottoman Turks were a factor in European politics, there would be no united Europe, no Respublica Christiana, no realization of the dream of the peaceful coexistence of rulers and peoples. Erasmus and his Hungarian, Polish, Austrian and Spanish followers had an alternative to offer Central Europe. From their point of view, the history of the period between 1526 and 1556 was a tale of conflicting alternatives. It is these that we shall try to reconstruct, with a view to encouraging further research.

***

On August 29 of 1526, Sultan Suleiman II won an overwhelming victory over King Lajos II. A force 20–25,000 strong, the Hungarian army had marched into battle under flags embroidered with pictures of the Queen of Heaven; at the end of the day, they had perished nearly to a man. Most of the lords spiritual and temporal – practically the entire political elite – had died in the battle. As had Lajos II, King of Hungary and Bohemia.[7]

All the more surprising, then, that on the very morrow, so to speak, of the Battle of Mohács, a whole new political elite stood ready to fill the vacuum. Most of these men were humanists and men of letters. Diets met and political decisions were made with no time lost, for the Hungarian question was more than that: it was the Bohemian question and the Polish question as well. Certainly, it was one of the principal questions of day-to-day international diplomacy.

A great many fine works have analyzed the ensuing royal election, and the outcome of Hungary's ending up with two kings. What has not been dealt with is what was perhaps the principal dilemma of the months that followed: negotiations with a view to mutual concessions, or civil war. The choice was between preserving intact the unoccupied parts of Hungary, and dividing them up among the powers that had defended them against the Turkish armies. Contemporaries saw Suleiman's victory at Mohács not as an isolated, one-time catastrophe, but as an event pregnant with consequences. The possibility of civil war in Hungary, and the question of its territorial integrity was of deep concern to the neighboring kingdoms, and indeed to everyone anxious about the future of Christian Europe.

Chancellor István Brodarics (1470–1539), Bishop of Szerém, who himself had barely escaped from the jaws of death, wrote an account (which

---

[7] Bárdossy: 1943, pp. 34–35. – Szakály: 1986. – Perjés: 1989a, pp. 225–267.

13

he subsequently published) of the days immediately following Mohács. He was charged to do so by Sigismund I Jagiellon (1467–1548), King of Poland and King Lajos's uncle, who wanted events documented for the conference at Olmütz, the most important international forum to be convened in the wake of the Ottoman victory: "The Sultan... set out for Buda... and burned to the ground the villages and towns he came across along the way... he had his men pillage all of Hungary on this side of the Danube.... The enemy which thus ravaged Hungary met with resistance only at Marót.... This was where our people had retreated, along with their wives and children... The enemy was obliged to bring in cannons; they shot the camp to bits, and slew everyone there.... Terror filled every heart, near and far, even as far as Vienna."[8]

The Venetian ambassador to the Sublime Porte had it from Mustafa Pasha, the Sultan's confidant, that Suleiman did not wish to conquer all of Hungary at that time; all he wanted to do was "to get his hands on the keys".[9] With his victory at Mohács, the road to Vienna lay open, and he could afford, for the time being, to go only as far as Buda. There he had the treasures of the royal palace loaded onto ships, and abruptly turned and went home, leaving not as much as a garrison in Buda, nor indeed in the entire conquered region between the Danube and the Drava.[10]

Three people reached out for the crowns fallen off King Lajos's head into the blood-soaked dirt of Mohács: Sigismund, who wanted the Bohemian crown; János Szapolyai, who would get the crown of King István the Saint; and Ferdinand of Habsburg, who would ultimately acquire both crowns.

As early as in his letter of condolence to his newly-widowed sister, Mary (1505–1558), Ferdinand made clear that he considered Hungary to be his rightful inheritance. Several treaties guaranteed his succession, and so did the Habsburg-Jagiellon marriage contracts of 1506 and 1515.[11] He found, however, that this was not a time when one could acquire the Hungarian crown by simple succession.

Suleiman, for his part, considered all of Hungary to be his by conquest; he placed an army of occupation in the Szerémség, the country's wealthy southern province, and left the border fortresses well-garrisoned. As things stood, he could be back at any time.[12]

[8]   Brodarics: 1527 (1977), p. 327.
[9]   Szalay: 1859, pp. 3–4.
[10] Brodarics: 1527 (1977), p. 328.
[11] Hermann: 1961. – Gonda–Niederhauser: 1977, p. 65.
[12] Káldy-Nagy: 1974, pp. 82–83. – Barta: 1983, pp. 19–20.

14

On November 10, 1526, János Szapolyai, Count of Szepes and Voivode of Transylvania, was elected King of Hungary at the Diet of Székesfehérvár by the overwhelming majority of the assembled estates; the very next day, he was crowned. The assembly cited a ruling of the Diet of 1505, which provided that a ruler be elected from among the sons of the realm should the king die without an heir. In reality, the decision was made on the grounds that the country lay open to renewed Turkish offensives, and Szapolyai was the only aristocrat with a considerable armed force still at his disposal. He was also the country's richest landowner. To boot, he was so popular with the nobility that even as a child he had been regarded as the heir to the throne.[13]

The problem of the Hungarian succession was, thus, inseparable from the Turkish problem. Even the brothers Habsburg, Ferdinand and Charles, had radically different ideas as to the best way out.[14]

Ferdinand made plans to take the country by force. He knew that if he had both Hungary and Bohemia he could put up a better fight against the Turks. As he wrote in his memoirs: "[The country] is the size of two kingdoms; it is not just its inhabitants that it provisions, it also provides Germany, Bohemia, Moravia and many other countries with meat and different foodstuffs". It would be a great disadvantage to the Hereditary Provinces "if we were to surrender this bulwark and bastion of Christendom, which has guaranteed us and our forebears peace and security over many years". To boot, Hungary had the world's best light cavalry, the only force capable of resisting the Turks.[15]

However, the Council meeting in Hainburg on October 14, did not consider Hungary's armed occupation to be feasible. Starting a war was neither acceptable, nor a real option, the councilors argued. Ferdinand had no money, nor did he have an army well enough prepared or equipped for such an exploit. But over and above that, the risks were incalculable: "The Turks and others might intervene".[16]

Charles V likewise opposed the idea of a military campaign. He saw the Hungarian situation as part of the larger picture, as related to the problem of the Ottoman Empire's military and diplomatic expansion.

The Ottoman armies, having conquered the regions surrounding the Mediterranean Sea, had made their way across the Balkans and into Hun-

---

[13] Brodarics: 1527 (1977), p. 291. – Kovachich: 1801. – Szakály: 1975, p. 40. – Barta: 1983, pp. 42–61. – Csáky: 1982.
[14] Wandruszka: 1989, pp. 23–24.
[15] Gévay: 1838–1842, I, pp. 55–63. Cited in Török: 1930, pp. 58–59.
[16] Jászay: 1846, p. 193.

gary, and effectively had Europe in a vice. The countries of Europe met the Ottoman challenge with a series of innovative reforms, but at the time, these attempts at modernization just made for new conflicts. After the French defeat at Pavia in 1525, King Francis I of France (1494–1547), refusing to countenance the enormous concentration of political and economic power that Charles V now had in his hands, had no qualms about asking for the Sultan's help against the Habsburgs. And, when the League of Cognac – an alliance formed in May of 1526 against Charles V by France, Venice, Pope Clement VII (1523–1534), and several of the Italian city-states – came upon the scene, Suleiman was accepted in the role of its silent partner, and influenced the course of European affairs in that capacity.[17] Charles V knew that only with a united Europe behind him would he stand a chance against the Turks in Hungary; on the other hand, the Habsburgs could not afford to let the Danube region out of their sphere of influence.

As soon as he got news of his brother-in-law's demise, Charles V sent out his ambassadors with a proclamation to the Hungarian estates. He told them that he had let his captive, the King of France, go free after the Battle of Pavia because he had agreed to join forces with him against the Turks. In fact, however, while he himself was in Italy in the spring of 1526 preparing to launch an assault on the Turks in order to relieve the King of Hungary, France had turned on him with the backing of the League of Cognac. He had set out for Hungary nonetheless, and received the news of the tragedy at Mohács along the way. Lajos II – Charles declared in his proclamation – was a hero and a credit to the human race, having died fighting valiantly for his homeland and the Respublica Christiana. In this, he, Charles, considered himself Lajos's heir. He, too, would give his life to unite Christendom against the Turks. He commended to them his brother, Ferdinand, "whom we stand by with our power, our authority, indeed, with our own person. Already we are in the highest state of readiness. All our strength, and that of our subjects, shall be focused on beating back the Turk from your doorstep as soon as possible, and, with God's help, keeping them away from your borders, in this way to place our brother in peaceful possession of these countries and provinces, and keep him in their possession."[18] Charles V also sent letters to the same effect to Ferdinand, the King of Poland, and Szapolyai.[19]

---

[17] Szekfű: 1935a, pp. 19, 33, 35. – Bárdossy: 1943, p. 15. – Kosáry: 1978, p. 17.
[18] Granada, Nov. 26/30, 1526. – Jászay: 1846, pp. 244–247.
[19] Charles V to Ferdinand, Granada, Nov. 30, 1526. *Brüsszeli Okmánytár:* 1857, I, nos 47–49. – Cf. Jászay: 1846, pp. 247–248.

It would, however, be overstating things to say that Ferdinand abandoned his plans for armed intervention at the Emperor Charles's behest, or that it was under his influence that he agreed to think in terms of election rather than right of succession.

Ferdinand's followers were rallied by Queen Mary – who had fled to Pozsony at the news of the lost battle – with the help of the two young privy secretaries, Tamás Nádasdy (1498–1526) and Miklós Oláh (1493–1568). Palatine István Báthori (1490–1535), Chancellor István Brodarics, and Ferenc Batthyány (1497–1566), the Ban of Croatia – the dignitaries of the realm who lived to tell of the Battle of Mohács – all recognized that there would be no containing the Ottoman armies without help from the rest of Europe. Elek Thurzó, the Lord Treasurer and a partner of the Fuggers, recognized something else as well: the fortunes of the Habsburgs were tied to the House of Fugger, and vice versa.

Every significant power play of the Habsburgs – the expenses of the conference in Vienna ratifying the Jagiellon–Habsburg marriage contract, the engagement gifts exchanged on the occasion of the double marriage alliance, and the expenses of Charles's election to the imperial throne – had been financed by the Fuggers. The Fuggers, on the other hand, had a powerful interest in owning Hungary's rich copper deposits, which, given that they owned the Tyrolian copper mines, would give them a monopoly of the European copper trade.[20]

The Habsburgs, thus, had every reason to try to get their hands on Hungary. The notion that they should was not entirely illogical from the Hungarian point of view, given the nearly a hundred-year-old tradition of establishing protective alliances in the region in the form of dynastic unions.[21]

In the fall of 1526, thus, the Hungarian prelates of the church and the high dignitaries of the realm made a regular contract with the young Habsburg archduke. Ferdinand had to recognize the country's integrity, and pledge to be bound by its laws, and to subject himself in all things to the dictates of the Hungarian constitution. On December 16 of 1526, the Diet sitting in Pozsony placed its faith in the political prestige and economic power of Charles V, and elected Ferdinand of Habsburg, King of Bohemia and ruler of the Hereditary Provinces, to be King of Hungary.[22] The expectation was that upon his return from the Italian campaign, the

[20] Makkai: 1960. – Hermann: 1976.
[21] Kosáry: 1987, pp. 22–23.
[22] *Magyar Országgyűlési Emlékek*, I, pp. 33–70.

Emperor would rally the forces of Europe, and launch a campaign against the Turks.

A king without a country was Ferdinand, the elected King of Hungary. For except for a few counties on the western edge of the country and three or four towns, all of Hungary was in János Szapolyai's possession. Ferdinand declared János to be a usurper, and initiated vigorous diplomatic and propaganda campaigns against him. He also made preparations to fight him. Eight thousand German infantrymen and two thousand cavalrymen were sent to Pozsony to keep the Diet loyal, and Ferdinand's men took the castle of Pozsony by a ruse.[23]

The Emperor Charles V, on the other hand, repeatedly urged his brother to come to terms with King János – "the Voivode", as he referred to him at that time. János Szapolyai himself was in favor of a compromise with the Habsburgs. The King of Poland, too, wanted to see the two parties come to some agreement, as did some influential aristocrats among both Ferdinand's and János Szapolyai's supporters. Thus, in early 1527, both sides began to prepare for negotiations.

THE OLMÜTZ CONFERENCE

King János's popular support lay with the counties, the towns and the lesser nobility. His leading courtiers were learned noblemen schooled in the best humanist tradition, men like the renowned legal scholar and ex-palatine, István Werbőczy (1458–1541), and some influential members of the old government: Péter Perényi (1502–1548), Ban of Temes, Lord Treasurer János Dóczy, and Pál Várady, Bishop of Eger. These men watched Ferdinand with apprehension, and feared for the country's sovereignty, knowing full well by what means he had bent the Austrian estates to his will.[24] Their fine appreciation of the weight of the Habsburgs' international prestige could not blunt the keenness of their disillusionment with their performance at Mohács: the brothers Habsburg had been incapable of mobilizing international assistance for their hard-pressed sister and brother-in-law. In early 1524 already, Charles, Ferdinand, and Lajos II had been unable to get from the Papacy the help they sought. There was also the feeling among the Hungarian political elite that Suleiman himself had attacked Hungary by way of striking a blow at the Habsburg emperor,

---

[23] Ferdinand to the Archduchess Margaret, Vienna, Nov. 24, 1526. *Brüsszeli Okmánytár:* 1857, I, 45–47. – Jászay: 1846, pp. 206–209. – Barta: 1983, pp. 109–111.
[24] Lhotsky: 1971, pp. 127–128.

and that the House of Fugger was to blame for the country's economic collapse.[25]

King János hoped to compensate Hungary's weakened security with diplomacy. His diplomatic corps was a veritable Central European United Nations: János Statileo was of Croatian-Dalmatian descent, as was the former chancellor, István Brodarics, who threw in his lot with King János, and Ferenc Frangepán, the "Italian" monk who delivered Pope Clement's somewhat reluctant recognition of János as king, and would enter his diplomatic service. Hieronym Laski (1496–1541) was the brother of the Erasmian Jan Laski, the Primate of Poland, and there was also another Pole, Prince Casimir of Silesia. Like the Erasmians among Ferdinand's supporters, all these men were painfully aware of the risks inherent in any *de facto* partitioning of Hungary between its two kings.

The first test of the will to unity was the conference at Olmütz. After lengthy preparations, the preconditions of an agreement were signed on April 14, 1527. Ferdinand was represented by Chancellor Leonhard von Harrach; King János by his chancellor, István Werbőczy. Werbőczy conjured up the spirit of Erasmus when he stated the purpose of the accord: to prevent the spilling of Christian blood. King Sigismund of Poland had been calling for a peaceful agreement between the two kings for a year, and now took on the task of mediation through his chancellor, Krzysztof Szydłowiecki. But the most persistent calls for an agreement were coming from Charles V.

On March 6, 1527, he had written to Ferdinand: "Many a good thing can be best achieved through peaceful means. It is better to be patient, than to trust to the wheels of fortune... It would be best to come to terms with the Voivode [King János], and content yourself with just the crown. To do so would spare us a great deal of expense and danger. But more than that, it would thwart the Voivode's scheming, forestall his joining forces with the Turk and, in return for tribute, getting Turkish help to ravage all Christendom, the Hereditary Provinces above all, by way of avenging himself on you, and pressing you so hard that you would never again be able to do Hungary harm."[26]

Ferdinand, however, had other plans. Writing to the Archduchess Margaret on May 27, 1527, on the morrow of his coronation in Prague, he told of his plans to rally his troops upon his return to Vienna, and his

[25] Acsády: 1896, p. 12. – Sinkovics: 1986, p. 156. – Barta: 1983, p. 67. For a later interpretation, see Rúzsás: 1976.

[26] Gévay: 1838–1842, I, p. 48. – Bárdossy: 1943, pp. 48, 52. – Lhotsky: 1971, p. 210. – Letters were exchanged relatively quickly, and quite safely: Rabe: 1982, p. 175.

determination to occupy Hungary, by force if need be.[27] It was about at that time that he must have received another one of Charles's missives admonishing him to negotiate: "Do not take the risk of war. Make peace with the Voivode, at whatever price. Just try to keep the crown. I hope that there will be peace within Christendom; if there is, I shall be able to be of help to you."[28]

The conditions of the agreement were worked out with great care. They were to form the basis of all subsequent negotiations. The parts of the country already under King János's *de facto* rule would remain his, but upon his death, the crown would devolve on Ferdinand. The widowed Queen Mary's marriage to King János Szapolyai was to set the seal on the agreement.[29]

The proposal would have guaranteed Hungary's integrity, for practically the entire country was, at that time, still under King János's rule. Several sources deemed to "know" that the Emperor Charles and Ferdinand had "endorsed" János's kingship.[30] The House of Fugger, always a sensitive barometer of the winds of change, had, in March of 1527, signed a lease with King János for the Hungarian copper mines.[31]

However one looked at it, the peaceful settlement of János and Ferdinand's conflicting claims seemed the only reasonable course to follow. For Hungary, any other course meant partition, and the loss of its independent statehood. For Charles, who had a holistic approach to the problems of Europe, the alternative meant civil war in Hungary, and an excuse for overt Turkish intervention. For the King of Poland, the prospect of fratricidal conflict in Hungary meant having to wage war against the Ottoman Empire in the very heart of Europe, to the peril of every country in the region.

That these were not exaggerated scenarios was soon apparent. The League of Cognac immediately recognized the opportunity to open a new front against the Habsburg emperor: Venice and France had already made efforts to win over King János.[32]

János, though encouraged from several quarters to seek the support of the Porte, the League's silent partner, still refrained from doing so. He

[27] Brüsszeli Okmánytár: 1857, I, 52–53.
[28] April 26, 1527. Gévay: 1838–1842, I, p. 71. Cited in Bárdossy: 1943, p. 52. – Lhotsky: 1971, p. 210.
[29] Szalay: 1859, pp. 52–73. – Bárdossy: 1943, pp. 50–52.
[30] Szalay: 1859, p. 79. – Bárdossy: 1943, pp. 51–52. – Hopp: 1992, p. 90.
[31] Hermann: 1976. – Kellenbenz: 1982, pp. 39, 42.
[32] Óváry: 1879, pp. 31–33. – Charrière: 1848–1860, p. 155. – Szalay: 1859, pp. 16–18. – Bárdossy: 1943, pp. 39–41. – Barta: 1983.

stood firm in spite of the Turkish delegation that called on him in Buda in late 1526, and in spite of diplomatic pressure from the Venetians that he seriously consider making terms with the Turks.[33]

But even while he was hoping to make an agreement with the Habsburgs, King János, like any good politician, hedged his bet, and sent an ambassador to Paris to present his plans for a French-Hungarian alliance.[34] And there is strong evidence that Chancellor Harrach's fear that "die Venedtiger und der Weida gantz ains sein" was far from groundless.[35]

"Civil war, according to Plato, is rebellion, not war", argued Erasmus, who thought few things quite as reprehensible as the sight of a Christian fighting a Christian, and nothing as unjustified as princes making war on the pretext of fighting for their rightful inheritance: "By the time you acquire a certain piece of territory, you will have despoiled your entire country and brought ruination upon it". On the eve of the Olmütz conference, Erasmus welcomed the possibility of the peaceful settlement of the Hungarian succession in a brilliantly argued pamphlet: "If the Christian princes were to agree among themselves, their rule would be more auspicious and more magnificent, and they could more easily free all Christians from the Turks."[36]

It is left to future researchers to uncover the ins and outs of the negotiations between Ferdinand and King János, and the reasons for its derailment. We do not know why the King of Poland lost interest in the role of mediator, why Werbőczy did not show up at the last round of the talks, and when the opponents of the agreement in Vienna might have got the upper hand of its supporters, and why.[37]

"PEACE HAS PASSED AWAY"

"Peace has passed away", is how Erasmus saw the failure of the Olmütz negotiations, thinking of its implications not just for Hungary, but for all of Europe. Ignoring the terms of the preliminary agreement, Ferdinand specified conditions that János could not but find altogether unac-

[33] Kosáry: 1978. – Perjés: 1989a, p. 104 ff. – Barta: 1983, pp. 103–104.
[34] April 26, 1527. Charrière: 1848–1860, p. 158. – Szalay: 1859, pp. 18–19. – Horváth: 1859, pp. 324–333. – Barta: 1983, pp. 141–143.
[35] Cited in Lhotsky: 1971, p. 211.
[36] *Erasmus's Letters:* 1906–1958, IV/1, pp. 217–218. – Trencsényi-Waldapfel: 1941 (1966), p. 102.
[37] Barta: 1986, pp. 289–290. – Csáky: 1982, p. 237.

ceptable. The ambassadors had hardly got home when, in early July, he marched against János with a force of fifteen thousand men. In Buda, in the meanwhile, István Werbőczy made the solemn announcement that King János had joined the League of Cognac.

Led by Casimir, Elector of Brandenburg, the Habsburg troops occupied all of Hungary without much resistance. In Transylvania, they won over the Saxons and the Székelys, and King János withdrew with his government to Poland. Ferdinand convened the Diet, and was crowned on November 3, 1527, in the presence of the majority of the estates.[38]

Without followers and without a country, János Szapolyai saw no alternative but to heed the advice of Venice and France and turn to the Sublime Porte, which had already indicated its willingness to help. The Polish king, Sigismund, did his best to dissuade him, and János, too, had agonized over the dangers the decision held for Hungary. János Szapolyai, however, was not an isolated anti-king, but a member of the League of Cognac, and a potential ally of France. This, possibly, was the reason that Hieronym Laski, his ambassador, was able to conclude the Turkish-Hungarian treaty of January 27, 1528 on terms so very favorable to János. Sultan Suleiman undertook to "return" all of Hungary to him, (i.e., retake the country from Ferdinand), and wanted neither tribute, nor gifts, nor services in return, but only János's commitment to the Turkish-Hungarian alliance. It was at that point that János appointed Lodovico Gritti (1480–1534) – the illegitimate son of the Doge of Venice who had made a career in Istanbul as banker and supplier to the Ottoman army – his plenipotentiary to the Porte. As an aide to the Grand Vizier Ibrahim, Gritti had helped to bring about the alliance. Subsequently, János would appoint him viceroy. It was in this capacity that he all at once began to recommend Ferdinand's cause to the Porte, thus confusing even further what was in any case a rather baffling political scene.[39]

Researchers today are of two minds as to whether the Turkish-Hungarian alliance was just a form of Hungary's subjugation, or whether it really did contain mutual guarantees, and are studying the terms of the treaty for both the formal and the real advantages that it might have held. But most of all, they are analyzing the forces and circumstances behind it.[40] Certain fascinating details have already emerged. In the course of the

[38] *Magyar Országgyűlési Emlékek*, I, pp. 133–156.

[39] Szalay: 1859, pp. 103–125. – Perjés: 1989a, pp. 118–119. – Kretschmayr: 1901. – Szakály: 1975, 1986c. – Kosáry: 1978, p. 147. – Barta: 1983, pp. 172–173, 242.

[40] Perjés: 1979, 1989a. – Szakály: 1975. – Kosáry: 1978, p. 147. – Barta: 1983, pp. 172–173, 242.

negotiations, for example, Laski rejected the Porte's demands for tribute with a direct reference to the power of Charles V; Suleiman, for his part, could not afford to leave behind a restive country, preparing as he was for a western campaign. And János, he had to keep in mind, was a member of the League of Cognac. Indeed, in the fall of the same year, Francis I's chancellor and the Transylvanian bishop, John Statileo, János's ambassador, signed the Franco-Hungarian alliance.[41] It follows from this that neither the Ottoman Empire nor the King of France recognized Ferdinand as Hungary's king. The person whose kingship they did recognize was János Szapolyai.

Over a hundred and fifty years of European history shows the Ottoman Empire keeping pace with the Christian West, advised of its plans, as often as not one step ahead, but at the very least, quick to respond to every new challenge. We see this at the outbreak of the Fifteen Years' War, in the evaluation of the negotiations preliminary to the Peace of Westphalia, and in the siege of Venice.[42]

On this analysis, Suleiman's military campaign of the year 1529 might have been an answer to Ferdinand's takeover of Hungary. Would the Ottoman armies have laid siege to Vienna if Ferdinand had not attacked King János, the Sultan's ally? Or was Ferdinand's own aggression just a convenient excuse? What historians do agree on is that Suleiman was determined to occupy Vienna. (A hundred years later, Kara Mustafa Pasha (1634–1683) would adopt his priorities, and make a renewed attempt to conquer the imperial city.) Several sources – and the logic of the events – suggest that to Suleiman's mind, the principal enemy was Charles V. In the final analysis, it was Charles that he was fighting in Hungary, no less than in the Mediterranean. If we consider all the locations on land and sea where Ottoman forces were engaging Christian troops in battle, we see the campaigns of this period as one gigantic pincer movement. Just how apt such an interpretation might be is borne out by the letter Suleiman sent to Ferdinand from Eszék on July 17, 1532: "I have decided to march against the King of Spain... My goal is not to proceed against you, but against the King of Spain. The King of Spain has been saying for a while now that he wants to march against Turkey. By the grace of God, however, I will turn my army against him...". And at the peace negotiations, Suleiman would treat with no one but Charles V.[43]

[41] Charrière: 1848–1860, I, pp. 163–165, 167. – For a comparison with the Turkish–Hungarian alliance, see Bárdossy: 1943, pp. 75–76.

[42] R. Várkonyi: 1988, pp. 2–3.

[43] "Caesar autem Karolus, si pacem velit querat eam a magno Caesare sed sine medio

The Ottoman campaign of 1529 had far-reaching repercussions. Ferdinand was practically totally driven out of the country. What he had left was a few counties, and a thin strip of land on the western and north-western edges of the country. He was obliged to leave Buda, the capital of the kingdom, once and for all. Never again would he set foot in the despoiled, but still magnificent Renaissance palace built by King Matthias Corvinus, and it would be another two hundred years before his descendants would visit the rebuilt castle. (Neither Leopold I (1640–1705) nor the young King Joseph I (1678–1711) visited Buda after the Turks were driven out of the country.) The Hungarian crown fell into Suleiman's hands, and he returned it to János with great pomp and circumstance.[44]

If the losses at Mohács had touched all Christendom, the siege of Vienna sent shock waves through it. But the heroic defense of the city brought home to all of Europe that all was not lost, though the Turkish army be at the gates of Vienna.

Hungary, for its part, became the battleground on which the two great rival forces of a divided Europe contended with one another. The body of the country was carved up into the Habsburg and the Franco-Turkish spheres of influence. The population was driven into the no-man's-land between the front lines, and waged a daily battle for survival. Stopping the Turkish expansion had become a matter of life and death for the nations of Central Europe.

At the meeting of the Imperial Diet in Augsburg in the summer of 1530, Charles V and the delegates of the Hungarian estates seemed to have very similar views of the Turkish problem. Charles V was the lord of Europe, having just the year before signed the Peace of Cambrai recognizing his victory over the League of Cognac, and having just been crowned Holy Roman Emperor by the Pope. Addressing the assembly, he noted how quickly the prophecies of the Hungarian delegations of the past ten years had come to pass: The Ottoman Empire had got a foothold in Hungary, the last bastion of Christendom. It was time for the princes and estates of the Empire to put up some serious resistance, "instead of the so-called emergency aid which, in fact, had never yet been delivered".[45]

Ferdinandi regis, non enim vult magnus Caesare quovis modo, per medium Ferdinandi regis ipsi Karolo Caesari pacem dare." Gritti, June 11, 1533. Cited in Bárdossy: 1943, p. 145. – Suleiman's letter: Gévay: 1838–1842, I, pp. 87–88. – Berindei–Veinstein: 1987. Cited in Perjés: 1990, p. 148. – As Pál Fodor (1991, p. 54) aptly noted, "Hungary was one site of the Ottoman-Habsburg rivalry".

[44] Szekfű: 1935a, p. 23. – Rázsó: 1986, p. 154.
[45] Károlyi: 1880, p. 280. – Bárdossy: 1943, pp. 88–89. – Kohler: 1982. – Luttenberger: 1982. – Kohler: 1990, pp. 160–164. – Gundmann: 1986, pp. 95–105.

The Hungarian delegation submitted a memorandum as to what they thought should be done. The first thing would be to install a modern system of defense. László of Macedon, Bishop of Várad, pointed out the particular propitiousness of the moment for a war against the Ottoman Empire. Miklós Oláh (1493–1568) wrote a humanist epistle to Erasmus, detailing the unbelievable brutality of the Turkish raids, specifically the carnage left in the wake of Mehmed Bey, the commander of Nándorfehérvár: "After the Turks had withdrawn, and [Elek Thurzó] went out to see what fiendishness they had committed, ... he found over five hundred little children hacked to death, or dashed to the ground. About fifty of them still had more or less breath in them; deeply affected by the tragedy of these half-dead little ones, and inflamed by the Turkish bestiality, he had them put into two wagons, and taken to his castle in Sempte, hoping to be able to heal them somehow. See, Erasmus, what ruthless tyranny oppresses a Christian people, and what grievous servitude weighs upon Hungary, once famous for its valor and conquests, and resplendent with glorious deeds; today, it has not one moment of security from the incursions and pillaging of the enemies of the faith."[46]

Erasmus himself issued a pamphlet urging the Imperial Diet to take action. The conflict between the Mohammedan world and Christendom was not of a religious nature, he wrote. With the Ottoman Empire's invasion of Europe, it was two radically different cultures that clashed head on. It was time for all Christians to realize that the Ottoman conquest of Hungary held incalculable dangers for all of Europe. It was time to learn to cooperate, and to make the best use of one's financial resources. And it was time for the princes of Europe to realize that peace within Europe was the first and foremost precondition of successful warfare against the Turks.[47]

The Imperial Diet, as we know, voted to deal with religious questions first, and assigned the Turkish question to a committee. In the meanwhile, there was a falling out in the assembly itself: the Protestant princes and estates walked out, having formed a unified front against the two Habsburg rulers. The Catholic estates stayed, and responded generously to the Emperor Charles's appeal, voting Hungary a new round of emergency aid (again, however, without earmarking the resources for it), and making vague promises to set up a joint army suitably trained and equipped for a major military offensive.[48]

[46] Augsburg, Oct. 13, 1530. *Erasmus's Letters:* 1906–1958, IX, p. 2396. – Klaniczay: 1982, p. 701.
[47] Erasmus: 1530. – Trencsényi-Waldapfel: 1941 (1966), pp. 110–112.
[48] Károlyi: 1880, pp. 280–281. – Bárdossy: 1943, pp. 88–90. – Kohler: 1980, pp. 135 ff.

Charles V's negotiations with the Persians in Barcelona, and campaigns around the Mediterranean leave no doubt that he had a good understanding of the strength of the Turkish war machine, and saw the Ottoman expansion as a global phenomenon. There is no other way to explain the fact of his continuing to advise Ferdinand to be tolerant in his dealings with King János, an ally of the Sultan's since 1528.

"Try not to antagonize the Turks, and refrain from making war until we have rallied somewhat.... I think our own forces insufficient against the Turks...." " Make peace with the Voivode. It seems to me totally superfluous for you to send new ambassadors to the Porte, if they have already decided to launch a new offensive; you haven't the time for it. You would do better to see to reinforcing the fortresses, and organizing the country's defence. Take care not to irritate the Turks, lest you yourself provoke the outbreak of hostilities", wrote the Emperor to his brother, commenting on Ferdinand's imprudent march on Hungary in 1527.[49]

The Viennese court, it seems, was totally unprepared for the Ottoman challenge. Ferdinand had no councilors with a sense for the kind of diplomacy that was conducted by the Porte. And he had no consistent Turkish policy. In 1530, he again offered to pay a yearly tribute to Suleiman if he would disown János, and recognize him, Ferdinand, as King of Hungary.[50] Then, he launched another attack on János. Soon Charles V's worst fears came true: Turkish auxiliaries overran the country, and laid it waste. In vain did King János ask for an armistice, King Ferdinand's troops under General Wilhelm Roggendorf (?–1541) took Esztergom, and then spent six unsuccessful weeks trying to take Buda. With centuries of experience behind him, the Venetian ambassador to Constantinople sent home the following sure prognosis: The siege of Buda has made peace impossible. Soon, Ferdinand himself was sending a desperate coded plea to Pope Clement: Suleiman's campaign is threatening to overwhelm not just Hungary and Austria, but all Christendom.[51]

In the summer of 1532, Ferdinand issued a proclamation to the estates of Hungary: the Emperor Charles V and he himself stand ready to face the Ottoman forces, to rebuff Suleiman's attack, and liberate all Hungary from the tyrant.

Indeed, an army of 130,000 had gathered to meet the host marching under Suleiman onto Vienna. Charles V, the German princes, the Austri-

[49] Gent, Jan. 11 and April 3, 1530. – Lanz: 1844–1846, I, pp. 262–263, and *Brüsszeli Okmánytár:* 1857, I, pp. 77–90. – Horváth: 1859, p. 333. – Bárdossy: 1943, pp. 52, 59, 88.

[50] Török: 1930, pp. 35–36. – Bárdossy: 1943, pp. 89–90.

[51] Jan. 7 and Feb. 16, 1531. Óváry: 1901, II, pp. 187, 190.

ans, and the joint Hungarian forces, however, did not move out of the plains around Wienerneustadt. Barely a hundred kilometers away, in the meanwhile, Suleiman and the entire Ottoman army spent three weeks besieging the fortress of Kőszeg. To this day, researchers have found no satisfactory answer to why the two great armies never met for the ultimate test of strength. The Christian plans had called for a decisive showdown; the armies had gathered at great expense. All Europe looked on, expectant, waiting for the Christian army to free Hungary of the Turks.

The year 1532 was an unusually arid one. Both armies were having serious problems provisioning the men, and the outbreak of an epidemic seemed imminent. The Christian soldiers were not receiving their pay on time, and the imperial troops – which comprised the bulk of the army – had been commissioned, by the Imperial Diet, to defend only the Hereditary Lands and the German principalities; nor could the assembled forces agree on a unified leadership.[52] Charles's navy had been successful. While Sultan Suleiman was busy under Kőszeg, the Spanish fleet took the fortress of Koron on the island of Morena. Neither side seemed willing to open up a new front in Hungary with only a fifty-fifty chance of success. The Hungarian domestic scene as well as the new Hungarian foreign policy made both Suleiman and Charles stop and think: they would be risking a great deal, and with dubious success.

CHARLES V AND KING JÁNOS

In 1531 already, János Szapolyai had sent to Charles V his memorandum[53] discussing the possible solutions to Hungary's problems. He declared himself mindful of the welfare of Christendom, and ready, as always, to arrive at a settlement; Ferdinand, on the other hand, had misinformed the Emperor of his intentions, had arrested the envoys he had sent to him, and had compromised the country's future with the use of arms. He, János, was still willing to make terms if Charles would take charge of the negotiations and then guarantee the agreement, for Ferdinand made nothing but trouble with his use of force. He appealed to Charles "to try to make his brother see things differently, adjuring him as both his loving brother and his emperor, and to try to keep him from disrupting all Christen-

---

[52] King Ferdinand to the Hungarian Estates. Pozsony, June 19, 1532. – To Commander Miklós Jurisics. Linz, Sept. 12, 1532. In: Kőszeg emlékezete: 1982, pp. 22–23, 49–51. – Szerémi: 1545 (1961), pp. 217–220. – Istvánffy: 1622 (1962), pp. 150–154.
[53] Zombori: 1980, pp. 619–620.

dom".[54] The Emperor Charles was the only one, János Szapolyai wrote, capable of bringing long-desired peace to Hungary. His concluding lines expressed the hopes of all Christians: "It is up to Your Majesty – who surpasses your brother in wisdom, authority and age – to tend to the needs of the Respublica Christiana and all Christian religions without prejudice and without favoritism, and according to the dictates of your own wisdom and authority."[55]

Why had János Szapolyai decided to circumvent both Ferdinand and Suleiman, and try to resolve his country's problems with Charles V directly? For over a year by that time, János's and Ferdinand's supporters had been meeting regularly in the attempt to stave off civil war. From these meetings, two guidelines emerged: the country had to be kept intact at all cost; and its rule by two kings had to stop. Either János or Ferdinand was to keep the throne – whichever one was capable of keeping the country intact. If neither of them was up to the task, they would elect a new king, and not even the thought of Turkish suzerainty – so Ferdinand's followers declared – would deter them.[56]

King János had learned, through bitter experience, to read Turkish foreign policy. He saw that not even the Turkish-Hungarian alliance of 1528 was a safeguard against the ravages of the Ottoman army. Gritti was working for Ferdinand, and thus was contributing to the country's partition. As for Ferdinand's military strength, it was nothing compared to the Ottoman forces. And yet, Ferdinand had as good as promised the recapture of the fortresses taken by the Turks, nay, the occupation of Constantinople to "our unfortunate and gullible Hungarians", observed János in his memorandum to Charles V.

"We two are weak", Charles V wrote to Ferdinand in Vienna, and the Christian princes would not be forthcoming with help in the foreseeable future.[57] The chances of an all-European cooperation seemed slimmer than ever: the Protestant princes of the Schmalkaldic League had gone on the offensive against Charles V, while the King of France was openly negotiating an alliance with the Sultan.

To fight against the Turks successfully, a country must be morally prepared for war, Erasmus was wont to say, and in 1532, Charles had to real-

[54] *Ibid.*, p. 620.

[55] *Ibid.*

[56] *Magyar Országgyűlési Emlékek*, I, pp. 326–330, 370. – Bárdossy: 1943, p. 103. – Perjés: 1989a, pp. 133–134.

[57] Gévay: 1838–1842, I, 5, pp. 64–66. – Lanz: 1844–1846, I, p. 605. – Bárdossy: 1943, pp. 105–106.

ize that the Ottoman forces could not be effectively engaged in a country divided against itself and rent by civil war.[58]

From Paulus Jovius, the Italian humanist historian, we learn of another dimension to the question. In the camp by Wienerneustadt, there was a violent exchange of words between the brothers Habsburg. Once it was decided that they would not be attacking Suleiman on his way home through Styria, Ferdinand wanted to take the assembled army into Hungary and attack King János. Charles, for his part, would not hear of it, and Ferdinand had to give up the idea of the Hungarian campaign.[59]

Psychologically speaking, one can understand Ferdinand's desperate plan. Hungary was part of the defensive system of his other possessions, and he relied on it as a source of foodstuffs as well. What is more, even with the Turkish presence, Hungary's trade and mineral resources counted for a great deal on the international credit market. Ferdinand's problems were but compounded by the difficulties he was having in Bohemia. In early 1533, thus, he again sent envoys to the Porte. Let the Sultan recognize him as King of Hungary, and he would make peace with the Ottoman Empire; if Suleiman met his first demand, the envoy was free to make practically any other concession.

The Grand Vizier Ibrahim and Gritti, presumably, had got word of the rapprochement and negotiations between Charles V and János. Furthermore, Hungary's strategic importance was as evident from Istanbul as from Vienna, to say nothing of its being a vital source of foodstuffs and manpower for the expanding Ottoman Empire. Gritti, too, was likely counting on some personal advantage to be derived from encouraging Ferdinand. Ferdinand's envoy, at any rate, interpreted the Porte's cryptic answer to mean that the Sultan would accede to his request in return for the keys to Esztergom.

The more wary of Ferdinand's Viennese councilors heard the news with justified suspicion. On March 22, 1533, Ferdinand called the high dignitaries of Hungary to council. The Hungarians rejected the idea of partition in no uncertain terms. Though it might serve the momentary interests of the Hereditary Lands for the Sultan to recognize Ferdinand's kingship over parts of Hungary, the very idea did violence to Hungary's most elementary interests, nor did it profit the dynasty. "While the country is partitioned, Your Majesty will never exercise his sovereign prerogatives. ...

---

[58] Erasmus: 1516 (1987), pp. 133–134. – Kárpáti: 1942. – Hantsch: 1959. – Kellenbenz: 1960.

[59] Jovius: 1532 (1982), p. 163.

There will always be another reason for war and internal strife within the country, nor will the troubles end until we recognize you as our sole king and leader. If, on the other hand, this does not come to pass, Hungary's fate will be sealed – and would be, even if there were no enemy at our door – and this will not be to Your Majesty's benefit either. Indeed, it will cause you constant concern and inquietude of spirit, and us, our ultimate destruction...." Again and again they implored Ferdinand "to deign to soberly reflect upon all this, lest if we partition this still intact, sorely buffeted, and all but lost country, Hungary should perish even in name." They advised Ferdinand to treat with the Sultan once he had a firm hold on the country: "Make as enduring an alliance with him as possible, and come to terms with him for the benefit of the country and Your Majesty's children".[60]

In spite of these pleas and warnings, Ferdinand asked Suleiman to partition the country, not excluding the possibility of the Sultan's getting Koron if he were to give all of Hungary to Ferdinand. "Totum Regnum Hungariae, quod gladio acquisivi donavi gratiose Joanni regi" (I have given all of the kingdom of Hungary, which I acquired through conquest, to King János), reads the Latin translation of Suleiman's reply to Ferdinand.[61] Suleiman, however, was busy with the war on Persia, and Gritti managed to get his consent to Hungary's partition along the lines of its *de facto* rulership, with he himself in charge of drawing the borders.[62] Ferdinand, for his part, interpreted the Porte's rather enigmatic replies as an unqualified diplomatic success: the Sultan had recognized him as King of Hungary. It seemed that he had also managed to short-circuit King János's rapprochement with the Emperor Charles, for at the news of Ferdinand's deal with the Sultan, the negotiations came to an abrupt halt.[63]

NAPLES, VÁRAD, TOLEDO

In March of 1536, two plenipotentiaries of King János's, Ferenc Frangepán (1483–1543), Archbishop of Kalocsa, and István Brodarics, councillor and Bishop of Veszprém, were admitted to the presence of the Emperor Charles in Naples. The envoys had come with János's latest recommendation. Let

    [60] Gévay: 1838–1842, II, p. 102. – Bárdossy: 1943, pp. 120–122.
    [61] Suleiman to Ferdinand, July 4, 1533. Gévay: 1838–1842, II, 6, pp. 138–139. – Török: 1930, pp. 72–73. – Bárdossy: 1943, p. 127.
    [62] Barta: 1988. – Kretschmayr: 1901. – Szakály: 1986c, p. 14.
    [63] Acsády: 1896, p. 104. – Török: 1930, pp. 70–72. – Bárdossy: 1943, pp. 115–123.

the Emperor send a strong and effective garrison to Buda and Temesvár. In the interest of the country's unity, János would renounce his claim to the Hungarian crown in Ferdinand's favor, on condition he were given his family estates: the Duchy of Szepes, the towns of Szepes, the mining towns, seventeen counties, and to boot, a Habsburg archduchess for a wife.[64]

The Emperor Charles had recently taken two important Mediterranean strongholds, La Goleta and Tunis. The new pope, Paul III (1534–1549), pinned on Charles his hopes of concerted Christian action against the Sultan, and kept a watchful eye on the Hungarian developments. His Holiness was a willing mediator between János and the Emperor, convinced as he was that Hungary's unity was the key to victory over the Turks in a continental war.[65] Charles V himself must have made his decision on the basis of similar considerations, nor did he see any way other than a compromise with János to guarantee the interests of the dynasty. Accordingly, he dispatched to Hungary his most outstanding diplomat, Johann Wese, the Archbishop of Lund, to engage in negotiations with King János.[66] János's representative was his chancellor, György Martinuzzi (1482–1551). Martinuzzi conducted the talks with great tact and discretion, pretending that they were the preliminaries to an armistice, lest the Porte's excellent intelligence agents get wind of their real purport.

The hope that an international anti-Turkish alliance was just around the corner certainly provided a positive backdrop to the negotiations. With the prospect of a Turkish war in the air, King János and Martinuzzi were all the more anxious to provide for the country's integrity. Just how important this was to contemporaries is well documented by a letter dated Sárospatak, August 24, 1537, which Péter Perényi (1502–1548) wrote to Elek Thurzó: "I so long for the two princes to come to an agreement that I would give up all the goods God has bestowed on me for this blessed concord, and give thanks barefoot, and with just the shirt upon my back, so God love me."[67]

The negotiations took place, with several interruptions, in Gyulafehérvár, Körmöcbánya, Rozgony, and Sárospatak; finally, an agreement was reached in Várad.[68] Ferdinand's suspicions and inflexibility were prob-

---

[64] Sörös: 1917, pp. 457–459.
[65] The reports of Morone, Bishop of Modena, papal legate to Vienna, 1536–1537. Óváry: 1879, pp. 9–21.
[66] Károlyi: 1879, p. 68.
[67] Sztárai: 1985, p. 117.
[68] Károlyi: 1879, pp. 131–231.

lems right through. For a start, he rejected the offered papal mediation, and insisted that János immediately surrender the entire country. Then he set about expanding his holdings and wooing supporters, and János, of course, responded in kind. The sparks of internal strife flared up again.

In 1537, Ferdinand decided to cut the thread of the negotiations with the sword, and ordered an attack upon the Turkish forces. General Katzianer (?–1539) was charged with taking the bridge over the Drava at Eszék, the main thoroughfare of the marauding Turkish forces in the south of the country. The campaign ended up costing Ferdinand 30,000 men in the most massive defeat suffered by the Christian forces since Mohács.[69]

In the meanwhile, the international anti-Turkish alliance initiated by Pope Paul III and Charles V was gradually taking shape. Hungary's politicians knew about the preparations, and had high hopes of the Holy League formed by the Pope, the Emperor and Venice on February 8, 1538. We can be quite certain that Miklós Oláh's two major works, the *Hungaria* and the *Athila* had a great deal to do with the nascent international alliance.

In the *Hungaria*, Miklós Oláh describes the country's topography, its fertile agricultural lands, rich forests, rivers and mineral wealth. He pointed out that it was Hungary which supplied Venice and the towns of the German principalities with meat – the implication being, perhaps, that even under Turkish occupation, Hungary remained an organic part of Europe. Oláh's *Athila* was also written with an eye to the needs of the moment. Oláh dressed the Huns in togas, and had them pay reverence to Venus, Jupiter and Mars. Thus invested with the culture of antiquity, they are the very fountainheads of European civilization. Athila was sent by God to chastise a sinful Europe. The sins are the sins of bad government: inequality, civil war, anarchy. Let the nations of Europe, therefore, reform their government, and stop fighting one another. Or they might again experience the scourge of God.[70]

By the time the Habsburg-Szapolyai treaty was signed in Várad in late February, and István Brodarics set out with the document for the court of Charles V, the year 1538 had turned into the year of peace in Europe. The formation of the Holy League was soon followed by a treaty between Charles V and the King of France.

By the terms of the Peace of Várad, Charles V and Ferdinand embraced János as a brother. They agreed that the country would remain unified in

[69] King Ferdinand to Queen Mary, Graz, Nov. 20, 1537. *Brüsszeli Okmánytár:* 1857, I, 385–386. – Acsády: 1897, pp. 120–121.
[70] N. Olahus: 1938.

principle, though for the moment it was under the rule of two kings. If János died, the Kingdom of Hungary and Transylvania would fall to Ferdinand and his sons; if they should all die, Charles's heirs would inherit the crown, and if Charles's direct male issue should die out, János's descendants would wear the crown. It was also agreed that if János should have a son, he would receive compensation.

The preambles to the peace documents all underscored the significance of Charles V's role in the agreement. "We, János... saw our Kingdom of Hungary in such danger and suffering so many hardships and blows that we could barely have hope of its survival. Even less could we hope to see it restored to the form that it had when Nándorfehérvár, the bastion of Christendom at the time, crumbled, and when, not much later, King Lajos himself perished, along with the flower of the country's youth.... The country was further rent by the murderous rancor of internal strife, with brother despoiling brother, so that in the end, even its enemies took pity on it.... Now, at last, God in His mercy has willed that the sun should shine on Hungary, as we bring our case before that most holy and most excellent Catholic prince and Holy Roman Emperor, the Lord Charles, the head of all Christendom, the only one, after God, whom we can expect to help Hungary, trusting to his guidance and supreme power".[71]

The fragile Peace of Várad was the result of the concerted efforts of King János and the Emperor Charles. János's motivation was the preservation of the country's integrity; Charles's was the dynasty's interest. What they had in common was the determination to defend the country against the Ottoman armies. By the terms of the treaty, it was up to Charles how and when to make the agreement public, provided he guaranteed the country's security. Indeed, by the time Charles himself signed the treaty in Toledo, Hungary was facing a new wave of Turkish attacks.[72]

How effective would the Peace of Várad be? It depended on how effectively the signatories could organize Hungary's defence before the Sultan got word of the agreement. King János, Martinuzzi, and the Emperor Charles were all of one mind on one thing: the treaty was not to be made public until they had mustered an immense army. In Istanbul, Martinuzzi kept up the double talk and the stream of gifts for the Sultan. When King János died in 1540, he had the infant János Zsigmond declared King of Hungary expressly to allay whatever suspicions Suleiman might have had. Few people in Vienna understood this tailor-made diplomacy quite as well

[71] In: *Brüsszeli Okmánytár:* 1858, II, 156. – Gooss: 1911, nos 12–16. – Bárdossy: 1943, p. 209.
[72] Sörös: 1917, pp. 346–347.

as the papal legate: "I, too, am versed in the way that King János is handling the [Turkish] situation.... I am very well aware with what consummate skill he keeps up his position vis-a-vis the Porte.... There can be no doubt that it is the only way to safeguard Hungary for Christendom; without him, the country would long have gone to the dogs."[73]

Ferdinand, however, remained distrustful, and demanded that the terms of the Peace of Várad be publicized with all speed. Then he set about giving force to his demands, dispatching an army of 30,000 men with orders to take Buda. At the same time, he sent Hieronym Laski to the Porte "to tell on" the peace treaty, as the romantic historians of the 19th century charged. Actually, it was more a matter of Ferdinand's having lost patience. In an impetuous and imprudent diplomatic move, he asked Suleiman to act on the terms of the Peace of Várad, and recognize him as sole King of Hungary. This is the report that Laski sent back of his audience with the Sultan: "He was almost too impatient to hear me out; my words stuck in my throat, for he practically drove me out of the hall. Certain members of his entourage advised him to cut off my lips and nose, and thus send me back to Your Majesty. Your Majesty should know that one can offer neither peace nor an armistice here, for tomorrow the Turks are already setting off to war... They are setting off, determined to take Hungary. Your Majesty has ruined everything with that army you sent; I told Your Majesty as much ahead of time, and even wrote to you about it, but Your Majesty chose to listen to other counsel."[74]

Though I have found no direct evidence to that effect, I simply cannot believe that the court in Istanbul did not know about the Peace of Várad. Negotiations were going on for years, more or less before the eyes of the Christian diplomatic community. And the Ottoman Empire had not only one of the most extensive spy networks in the world, Istanbul itself was a veritable diplomatic center for the coming-and-going envoys and ambassadors of Europe.[75]

All Hungary was shaken by the news of the imminent Turkish strike. Archbishop Ferenc Frangepán sent a dramatic missive to the Emperor Charles, asking him to stand by the guarantees he undertook in the Treaty of Várad. "We know no one in the Christian world but Your Imperial Majesty who could heal our wounds and protect this noble member of the

---

[73] Papal Legate Jeromos Rorario to Cardinal Farnese. Villach, Oct. 11, 1539. Óváry: 1879, p. 76. – Sörös: 1917, pp. 348–349.
[74] Laski's report: HHStA Turcica I. fasc. 5. Konv. – For Gy. Kenéz's translation, see Tardy: 1977, pp. 271–274.
[75] Bárdossy: 1943, pp. 250–251. – Bessenyei: 1986, pp. 81–82.

community of Christian states." Central Hungary, a lowland, stands exposed to the Turkish onslaught: "The country is finished if, Heaven forfend, Buda, too, falls to the Turks."[76] The archbishop made several suggestions: they could ask for an armistice, or offer the Sultan a yearly tribute; in the worst instance, they could fight to forestall Hungary's tragedy. It would be a great help if Charles could make a deal with the French. The country needed to be united under Ferdinand; there was no other way to keep it out of Turkish hands. Frangepán – who had changed sides and was now pro-Ferdinand – delivered much the same message on October 10, 1540, at the conference held in Wienerneustadt to discuss the crisis in Hungary, firmly believing that Charles and Ferdinand together had an armed force strong enough to protect his country.[77]

On April 5, 1541, the Imperial Diet convened in Regensburg to discuss the issue of aid to Hungary. The Hungarian councilors and Ferdinand's ambassadors were received in a personal audience by Charles. The Emperor was tense and nervous, but Ferdinand's envoys brought him reassuring news: the Hungarians were overstating the Turkish danger.[78]

Then came the news that the Sultan had routed Ferdinand's army, and was marching on to Hungary. Finally, Ferdinand himself arrived in Regensburg. This was the moment that Frangepán, building on the common core of Erasmianism, rose to give his dramatic address to the Imperial Diet. Hungary's destruction, he said, would be Europe's loss. The Ottoman Turks knew no peace: spreading their faith by force of arms was, for them, a religious precept. Even in times of "peace", they lived by plundering, as the wholesale destruction of southern Hungary so clearly showed. Right and law, for them, was a matter of the whim of the moment; they dishonored the human body, appropriated the work of one's hands, and destroyed learning, tradition, and all that was noble. Suleiman was determined to conquer all of Europe; it was time for Europeans to make peace among themselves. "Have done with your senseless disputes, and your vain discords; at least in these hours of danger have done with your enmity toward one another." It would forever redound to their glory if the assembled would free all Christendom from the present great danger, and, under the leadership of the Emperor Charles and King Ferdinand, would defend Hungary.[79]

[76] Sörös: 1917, pp. 552–554.
[77] Bucholtz: 1831–1836, V, pp. 132–134. – Hopp: 1992, p. 100.
[78] Károlyi: 1880, pp. 292–293. – Óváry: 1879, pp. 129–130. – Sörös: 1917, pp. 565–566.
[79] The address immediately appeared in print. Latin editions came out in Augsburg, Wittenberg and "no place"; German editions in Regensburg and Ingolstadt. In 1542, there was an Italian edition, n.p. Cf. Sörös: 1917, pp. 564–571.

Time was running out, and Charles made haste to send a formal delegation to meet Suleiman. The envoys arrived too late. Camped under the castle of Buda, Suleiman had already asked the queen and the high dignitaries to bring the infant János Zsigmond into his camp; in the meanwhile, his men had occupied the castle, and quickly put the standard of Islam atop the tower of the Church of the Assumption. He had good reason to hurry: he wanted to present Ferdinand with a *fait accompli*, and forestall the decisions of the Regensburg Diet.[80]

The news of the fall of Buda reverberated throughout Europe. For the first time since Mohács, probably, Charles and Ferdinand acted in concert. In 1542, they sent a force of 60,000 imperial and papal troops to Hungary. The army, however, fell apart before it actually achieved anything.[81] In response, Suleiman reinforced the garrison in Buda, and returned in 1543 and 1544 to add to his Hungarian conquests. He took several important fortresses, and actually occupied the central third of the country. Charles V made peace with the King of France (at Crépy, in 1544), but was unable to send an army to Hungary. He had first to make peace with the German principalities, and put an end to the religious wars.

After Charles V had defeated the Schmalkaldic League in 1547, György Martinuzzi, the viceroy of Transylvania, appealed to the Emperor on several occasions, asking him to liberate Hungary from the Turkish yoke, and take possession of the country according to the terms of the Peace of Várad.[82] By that time, however (June of 1547), the Sultan had made peace with the Habsburgs in preparation for his Persian wars. The Ottoman-Habsburg treaty was a global agreement extending to the Mediterranean region, Venice, as well as France. In Hungary, the treaty consolidated the status quo. Sultan Suleiman declared himself to be the lord of all Hungary by virtue of conquest, but offered – in lieu of a yearly "gift" of 30,000 gold pieces – to let Ferdinand rule the parts actually in his possession. The rest of the country remained under Islamic rule.[83] The Ottoman-Habsburg treaty legalized everything that had happened in Hungary after 1541, including the country's partition. The parts under Ferdinand's rule consisted of a vaguely determinable number of counties, and truncated parts of Croatia and Slavonia. Rich in mines, and boasting many towns, trade routes and tolling places, Ferdinand's "Royal Hungary" in-

---

[80] Sinkovics: 1986, pp. 220–221. – Perjés: 1989a, pp. 162–167.
[81] Károlyi: 1880.
[82] *Martinuzzi levelei és iratai:* 1878–1882, pp. 554–559, 253, 270–281. – Barta: 1988, pp. 241–287.
[83] *Brüsszeli Okmánytár:* 1858, II, 142–138. – Thúry: 1896, II, pp. 396–400.

cluded the most developed, and most densely-populated parts of the country. The western and northern edge of pre–1526 Hungary, the country's "collar" as contemporaries were wont to call it, was a strip that was difficult to defend; certainly in the northeastern counties, Ferdinand's rule was nominal, at best.

CHARLES V'S VISION OF TRANSYLVANIA

The peace treaty of 1547 gave Prince János Zsigmond the substantial eastern part of the country: Transylvania, the parts beyond the Tisza, and the town of Kassa and the counties that served as its hinterland in Upper Hungary.

The central part of the country, about a third of old Hungary, was placed under direct Ottoman rule.

Hungary's partition was made an established fact by the treaty of 1547. It put an end to the uniformity of the country's institutions, and made for insecurity in every sphere of life.

The councilors around János Zsigmond and Ferdinand's Hungarian advisers protested the illegality of having had no part in the negotiations: the Emperor Charles and Suleiman had decided on the country's tripartition without consulting them.

György Martinuzzi, for his part, was determined to restore the country's unity as provided for in the Peace of Várad. Under the circumstances, of course, the part under direct Turkish control was out of the question, but there were the western, northern, and eastern parts surrounding it. After protracted negotiations, an agreement was reached in 1551, just as Suleiman was preparing to occupy the southern part of Transylvania. Ferdinand had a three-thousand strong army of Spanish and German soldiers march into the country under Johann Castaldo (1500–1562); Queen Isabella (1519–1559), the mother of the eleven-year-old János Zsigmond – King János II – abdicated in her son's name, handed the Holy Crown of Hungary over to Castaldo, and betook herself to Poland.

The parts of Hungary not overrun by the Turks were, in principle, under Ferdinand's rule from 1551 to 1556. Charles and Ferdinand, however, did not see eye to eye on the question of Transylvania, and had not since 1541.

Charles did not approve of Ferdinand's attempts to acquire Transylvania. He was much more realistic in his evaluation of what could be achieved than his stubborn and contentious younger brother. A number of books have been written about the misery and ruin that the ill-equipped

Habsburg armies brought upon the population of Transylvania. Knowing that the Sultan was preparing to attack, Martinuzzi tried to cajole him out of it. Ferdinand, suspicious of Martinuzzi's real intent, had the friar murdered. The man struck down by the assassin's hand had been more than just a brilliant statesman; he was also the Bishop of Várad and a cardinal of the Church of Rome, and Ferdinand's rash deed would get him into serious difficulties with the Holy See.[84] As for the Sultan's reactions, they followed the established pattern for unification attempts: another violent offensive.

In 1552, accordingly, Suleiman sent two immense armies into Hungary expressly with a view to adding to his territorial acquisitions there. In vain did Ferdinand send his brother one letter after another appealing for help, the wars with the German princes tied down all of Charles's armed forces.[85] Hungary was left to defend itself the best it could. Several fortresses – Temesvár, Szolnok, and Drégely – fell to the Turks at this time, who thus added several counties' worth of territory to their Hungarian possessions.

The successful resistance put up by the fortress of Eger under the leadership of István Dobó (1500–1572) – appointed commander by Miklós Oláh, by then the Bishop of Eger – was more than just a heroic victory for what was left of truncated Hungary. Eger's having withstood the siege of the combined forces of Ali Pasha and Ahmed Pasha was a symbolic act of Europe-wide significance. So was the defenders' taking the captured Turkish military standard up to Vienna to the King, a token, as it were, of the Turks' vincibility. More than just a symbol, Eger was the fortress protecting the trade route between Poland and the Kingdom of Hungary, and shielding Kassa and all Upper Hungary. Keeping it out of Turkish hands was a must for the region's livelihood and international trade.

In 1556, it seemed that the brothers Habsburg had wearied of fighting Suleiman for Hungary. Ferdinand announced to the Porte that he was renouncing his claim to Transylvania, would be withdrawing his troops and would hand over that part of the country to King János II. The Emperor Charles V relinquished all his titles, and retired to a monastery; the title of Holy Roman Emperor devolved on Ferdinand.

János II, then sixteen, was brought back from Poland to Transylvania in triumph as the elected King of Hungary. He probably had with him the copy of Erasmus's *Institutio* that had belonged to Lajos II and then his

---

[84] Barta: 1988.
[85] King Ferdinand to Queen Mary, Passau, June 26, 1552, and to Emperor Charles, Passau, June 28, 1552. In: *Brüsszeli Okmánytár*: 1858, II, pp. 333–336. – Lutz: 1964. – Lutz-Kohler: 1986.

father; Queen Isabella is unlikely to have left it behind when she had to surrender Buda to Suleiman. But Erasmus's injunctions as to the nature of good government and the necessity of avoiding civil war were, by then, just pious wishes, and would be just that for over the next hundred years.

Ferdinand consolidated his power in what was left to him of Hungary. He set up the vital organs of central government, enlisted the help of the Diet to smash the power of the dozens of petty kings lording it over various parts of the country, and organized the defence of its borders with the assistance of the towns and counties.

The new system of border fortresses made the best of the country's topography, and was built on the line where the plains met the mountains, making full use of the protection provided by the waterways. Up-to-date and designed by Italian, Dutch and German military engineers, the building of the series of strongholds was financed to a great measure by the German principalities and the Hereditary Provinces. The great landowners also contributed to their utmost; the serfs provided the labor and the towns and counties the organizational know-how. The strength of these border fortresses lay in the fact that they formed a system, and that they provided basic facilities for the housing, feeding, and personal hygiene of hundreds – some of them thousands – of people.

Ferdinand never was able to do the job he was elected to do in the first place: he never could retake as much as an acre of land from the Sultan. For all that, the aristocracy of Royal Hungary, and its highest church and state officials, accepted King Ferdinand: they respected him for his industry, and admired him as a devoted family man. And they hoped that once his son moved to Hungary, he would dress as a Hungarian, and would learn to think and feel like a Hungarian king. But they never did expect him to reunify the country, or break the stranglehold of the Ottoman Empire. That expectation would always be associated with the person of Charles V.

HOROLOGIUM PRINCIPUM

The poet-musician Sebestyén Tinódi Lantos (1505/10–1556) immortalized the history of the decades we have been discussing – the fall of Buda, the loss of Temesvár, the defense of Eger – in a series of "histories in song". What most people do not know is that the first Hungarian "reporter" devoted an entire song to the Emperor Charles V, a song set in the days of his wars with the Schmalkaldic League. Several of the thousand heroic Hungarian hussars fighting on Charles's side engage the emperor in conversation, and urge him to come fight the pagan in Hungary. The answer Tinódi puts in Charles's mouth is a faithful reflection of the imperial variant of the contemporary Habsburg-Hungarian relationship: he had often planned to come, he would gladly come, but first he had to deal with enemies closer to home. But he does make this promise to them:

> "Stouthearted braves, if it's given me to live
> My best help to your dear country I'll give."[86]

To the Hungarian mind of the 16th century, the Emperor Charles was the personification of *humanitas Erasmiana*, and of the much hoped-for, all-European cooperative action that never did come. A hundred years later, it was this image of Charles V that Zrínyi conjured up.

The humanist scholar János Zsámboki (1531–1584) celebrating the victory of the Holy League over the Ottoman Turkish fleet in the Gulf of Lepanto (1571) in his *Arcus aliquot triumphalis* (published in Antwerpen, 1572), took the opportunity to direct attention to Charles V even in the Dedication: "To Don Juan de Austria, the son of Charles V". Then, in a prophetic vein: "Posterity shall hold this event in high regard someday, when the swirling tide threatening to sweep away the very name of Christian will have been annihilated". Zrínyi, we know, had a great fondness for Zsámboki's edition of Bonfini; whether he ever read this particular book of his we do not know.

We do know, however, that he had in his library Antonio Guevara's *Horologium Principum*, a work of political philosophy that appeared in 1529, the year of the first siege of Vienna. Guevara was Charles V's court chaplain, and one of his chief advisers. János Draskovich (?–1613), Ban of Croatia, the first Hungarian translator of Guevara's work, in his Dedication to his "beloved mate", Éva, the humanist historian Miklós Istvánffy's (1538–1615) daughter, tells her that Guevara had explained to Charles V in a letter why it was that he gave his work the title *Horologium Principum*, "Clock of Princes": "Even as people measure time and divide the days into hours, so should princes and the leaders of men keep themselves to certain regulations and limitations – as, indeed", he added, giving a new formulation to the old Erasmian tenet, "the law of the living God, and the peace and tranquillity of their own peoples requires".

---

[86] Károl császár hada Saxoniába, ott kúrfirstnak megfogása (1546). Tinódi: 1554 (1984), *Cronica*, p. 347.

As Erasmus's *Institutio* was once the intellectual bond between a partitioned Hungary and the rest of Europe, so in the latter decades of the 16th century, Guevara's work would be one of the most popular works of political theory in Transylvania and Royal Hungary. András Prágai (?–1636), court chaplain to Transylvania's Prince György I Rákóczi (1591–1648), translated the entire work under the title *Fejedelmeknek serkentő órája* (Inspirational Clock of Princes), which appeared in Bártfa in 1628. On the hundredth anniversary of the first Ottoman siege of Vienna, it was being read throughout Hungary.

*

An allegory of Hungary partitioned by the Ottoman conquests, with the graves of the kings and heroes who fought against the Turks. A famous woodcut by Johann Nel in Martin Schrott: *Wappenbuch des Heilig(en) Römisch(en) Reichs und allgemeiner Christenheit in Europa.* Munich, 1582.

41

The story of Charles V and Hungary as told above is necessarily sketchy, and a great deal more is to be learned even just from the sources that we have referred to. What is amply evident, however, is that it was no mere whim on Miklós Zrínyi's part when he invoked the memory of Charles V as he and his confederates tried, in the 1650s and '60s, to rally support for an international anti-Turkish alliance.

For Zrínyi, Charles V was the ruler destined to unite all of Europe. He reproached him for the missed opportunities, but admired him for having clearly recognized the need to contain the Ottoman Empire.

We have no evidence to indicate that Zrínyi and his associates knew of the differences of opinion between Charles V and Ferdinand. We do, however, have a great deal of evidence that throughout the century of the tragedy at Mohács, many leading aristocrats, men of letters and members of the nobility did everything in their power to avoid civil war, and prevent Hungary's "internal partition". Erasmians one and all, they were firmly convinced that Hungary's internal unity and tranquility was also in Europe's interest.

In Zrínyi's time, the challenge to Europe was still what it had been a century earlier. One of the most influential of the pamphlets to appear in the years of the international anti-Turkish alliance of the years 1663–64 was the anonymous *Le Mars à la mode de ce temps*.[87] The author has a Catholic slant on international relations, and makes several references to Charles V, whose unfinished business of freeing Christendom from the Turkish yoke had been taken on by Zrínyi. "If Zrínyi should die", the anonymous author wonders, "then what shall become of Christendom?"

[87] *Le Mars à la mode de ce temps*: 1663–1664, Liège, "Dans le Royaume de Vulcain", 1672. OSZKK, App. H. 971.

Religious Tolerance
in the Principality of Transylvania
∞   ∞

The dawn of the modern age was accompanied in Europe with the dual experience of revival and division. The Christian world reacted to the advance of the Ottoman Empire with a number of revivals. This, however, brought new discords to the surface. With the great achievements of the Renaissance and the Reformation, namely, printing, education in the vernaculars and free scientific enquiry, rulers and ruled, scholars and laymen just about learning to read, royal courts, towns and villages all lived through these changes in their own ways. Part and parcel were crises and afflictions that derived from religious conflict. Erasmus, in 1516, clearly shows the disintegration of mediaeval unity – the *universalis Christiana* with this sound observation. *"In the past it was the office of preachers to weed out root and branch quarrelsomeness from the soul of the people. Now the English loathe the French, just because they are French, the Scotch the English because they are English, the Italians the Germans, the Suebians the Swiss and we can say this about the others too. Every land loathes every other, and so do cities. Why is a wedge driven between us by these many foolish names, why are we not welded together by that common word: Christ."*

Hungary lived through the breaking up of the old European unity suffering a disaster that affected its very existence. The Hungarian army that met the host of Sultan Suleiman in August 1526 on the battlefield of Mohács was practically wiped out. Along with most of the country's church and secular dignitaries, Lajos II, King of Hungary and Bohemia was killed. The body of a strong and respected mediaeval country was first cut in two by the new frontier between the Ottoman and Christian worlds; then, as the vacant Hungarian throne attracted two claimants, János Szapolyai (1478–1540), the voivode of Transylvania, and Archduke Ferdinand of Austria (1503–1564), lord of the Austrian hereditary lands, what was left

"Pro quiete regni — for the peace of the realm. (The 1568 law on religious tolerance in the Principality of Transylvania." *The Hungarian Quarterly*, 34 [130] (1993), pp. 99–112.

of the kingdom was further divided, ruled in the West by King Ferdinand and in the East by King János. The two parts were separated by a triangle occupied by the Turks, the peak of which extended far beyond Buda. The shadow of a divided Europe fell heavily on this Hungary, now sundered into three parts; she could get no help against the Turks from a Western world divided by a struggle between the Bourbons and the Habsburgs and by religious strife.

The events that led up to the 1568 Diet reached back in many respects to the Hungarian attempts to achieve unity. King János was recognized by France, which even took him as an ally, his country became a protectorate of the Porte, and he was helped by his brother-in-law, King Sigismund of Poland, was received with understanding by the Holy See, and established direct contact with the Emperor Charles V, who recognized the need for a new unity of Europe. At all costs, János wanted to avoid civil war, and his religious policy was marked by openness, enhanced by the fact that his wife, Isabella, had been brought up in the spirit of Italian and Polish humanism. The speeches delivered by his envoys were imbued with the spirit of European unity. In April 1541, at the Imperial Diet of Ratisbon, the princes engrossed in religious struggle listened to a Hungarian proposal: *"Put an end to senseless polemics, leave off purposeless and senseless enmity! Abandon mutual hostilities at least at the hour of extreme peril. Should Hungary perish, the whole of Europe would suffer the consequences!"*

When Suleiman's Janissaries occupied Buda in 1541, King János was already dead. Isabella, the widowed queen, fled to Transylvania with her infant son. She also took with her a copy of an important work by Erasmus, the *Institutio Principis Christiani* (The Education of the Christian Prince) which Erasmus had dedicated to Charles V, at the time sixteen years of age. The copy Isabella took to Transylvania bore the following note: *Sum Johannis Regis Electi Hungariae* (I belong to János, the elected king of Hungary). It has not yet been fully clarified to what extent the principles of the work had influenced King János; what is certain is that they did prevail in the education of his son. This is all the more important as few princes have been entrusted with a greater task, or under more adverse conditions, than the young János Zsigmond, who had to create a state.

The Principality of Transylvania came into being out of the eastern parts of János Szapolyai's kingdom. Buda, together with the fertile plains, the eastern part of Transdanubia and the lower tip of Transylvania, was under Turkish rule. In 1570, János Zsigmond renounced the crown and became Prince of Transylvania. Along with maintaining the traditions of the Hungarian royal court, Transylvania had to undertake all the duties that fell to Hungarian statehood. The law decreeing religious tolerance was born with the Transylvanian state in 1568, as part of the very process of building that state.

The constitution and institutions of the new state were created between 1541 and 1570. At first, the Transylvanian Estates (known as the "three nations", consisting of the nobles [Hungarians], Székelys and Saxons, with mediaeval institutional privileges), led by György Martinuzzi (1482–1551), the Bishop of Várad and chancellor, who as regent governed on behalf of a ruler then still a minor, managed to get Suleiman and Ferdinand I to recognize their right to elect a prince; they established the country's economic independence and defence, developed channels of international mediation and diplomacy, and set up a flourishing princely court in Renaissance spirit. The Szeben Diet of 1566 set down the basic principle of policy: *"The cure of the country rests equally on the law and on arms."* The new value assigned to the law, placing it above arms, tallies with Erasmus' requirement that the prince must try to ensure domestic peace by the rule of law.

The law had to be enforced to ensure domestic peace as the young Transylvanian state was not only threatened by foreign powers but by the spectre of civil war as well. The sanctity of private property was strictly protected: the theft of a few bunches of grapes or of a sheep was punished by hanging. Those taking the rogue's part or protecting the criminal, be they Székely, Saxon or nobleman, *"must be punished with the same punishment as are the thieves, indeed, they should be hanged even higher..."* At the same time, a whole range of laws were passed on the prevention of crime and on clemency. Help had to be provided to the poor, the abject, the injured; the punishment of forfeiting property could not be extended to heirs, the sins of the fathers could not be visited on the children and grandchildren. Rehabilitation was due to well-behaved criminals after a year, and after three years the mark of punishment was annulled once the criminal had atoned for his crime. These were humane laws, and seemed to echo Erasmus' *"the law only serves public welfare"*. It was in the basic interest of the young Transylvanian state to create domestic peace, law and order. The law on religion passed by the Torda Diet fits well into this conception of the polity.

Earlier historians tended to derive the law of religious freedom from János Zsigmond's Polish and Italian upbringing, his classical education and possibly his preference for literature and music over the martial virtues, for which he was even considered by some as a "weak", enervated ruler. János Zsigmond was indeed an educated prince. When he was 17 years old, the Venetian envoy, Paolo Tiepolo wrote of him that *"he may become one of the most eminent princes of the age"*. Dionigi Atanagi, the Roman humanist, dedicated an anthology to him in 1565, which included two sonnets by Michelangelo. The prince spoke fluent Italian and was a skilled musician: as a boy he was presented a virginal by the Saxons of Szeben, and he welcomed Bálint Bakfark, the Brassó-born virtuoso lutanist and famous master of polyphonic music, at his court. The princely court at Gyulafehérvár was a microcosm of this divided Europe, a meeting place of languages, religions and schools of thought. But the law on religion was not passed by the Prince alone, under the influence of one of these schools, as had earlier been thought; it was the outcome of a concerted effort by the Diet and the Prince.

The blurred features of two generations appear against the background of the law: the survivors of Mohács and the first generation born after the catastrophe. Among them were István Báthori, the Captain-General of Várad, and later Prince of Transylvania and King of Poland, Kristóf Hagymássy, the national Captain-General and Lord Lieutenant of Central Szolnok County, Michael Hermann, the Chief Magistrate of Brassó, and Peter Haller, a Saxon and mayor of Szeben. Johannes Honterus, the humanist scholar and founder of the Lutheran Church of the Saxons, was no longer alive at the time of the Torda Diet, but his spirit lived on in his pupils. Giorgio Blandrata, a follower of Miguel Serveto, who had been forced to flee his country and who had found refuge in Transylvania, where he became the court physician, was presumably a member of the princely council. One of the catalysers of the law in all probability was Ferenc Dávid (cca 1510–1579), a theologian educated in the humanist atmosphere of the princely seat of Gyulafehérvár and at Wittenberg University, whose life brought him from the rectorates of the Latin schools at Beszterce and then Kolozsvár, to the court-chaplaincy. Dávid established Unitarianism as part of an anti-Trinitarian trend.

Transylvania accepted the Reformation at a very early stage, but this did not lead towards a dominant single faith; rather, it gave rise to the speedy establishment of various denominations in a region where Rome and Byzantium met and overlapped. Transylvania had always had powerful commercial and cultural links with other parts of Europe. The Saxons, with their many towns, had close links with other German-speaking areas.

The Hussites, the Renaissance and Humanism, and the spirit of reform associated with the Franciscans had all found a ready response there.

By 1568, the great tide of the Reformation had already engulfed the whole principality. Szeben, a centre of the Saxons, had been Lutheran since 1526; by 1542 Honterus had organized the Saxon Church. In the 1550s,

Calvinism gained ground, mainly among the Hungarian lower nobility. Roman Catholicism, in a minority, still survived among a few aristocratic families such as the Báthoris, and in enclaves in the Székely Country. In the early 1560s, anti-Trinitarianism appeared, midst stormy religious debates, particularly in Kolozsvár and Torda and the Székelys of Udvarhelyszék. The greatest in number in the principality were Protestants of one sort or another, but none of the denominations was able to achieve dominance, nor did religious division follow precisely the borders set up by social conditions or by feudal society. The 1568 Diet assembled at a time when conditions were ripe for a settlement by law of the religious situation.

Europe had been trying for decades to cope with the chronic crises of conscience that were occasioned by religious conflicts. One of the solutions was thought to lie in the creation of a country with one religion, but violence, coercion and the familiar methods of mental terror led to repeated crises. The Augsburg law of 1555 was the other, which with the principle of *cuius regio eius religio* placed the conscience of subjects into the hands of the prevailing power. Torda opted for a different way.

The first sentence of the 1568 law refers to the fact that the Diet had previously already passed laws concerning religion, and it "reaffirms" these. The religious laws of 1545, 1548, 1552 and 1564 recognized the new denominations and guaranteed their functioning. Furthermore, the laws passed in 1544 and 1545 also tried to lay down a *status quo,* and put an end to further innovations.

The third group of laws directly anticipated the spirit of the 1568 law. They express the demand to accept other people's religious convictions and respect the individual. The Torda Diet took a typical stand in 1545. György Martinuzzi, the Regent, wishing to stem the Reformation which had spread like wildfire among the Saxons, summoned Honterus to attend the diet. However, the princely council, including its Catholic members, observed that the whole Saxon nation had already accepted *Libellus Reformationis,* and opposed the Regent with the Estates also taking the side of Honterus. At the same time, they laid down in law that the priests of the old religion, that is Catholic priests, could not be hindered or restricted in the practice of their office, nor could they be molested. Punishment was due to people who scandalized or offended others. According to the 1557 law, everybody was free to follow the religion he chose, whether it included the old or new liturgies, but followers of the new denominations were not to incommodate the adherents of the old. The Torda decree of 1563 is worthy of particular attention. For the first time the use of churches in parishes with adherents of various religious denominations was regulated. Accordingly, the various denominations among the Székelys were to use the church jointly by holding divine services in turn, each minister of religion waiting until the other concluded his service. They had thus sought peaceful solutions even earlier and had tried to establish the mechanisms of mutual tolerance.

The 1568 law went further in four respects.

The new law left Biblical exegesis to the preachers: *"the preachers are to preach the Gospel everywhere, each according to his own interpretation"*.

The choice of religion and of the preacher became the right of the parishes, of the shared institutions of the faithful. In other words, it was not any form of temporal authority – the state or the landlord – which decided on their spiritual matters, but the towns, market-towns and villages themselves: *"and the parish, if it wants to accept it, should do so, but if not, nobody should force it by compulsion, but it should have a preacher whose teachings are to its liking"*.

The law protects the preacher who expounds the Gospel according to his own interpretation, and it also protects the parishes which take the decisions: *"none of the superintendents nor anyone else should offend the preachers, no one should be abused by anyone for his religion, in keeping with the previous constitutions, and no one is permitted to threaten anybody with captivity or removal from his post because of his teaching"*.

Finally, perhaps the most important aspect of all, the law leaves religion to the conscience of the individual, i.e., it sets down the principle of freedom of conscience: *"Because faith is the gift of God, it springs from listening, which listening forwards the word of God"*.

Interestingly, the reason directly given in the law for these decisions of great consequence is freedom of conscience. Implied is also public interest: the first sentence refers back to the previous laws, and so the reason given at the 1564 Diet remains valid, *"pro quiete regnicolarum"*, a looser interpretation of which would be *pro quiete Regni*, that is in the spirit of the law, in the interest of the peace of the realm.

For nearly a century now, there has been a debate among Hungarian historians over the character of this law. Is it really the first (and a particularly early) formulation of religious freedom and tolerance in modern times? And if it establishes freedom of worship, is it not biassed at the expense of the Catholics, and particularly of the Orthodox Romanians, who at the time made up about 25 per cent of the inhabitants of Transylvania?

The Diet did not, and could not make provisions on returning goods and chattels that had been taken from the Catholic Church. This would have been contrary to the spirit of the law, which wished to stabilize the conditions established, and which set down that it is the individual and the parish that make decisions on religious matters, and the Prince, and hence temporal authority, has no right to interfere. At the time of the Diet, the Transylvanian bishopric had long been vacant. That was partly due to reasons outside of the Transylvanian Principality, as there was a dispute between the Holy See and the Habsburg king on the question. The Vienna court referred to the Papal bull of the Council of Constance and considered the nomination of bishops as its right. The Holy See, on the other hand, did not accept a state of affairs in which its only part in selecting the successors of the Apostles would be to take note of the filling of the bishopric; no trace was found of the bull among the papers of the Council, and the process was in conflict with canon law. In this context the Catholic Church meant the threat of the enforcement of the power of the Habsburg Emperor and King in the Principality, and alarming signs of religious persecution were already evident in royal Hungary. The young Transylvanian state had to defend itself against the influence of the foreign power; it could not afford a civil war to rage within a fragile country. Nevertheless, the Torda law included no form of prohibition, and its principles concerning freedom of conscience and the respect for religious conviction were valid for all the religions, including the Catholics.

Neither the social nor the ecclesiastical conditions allowed for an institutionalized acceptance of the Orthodox religion. Orthodox Transylvanians were subject to the bishopric of Wallachia; the Romanians had no hierarchy within the Principality and their ecclesiastic language was church Slavonic. Some of the Romanians practised transhumant animal husbandry, with a seasonal movement of sheep between the pastures on the slopes of the Carpathians, within the territories of the Transylvanian Principality and the Romanian Principalities in Moldavia and Wallachia. Nonetheless, Transylvania designated a bishop at the head of Orthodox Romanians in Transylvania, and first the Saxons of Szeben, then those of Brassó set up printing presses and promoted the translation of various religious texts, including the Bible, into Romanian, with the intention of spreading reformed faith. A special paragraph of the law the Torda Diet passed in 1568, compelled Orthodox believers to accept the bishop appointed by the Prince. This, of course, asserted the influence of the state, but at the same time the 1566 ruling also remained valid: *"concerning religion, it has been established that in keeping with the previous articles, the preaching of the Gospel should not be hindered among any of the nations"*.

A real novelty of the 1568 law is the confidence it places in the people. It confides in the individual's ability to take his own decision, all by himself, without any outside influence, by listening to his inner voice. It has confidence in the inhabitants of towns, market towns and villages that they are able to choose and protect the peace of their parish. In fact this places responsibility on the people. Man is responsible for the creation of his own spiritual peace and for creating the conditions under which people of different faiths can live peacefully alongside one another. It grants confidence to people in themselves and in their fellow-beings when it lays down that they should respect the religion of the other man, as the other man too, respects his. All this called for neither more nor less than for the communities to learn how to deal with their daily conflicts and to develop skills in solving the conflicts arising from their being different.

The basic principles of this law prevailed all during the existence of the Principality, despite the changing and often tragic and serious condition of Transylvania.

The law reiterated repeatedly (1570, 1572) that the Prince cannot interfere in religious matters, while it is his duty to punish the "innovators", that is not to allow any change in the basic spirit of the 1568 law. One reason for this conservative element was to prevent temporal power to allot undue advantage to any one of the religions over another if, or whenever, power came into different hands. Of course, it was impossible for all this to succeed in its pure form. New solutions to the issues were particularly called for by changing conditions.

But the majority of new decisions were taken in the spirit of the Torda law of religious freedom. In the grave situation of the 17th century, Transylvania remained a receptive country. It offered refuge to the Anabaptists who were expelled from Moravia, the Unitarians from Poland, and fugitives from the Hungarian kingdom, regardless of religious denomination. It received enterprising merchants, Armenians, Jews, Greeks, members of the Levant Company, and the Orthodox from the Wallachian Principality. The spirit of respect for the human dignity of people of different religions is reflected in the letters patent Prince Gábor Bethlen (1580–1629) granted to the Jews: "*They will be granted religious freedom which they can practise according to their ritual custom but without disturbing others*". The patent issued in 1623 also sets down that they may move about without any distinguishing mark "*in Christian apparel*", since any discrimination is "humiliating". The patent ensures several economic advantages and the right to integration, and concludes: "*These are the privileges which we have ordered for the aforementioned people of Jewish religion, to be executed readily and with respect*".

Recent studies have justified the report by the Calvinist Bishop János Keserűi Dajka (cca 1580–1633) of Transylvania, according to which Gábor Bethlen was surrounded by many people of different religions, "*by virtue of the country's laws"*, and more than half of his councillors were Catholics. In his testament, the Prince reiterated the basic principle of the Torda Diet; it sets down that the country's perils can be avoided if they respect God, maintain unity among themselves, and *"do not quarrel with each other over religion, but leave that to the judgement of the high Priest in heaven, where He will repay everyone according to his deserts: let them not be priests and let them not save others by force; they should let them live in freedom according to the country's constitution, accepting whichever of the four accepted religions."*

Prince György II Rákóczi (1621–1660) confirmed the liberty of conscience and the right of serfs and villages to freely choose their religion, in his code issued in 1652, called the *Approbatae Constitutiones*, which forbids all forms of pressure.

The spirit of the law prevails in the assistance and rights granted to Orthodox Christians. Prince Mihály Apafi (1632–1690) confirmed the financing of the Romanian school founded in Fogaras by Prince György I Rákóczi (1591–1648) and his Consort, Zsuzsanna Lorántffy (1600–1660), and provided princely protection to the first, and highest standard, establishment for educating Romanian priests and teachers. He also summoned the Romanian bishop to the Diet.

The influence of the law on religion of 1568 could be felt in the Habsburg kingdom as well. Cardinal Péter Pázmány (1570–1637), the leading figure of the Counter-Reformation, and Archbishop of Esztergom, was familiar with conditions in Transylvania and had the cause of the Principality at heart. He also maintained close contacts with Prince Gábor Bethlen. In a recently published *Opinio*, dated 1608, Pázmány wished to uphold the exercise of free religious choice in opposition to the extremists. Miklós Zrínyi (1620–1664), Ban of Croatia, general, poet and politician, stressed, in the knowledge of religious conditions in Transylvania, that since there were various religions in the Kingdom as well, the reform of the country should be started by putting an end to religious animosities and ensuring the free practice of religion. The Habsburg government came to a *modus vivendi* on the question of religion after the uprising led by Imre Thököly (1657–1705). But while in Transylvania free choice of religion was the legal right of serfs as well, the compromise arrived at in the Kingdom tried to attend to the grievances of Protestants in a law passed by the Sopron Diet of 1681, by paying due regard to seigneurial rights as well. Finally, after the Turks had been driven out of Hungary by the Holy League, Ferenc II Rákóczi (1676–1735) led an insurrection against the absolutist Habsburg Emperor and Hungarian king, at the time of the War of Spanish Succession. Rákóczi organized a new Hungarian state in the Kingdom, and he asserted the spirit of the Torda Diet there as well. The Szécsény Diet in 1705 declared the general principle of religious freedom, restricted seigneurial rights, and took stock of churches according to parishes, taking into consideration the religious division of the inhabitants and allotting the church to the majority denomination, but obliging them to help the minority in building their own church. The hospitals and alms houses, whichever denomination they may have belonged to, were compelled to receive the poor regardless of their denomination.

The law passed by the Torda Diet and freedom of worship created the conditions for freedom of education in the vernacular, since schools, printing presses and gifts, and stipends for study abroad, the pulpit and all the important means of institutionalized education in the vernacular, were in the hands of the churches. The national cultures of peoples of different languages, living side by side, in enclaves, and in mixed areas, were nurtured by the free development of their own vernacular tongue.

As a mark of the influence of the 1568 law, Comenius (Jan Komensky, 1592–1670) seems to have been searching for a solution in a similar direction. He had close links with Transylvania and was aware of the fact that the Principality was the only one of the countries in the region where freedom of conscience and the free exercise of religion were assured by law, and where the children of the three nations, Hungarians, Saxons and Romanians, could study in their vernacular. Comenius came to Hungary after he had learned that his homeland, Bohemia, was left out of the Peace Treaty of Westphalia, which meant for him and for his co-religionists that – as he wrote it – having lost the independence of their country, they will *"never be granted liberty of conscience"*. He started to draw up a comprehensive programme in the Calvinist college of Sárospatak, the bridge-head of the Transylvanian Principality, with a view to mutual understanding between the peoples of Central Europe, divided in religion and language. Mátyás Bél (1684–1749) examined the towns and villages in the Hungarian kingdom under different conditions, but with similar notions in mind, when he recorded the religions of the inhabitants, and described how followers of the various denominations were living together, as it was his conviction that religious tolerance constituted one of the main conditions for prosperity in the region.

The idea of civic tolerance began to crystallize in the debates of the late 17th century. There is no evidence whatever that French, English and Dutch authors were familiar with the conditions of the Principality, although the awareness of religious freedom in Transylvania often featured in reactions abroad to the rebellions in Hungary and to political polemics. But it is unlikely that the knowledge of the law passed by the Torda Diet had reached, say, Pierre Bayle (1647–1706) when, a good hundred years later, he wrote: "*Nothing would be more suitable to turn the world into a bloody theatre of chaos and butchery than to accept the principle that all those who are convinced of the truth of their religion have the right to wipe out everybody else... It is obvious that true religion, whatever it should be, cannot grant the right for violence against others...*" A similar conceptual congruence can be observed in Bayle's opinion stressing the sovereignty of conscience: "*On the subject of religion the rule of judgment lies in the conscience and not in reason.*"

It can be taken for granted that John Locke was also unfamiliar with the religious conditions in Transylvania when he wrote his *Epistola de tolerantia* in 1685, when in hiding in Amsterdam. Bayle taught philosophy in Rotterdam from 1681 onward and dozens of Transylvanian students were studying at universities in the Netherlands. Amsterdam granted asylum to Comenius and to Polish, Bohemian and Moravian fugitives. Anyway, the thoughts expressed under the ogive arches of the Torda church in the winter of 1568 were a distant prelude to Locke's ideas: the authorities, the state may not interfere in the faith of the individual. "*...no man can so far abandon the care of his own eternal salvation as to embrace under compulsion worship or faith prescribed by someone else, be he prince or subject. For no man even if he would, can believe at another's dictation... the care of souls cannot belong to the civil magistrate, because his power consists wholly in compulsion. But true and saving religion consists in the inward persuasion of the mind, without which nothing has any value with God and such is the nature of human understanding, that it cannot be compelled by any outward force. Confiscate a man's goods, imprison or torture his body: such punishments will not make him change his inward judgment of things.*"

Cardinal Péter Pázmány the Diplomat

Cardinal Péter Pázmány Archbishop of Esztergom (1570–1637), the highest church dignitary of the Kingdom of Hungary, wrote his last letter to György I Rákóczi (1591–1648), Prince of Transylvania. He asked Rákóczi to maintain at any price, if necessary even by dissimulation, the peace and security of Transylvania in the face of any new act of conquest on the part of the Ottoman power.[1]

What principles are implied in these ideas amounting to a political testament? What did the statesman do and what was it that he could not do but only would have liked to do when, a few days before his death, he sent from the Kingdom of Hungary, which was in close relationship with the Habsburg Empire, a political programme to the ruler of the Principality of Transylvania or – in contemporary terms – "the other Hungarian country"?

What could he judge correctly, and what was he mistaken in? What did he feel he should, even after several decades of strenuous political exertions, pass on unfinished to the next generation?

Pázmány, the victorious pioneer of the Counter-Reformation in Hungary, was portrayed by Hungarian historians of earlier times mostly as a staunch adherent of the Habsburg dynasty. But his letter to György Rákóczi hardly fits into this picture, since even in the dark days of parting with the world, in the doorway between death and eternal life, he was concerned with the Turkish menace and the future of Protestant Transylvania.

Pázmány's statesmanlike ideas and decisions, endeavours and deeds, everything covered, in the 17th century, by the concept of politics, the art

"Erdély és a török kérdés Pázmány politikájában." In: *Europica varietas – Hungarica varietas*. Akadémiai Kiadó, Budapest, 1994 (Transl. by Sándor Simon).

[1] Pázmány to Prince György I Rákóczi of Transylvania. Pozsony, March 11, 1637. Holograph original in the Transylvanian Museum Archives, Sándor Mike coll. No. 9. Cf. *Pázmány's collected letters*: 1910–1911, II, pp. 757–758.

of possibilities – all these have so far been hardly studied at all by writers of history, although it is undeniable that Pázmány was one of the most fascinating personages of Hungary's 17th-century history. Born the son of a Calvinist deputy lord-lieutenant of the County of Bihar, he turned Catholic practically as a child and joined the Order of Jesuits, then became Archbishop of Hungary in 1616 and finally died as a cardinal. He was an influential religious polemist, reformer of the Catholic Church, founder of a university, theologian, author, organizer, orator, educationalist, a modern agriculturist, the embodiment of an original mentality, representation and conduct of life. Also, he was the "father of Hungarian prose". His fascinatingly rich lifework is a subject studied, in a virtually interdisciplinary workshop by successive generations of experts in ecclesiastical and literary history, historians, philologists, writers. The monograph written in the 19th century by Vilmos Fraknói (1843–1924) was followed by a great number of specialist studies throwing light on more and more, as yet unexplored, fields of Pázmány's ecclesiastical and literary activity, and in the course of time even a fuller, up-to-date reconstruction of his path of life turned out to be a task beyond the capacity of several generations. Today we can see the lifework of the author, the theologian, the prelate and the polemist in harmonious unity, while the figure of the politician has had little interest for the researchers.[2]

Pázmány's view on Transylvania and the domination of the Ottoman power was usually illustrated by his statement recorded in the "Autobiography" of János Kemény, a politician of the Principality: "It would be a wretched man who would urge you to break with the Turks, to be kicking against them, until God takes pity on Christendom otherwise, because you live in their jaws... Our credit with the German nation lasts as long as a Hungarian Prince makes his authority felt in Transylvania; afterwards we shall forthwith fall into contempt, and the Germans will spit under our collars..."[3]

Did János Kemény record Péter Pázmány's words authentically? This question has been debated calmly but persistently for more than a hundred years now. Fraknói failed to give an answer, while Sándor Szilágyi (1827–1899) and Vencel Bíró (1895–1962) tried to find one by examining Pázmány's personal contacts with two Princes, Gábor Bethlen and György

[2]   Fraknói: 1868–1872. The matter is clearly elucidated by László Polgár, S.J. in his "Pázmány Bibliography." Altogether 25 items at pp. 413, 473–475 belong under the heading "The statesman educator of the nation." Polgár: 1987.
[3]   *Kemény Önéletírása*: 1657 (1980), p. 100.

Rákóczi. A few historiographers, for example Gyula Szekfű (1883–1955), questioned the authenticity of the statement. Others, among them István Hajnal (1892–1956), accepted it only with some modifications. On the other hand, Sándor Sík (1889–1963), analysing the text from a stylistic point of view, recognized it to be an original opinion of Pázmány's, but referred the matter to an up-to-date historical scrutiny. "In any case, this bluntly sincere utterance may give food for thought to those who suppose Pázmány's political thinking and action to have been not only uniform but rigid, biassed, one-sidedly dogmatic."[4] The method and the underlying principles of a solution of the problem were outlined long ago by the young Hajnal. What he demanded was a critical study of the sources purified from the fallacies of historicism, an unprejudiced survey of 17th-century Hungarian political trends, up-to-date biographies of historical personages, because amidst party strifes the barons and noblemen "were certainly more concerned with the problem of the nation's survival and the grim hope of renewal than can be told today from the source material that has come down to us." On the other hand, Szekfű in his Bethlen monograph already devoted great attention to Pázmány's Transylvanian politics and hinted concretely that various ambassadorial reports had been indicative of Pázmány's role as an important factor in international diplomacy.[5] But the period between the two World Wars proved to be too short a time; and even Pázmány's opinions quoted in Fraknói's work failed to direct the attention of historical science specially to his politics and international activity. Thus, towards the end of that period the topic of specialized research still to be done was indicated by Sík also with the title of his fine essay "Pázmány and Transylvania."[6]

In the two decades following World War II the continuity of research on Pázmány was maintained by the workshop of Jesuits in Rome. Its modern renaissance was launched by Miklós Őry, S. J. (1909–1984), with his work built upon an extensive exploration of the sources.[7] The results of recent studies of historical topics and ecclesiastical, literary and cultural

[4]   Hajnal: 1929, p. 7. – Szekfű: 1929 (1983). – Sík: 1940, p. 5. – Fraknói: 1868–1872, 1886. – Szilágyi: 1870. – Bíró: 1914.
[5]   Hajnal: 1929, p. 4. – Involuntarily though, Szekfű hindered research on Pázmány by stating as his opinion that "Pázmány's outward life is entirely clear to us today." In his biography of Bethlen, discussing Pázmány's Transylvanian policy in more detail than before, he does not quote Pázmány's above statement, but his remark on János Kemény's "biographic gossip" leaves no doubt as to his judgement. Szekfű: 1929 (1983), p. 275.
[6]   Sík: 1940, p. 5.
[7]   Őry: 1970.

history[8] already make it imperative to answer the question: What was the pragmatic policy summed up in Pázmány's pithy utterance with regard to Transylvania and the Turks that Kemény found worth recording for posterity?

The points of orientation in my investigations are determined by the long-range trends of 17th-century Hungarian political culture. The politics associated with the names of Ferenc I Rákóczi, Palatine Pál Esterházy, Mihály Apafi, Prince of Transylvania, Palatine Ferenc Wesselényi, Archbishop György Lippay and primarily Miklós Zrínyi have led me also to hitherto unknown or less known domains of 17th-century Hungarian history. Where is the origin of political devices like co-operation between the Kingdom and Transylvania, their endorsement of common political aims, the theoretical methods and techniques of peace-making, the range of international activity for Hungarian political culture, continuous readiness and painstaking preparation for the expulsion of the Turks and for the unification of the country.[9] It is in this theoretical frame of reference that I examine in my essay the affairs of the Principality of Transylvania and the restriction of the Ottoman power as part of Pázmány's politics.[10] My only aim is to show that Pázmány the polemist, writer and prelate is, in his capacity as politician, an integral factor of Hungarian political culture as well.

I. VÁRAD: BORDER FORTRESS OF THE CHRISTIANA RESPUBLICA

By his education Pázmány had been prepared for conditions different from those of the political medium he was to work in. His life spanned the great break line of the changes in political power relations: he was born in a Europe celebrating the triumph of Christendom over the Turks at Lepanto

---

[8]   Lukács: 1987. – Szabó: 1987. – Benda: 1978. – Hargittay: 1980, 1987. – Bitskey: 1977, 1986.

[9]   For the first presentation of these problems see my essay "Turkish dominance and Hungarian foreign politics" (1975) which I summed up and supplemented with a bibliography of my relevant part studies in: *Magyarország története 1526–1686*, II (1985). See the chapter entitled "Attempts at Unification." See also R. Várkonyi: 1986a.

[10]   See Polgár: 1987. (Here I express my thanks to Ildikó Horn, István Hiller, Éva Lauter, Árpád Kulcsár, Katalin Tóth, Gábor Várkonyi, former pupils and now colleagues of mine, who as university students freshly applied this research method still new at the time and have since enriched it, as can be seen also from their works referred to in the present essay, with new viewpoints and results.)

(1571) preparing at the same time to continue fighting against them, and when he closed his eyes nobody knew as yet when the Thirty Years' War would be over, when the opportunity would arise again for the European countries to join forces against the Ottoman power. Still, without the promptings of his childhood and early youth Pázmány's politics cannot be fully appreciated.[11]

When he was a boy, Várad, his native town rising on the western border of the Principality, was still a flourishing island-like peace, a bustling commercial centre. It was a connecting link between the parts of the country split up into three: the Principality, the intermediate territory integrated with the Turkish Empire, and the narrow semicircle in the west and north of the Kingdom of Hungary. Várad was a quasi-embodiment of quondam Hungarian unity: people living under the rule of the King of Hungary and Habsburg Emperor met here with the inhabitants of the Principality and the Turkish sultan's subjects. Its market was frequented by Hungarians, Saxons, Romanians – by handicraftsmen, peasants, noblemen, mountain shepherds. The streets between its title-roofed houses with glass windows were swarming with Greek, Turkish, Polish merchants. Going to and for in the fortress were imperial officers, Italian military engineers, soldiers coming from far, refugee burghers from Buda, Székely carters, Saxon brickmakers, stone-cutters and Franciscan carpenters. Masters educated at various universities of Europe taught in its schools, and learned prelates lived in the episcopal palace. The chief justice of the town was a man of letters, Balázs Weres, who had published a Werbőczy translation in Debrecen in 1565, five years before Pázmány's birth.

Várad's strategic importance increased after the occupation of Buda. Being second in rank to the Prince, its commandant-in chief was governor of the whole "Partium", (the territory on the western fringes of Transylvania which had been originally "parts" of the Kingdom of Hungary), and held the office of lord-lieutenant of the County of Bihar which was the immediate stepping-stone to the Princedom in terms of dignity and power. István Báthori (1553–1586) was the first commandant-in-chief of Várad to ascend the princely throne – precisely in the year of Pázmány's birth.

Barely a generation after the Mohács disaster (1526) Várad was an exceptionally open-minded community. A cradle of Hungarian humanism, it managed to ride out the storms of the election of two kings without any cultural losses. It was made the scene of the new national politics by the peace of Várad. Maybe already King János but certainly Queen Isabella

[11] Őry: 1970, pp. 11–12. – Zimányi: 1983.

intended to make it the capital of the eastern part of Hungary, of "the other Hungarian country". Her place, the *palatium reginae*, furnished in the left wing of the episcopal court, with its apartments, fine painted ceilings and its bathroom satisfied the requirements of the Renaissance. The cathedral with its liturgical order likewise made it understood that Várad was an episcopal see, the spiritual border fortress of the *Christiana Respublica* in the Turkish frontier zone. The equestrian statue of King László the Saint erected there came to be both an inspirer and commentator of hymns and prayers. The artistifically creative influence emanating from it is eminently testified by an ornamental stove-tile imprinted with the figure of the holy king.

The town instantly embraced the Reformation and became the centre of Protestantism barely a generation after the battle of Mohács. In Pázmány's childhood years the Church of the Holy Ghost in the western section of the town was a place of Protestant worship, and the Protestants had a college in the former Dominican monastery, moreover, a printing press and even a hospital. Péter Pázmány was a pupil of the thriving Protestant school, he enjoyed the protection of the beautifully situated and rich town on the banks of the river Körös, and could have only heard about the devastating Turkish attacks in the borderland.

Safety and Turkish menace! Unity and division! John Calvin's rational faith and the notions of the miracles surrounding the figure of the holy king! All these were experiences of a twofold nature. And if a child's imagination is expanded by the diversity of the world he faces and the richness of life he stares at in wonder, Pázmány can be said to have had a lucky childhood.

Situated in the eastern border region of Central Europe, Várad provided also the first "experiences of Italy" as well. In the 1570s Várad was strengthened by fortifications to an unprecedented extent. The building operations took place under the direction of an *architectus Italus* and the military engineer Colonel Domenico Ridolfini from Camerino. As was usual at the time, the contractors brought the workmen and skilled labourers with them. They directed the multitude of stonemasons and foremen-builders, carpenters and brickmakers, bondservants and carters summoned from the town and from more remote places of the County of Bihar to work at the modernization of the fortress of Várad.

The construction was an undertaking of nation-wide interest carried out with a considerable outlay and with all possible speed, under the direction of István Báthori who was Prince of Transylvania from 1571, and King of Poland from 1576. It was a concern of national assemblies. As a child Pázmány must have heard a lot about it in the environment of his father, the deputy lord-lieutenant. Erected before his very eyes were the new bastions: the Prince Royal Bastion, the Truncated Bastion, the Earthwork Bastion and the Golden Bastion, its pediment ornamented with the gilded Báthori coat-of-arms which could be seen intact as late as 1943. The lion holding the coat-of-arms is the personification of courage in the symbolic language of the age. The precipitate pace of construction and its monumentality made people aware of the threatening force of the Turkish menace which it was intended to check, demonstrating at the same time the superiority of the builders' craftsmanship, and transmitting the message of Italy with the introduction of up-to-date military engineering into Transylvania.[12]

Even today we do not know for certain why the Calvinist deputy lord-lieutenant of the County of Bihar sent his talented son to the Jesuit college of Kolozsvár. But it is perhaps more important to note what recent research has proved that in 1583, the time when Pázmány began his studies at Kolozsvár, the college was very much under the spiritual influence of Báthori, then already King of Poland. A very efficient professor of the college, the preacher István Szántó, was a follower of Báthori. Opposing the conceptions of one of the strongest pro-Habsburg parties he supported Báthori's plans with ardent Transylvanian patriotism; he thought that international co-operation could liberate the country from Turkish domination, rouse the population of Hungary and restore the one-time unity of the country.[13] There is no direct evidence to prove that Pázmány knew, even at a later date, of István Báthori's plan for an anti-Turkish international alliance. It is hardly conceivable, however, that his superiors should not have known about and been concerned with Báthori's conception which was to unite the forces of Poland, Transylvania, the Romanian voivodeships and the Habsburg Empire with the assistance of the pope.

[12] Pázmány's memories of Várad as reflected in his writings are summed up and discussed in detail by Őry: 1970, pp. 11–12. We have reconstructed a few crucial points of the double experience on the basis of Jolán Balogh's monograph on Várad. The data she collected on the large-scale work of construction in Várad coinciding with Pázmány's childhood years are still to be analysed further. Balogh: 1982, I, pp. 31, 43 ff; II, pp. 79 ff.

[13] Since the publication of Miklós Őry's work (Őry: 1970) new points of view regarding Pázmány's stay in Kolozsvár have been proposed by Barlay: 1986, pp. 121–144. Contrary to the generally accepted view that the 12-year-old Pázmány was sent to the Jesuit college of Kolozsvár under the influence of his Catholic foster mother, Borbála Telegdi, or becuase of the visit of Várad by Antonio Possevino (Bitskey: 1986, pp. 10–11), Jolán Balogh is of the opinion that it was in 1576, at the time of the building operations, that the Jesuits established themselves in Várad, and that "young Péter Pázmány coming from Bihar started out of their circle to embark on the road of the Counter-Reformation." Balogh: 1982, I, p. 49; II, pp. 82–83.

II. AN EXPERIENCE OF TRANSYLVANIA
GAINED IN ROME

Pázmány, who asked for admission to the Jesuit Order in 1588, spent half of the nine years of his training in Rome. As has been established by Miklós Őry's researches, it was in the spring of 1593, that after finishing his studies in Cracow and Vienna, Pázmány arrived in the Eternal City. That was the year when the Fifteen Years' War broke out.

For the first time since Lepanto the Christian world went to war once more against the Turks. The war seemed to be the continuation of the preparations broken off because of István Báthori's death in 1586. Not only had Báthori mapped out the plan of an international war but he had taken consistent diplomatic measures as well with the view of making the necessary preparations for it. The same purpose was served by his effort to have his nephew, András Báthori, appointed cardinal, then by his second journey to Rome, to Pope Sixtus V who, like his predecessor, Gregory XIII, espoused the plans and decided also to grant the necessary subsidy for the war, and even paid out part of it. The Jesuits – among them István Szántó, János Leleszi and Alfonso Pisa – also espoused the cause out of staunch patriotism; András Báthori received a loan of several thousand thalers from the local Jesuits to defray some of his expenses in Rome. According to the plans the armies of several European countries were expected to go into action, and so was the fleet of the Christian League. Though the sudden death of the King of Poland interrupted the preparations, local skirmishes continued and planning dragged on, until the Ottoman power struck first, as usual, and by launching a general attack, forestalled the war that was about to start as a joint undertaking of united Christendom.

Thus the war against the Turks was a cause embraced by Rome as well right at the moment of its outbreak. The young Prince of Transylvania, Zsigmond Báthori (1588–1597, 1602) obeyed the orders of his uncle when, contrary to the warning from the Sublime Porte, he did not go to war in support of the Turks but, in the middle of 1594, crushed the party opposed to the anti-Turkish war and sent his emissaries to Pope Clement VIII and to Rudolf, Holy Roman Emperor and King of Hungary (1576–1612). The anti-Turkish alliance between Transylvania and the Habsburgs was concluded with the help of papal diplomacy (28 January 1595) as a result of P. Alfonso Carillo's lengthy preparatory efforts. During Pázmány's years in Rome there was a lively contact between the Holy See and the Principality: nuncios went to Transylvania, and Báthori's envoys paid visits to the papal court. The evidence Miklós Őry has found proves that Jesuit scholastics in Rome followed the events of war with attention, and when Győr was occupied by the Turks or when Esztergom was taken by the Christian forces, they undertook to do severe penance, expressing thereby that in spirit they were taking part in the struggle.

However, the battleground of key importance was Transylvania and Wallachia. While on the territory of the Kingdom a certain state of equilibrium was maintained between the opposite parties in 1593–1594, the Christian forces appear to have gained the upper hand in the south-eastern area. Having come to terms with the voivodes of Moldavia and Wallachia and joining the Christian League, Báthori scored a number of victories: the Transylvanian troops recaptured Lippa and Jenő, together with the forces of Wallachia they took Targoviste after a three days' siege, and defeated the troops of Grand Vizier Sinan at Giurgevo. But after the great victories of 1595 came the bloody events of an internal civil war. Zsigmond Báthori managed to raise a highly efficient army by emancipating Székely commoners who joined his forces. However, he was not strong enough to put the princely decision into practice. The movement of the Székely commoners trying to assert their right by legal means was quelled by the nobility who insisted on exacting villein services from them. The ruthless reprisal known as the "bloody carnival" was followed by an internal war lasting several years. In this way Transylvania which had won the first few victories in the Christian–Turkish conflict, became a de- . fenceless victim of the protracted war, and the people of the country suffered no end of unprecedented reprisals, persecutions and ravages.

In the years of Pázmány's stay in Rome his superiors practically kept abreast of what was going on in Transylvania. News of the battles and jubilant accounts of Báthori's victories describing them in detail are to be found in the letters regularly sent by the Jesuit missions of the Principality and in P. Alfonso Carillo's reports, which have in recent years been discovered, collected and published by the Jesuit László Lukács. We consider it impossible that Pázmány should not have had information about all that. He had relatives living in Transylvania, and till then he himself had spent the greater part of his life there. As can be concluded from his later decisions and opinions it was there, in Rome that he fully realized how fundamentally important it was to have a strong, well-knit international alliance for pressing back the Turks; however, Transylvania was too frail and weak to bear the greater part of the burden of the alliance as István Báthori had envisaged. Even so the war demanded tremendous sacrifices in men of the mutilated country, which, in order to survive, was in need of internal reforms and unity in the first place. It is perhaps by thinking about the fate of the cheated Székely commoners that he got so far as to stand up for the heyducks.[14]

He had to deal more thoroughly with the Transylvanian changes if only because his superiors had planned as early as 1595 to send him to Transylvania. For the time being, however, he was given a task apparently quite apart from his future mission. Miklós Őry's research has made it clear that in the school-year 1594/1595 he was a professor's assistant at the English college in Rome. Would it be accidental that the beginning of the Principality's English connections and Pázmány's appointment to his post at the English college coincided in time? Báthori delegated his envoy István Kakas to the Queen of England with a view to obtaining support in anticipation of an attack of the Porte and entering into contact with the Persians through the agency of the English resident in Constantinople. The Christian League counted upon Persia which was then growing in strength, and it reckoned with an attack to be launched by Shah Abbas from Eastern Anatolia. It is obvious that more thorough research would be needed to clarify whether Pázmány's commission to teach at the English college fitted in with the more comprehensive plans considering his future functions, and whether it served as a sort of training for the implementation of those plans. And was there any connection between Pázmány's English contacts and the lively, unflagging interest he would later show in Persian affairs?

If we examine the long-term plans of Europe preparing to force back the Turks and if we reconstruct, in this context, the attempts made by Hungarian politicians to reoccupy Hungary, to restore the unity of the country, it cannot be doubted that Pázmány, too, was attracted towards those two distant countries by something more than mere autotelic or accidental curiosity. Later on, the barons and members of the lesser nobility engaged in politics in the circles of Palatine Miklós Esterházy and then

[14] Nagy, L.: 1983. – Demény: 1977. – Őry: 1970, p. 131. – Lukács: *Monumenta*, 1987, IV, pp. 3–8. – P. Sz. Szántó to P. Acquaviva, Vienna, Oct. 28, 1594. – Ex litteris annuis provinciae Austriae S. I. Anni 1594. – P. A. Carillo to P. L. Maggio, Monostor, May 16, 1595. – P. M. Pollardt to P. B. Viller. Szamosújvár, Oct. 24, 1595. P. A. Carillo to P. B. Viller, Kolozsvár, Nov. 2, 1595. P. C. Acquaviva's congratulations on Báthori's victories, Rome, Jan. 13, 1596. In: Lukács: *Monumenta*, 1987, IV, pp. 94–103, 118–120, 137–138, 162–163, 165–166, 190–191. See also Veress: 1929–1933, II, pp. 150–157, 174–178. On the victories at Temesvár, Lippa, Giurgevo and elsewhere: Veress: 1929–1933, II, pp. 186–190, 207–213. – On Pázmány's mission to Transylvania, P. C. Acquaviva to P. L. Maggio. Rome, July 15, 1595. In: Lukács: *Monumenta*, 1987, IV, pp. 152–153.

Palatine Pál Pálffy were characterized by extremely wide international interests. Zrínyi always counted upon the Persians in his strategic plans to expel the Turks. As is known, it was by the cover-name "Kazul Pasha" that he kept mentioning in his writings the power threatening the eastern confines of the Ottoman Empire. His secretary of Irish birth, Mark Forstall, often exchanged letters with his brother, and he was thereby informed about developments in English political life. Though in his pamphlet *An Antidote to Turkish Opium* (1663) Zrínyi spoke of England as a different, remote world, and, reckoning with realities, stated that we could not expect military assistance from there, at the same time English politicians were informed, probably through Regensburg, about all the events of the 1663–1664 war. It is also beyond doubt that the extremely rich contemporary English literature dealing with Zrínyi must suggest the existence of foreign relations still to be explored. Further examination is necessary to clarify an interesting phrase found in the coded correspondence of Hungarian politicians organizing against the Turks. A cipher key used in 1663–1664 contains the following phrase: "The Crown = Gift from England."[15]

Reckoning with the actual power relations, Hungarian politicians always knew that an anti-Turkish war could be waged successfully only if several countries joined forces. And in the anti-Turkish international alliance they counted upon the Holy See in the first place. The antecedents of all these are already to be found also in the Hungarian politics of the time of the Fifteen Years' War.

In 1596, the year when Pázmány was ordained priest, the Hungarian barons and members of the lesser nobility, the Estates whose 90 per cent were still Protestant, petitioned the pope to render them assistance, both diplomatic and financial, in bringing to success the war for forcing back Ottoman power.

Pázmány's superiors considered on several occasions that they would send him to Transylvania. Yet nothing came of it and contrary to the expectations of his vice-provincial he never became a preacher to serve the cause of Europe and Hungary from the pulpit of the cathedral of

---

[15] Őry: 1970, pp. 91 ff. Concerning the fact, that in matters of theology and mainly church doctrine, Pázmány was a follower of the Leuven and the English trend rather than of the southern, Roman line, see *ibid.*, p. 118. On Báthori's English connections, too, see Veress: 1929–1933, IV, pp. 25–29. – Demény: 1977, p. 16. – Kara: 1987. – S. Lauter: 1989. – Fodor: 1989. – *Angol életraj Zrínyi Miklósról:* 1987, and its criticism in Gömöri: 1988, pp. 65–93. – For the code list, which has been pointed out to me by Árpád Kulcsár, see MOL P 659, fasc. 51. Teleki Arch. Missilis dept.

Gyulafehérvár, seat of the Principality under Turkish protection.[16] The modification of his career coincided and was probably connected with a radical change in international and domestic conditions.

In Europe the dawn of the 17th century was marked by the disenchanting light of crises. Fernand Braudel (1902–1985) points out that the reason why the Lepanto victory could have no sequel was that it was not enough to defeat the Turks at sea, since the power of the Ottoman Empire was deeply rooted in vast inland regions of the continent. The Fifteen Years' War, on the other hand, demonstrated also that the Ottomans could not be defeated on land alone. Europe had been economically exhausted in the long-lasting warfare. The Christian countries eagerly looked for new ways to establish a state of equilibrium: instead of fighting against the Turks, they wanted to trade with them, and they were grinding their swords against one another.[17] International power relations were shifting, and the Bourbon and Habsburg dynasties turned against each other to maintain their superiority. The Peace of Zsitvatorok which put an end to the Fifteen Years' War stabilized for decades to come the frontiers and co-existence of two weakened powers, the Ottoman Empire and the Habsburg Empire – with Spain also included in the text of the treaty.[18] Lepanto and the Fifteen Years' War were nevertheless grandiose events, materializing for Pázmány's generation the possibility of achieving the initial victories over the Turks and of forming an international alliance. Also, Lepanto and the Fifteen Years' War became an integral part of Hungarian politics and public thinking and lived on in the international symbolic language of the period as a directly transmitted tradition. The separate statehood of the Principality of Transylvania was consolidated, while the narrow crescent of the Kingdom of Hungary began increasingly to be integrated with the Habsburg Empire. Political and economic motives made the Habsburg dynasty interested in keeping the eastern frontiers permanent. The territorial division of medieval Hungary had become a serious reality.

---

[16] The reason of the change is explained in different ways: "there is always something to interfere." Őry: 1970, p. 144. – The superiors were afraid to send the highly educated Pázmány to dangerous Transylvania. Bitskey: 1986, p. 41.

[17] Braudel: 1949–1965, quoted by Zimányi: 1983, pp. 213–214, – Carter: 1964, pp. 11 ff. – R. Várkonyi: 1986b.

[18] Nehring: 1986. – Galavics: 1986 and R. Várkonyi: The opponent's opinion on Géza Galavics's academic doctoral dissertation.

III. THE NEW SPHERE OF ACTIVITY
OF HUNGARIAN POLITICAL CULTURE

How far did Pázmány reckon with the big change in international relations? His judgement of the situation was sharp according to Szekfű, clear
according to Hajnal, and downright *kuruc* in conception – that is, opposed
to the Habsburg dynasty and supporting state sovereignty – according to
Gyula Kornis.[19] Dezső Kosztolányi characterized him as a person reckoning with realities. In Pázmány's writings, he stated, "there is no display
of fireworks: all is real".

It may not have been easy to prognosticate realistically amidst the critical
conditions. In 1616, when Pázmány became Archbishop of Hungary, he
still greeted Palatine György Thurzó by saying: "May the Lord give real
peace unto Christians, so that they might muster more strength against
the natural foe, if need be."[20] And even though he was mistaken in hoping for an anti-Turkish war before long, he shared this error with a future
fellow-cardinal and principal political opponent of his. For it was precisely
in 1616 that Richelieu turned to the pope and the Habsburg government
with a plan of an anti-Turkish international coalition.[21] Rome's answer was
long in coming, while Vienna rejected the plan. In Bohemia the conflict
between the trade interests of the Estates and the Habsburg government
foreshadowed the battle of Fehérhegy (Bila Hová, the Whitehall) and the
Thirty Years' War which were to bring about a tragic change in Czech development. The policy of France was already characterized by a new Turkish orientation, and the sensitive instruments of secret diplomacy everywhere registered the imminent upsetting of the European balance of power
to the detriment of the Habsburgs.[22]

Pázmány's decisions indicate that he also reckoned with the change in
the main trend of international politics. He sized up the short- and long-
range developments at the same time. "I am as much concerned about
Transylvania as about Győr", he stated and in defining his political attitude he always envisaged the unity of the separated parts of the country.[23]

[19] Szekfű: 1935b, p. 24. – Hajnal: 1929, p. 9. – "This is already a kind of prelude to the
lamentation of kuruc times from the lips of a proimperial archbishop." Kornis: 1935. –
Kosztolányi: 1920, p. 914.

[20] Pázmány to Palatine György Thurzó, Prague, Aug. 20, 1616. In: *Pázmány's collected
letters:* 1910–1911, I, p. 60.

[21] Djuvara: 1914, pp. 190–201.

[22] Polišenský: 1968. – Šmerda: 1989, p. 48. – Bóka: 1983, pp. 93–94.

[23] Péter Pázmány to Prince György I Rákóczi, Pozsony, March 30, 1964. in: *Pázmány's
collected letters:* 1910–1911, II, p. 478.

To expect the unification of the country within a short time proved to be a vain hope. Society had lost too much blood. The decrease in population was disastrous. The security of the inhabitants had been shaken and, as Pázmány wrote, their mode of living needed reforming.

Pázmány's rational thinking was emphasized already by Szekfű. Pázmány scholars noticed long ago that the archbishop's innovatory endeavours had not been confined to the reformation of the Catholic religion: namely – although his activity was focussed on the resuscitation of Hungarian Catholicism – he was working hard on the improvement of the whole of Hungarian society. More than once he criticized the social conditions, the absence of internal order, the lack of discipline among the soldiers, he often castigated, as Zrínyi would do later, the disorderliness of Hungarians, their dissension, their ignorance – altogether, their vices.

He demanded order almost ruthlessly, and at the same time, as a competent politician, he did everything he could by the force of words and ideas to restore the impaired self-respect of society. At the time of the 1632 epidemic of the plague, for example, he ordered that whoever failed to meet the requirements of hygiene might be punished with excommunication.[24] And he spared no effort to fill people with courage, hope and self-confidence.

A typical feature of ideas in the 16th–17th centuries is the consciousness of collective guilt. Guilt deserves punishment, a guilty country or a guilty community deservedly receives punishment from God or His vicar on earth – the monarch. This idea appears in various ideological forms. E.g. it was in Pázmány's time that the ideology of the Czech Estates' collective guilt was formulated, according to which the whole country was "put in the dock" because of the Prague uprising. Hungary inherited from the 16th century the body of arguments which maintained that the coming of the Turks to Hungary was a visitation of God for the sins of the Hungarian people. Also Pázmány himself was often concerned with the notion of God castigating people for their sins, but in essence he questioned the idea of a "guilty nation". According to Péter Alvinczi, a Calvinist theologian and pastor of Kassa, the loss of the battle at Várna (1444) was a visitation of God for the violation of an oath by King Ulászló I of Hungary. Pázmány gave a rational explanation: the battle was lost because the Turks were stronger and the king did not take the military commander's advice. In Pázmány's writings the vices of the Hungarian nation are

---

[24] Pázmány to the town council of Nagyszombat and to the whole borough. Sellye, Aug. 22, 1632. In: *Pázmány's collected letters: 1910–1911*, II, p. 348.

always specified, and are never supertemporal and unalterable. He stresses particularly that these sins cannot incur so intense a wrath of God that it would make Turkish domination final and everlasting. "Because, even if a Christian country has done wrong and really pays the penalty, it should not let the innocent community be brought into bondage to the pagans and exposed to spiritual perils..."[25] It can be said with absolute certainty that Pázmány's writings and sermons were intended to awaken people to the consciousness of their ability to act.

The cardinal's decisions show that first and foremost he endeavoured to widen the scope of Hungarian political activities to an unprecedented extent.

The formidable religious polemist was tolerant in political matters. In view of Turkish presence in the country he argued, as early as 1608, in favour of religious freedom.[26] He was on good terms with Palatine György Thurzó, a Protestant. It is characteristic, for example, that in 1616 he stood up for the Protestant heyducks against the Protestant Palatine, when he pointed out – maybe the first among Hungarian statesmen to do so – that Várad was one of the targets in the Turkish plans. If Transylvanians were not on the alert, the city of King László the Saint could easily become Ottoman possession.[27]

In politics Pázmány was guided by the interests of the country. In 1622, after the death of Palatine Forgách, he recommended Batthyány, who was likewise still a Protestant at that time, against two Catholic candidates.[28] He had serious conflicts with the Lutheran Palatine Szaniszló Thurzó, though not because of religious affairs but on account of the internal reform and Transylvania.[29] In the interest of the negotiations for an agree-

---

[25] "On the duty of Christian knights." In: *Pázmány's works:* 1983, p. 305. Cf. Šmerda: 1989, pp. 57–60.

[26] Pázmány's Opinion of July 1608 is also published by Benda: 1978, pp. 225–229.

[27] "De Varadino Turcis tradendo, quae sint ipsius consilia, nescio. Illud scio Illustrissimam D. V. intelligere, quantum juramento ipsius tribui possit, quamque periculosum sit civitatem ipsam iam Turcis replevisse. Quid si occulta obsidione eos, qui in arce sunt, per Turcas civitatem occupantes in potestatem redigere velit? Etiamne tum prohibendi Haydones, qui suo periculo tam insignem Ungariae portionem defendere volunt, ne vim injustam justis armis propulsent? Ego certe Varadinum, et eum, qui ei adiacet, tractum, dignum censeo, pro quo Christianitas universa diu depugnet..." Pázmány to Palatine György Thurzó, Pozsony, Nov. 14, 1616. In: *Pázmány's collected letters:* 1910–1911, I, p. 82.

[28] Várkonyi: 1988, I, p. 152.

[29] Szekfű: 1929 (1983), pp. 206–207. – In 1618 Pázmány included also Szaniszló Thurzó among the possible candidates for confidential posts and high offices. His proposal submitted to junior King Ferdinand II, Pozsony, May 28, 1618. In: *Pázmány's collected letters:* 1910–1911, I, p. 153.

ment on Transylvania he was then ready to permit Protestant serfs on his estate in the County of Somogy the free practice of their religion, and in the cheerless years of the Thirty Years' War he suggested several times that the Habsburg monarch should make peace with the Protestant Princes. A less known detail of his missionary activities is elucidated by what happened to Kőszeg.

Together with Miklós Esterházy and Chancellor István Sennyey, Pázmány stood security with the imperial government for the Protestant borough of Kőszeg when Prince Gábor Bethlen, joining in the Thirty Years' War on the side of the Czech Estates, set his troops in motion to the Kingdom of Hungary. What is more, it was largely due to the Archbishop's support, that at the Diet of 1622 Ferdinand II renewed all the municipal rights of the borough. Later on, between 1627 and 1633, Kőszeg endured the Habsburg government's campaign intended to enforce conversion. By his *General-Mandat* applied in Lower Austria, Ferdinand II ordered the Protestant clergymen and schoolmasters in 1627 to leave Kőszeg, since there was nothing to move the emperor to "permit here (i.e. in the town) the practice of any other" than the Catholic religion. New and new orders issued in response to the stubborn resistance of the borough, the imprisonment of aldermen, negotiations carried on by delegated commissioners left no doubt than the imperial decrees aimed at suppressing the self-government of the borough and severing its ties with the Kingdom of Hungary. By enforcing the principle of *cuius regio eius religio* the monarch would in effect have brought Kőszeg, a town pledged to Lower Austria, though invariably belonging to the diocese of Győr, under the power of the central government: moreover, it is evident from the phrasing of the *General-Mandat* that this same fate was in store for a number of other boroughs and demesnes situated within the boundaries of the Kingdom of Hungary. It is obvious that the court-promoted drive of the Counter-Reformation was guided also by economic interests: thereafter the Kőszeg burghers were obliged to pay taxes not to the Hungarian Treasury but to the Court Treasury. The Habsburgs regarded the boroughs as sources of income elsewhere, too.

Still in 1622 Pázmány intended to found a Jesuit college at Kőszeg, but he changed his mind and chose Győr instead. Earlier he thus openly stood by Protestant Kőszeg, and later displayed no kind of co-operation with the Habsburgs in the state-supported Counter-Reformation. How does all this fit in with his missionary activity for the conversion of Hungarian barons? He knew full well the policy of the Habsburg court, he was aware of the disagreement in the circles of the court aristocracy controlling the government. The interests which aimed at incorporating the Kingdom of

Hungary, and abolishing its independent statehood, by means of the state-supported Counter-Reformation, threatened also the sovereignty of the Hungarian Catholic Church. The obvious way of warding off the menace was to strengthen the Hungarian institutions which should take over the work of re-Catholicization. The reformation of the Hungarian Catholic Church followed at least as much from the intention of reforming the country as from the spirit of the Council of Trent. It became plain that the Hungarian aristocrats could obtain higher government posts, and expect to represent the affairs of their country at the highest level within the framework of the Habsburg Empire, only if they professed the Catholic religion. A war against the Turks could be started only through international co-operation, and a league of the Christian countries seemed unfeasible without the aid of the diplomacy of the Holy See. In addition, there were other factors among his motives, such as concern for the Latin language, for Humanism. And the case of Kőszeg made it clear that the circles holding extreme opinions in the Habsburg government would not tolerate any kind of consensus between Catholicism and Protestantism.

Without contesting the priority of Pázmány's religious conviction in his work for the Counter-Reformation, in view of his political practice, we have to investigate more carefully, and analyse more thoroughly than before, his national motives taken in the contemporary sense. We have to reckon with Hungarian political traditions. A fundamental principle of 17th-century Hungarian political thinking was that power should be divided and controllable. It is interesting to see later Hungarian politicians, such as István Zrínyi and Ferenc II Rákóczi, backing up this Hugo Grotian principle by quotations from Chapter IV of István the Saint's *De morum institutione*. István, the founder of the state, is in Pázmány's opinion one of the pivotal figures of Hungarian politics.[30]

[30] Evans: 1979, pp. 41 ff. – Bariska: 1982, pp. 54–90. – Pázmány to Ferdinand II on the Jesuit college to be founded at Kőszeg (no date). The king referred Pázmány's proposal written in his own hand to the Court Treasury in Vienna. The date of receipt by the Treasury: July 22, 1622. – On the relentless crushing of the opposition of the Győr Chapter objecting to the establishment of the college at Győr, see also Pázmány to Miklós Dallos, bishop of Győr. Pozsony, Oct. 16, 1626. Both in: *Pázmány's collected letters:* 1910–1911, I, pp. 298–299, 543–545. – An essay pointing beyond Szekfű's statement ("The number of his acts of conversion and their results are not sufficiently known to us") on the effectiveness and methods of conversions by Pázmány, and arguing somewhat with Fraknói is: Őry–Szabó: 1983, pp. 45–47. – In Pázmány's opinion, according to Szekfű, religion is above politics. Our analyses vindicate the recent views. Two qualitatively different activities are at issue, and their rating is anachronistic. Cf. Rónay: 1974, pp. 51–52.

Examining the problems of Transylvania and the Turkish question in relation to the Habsburg government, we can find it remarkable in Pázmány's politics to what a great extent he always reckoned with the fierce and desperate fight carried on in this respect by the court parties against one another. He availed himself of the possibilities given by the situation of the moment, but in doing so he always riveted his eyes on the gate of the future. All that could be done under the pressure of the daily routine was a preparation for the great trial of prime necessity, for the long-term chance of expelling the Turks and restoring the unity of the country.

Speaking of Ferdinand II's election at the Pozsony County meeting in 1617, Pázmány presented to the mostly Lutheran members of the lesser nobility the following alternative: "We must either fall into the jaws of the pagans, or seek repose under the wings of the neighbouring Christian Prince."[31] Here the key word was "repose", but not in the sense of acquiescence. As follows from several of Pázmány's relevant disquisitions, this meant that the Hungarian people should take repose in order to gather strength. Why? He articulated his view on a number of occasions in these words: "Because I wish these few Hungarians would be saved for better times."[32]

The notion of a country jammed between two great powers was a political stereotype already in the 16th century.[33] Pázmány's apposite metaphor was later taken over by many authors, even Protestant pamphleteers: "we must suffer both from protection and from enemy like a finger jammed between door and threshold unless we keep quiet."[34] This notion has more than once been brought up in Hungarian political literature in justification for inefficiency, helplessness and lethargy.[35] Pázmány's programme, on the other hand, was not one of passive endurance and sufferance, but a very active programme for a more remote end. This remote

[31] Pázmány's address to the Pozsony County meeting in support of the election of Ferdinand II. In: *Pázmány's works:* 1983, I, pp. 397–398.
[32] Pázmány to György I Rákóczi, Érsekújvár, Jan. 5, 1633. In: *Pázmány's collected letters:* 1910–1911, II, p. 388.
[33] Bitskey: 1977.
[34] Pázmány to the Estates of Upper Hungary in Bethlen's camp. Pozsony, Oct. 22, 1626. In: *Pázmány's collected letters:* 1910–1911, I, p. 546.
[35] "We are pinning between the Turk and the German. / One is a domestic cross, the other is a mere plague, / This is like a snake in our bosom, / The other is a blood-sucking, insatiable bear." Thököly's council of war. Varga: 1977, p. 212.

end was outlined in his address to the Pozsony County meeting, too: a ruler must be elected whose relatives are Christian Princes able to render assistance against the Turks.[36] Surely, there was no politician, general, or thinker who believed that a single country, even the Habsburg Empire was strong enough to fight the Ottomans successfully with no help from others.[37]

Seeing that the Turkish question was an all-European affair at the time, a most urgent matter for Hungarians to be dealt with and settled at none but an international level, Pázmány's international orientation must be regarded as a remarkably original feature of his politics.

I wonder whether his superiors directed his training deliberately so as to enable him to hold his ground in the forums of international politics. He knew Spanish well, he spent a year at the English college in Rome. Jesuit education included, as a rule, the development of statesmanlike abilities in the students. A survey of Pázmány's career shows the great significance of the fact that his training in Rome coincided with the most active period of the Jesuit Order's Transylvanian policy and with the Fifteen Years' War. Nor can it be disregarded that it was the situation in Hungary during the early decades of the 17th century that determined Pázmány's objectives in the international political arena.

In his Pázmány monograph Vilmos Fraknói (1843–1924) already made frequent references to diplomatic sources, but the task he had set to himself was to portray the prelate, not the politician.

Gyula Szekfű was the first modern historiographer to take notice of Pázmány's diplomatic activity as well, but he did not regard it as something really important from the point of view of the cardinal's course of life and political career. Following the old-established interpretative tradition of Hungarian historiography instead, he found it more important to emphasize the Habsburg–Hungarian differences and Gábor Bethlen's armed struggles. The history of Hungarian foreign relations as yet unwritten, he had nowhere to fit in Pázmány's activity in the capacity of a diplomat. In Szekfű's days, and for a long time after, historiography in Hungary was still the history of wars and battles.

"Thus far our historiography has either not or only rather superficially examined the 17th-century foreign relations of the Kingdom of Hungary. The general view has been that the Habsburg court had completely monopolized the conduct and control of foreign affairs concerning Hungary,

---

[36] Pázmány's address. In: *Pázmány's works:* 1983, p. 397.
[37] R. Várkonyi: 1986b, pp. 20 ff.

and the Hungarian Estates had no influence upon shaping the course of diplomatic affairs. By this token it has seemed needless to look into the 'non-existent' foreign relations of the Kingdom of Hungary. At the same time, the work of assessing Habsburg diplomacy from the Hungarian point of view has not been done either."[38] On the whole, the politics of the Kingdom of Hungary have for long been regrettably "written off". They have been labelled unimportant or "loyal to the court", "pro-Habsburg" or "retrograde", "reactionary" or even "antinational". Occasionally they have been described by illustrative methods, made to appear to safeguard the conservative feudal institutions or serve Habsburg absolutism in the traditional old sense within and outside our boundaries alike. More subtle recent descriptions still fail to deal with foreign relations altogether.

Pázmány was not a lonesome politician. The work of examining his chancellery and his party in detail is still to be done. Together with Palatine Miklós Esterházy, his contemporary, he fought hard struggles in defence of the sovereignty of Hungarian state power against the extreme views of government organs in Vienna. Moreover, he endeavoured, using the tug-of-war methods of compromise, to retake from the centralized forums of the increasingly absolutist Habsburg power the functions of the high dignitaries of the kingdom, namely the palatine, the archbishop, the lord chief justice, the ban, – as well as those of the new Hungarian central organs of government, including the Hungarian Treasury. Feudalism and absolutism in Hungary were not so simple phenomena as e.g. in Spain or France. Under the prevailing historical conditions the protection of the constitutional forums of the Kingdom of Hungary, served, like the struggle of the Czech Estates, to safeguard the country's statehood by preventing its annexation.[39]

Pázmány and his contemporaries protected the country's ability to act in the capacity of a state in its own right. They saw the solution not in giving up the interests but in reconciling them. They were perhaps the first to realize that the Habsburg Empire and the Kingdom of Hungary could normalize their relations only if the statehood of the country was maintained and their interests were mutually recognized. This is how the archbishopric could become one of the mainstays of Hungarian diplomacy. The importance of Pázmány's foreign contacts can be appreciated only if we know that in certain quarters of the imperial court repeated efforts were made to obtain control over the foreign relations of the Kingdom of

[38] Hiller: 1988, p. 125.
[39] Makkai: 1985, I, pp. 785 ff., 894 ff. – Benda: 1975. – Šmerda: 1989, pp. 48, 60.

Hungary, then to limit them by various prohibitions. At the same time the court was unable to monopolize Hungary's foreign relations entirely, if only because the European forums highly appreciated the dignity of the palatine and the archbishop. And sometimes the interests of the dynasty expressly required the diplomatic services of the high dignitaries of the Kingdom, and also for purposes of official display esteemed so important at the time the court could not dispense with the ritual presence of the notabilities of the Kingdom. It would have been, in fact, a scandal if in the corridors, lobbies and reception halls of the Burg ambassadors, residents and secretaries of nunciatures could not have entered into conversation with Hungarian noblemen. It is also beyond doubt that the Hungarian Estates were already divided at that time. There were some who saw or sought the solution in an "all the same anyway" attitude of detachment, isolation and inertia, or in armed resistance. On the other hand, Pázmány was one of those who worked hard at reaching an agreement, on establishing extensive international connections.

It followed from his archiepiscopal dignity and his special talent that he was reckoned with all over Europe and had authority also with the Princes of Transylvania.

Where did the archbishop get his particularly fresh and detailed international information? Who were his aids in performing his office? Who were those "friends" of his in Constantinople who supplied him with practically first-hand information about the Turkish affairs? Further research could provide the answers to these questions.

Pázmány criticized Prince Gábor Bethlen's first attack by weighing up the power relations in the wider international arena. He was exasperated by the concomitant tragic circumstances of the campaign. He was convinced that there were neither internal nor external guarantees for the Hungarian Estates of the Kingdom to enter the war with the chance of success on the side of the enemies of the Habsburgs. The territory of the country was a long narrow stretch. Contemporaries called the Kingdom "the collar of the country". This may have been echoed by "under our collars" in the phrase handed down by Kemény as Pázmány's, and truly characteristic of him which has been the subject of so much guesswork ever since. The Kingdom was difficult to defend against the Turks who were ready to pounce on it.[40] The archbishop of Hungary considered foreign relations and negotiations to be the preferable means of diplomacy on an international scale.

[40] He sums up his view quite clearly in his letter addressed to Szaniszló Thurzó from Vienna on March 17, 1620. In: *Pázmány's collected letters:* 1910–1911, I, pp. 226–228.

He was a permanent mediator between Prince Gábor Bethlen and the Habsburg ruler. It was he who initiated the Peace of Nikolsburg between Austria and Prussia, and he conducted the negotiations. If we examine his moves and those of the great Prince of Transylvania, it looks as if two powerful politicians were putting their heads together, bending over the map of the dismembered country. Or as if it were a game of chess between pupils of Machiavelli, the undisputed master of the science of politics, an author represented in the archbishop's library as well. Pázmány shared Prince Gábor Bethlen's concern about the country: "For if we are not grieved by our own nation's decline and destruction, I don't know who can be." This is a thought living on throughout the century, being repeated practically word for word in the writings of Palatine Ferenc Wesselényi (1655–1664), Miklós Zrínyi, Chancellor János Bethlen of Transylvania, and Prince Mihály Apafi (1661–1690). The archbishop's writing in which he proposed peace negotiations must probably have been circulated in manuscript. This shows him to have been in full agreement with what the Prince and public opinion demanded: the German soldiers should be withdrawn from the country.[41]

Transylvania was only to gain by the peace negotiations. There were recurring articles in the documents of the agreement such as: If the Turks attack Transylvania, Vienna sends help and guarantees its interests on a constitutional basis; and once the Turks have been driven out of the country, it will include in the peace treaty the guarantees of the Principality's independent statehood.[42]

Pázmány and Bethlen were authors of a new and as yet unknown or very little appreciated chapter of Hungarian politics: that of the co-operation between the Kingdom and the Principality in the interest of survival. In looking into the peace-making technique and theoretical conceptions of Pázmány and Bethlen, we can rely on two sources. One is the old-established Hungarian tradition, the other is the European practice.

As early as 1538 the principle of mutual forgiveness had been included in the articles of the Peace of Várad: the opposing parties restored the real estates taken from each other's followers, provision was made for settling accounts on both sides, while donations were recognized, and prisoners released. In the 17th century this tolerant attitude lived on in the practice of concluding peace treaties regulated by most elaborate international norms in accordance with the theoretical works of Justus Lipsius and

[41] Bitskey–Kovács: 1975: Pázmány to the States of Upper Hungary in Bethlen's camp, Pozsony, Oct. 22, 1626.
[42] Bíró: 1914.

Grotius. István Bibó was the first to point out that the peace-making techniques and principles of the 16th to 18th centuries differed entirely from the practice of the 19th and 20th centuries. Those earlier times had not yet known the punitive sanctions of peace treaties characteristic of the 20th century, which imply that the loser is brought to bay and punished. In the 16th to 18th centuries the primary goal of concluding peace treaties was that the "peace" should be good for all concerned and "perpetual". It was considered achievable by the mutual reconciliation of interests and international guarantees: particular attention was paid to the interests of small countries, and various securities were provided to relieve tensions.

An international recognition of the statehood of any country was ultimately brought about by its inclusion in the provisions of a general universal peace treaty. This principle will be seen in its most elaborate form in Ferenc II Rákóczi's diplomatic activity as a preliminary to peace, and its origins can be observed in the peace negotiations of Pázmány and Bethlen. In his wars Bethlen insisted on subjecting international treaties to stipulations of future agreements in order that, by applying them, he could introduce Transylvania into Europe and make Christendom recognize, by including it in an international peace treaty, the independent statehood of the Principality that had grown up under Turkish protection.[43]

The question is raised with good reason: if Pázmány himself also helped Transylvania grow strong and receive diplomatic assistance in its independent development, how did he reconcile this with the idea of a Hungary delivered from Turkish yoke?

As to Pázmány's associates in the political field, we know very little about them. His workshop and intellectual environment have not yet been explored with scholarly thoroughness. It is obvious that he was not a solitary politician, he also had followers of the same cast of mind round him, and his chancellery was staffed with men who shared his views. It was in this invisible workshop that the theory of the virtual unity of Hungary living under the rule of three powers was worked out. The separate areas of the country under the sway of different powers were parts of the Holy Crown and economically dependent on one another. It is in this sense that Pázmány regarded the independent Principality of Transylvania as an integral part of Hungary.[44]

Early in 1627 Gábor Bethlen repeated his offer to the archbishop and the palatine: Transylvania was willing to take part in the anti-Turkish

---

[43] Szekfű: 1929 (1983), pp. 138–140, 177–178. – Bibó: 1934. – R. Várkonyi: 1980b, 1981.
[44] Hargittay: 1980, 1987.

war to be launched. He asked Pázmány to transmit his plan to the monarch.[45] The circumstances were not ordinary. The Porte was still at war with the Persians. The Peace of Zsitvatorok had already expired the preceding year. Contemporaries thought the Thirty Years' War was drawing to a close.[46]

It was not for the first time that the offer was made, and it did not surprise the high dignitaries of the Kingdom of Hungary, who were aware of the difficulties and the court's fear of making war on the Turks. Their prestige and power, however, had increased in the past few years. When at the Diet of 1625 Pázmány put the Hungarian crown on the head of 17-year-old Archduke Ferdinand, this act of the coronation could be seen as an important occurrence fitting in with a large-scale project. This he had been preparing in common with Miklós Esterházy over several years in order that, by bringing about an alliance between Spain and the Austrian Habsburgs, they should establish an international power bloc that could ultimately fight the Turks successfully.[47] Even the English ambassador interpreted the coronation as an act giving the Habsburgs larger freedom of action in fighting with the Turks, since the junior king of Hungary was not bound by his father's agreements with Constantinople.[48]

Is it conceivable that this could explain somehow the peculiar phrase "the crown = a gift from England" included in the code to be used later by Zrínyi and his associates?

Hungary gained by this compromise a royal diploma and received a particularly gifted palatine in the person of the young Esterházy. All this added to the international weight of Hungarian politics: the Spanish court conferred on the palatine the Order of the Golden Fleece, Pázmány was granted a Spanish annuity which he regarded as a glory to the Hungarian nation. And the appreciation of Hungary was served by the petition which the Estates submitted to Pope Urban VIII requesting him to propagate the cult of King István the Saint all over the Christian world.[49] It is possible that Pázmány's appointment as cardinal (1629) also fits in with this process.[50]

[45] Szalay–Salamon: 1863–1870, III, pp. 44–45. – Fraknói: 1886, pp. 166–174, 216. – Szekfű: 1929 (1983), p. 236. – Péter's study in Makkai–Szász: 1986, II, pp. 662 ff.
[46] Rudolf: 1977. – Polišenský: 1971.
[47] Hiller: 1988, pp. 111–147.
[48] The reports of the English ambassador to Constantinople (Roe: 1740) were already used by Szalay (1869–1870), but not exhaustively. Cf. Szekfű: 1929 (1983), pp. 200, 270.
[49] Frankl: 1869. – Pázmány to Pope Urban VIII, Sopron, Nov. 29, 1625. In: *Pázmány's collected letters:* 1910–1911, II.
[50] "I wish good luck... to all Hungary as well; because I am convinced that your pro-

Pázmány's diplomatic activity of several years pursued in common with Palatine Esterházy ultimately helped prepare an action against the Turks. This, of course, covered all that was included in the political culture of the period: the efforts made to gain advantages at negotiations: promoting the cause of peace in Europe, and keeping abreast of the rapid shifts in power relations.

In the spring of 1626 the Hungarian councillors held a conference in Vienna, and Palatine Esterházy's "Opinion" on a reform of the Hungarian armed forces was drawn up. In the middle of the year a secret conference was convened at Pázmány's place who attended it and what was it for? A hypothesis may be justified by an autumn consultation. Sitting at a common table in the archiepiscopal palace at that time were Councillor Maximilian Trauttmannsdorf as well as Questenberg and Wallenstein. All of them were pondering the chances of a war to be started against the Turks. Questenberg was the Habsburg government's expert on Turkish affairs, Trauttmannsdorf urged, among other things, the reinforcement of the Habsburg army, and Wallenstein was a general of singular abilities which could have been put to good use in military operations against the Ottoman forces. The war between the Habsburgs and Transylvania entailing great sacrifices and failures on both sides was at long last brought to an end. On 20 December 1626 the Peace of Pozsony and the convention of Tokaj were concluded with Bethlen.[51]

Constantinople regarded the agreement as an alliance directed against the Porte and ordered troops to be concentrated in defence of Buda. In the summer of 1627 Esterházy, again in agreement with the Hungarian councillors, presented his "Memoriale" to the court. They demanded far-reaching internal reforms, aid from the German Empire: for years the country had not received the *Türkenhilfe* (subsidy to fight the Turks), so the emperor should give orders to pay it again. The incomes of the country should be spent on the armed forces, the border fortresses should be put in good

---

motion will do much good to the whole of Christendom and mainly to this country." Ferdinand II's holograph letter is published by Fraknói: 1868–1872, II, p. 328. The same author comments on the antecedents of the cardinal's appointment, on the remarkable attention displayed by diplomatic missions, as well as on Pope Urban VIII's letter of appointment dated Nov. 29, 1629.

[51] Evans: 1979, pp. 175–176. – Szekfű: 1929 (1983), p. 232. – Characteristic of Pázmány's comprehensive notions is his memorial addressed to Cardinal Barberini and criticizing the pope's secular policy. Vienna, Aug. 24, 1629. In: *Pázmány's collected letters:*1910–1911, II, pp. 55–66. – Concerning his negotiations in 1626 as reported by the nunciatures see Fraknói: 1868–1872, II, pp. 187–190.

repair and equipped, the resources of mines should not be exploited by private individuals, the secrets of the Crown must not be sold out to the prejudice of inland laws. The interest of the neighbour countries and of all Christendom alike required that Hungary should use all its strength to turn against the Turks.[52]

Opinions about the Turkish question were divided in the Habsburg government all the time during the critical years from 1626 to 1628. The policy pursued in Vienna against Constantinople was always affected by the affairs of the Kingdom of Hungary and the Principality of Transylvania. The information gathered by the English ambassador was forwarded by the nuncio of Venice to the doge, to the effect that Wallenstein was preparing to besiege Buda. Bethlen's international prestige was greatly enhanced by the Hague coalition and the Westminster covenant, but since European diplomats were unable to see the Transylvanian conditions in their reality, and the grave situation of the Prince of the country under Turkish protection, they could neither follow nor understand his politics. His plans were received with distrust in Vienna.[53] At the same time peace talks between the Habsburgs and the Turks began, but were carried on with more interruptions than any time before. Neither side wanted to renew the Peace of Zsitvatorok, feeling that a new agreement would be needed. The excellent diplomacy of the Porte sensed the potential dangers of an anti-Turkish war.[54]

V. LONG-TERM PLANS

The political culture of the period was characterized by its variety. Diplomatic action was usually taken along several lines simultaneously. If we want to take our bearings among the intricacies of tentative efforts, fumbling endeavours, tests of strength, attempts to detect the opponent's de-

---

[52] Miklós Esterházy's Memorial, June 2 1627. Recently published by Péter: 1985, pp. 73–82.

[53] Szekfű: 1929 (1983), pp. 200–201. *Calendar of State Papers* (Venetian), vol. XX (1627–1628), No. 123.

[54] Jászay: 1838. Contrary to the generally adopted view that the Turkish–German treaty of peace was concluded in September 1626: "Though the peace of Szőny had been *drawn up* by September 13 1627 (italics mine), yet as appears from its articles, a few delicate point under discussion were reserved for further negotiations, and the ratification of the instrument already drawn up was also more questionable for the Turkish Porte than in the usual instances of concluding a peace treaty." Szalay–Salamon: 1863–1870, II, p. 175.

signs, pieces of false and misleading information, we must know that these were all ingredients of more comprehensive and far-reaching schemes.

Pázmány's standpoint has for long been judged in the light of one or another detached particular of contradictory documents. Thus a few Hungarian historians of earlier years – Mihály Horváth (1809–1878), Sándor Szilágyi (1827–1899), Vilmos Fraknói (1843–1924) – expressed the unanimous opinion that Pázmány rejected Bethlen's anti-Turkish plans. The difference between them was only in their replies to the whys and wherefores. According to Mihály Horváth and Sándor Szilágyi what the cardinal had at heart was "the suppression of Protestantism rather than the expulsion of the Turks". Fraknói was of the opinion that the reason why not even Wallenstein could persuade Pázmány into espousing the plan of the Prince of Transylvania was that he entertained a chronic distrust and was convinced that "the maintenance and consolidation of the Hungarian element demanded the preservation of peace in the first place". Szekfű recognized that Pázmány urged Gábor Bethlen to collaboration against the Turks, but he did not trust the Prince. On the other hand, if we integrate the partial data with long-term politics, we can see that Pázmány regarded the anti-Turkish war as an all-European venture. In his opinion the primary condition was international assistance, a combination of European forces. He stressed on a number of occasions that if the clash took place only between Germans and Turks, and the war were waged on Hungarian territory, it would threaten Hungary with utter destruction. Only in the full context of his political conception is it possible to understand the letter he sent to Bethlen by János Kemény. The key sentence of the letter written in extremely cautions terms about the Turkish question is: "if the Turks wish to make war, this side will, perhaps, not be behind in answering them..." Then he summed up his view after surveying the conditions in Europe as follows: "It is conceivable that God will bring about a general peace in the Christian World. If it be so, we might then be able to stand up to the Turks as well. The reason why I have brought this up is that I wish Your Majesty to understand the state which Christendom is in. And, by comparing it with that of the Turks, to form a wise judgement on how wonderfully favourable an opportunity it would be for Europe to get rid of the Turkish yoke, an aim for which I would not hesitate to lay down my life."[55]

[55] Pázmány to Prince Gábor Bethlen, Nagyszombat, Dec. 28, 1627. In: *Pázmány's collected letters: 1910–1911*, I, pp. 670–671.

It can be taken for certain that – as was usual at that time – Pázmány sent with this letter to Bethlen also a message "which he could not leave to his pen" and which in 1657, i.e. two decades later, enriched with much uncommon experience, János Kemény committed to paper, in his "Auto-biography".

This cautious message is characteristic of Pázmány's analysis of the international situation, too. He took special care in writing about Richelieu's victory over the English and noted that the naval force of Spain was on the side of the French. It can safely be said that both the cardinal and the Prince were aware that the cause of the anti-Turkish international league already depended mostly on France. Still present in the court of Louis XIII was Sully who had earlier, in 1609, worked out the plan of an all-European confederation of anti-Turkish forces including all countries from France to Transylvania. But the Chancellor Cardinal Richelieu already spoke disparagingly of Sully and was preparing to match the power of his monarch with that of the Habsburg emperor in the Italian theatre of war. Pázmány, however, used all means to prevent a Habsburg–French collision in Italy. That same year Bethlen also launched a large-scale international action. The journey made by the Prince's nephew, Péter Bethlen, was in reality a diplomatic tour, and as members of his retinue related in detail, the important places they visited during this mission were Belgium, Spain, the French court and Venice. Pázmány himself also paved the way for the Prince's nephew on his tour.[56]

Subsequent events again caused the long-term plans to be put off. Louis XIII went to war in Italy, Bethlen died. Vienna responded to the French onslaught by forging a Hispano–Austrian axis and hastened to put an end to the long-drawn-out negotiations with the Turks: the peace between the Habsburgs and the Turks was ratified in 1629. But the victories scored by Gustavus Adolphus brought to light the deep crisis of the Habsburg Empire. The Swedish armed forces routed the imperial army. Tilly died from his wounds after having suffered crushing defeats (1631–1632). They in the Burg already reckoned that the situation established after the battle of Fehérhegy would change to the contrary. At the same time Richelieu was facing internal revolts and had to reckon with the possibility that the successes of the King of Sweden who had dashed forward to the Rhine might threaten France's interests too.

All Europe expected the solution of the crisis from Pope Urban VIII. Pázmány was fully conscious of the serious situation. His proposal for

---

[56] Djuvara: 1914, pp. 163–171. – R. Várkonyi: 1986b, pp. 21, 49.

coping with the crisis was quite unlike the plans of Richelieu or those of the statesmen of the Habsburg Empire.

King Ferdinand II asked the pope for help against the Swedes and sent Pázmány at the head of a delegation to Rome. This time, on 10 February 1632, the archbishop submitted a grandiose plan to the court. He was of the opinion that the crisis of the Christian countries of Europe had been brought on by the excessive predominance and superiority of the Spanish and Austrian Habsburgs. Relying on support from the pope, the Catholic powers – Spain, France, Venice, the German Principalities and the Habsburg government – should form a league in order to expel the Turks from Europe. The controversial issues should be settled jointly by means of negotiations, and the status of the territories retaken from the Turks should be decided by common agreement. Pázmány can be supposed to have known Sully's scheme. He could also reckon upon Miklós Esterházy's *opinios*. A completely new idea is to be found in his argument that an all-European balance of power was required for pushing back the Turks.

The King did not accept Pázmány's plan. His government could see only one way of solving the crisis: by defeating the Swedes. The pope should give financial and diplomatic aid for this purpose. At the same time Richelieu, who already wielded great influence in the papal court, was working hard on making the French orientation in Rome prevail against the Habsburgs.

Why did Pázmány undertake this mission to Rome when officially he had to represent there a position contrary to his settled conviction? Since the outbreak of the Thirty Years' War the Hungarian archbishop had been doing his utmost to end the war as soon as possible. He could not be expected to represent, simultaneously, the demand for assistance against Sweden and the plan of an anti-Turkish war based upon an all-European peace. The two lines of action precluded each other. However, knowing as we do the rational thinking of the age and Pázmány's long-term political conception, we cannot totally reject the hypothesis that he pursued this double objective. On the basis of sources available to us we can suppose that the reason why Pázmány undertook the mission, futile as it might be at a short term with regard to his plan of an anti-Turkish league, was that he hoped to see the end of the war in the west very soon.[57]

---

[57] Pázmány's proposal submitted to King Ferdinand II. Pozsony, Feb. 10, 1632. In: *Pázmány's collected letters:* 1910–1911, II, pp. 245–246. – Relatio Legationis Romanae, quam obivi iussu Cesareae Maiestatis anno 1632. Mednyánszky: 1830. – Pázmány did not even submit to the pope his plan of an anti-Turkish war. Frankl: 1871. – Leman: 1920.

His last acts show that, even in spite of initial defeats, he died convinced that, in the long run, the future looked promising.

In 1634 the Hungarian Diet preparing for internal reforms had to be postponed because of the news of Wallenstein's assassination, while on László the Saint's Day the then 14-year-old Miklós Zrínyi, talking in the spirit of Pázmány's ideas at István the Saint's Cathedral, quoted László the Saint on the tasks of his own age, on internal reforms and on the anti-Turkish international league to be established with the pope's assistance.[58]

In 1635 France declared war on Spain. No one could see as yet when the new French phase of the Thirty Years' War would be over. In Hungary the War Council's orders followed one another to the effect that the peace between the Turks and the Habsburgs was eternal and inviolable, and fighting on the Hungarian borders was prohibited. Again, the cause of an international alliance for an anti-Turkish war seemed to have been swept from the table of European politics for an indefinite time. Pázmány founded a university, and in the deed of foundation he already laid down where the university should be located after the country's reoccupation from the Turks. "And if with the passing of time (if God delivers Hungary from the Turkish yoke) a more appropriate town were found for the University..."[59]

He could close the last year of his life with a political success which, though apparently insignificant, was truly far-reaching.

Early in 1634 Prince György I Rákóczi informed King Sigismund III of Poland that Constantinople was preparing for an unprecedented large-scale attack on him. The plan was proof of the consistent and rational attitude of the Ottoman government. It could be seen that a sort of parallelism existed between the policies of the Sublime Porte and those of the Christian countries. If Christian Europe prepared to join forces against the Ottoman world, Constantinople would respond with an attack. The plan of an attack on Poland was a response to the international anti-Turkish schemes of the preceding years.[60] Poland had already figured in former plans as one of the most important bulwarks of the international anti-Turkish alliance, an indispensable factor reckoned with in all projects. From Turkish territories the road to Poland led through Transylvania, so Rákóczi ought to help the grand vizier's army with troops and provisions. Tran-

---

[58] Oration on László the Saint (translated by Péter Kulcsár). In: *Zrínyi könyvtár:* 1985, I, pp. 449 ff.

[59] The deed of foundation of the University of Nagyszombat, 12 May 1635 (translated by Sándor Sík). In: *Pázmány's collected letters:* 1910–1911, I, p. 372.

[60] Szilágyi: 1893, pp. 251–252. – Nagy, L.: 1983. – R. Várkonyi: 1988.

sylvania could not be dispensed with even if the attackers chose to penetrate into Poland by starting a campaign from Hungarian bases or through Moldavia. But the interest of Transylvania required that Poland should preserve its sovereignty, or else the Principality would also sink to the level of the Romanian voivodeships. György I Rákóczi had ascended the princely throne amidst serious struggles, and his rule was not yet consolidated. The Porte was of the opinion that it could easily bring about the Prince's downfall and, by turning to advantage István Bethlen's aspiration for power, support the latter's candidacy against Rákóczi with the aid of the troops of the pashas, for it needed an obedient Prince for the success of its venture against Poland.

The conflict between Transylvania and the Turks naturally caused great excitement among the Hungarian politicians of the Kingdom and the statesmen of the Habsburg government. Opinions were divided. The conflict might upset the peace between the Habsburgs and the Turks and spark off another war: Palatine Miklós Esterházy was not the only one to support cautiously, but consistently, the designs of the Porte and back up István Bethlen. On the other hand, Archbishop Péter Pázmány openly stood up for the cause of György Rákóczi. "I am very pleased to see" he wrote to Rákóczi, "that the Transylvanian Estates showed true loyalty and good intentions to Your Excellency."[61]

Pázmány's standpoint deserves a thorough analysis. Was he aware of the interdependence of Transylvania and Poland? Who else but he could have reckoned with it, for Poland had been an important station of his youth: from both Vienna and Graz he could have a clear insight into the interrelated interests of the countries of the region in opposition to the Ottoman Empire.

The Turkish–Polish–Transylvanian crisis was drawn out over months, causing alarm in the Habsburg government and among the pashas of Turkish fortresses alike. Finally, on 6 October 1636, György I Rákóczi succeeded in defeating the Turkish troops in the region of Nagyszalonta–Madaras. The clash was practically an insignificant feat of arms, and it was not for this reason that Constantinople put off its plan of an attack on Poland: it was guided by weightier political considerations. However, Pázmány attached great significance to the victory. His almost childish joy is reflected in what he wrote to his most confidential friend István Pálffy as follows: "Surely, I cannot remember an instance in Christendom, when so small a number of Hungarians, having no German troops with them, should have

---

[61] Pázmány to Rákóczi. Cf. Szilágyi: 1870, pp. 151, 159.

achieved so great a success. We must thank God for having so much humiliated the conceited, arrogant pagans."[62] That György I Rákóczi emerged from the Turkish–Transylvanian conflict grown in power added to the cardinal archbishop's most personal prestige.

Bethlen had already realized that Transylvania needed regional bases in the kingdom and endeavoured to build a bridge leading to Poland by taking possession of Munkács. The north-eastern part of the country with the castle and demesne of Munkács in its centre, had developed into a territory of key strategic importance in the country living under the sway of three powers. At the junction of the three parts of the country, in the immediate vicinity of Poland, it served as a gateway to Europe. After Bethlen's death Rákóczi secured the castle by way of mortgage. But the castle was likewise claimed by its former owner, Count Miklós Esterházy. Amidst the big tug-of-war Pázmány openly took sides with Rákóczi against Esterházy. He put all his authority into the scale and used even his connections in Vienna and Rome in support of the Prince of Transylvania.

I wonder whether it is not an exaggeration if we explain Pázmány's exertions in the matter of Munkács not by personal prejudice but by political considerations. Historical literature has dealt extensively and in detail with the fact that in the second half of the 1650s the relationship of Pázmány and Esterházy deteriorated in a marked manner. Often even by exaggerating their differences, historians attribute them to various, mainly personal reasons. An objective analysis verifies Szalay's opinion: in the cause of Transylvania Esterházy became a victim of a political adventurer, and Pázmány decided not against the palatine's person but against hazardous political adventures.[63] The existence of a strong Principality of Transylvania establishing direct contacts with Poland as a hinterland was in the interest of both. Munkács was at the same time a secure base of retreat for the Prince of Transylvania exposed to Turkish attack. The future vindicated Pázmány's judgement. But it is a fact that the politicians of the following decades were growing up in the environment of Esterházy, and later several of them would maintain the archbishop's principles, too.

Pázmány's basic political principle is well illustrated by a passage of a letter he wrote to Esterházy: "It would be worse than bondage if there

[62] Pázmány to István Pálffy, commandant of Érsekújvár, Pozsony, Oct. 20, 1630. In: *Pázmány's collected letters:* 1910–1911, II, p. 781.

[63] Szekfű: 1935b, pp. 45–46. – As to the conflict between the holder of church property and the secular proprietor, the pro-Habsburg statesman and the reformist politician, see Péter: 1985, pp. 180–183. Szalay–Salamon: 1863–1870.

were no *libera opinio* and *vox* among us."[64] As a political personality Esterházy differed from Pázmány. He held his opinion to be indisputable if only because of the authority implicit in his elevated position of palatine. On the other hand, Pázmány was of the view that the freedom to form and appraise opinions was indispensable for good politics.

Prince György I Rákóczi was informed by Pázmány's trusted follower and pupil, Bishop György Lippay, that the career of Hungary's cardinal archbishop had come to an and. Having lost his political supporter, the Calvinist Prince bowed his head with the utmost appreciation before the deceased cardinal:

"We are writing the truth to Your Eminence, namely, that we felt so much assured of His Eminence's good will, and his love for his country and nation in the effectuation of His Majesty's gracious command that, if others, too, had been of the same mind, our poor country and we ourselves should not have to face a gate opening so wide on our future destruction."[65]

[64] Pázmány to the archiepiscopal delegate sent to Miklós Esterházy, Oct. 3, 1636. Cf.: "It would be bondage if we ought to propse all that others propose." Pázmány to Palatine Miklós Esterházy, Nagyszombat, Aug. 9, 1633. Both in: *Pázmány's collected letters:* 1910–1911, II, pp. 707, 438.

[65] Letter from György I Rákóczi to György Lippay, Dés, May 23, 1637. Duplicate copy in the manuscript dept. of the Batthyány library of Gyulafehérvár. Cf. Szilágyi: 1893, p. 277.

Prince Bethlen
– Westphalia – Utrecht

ഔ   ର

"After so much fighting, pity for the ills of our desperate and decimated nation makes me think that we must, if we are not to perish, follow the paths of peace."[1] This was the life-long programme Gábor Bethlen declared in the first year of his rule. And on his death, this was how a report summed up the essence of his policies: "There's nothing he set more store by than [...] the quietude of peace."[2]

Few rulers have committed themselves to peace as often and as unequivocally as Gábor Bethlen. There was nothing he wanted to be called, he wrote, but the Prince of peace. "We have diligently endeavoured not only to free our poor country and all its estates from the ills of internal strife, but also, as befits a true and patriotic Prince, have spared no pains and no expense to win for our country from mighty foreign princes a precious and permanent peace, giving never an excuse for quarrel, but content with our lot, and wanting all our lives only to be called the Prince of peace."

For Bethlen, peace was nothing else but a work of "greatest wisdom and intelligence"; it was sensible policy and not a supra-historical moral category or a privileged emotional state. It was state interest, the interest of the commonwealth, of Christendom, of Europe itself. His was a modern approach consonant with Hugo Grotius' insistence that the small and weaker nations have just as much right to make peace as the stronger

---

"Gábor Bethlen and Transylvania under the Rákóczis at the European Peace Negotiations 1648–1711." In: *Forschungen über Siebenbürgen und seine Nachbarn. Festschrift für Attila T. Szabó und Zsigmond Jakó*. Ed. by K. Benda, T. Bogyay, H. Glassl, Zs. Lengyel. München, 1987.

[1] Gábor Bethlen to Ferenc Batthyány, Kolozsvár, Nov. 19, 1613. MOL P 1314 Batthyány family archives, Missiles. No. 6610. Quoted by Kállay–Papp: 1980, p. 38.

[2] Catherine of Brandenburg to the city of Kassa, Nov. 17, 1629. *Történelmi Tár*: 1887, p. 50.

ones.[3] Like his great contemporary, Bethlen had in mind all Europe when he spoke of peace, and he saw his country's position in terms of the correlatives of internal peace and external security. He was never concerned only about the momentary Turkish–Hungarian, or Habsburg–Transylvanian relations but also about their implications for the long-term peace of Europe and the long-term development of his country. All concessions and compromises of the moment were for him but means in this long-term work of construction. And such a long-term construction was the only way for a country, located at the crossroads of the power-struggles of the two great empires, to secure its own internal and external peace.

In the Deed of Foundation of the College of Nagyenyed we read: "The worse fate of our country and of our children can be avoided only if we take care to provide for scholars to render us useful service."[4] Bethlen sent young men to study abroad, hoping thereby to educate generations of scholars and politicians, equipped to work out the theory of his concept of peace and to carry it through in practice.

The traditional idea, that the educated should rule, was developed in the 17th century as applied to the state: the state was able to meet its tasks only with the help of educated men.

One fine expression of this conviction was voiced by the court chaplain, István F. Tolnai, in 1663: "Without schools and colleges, I know not where the peace of our country would stand. The peace of our homeland depends on wise, intelligent, informed princes and lords, and on the wise servants surrounding them like pillars. But these are reared in schools and colleges, as flowers are reared in enger some delightful and verdant garden."[5] Gábor Bethlen was, thus, in the vanguard of the spirit of his times by placing the cause of his country's peace in the hands of well-trained politicians and the lay intelligentsia, then on the rise.

Bethlen's ideas were given rounded formulation by Gáspár Bojti Veres as follows: "The watchful care of intellect can order anything, / And harmony and happy peace can thus bloom on earth; / Long live the good name of all lands, and let there stand watch, / As guardians over every zone, the boundaries set by reason."[6]

[3] Gábor Bethlen to Udvarhelyszék, 1615. In: *Erdélyi Magyar Szótörténeti Tár*: 1975, I, p. 722. – Gábor Bethlen's instructions to his envoys to Vienna, Besztercebánya, Jan. 12, 1624. In: Szilágyi: 1873a, pp. 36, 40. – Cf.: Barcza: 1980, pp. 100–105, Herczegh: 1980, p. 37.

[4] Quoted by Juhász: 1979, in: Jakó–Juhász, p. 10.

[5] Tolnai: 1664, p. 23.

[6] "Panegyris. Gáspár Bojti Veres: Dicsőítő költemény Bethlen Gáborhoz" (An ode of praise to G. Bethlen). In: Tóth: 1980, p. 111.

Peace, as the centre of a theory of international relations, was to be formulated later by the Hungarian Cartesians.

János Nadányi, one of the Várad Cartesians, who had studied at Leyden and later taught at Enyed gave the following definition of peace in his dissertation of 1660, *De jure pacis:* peace was the quiet liberty of human affairs, "tranquilla rerum humanorum libertas".[7] Nadányi quoted generously from Grotius; his work, dedicated to János Apáczai Csere, the Cartesian philosopher and pedagogue, left no doubt that his concept of peace referred to domestic and foreign affairs alike. The generations of Transylvanian Cartesians, who were to answer the question of "What is peace?" with "Intellect put to its proper use", were drawing the logical conclusion not only from a philosophical system, but also from years of indigenous political experience. Their idea of peace was based on the *recta ratio* concept, on the concept of a modern state capable of keeping internal order. Its basic principle was the idea, that within the country, too, the national interest was to have precedence over particular interests. Burghers, peasants and soldiers were all to receive due attention, and on the international scene, each nation and people its rights. Peace was to be made not with sanctions, but with agreements that guaranteed tranquil development. For the Transylvanian Cartesians, religious tolerance, the freedom of investigation and the free use of one's native language, as well as the checking of the landowning nobility's abuses of power were not just internal matters, but the preconditions of the country's presence on the European scene, and as such, international requirements. A state, strong enough to guarantee domestic peace and an up-to-date educational policy, was the price of admittance to the international forums, and the precondition of Transylvania's ability to communicate with the rest of Europe.

Was the above the wishful thinking of a small group of intellectuals with no real influence on the course of actual events? In fact, there were spirits kindred to the Transylvanian Cartesians within the Kingdom of Hungary. Péter Pázmány, Archbishop of Esztergom, a leader of the Hungarian Counter-Reformations, had a concept of peace in many ways identical to that of the Protestant Prince. And Palatine Miklós Esterházy had written to Prince György I Rákóczi as early as 1644 thoughts reminiscent of Bethlen's: "We need tranquillity (peace); nothing else will sustain this decimated nation of ours."[8]

---

[7] Nadányi: 1660. 11 theses. Cf. our contribution "Gondolatok a békéről a 17. századi Magyarországon" (Thoughts on peace in 17th century Hungary), to the discussion on the concept and interpretation of peace at the 15th International Congress of Historians.

[8] *Magyarországi palatinusnak ...:* 1645, p. 15.

Gábor Bethlen was convinced that if the young Principality of Transylvania wanted to come up to its enormous responsibility, it had to step into Europe, to win international recognition of its statehood, and to gain the freedom of movement of an independent power.

To contemporaries, his diplomacy was a series of attempts, of changes of direction, of experimentation and of matters left incomplete. Looking back today, however, we can see the broad outlines of a definite policy. We find some long-term insights, and one weighty result: the Principality emerged from isolation, and became a factor in Europe.

How did Bethlen manage to make a nation of European weight of this small state of the times?

One of the consequences of the 17th-century reshuffling of the balance of power was that the small or not quite independent nations acquired an increased importance within the new constellations that emerged. The theorists of state were busy evaluating the differences in power, national product, geo-political position and relative political weight within an area from one country to the next, and devised their policies accordingly.

Grotius drew up his plan for an international body responsible for the peace of Europe, by keeping the security of the small nations very much in mind. Every country was responsible for the other; the affairs of belligerent powers were to be settled by the international body. Grotius insisted that small countries were entitled to more attention and more international protection.[9] In the 17th century, a great many people read Justus Lipsius in Hungary and Transylvania; there was even a Hungarian translation of his work. His popularity was due partly to Lipsius' having dealt with the position of countries living between "two powerful neighbours", as he put it. Lipsius' theory was, that neutrality was as impossible a course of action for small nations as inactivity: "for you will only fall prey to the victor".[10]

Bethlen was a realist able to take modern diplomatic action and to take advantage of the opportunities of being a part of Europe. The results are known. The road to it we can deduce: "All my mind and all my discourse I've turned to the issue of how I can achieve permanent and perfect peace for my native land and nation."[11] Bethlen had a fine sense for the relative

[9] Grotius: 1646, 2.I/1–2, IV/8.
[10] *Justus Lipsiusnak ...*: 1641 (1970), pp. 384, 263. Cf.: Nagy: 1979. For the methods and significance of 17th and 18th century peace treaties as compared to 20th century methods, see Bibó: 1934.
[11] Secret instructions to Farkas Kamuthy. Besztercebánya, Jan. 11, 1624. Quoted by Szilágyi: 1873a, p. 45.

weight of the sword and of the olive branch: the economic and cultural community of interest expressed in the common diplomatic language. The key concepts of his diplomacy were international mediation, international guarantees, the alliance of other nations and their guarantee of the peace treaty to be made, and the recognition of statehood by the settlement. Bethlen had but one purpose with all this: Europe was to recognize the Principality, and guarantee its statehood in international treaties. He strove constantly to have Transylvania included in the peace treaties of the various powers, this being one form of the international recognition of statehood. For instance, he joined the English–Dutch–Danish alliance only on condition that they would make no peace without him. In all his instructions to his ambassadors, Bethlen emphasized that he would spare neither pains nor expense "to win an untrammelled and unconditional holy peace".[12] He thought of all eventualities. The secret clause of the Nagyszombat agreement deals with the possibility of the Habsburgs reoccupying the part of Hungary under Ottoman rule with the help of an international coalition. "If peace should be made, he shall not be excluded from it, but shall be a party to it",[13] is the way paragraph 8 defined Hungary's and Transylvania's right to state representation in the Habsburg–Ottoman peace treaty.

How far was Gábor Bethlen's endeavour to have Transylvania's independence guaranteed by international agreements that his successors could build on?

In the early 1640s, on the eve of the Treaty of Westphalia, Transylvania was in a relatively favourable position as the ally of France and Sweden. It is an open question, however, why Prince György I Rákóczi abandoned the international alliance at a time, when his own and his allies' military successes made it evident, that an all-European peace was just around the corner, why he agreed to a separate peace with the Habsburgs in 1645.

Rákóczi himself explained his peace negotiations in terms of Bethlen's prime goals: he wanted nothing more, he wrote: "than to see our dear native land and our decimated, almost exterminated nation have the quietude of peace in our times".[14] And he as much as quoted Gábor Bethlen when he declared: "Greater and more desirable than all victory and all spoils we hold to be the tranquillity and peace of our dear, sweet native land." As already referred to, Miklós Esterházy, too, had expressed this

[12] Miklós: 1929, p. 605.
[13] In: Szilágyi: 1867, p. 75.
[14] György I Rákóczi's instructions of June 17, 1644. In: Szilágyi: 1885, p. 14.

sentiment in his debates with Rákóczi: for all their differences in the means they adopted and for all they clashed on points of detail, their goal was a common one: "If the House and its foundation should stand, we can sweep and rearrange it, too; but if it should fall, in vain all our goods and all our efforts."[15]

We know, that György I Rákóczi made peace with the tacit support of his allies. The Habsburg government had made unprecedented concessions: it recognized the Principality's independent statehood, ceded territories and fortresses, and guaranteed religious freedom to the Protestants living in the Kingdom of Hungary, the serfs included.[16] What is more, Transylvania was included in the Treaty of Westphalia as well; admittedly, just about at the tail-end and only as France's ally – but nevertheless. Given the international conventions of the time, the treaty can, thus, be considered a valuable political concession in the history of the Principality of Transylvania and a partial realization of Bethlen's aims.

Indicative of the long-term effects of Gábor Bethlen's lifework was the fact, that even Prince Apafi, who ruled at a time incomparably less propitious for Transylvania, was able to get the French king to include his country in the Peace of Nijmegen.[17]

Likewise in the best tradition of Gábor Bethlen's rule was the declaration Ferenc II Rákóczi addressed to the peoples of the world: dated June 7, 1703 and sent out at the beginning of 1704, Rákóczi laid the issue of Hungary's and Transylvania's internal peace squarely at the door of European politics. Emphasizing his nation's right to peace, he condemned the Habsburgs for the way they ended the war with the Turks at Carlowitz in 1699. The Peace of Carlowitz had decided Hungary's fate "sine nobis, de nobis", he wrote, i. e. without the country's having had a say in the matter.[18]

Ferenc II Rákóczi was, thus, continuing Bethlen's policies, and was asking for no more than was commonly recommended by contemporary theorists of state, when he agreed to joining the War of the Spanish Succes-

---

[15] György I Rákóczi's instructions of June 17, 1644. In: Szilágyi: 1885, p. 15. Also: *Magyarországi palatinusnak ...:* 1645, p. 34.

[16] Zsilinszky: 1890.

[17] Louis XIV to Prince Apafi concerning the Treaty of Nijmegen, June 8, 1679. MOL P 1239, Apafi Gyűjtemény 3. 4. Reports of Winchilsea, English ambassador to the Porte, of 1661–1665; and Apafi's letter to Charles II of Britain. For a summary, see: Angyal: 1900, pp. 507–508.

[18] "Kiáltvány a világ népeihez" (Proclamation to the peoples of the world), paragraph 4 [1704]. In: *Ráday Iratok:* 1955–1961, I, p. 99.

sion, on condition that France included Hungary and Transylvania in the international peace treaty.[19]

The Treaty of Linz was, thus, in keeping with the Treaty of Westphalia and with the modern approach to peace. Keeping in mind the new techniques in international agreements, it was clearly one link in the chain of treaties ending the Thirty Years' War.

It was similar considerations that led Ferenc II Rákóczi to do everything in his power to make sure that Transylvania would be included in the Treaty of Utrecht.

In a proclamation of August 19, 1710, Rákóczi expressed his determination to start peace negotiations shortly, and expressed his hope that with English, Dutch and Russian mediation, the war would soon conclude with an inter-state treaty. A pamphlet that appeared on July 30 emphasized that the balance of power in Europe, too, required support for Hungary's right to the modern forms of peace. The pamphlet, "The letter of a Polish royal councillor" followed Grotius in elaborating Hungary's and Transylvania's demands for internal peace and external security. After a summary of the peace negotiations to date, the pamphleteer concluded, that the balance of international power tied in with Hungary's and Transylvania's independent statehood.[20]

The origins of the theory of the balance of power go back, as we know, to the restructuring of the power relations in Europe. Gábor Bethlen had built his diplomacy around it, too, using it to support his great goal, the preservation of his nation's statehood.

The Transylvania of Ferenc II Rákóczi not only venerated the memory of Gábor Bethlen, but strove to emulate him as well. He was called "Guardian Prince", "the refuge of the nation", "the nation's hero",[21] and his policies were a living example to the politicians working at the establishment of an independent Hungary. Typical is the way the diplomat János Pápai referred to him at the Szécsény Diet in 1705, when the Upper House defeated the motion on the proclamation of an interregnum: "Had Gábor Bethlen been in this situation, he would have arranged matters in Hun-

[19] Köpeczi: 1966, pp. 46, 239. – Perjés: 1980, p. 130.

[20] The author of the pamphlet and the circumstances of its writing were identified by Benda: 1979, p. 252. That its appearance tied in with the initiation of the peace talks was clarified by R. Várkonyi: 1980a, pp. 187–188.

[21] Rákóczi's instructions to the envoys sent to the King of Sweden and the King of Prussia, Jan. 27, 1704. *Ráday Iratok:* 1955–1961, I, pp. 96, 121. – Fejedelmi előterjesztés a marosvásárhelyi országgyűlésen (The Prince's referendum to the Diet at Marosvásárhely). *Ráday Iratok:* 1955–1961, I, p. 101.

gary so that the Hungarian crown wouldn't be in Austria now."[22] And when it was rumoured that the Czar wanted to make Rákóczi King of Poland, the diplomats responded: "This is similar to the foolishness when the Germans spread the word at the Sublime Porte that Gábor Bethlen wanted to unite Transylvania, Wallachia and Moldavia, and *vult apellari rex Daciae*."[23]

During the years of the Rákóczi war of independence, Gábor Bethlen was the measure not only within the country, but also on the international scene. Instead of Western examples, let me refer here to Constantin Cantacuzino, the Chancellor of the Voivode of Dacia, who expressed his disapproval of the Kurucs' willingness to engage in larger-scale battles to István Dániel, one of Rákóczi's diplomats: "Constantin Cantacusen [...] concerned about the Hungarian alliance and the reasons for it, once he was reassured on that account, bid me warn the leaders of the alliance to recall the last will and testament of the late Gábor Bethlen of happy memory, and in keeping with the rules therein, refrain from engaging the enemy in open battle, for it is in fact the case that the allied Hungarians are in no way a match for the enemy, and so the enemy inevitably defeats them."[24]

How far did Rákóczi follow Gábor Bethlen's concept of peace in his own attempts to make peace? The question is of great importance, for the issue of Transylvania's independence was central both in the Habsburg–Hungarian negotiations for a settlement, and later at the Utrecht and Rastatt peace negotiations.

Ferenc II Rákóczi a descendant of Transylvanian princes, had a clear claim to Transylvania; but in his plans for the war (1700–1702), and even during the first month of the war itself (1703), he did not exclude the possibility that Thököly, chosen Prince of Transylvania in 1690, might return from Turkish exile. However, as it became clear to Rákóczi that he would be received at the courts of Europe only as Prince of Transylvania, i. e. as the head of a state already recognized in the past, he was extraordinarily consistent in his insistence on the title of Prince. Nevertheless, he attached great importance to having the title not in virtue of being a Rákóczi, but by election (1704), and with the Diet confirming him in his power (1707). He hoped thereby that the European powers would renew with him, as lawful ruler, the Principality's old international agreements. Since he had

---

[22] János Pápai to Ádám Vay, June 9, 1706. *Ráday Iratok:* 1955–1961, I, p. 619.
[23] The letters of János Pápai and Ferenc Horváth, envoys to the Porte, to Ferenc II Rákóczi, June 6, 1707. *Ráday Iratok:* 1955–1961, II, p. 322.
[24] "Dániel István naplója" (István Dániel's diary). In: *Rákóczi-Tükör:* 1980, I, p. 50.

no illusions as to the military strength of his part of Hungary considering the Habsburg military potential, he necessarily attached great hopes to diplomatic means, and especially to the traditions of Transylvania's independent statehood.

Administratively speaking, Rákóczi treated Transylvania as a separate country. Though he could never consolidate his military hold over the Principality, and also had a strong internal opposition to contend with, he established an independent administrative system in the state of Transylvania. The two countries – the part of the Kingdom of Hungary that was his, and Transylvania – were joined not only by Rákóczi's person but also by a confederation. The confederation document contained important stipulations regarding the eventual peace treaty itself. The basic principles were worked out at the meeting of the Council in Miskolc in February 1706, and then in the course of preparations for the Habsburg–Hungarian peace negotiations through 1706. The essence was that the Habsburg settlement should restore and guarantee Transylvania's independent statehood. Rákóczi and his close advisers insisted on this for three reasons. Firstly, for the sake of the internal peace of the Principality; secondly, because the integrity of the Kingdom of Hungary depended not only on the guarantees of foreign countries but also on the internal guarantee of a likewise independent Principality. The last argument was that an independent Transylvania, guaranteed by other nations, was in the interest of the balance of power in Europe, i. e. it was a matter of international interest. Rákóczi did not insist on his personal power: if Transylvania's independence was restored, he was willing to renounce his claim to it, and was even willing, under certain circumstances, to trade his estates. In principle, he was consistent in this stand throughout, although under the rapidly changing circumstances he did modify his position on matters of detail.[25]

It is interesting to note, how far Rákóczi and his close advisers believed in the superiority of principles and reason over the force of arms. Rákóczi's instructions to his ambassadors and Chancellor Pál Ráday's reports, all show flexibility in their interpretation of Bethlen's balance of power concept. For instance, we read that while in their days Bocskai and Bethlen

[25] On Thököly's rule: R. Várkonyi: 1983. – Károlyi okmánytár: 1987, V, pp. 387–388. – The letter of alliance of the Hungarian and Transylvanian Estates. Huszt, March 8, 1706. In: *Ráday Iratok:* 1955–1961, I, pp. 531–532. – The peace conditions of the allied Estates, May 1706. In: *Ráday Iratok:* 1955–1961, I, p. 587. – R. Várkonyi: 1980a, pp. 186–187.

had been "the cornerstones of the balance of power" between Turks and Habsburgs, today, an independent Hungary and Transylvania would serve a more extensive European security.[26] Pál Ráday, in one of his famous pamphlets, the *Explosio*, explained that peace was a right rooted in natural law; for this reason, peace could be made only with international guarantees, as Gábor Bethlen's agreement with Emperor Ferdinand II also illustrated.[27]

Rákóczi's diplomacy adapted itself to the extraordinarily adverse circumstances with remarkable agility; as a consequence, he was able to keep the issue of Hungary and Transylvania on the agenda at both The Hague (1709) and the Gertruydenberg (1710) peace conferences. At the end of the summer of 1710, Rákóczi asked the Queen of England and the Dutch Estates, who had offered their mediation, to continue to intervene on behalf of the two Hungarian states, the Kingdom and the Principality, so that they might make peace with their independence guaranteed. At the same time, they published an imperial document of 1706 recognizing Transylvania's right, too, to make peace with international mediation.

The customary negotiations preliminary to the peace conference itself started in the autumn of 1710 amid circumstances particularly unfavourable to Transylvania. England and Holland offered to mediate; but Prince Eugene of Savoy, who had the final word at the time on the Habsburg side, felt that the interests of the dynasty were incompatible with even partial guarantees of either Hungarian or Transylvanian independence being given by the international treaty to be concluded. The ideas of guarantees and mediation were, of course, diametrically opposed not only to the dynastic principle, but also to the estates principle. Understandably, thus, their advocates urged an imminent settlement, while Rákóczi and his advisers insisted on mediation and guarantees as the only hopes of a secure peace, and tried to play for time until the beginning of the European peace conference which was to end the War of the Spanish Succession. At the time of the negotiations, imperial troops were already stationed in Transylvania; Rákóczi's own remaining Transylvanian troops, a force of about 4,000 men, were stationed in Moldavia. It was a small and very poorly equipped army which Rákóczi hoped to build on, in his plans to ally among others with Moldavia and Wallachia, and, with his back to the Turks, win time until the beginning of the European peace conference.

---

[26] Rákóczi's instructions to Ráday sent as envoy to the Swedish and Prussian rulers, Jan. 27, 1704, and Ráday's memorandum to King Charles XII of Sweden, April 1704. In: *Ráday Iratok:* 1955–1961, I, pp. 123, 138. – Explosio. In: *Ráday Iratok:* 1955–1961, I, p. 647.

[27] R. Várkonyi: 1980a, pp. 186–197. For the Szatmár peace document with the signature of the Transylvanians, see Lukinich: 1925, pp. 419–420.

His plans, however, failed because of changes both on the domestic and foreign political scene. The Turkish declaration of war put Transylvania once more in a danger zone; and the English and Dutch mediators presented Rákóczi's plans for Transylvania to the Habsburg government fatally simplistically. On April 29, 1711, Count János Pálffy, Ban of Croatia, Commander in Chief of the imperial troops in Hungary, and Sándor Károlyi, Commander-in-Chief of Rákóczi's troops left in Hungary, came to an agreement amid circumstances we need not go into here. This Peace of Szatmár was a compromise between the dynasty and the aristocracy, between the emperor and his penitent vassals, for which penitence they received pardon. By the terms of the agreement, Transylvania was restored to its pre-war status, belonging in theory to Hungary, but in practice coming under central imperial rule. The agreement was signed by a number of officials and representatives of Rákóczi's Principality of Transylvania.[28] Rákóczi himself held the conclusion of the hostilities to be not peace, but "convincing by force of arms"; the Transylvanian lords, he felt, had signed the document because "the knife was at their throats", and he felt it was not yet too late to have Hungary's statehood and Transylvania's independence guaranteed in the European peace to be made.

Rákóczi elaborated his position in the Rákóczi Memorandum commenting on the preliminary negotiations of the Treaty of Utrecht and in the letters sent to the representatives and diplomatic attachés of the powers taking part in the conferences that began in January 1712. In the matter of Transylvania, he reiterated his old principles. He needed to have his title as Prince recognized, but did not insist on ruling Transylvania; he was prepared to exchange his estates for other estates abroad, if they guaranteed Transylvania's independent statehood. These writings all make reference to the principle of the balance of power and show that Rákóczi wanted not personal power, but independence for the Principality in some form or another. For Rákóczi, the French–English talks went beyond settling the affairs of the two sides; Utrecht was a holy place, where decisions had to be made not according to the will of this or that party, but in the interest of the whole world. Rákóczi's efforts were not entirely in vain, but success eluded him. He received a great deal of encouragement; but a Prince without a country, and a country without independence could hardly be a factor to be considered at a European peace conference. The powers of Europe, especially the Protestant powers concerned about the fate of their co-religionists, were not entirely happy with the Habsburg–

[28] Szalay: 1864. – Fiedler: 1858, B: 11. – Fontes Rerum Austriacarum B.: 17. p. 259. – Márki: 1910, III, p. 304. – Köpeczi: 1966, p. 236.

Hungarian settlement, but the Habsburg's intransigence finally made them drop the matter of Transylvania, for it was jeopardizing the success of the entire peace conference. By the time France finally signed the treaty on April 11, 1713, the issue of Transylvania was a dead one in Utrecht.[29]

The Transylvanian question was again put on the agenda in the course of the Rastatt peace conference (November 1713–March 1714). When Prince Eugene of Savoy demanded guarantees for the Catalans at the behest of Emperor Charles III, Marshall Villars, the French delegate, followed his king's highly provisional instructions by demanding Rákóczi's Transylvanian Princedom in return. The French position was rather tentative, the Habsburg one all the more clear-cut; and in order that the negotians might proceed undisturbed, both sides gave up their demands. Thus Transylvania was left out of the Treaty of Rastatt as well.

***

"After the long years of exile, we should like to enjoy the blessings of peace", wrote the great Prince, Gábor Bethlen, at the beginning of his rule. The same thought directed Rákóczi in 1712 to address a pamphlet on Transylvania to the powers of Europe, which were about to conclude nearly a decade and a half of hostilities. The pamphlet, *Déduction des droits de la Principauté Transilvanie*, probably printed in The Hague for distribution among the delegates at the Utrecht conference, was theoretical discourse on the relationship between internal and external peace, and it gave a broad overview of the peace treaties of the 17th century and their implications for the small nations. It summarized – not quite accurately but essentially correctly – the results of Bethlen's international policies: "Since the Pope, the King of France and the King of Spain guaranteed the promises Emperor Ferdinand II made to Bethlen, Prince of Transylvania, and his Hungarian allies, [...] since György Rákóczi, Prince of Transylvania, was included in the Treaty of Westphalia as an ally of the Queen of Sweden, and since it was Emperor Leopold himself who had the Prince of Transylvania included in the Treaty of Nijmegen, there is ample grounds for the Prince's and the Estates' conviction, that the guarantors of the above treaties agree that Transylvania's being deprived of her freedom is an infringement of the provisions of the above treaties."[30] Rákóczi reiterated Gábor

---

[29] Köpeczi: 1966, p. 245.
[30] "Déduction des droits de la Principauté de Transylvanie" [1712]. In: Köpeczi: 1970, p. 385.

Bethlen's principle that no nation's peace can be guaranteed at the expense of another's. "We assume that the powers now at war desire nothing more than peace for their peoples after such a bloody war, and keeping in mind the future as well, wanted a stable and lasting peace which posterity, too, can enjoy."[31]

Ferenc II Rákóczi, a descendant of Transylvanian princes, had a stake: the nation's peace. This, however, was but one aspect of the history of their times. The real picture includes the other aspects of Hungarian politics as well: short-term gains, over-hasty decisions, indifference, procrastination, spectacular strong-arm gestures, the will to rule, the willingness to gamble, the politics of bitter revenge. In the 17th and 18th centuries, too, along with the realization of the need for coexistence, for peace, and international agreements and security, there went, like shadows, the spirit of mistrust, and a passion for lording it over the weak.

[31]   Köpeczi: 1970, p. 386.

Zrínyi, "the Hero
upon whom Providence Hath
Devolved the Fate of Europe"
ഏ ൙

"The Excellent Count *Serini* seems to be the Heroe, upon whom Providence hath devolved the Fate of *Europe*... Upon [his] success or overthrow the *Western* world seems to stand or fall",[1] opined the mysterious O.C., addressing "All the Admirers of Count Nicholas Serini, The Great Champion of Christendom" in the opening pages of *The Conduct and Character of Count Nicholas Serini*,[2] a book published in London, in 1664.

The above characterization, obviously, raises the question of the historical significance of Miklós Zrínyi (1620–1664), Ban of Croatia, as well as the question of his relevance to the Europe of his times. It is primarily this latter issue that I shall be focusing on in what follows.[3]

THE PROBLEM

The Conduct and Character of Count Nicholas Serini, the documentary evidence of Zrínyi's international fame and the source of his reputation as Europe's providential champion, has been familiar to Zrínyi scholars for much of this century. Sándor Apponyi gave a brief outline of the book in the catalogue of his collection published in 1927, and ever since, it has been a staple of bibliographies, studies on Zrínyi, and analyses of the international reaction to Hungary's role in the Ottoman wars.[4] In one rela-

[1] *The Conduct and Character of Count Nicholas Serini* (hereafter: *The Conduct and Character* ...): 1664.

[2] *The Conduct and Character of Count Nicholas Serini*. In Hung. in: *Angol életrajz Zrínyi Miklósról*: 1987, pp. 69, 70.

[3] I outlined the direction my research was taking in two earlier papers: one presented at the fifth national conference of literary historians on Zrínyi and Szigetvár held in Sopron, November 18–20, 1994; the other at the February 8, 1995 meeting of the Renaissance Study Group of the Institute for Literary Research of the Hungarian Academy of Sciences. The present study builds on the results of earlier publications on Zrínyi: *Zrínyi könyvtár*, vols I–IV: 1985-1991; *Zrínyi dolgozatok*, vols I–VI: 1983–1989; *Monumenta Zrínyiana*: 1991.

[4] Kosáry: 1946. – Klaniczay, T.: 1964, pp. 776–777. – Jones: 1966, pp. 298–305. – Köpeczi: 1976, p. 110. – Cf. *Angol életrajz Zrínyi Miklósról*: 1987, pp. 15–17, 19.

tively recent review. the authors noted: "The writer of the preface, the uni-dentified O.C., appears to be cultivated and well-informed. He appraises Zrínyi's activities in their European context, and makes bold to declare that it is Zrínyi 'upon whose success or overthrow the Western world seems to stand or fall'".[5]

The book consists of four parts, two of them devoted to Zrínyi. The third part tells of two other "scourges" of the Ottoman armies: George Castriot, the fifteenth-century Albanian chief and national hero; and the fourteenth-century Mongol leader, Tamerlane.[6] The 1987 facsimile edition includes excerpts from *A Short Relation of the Rise and Progress of the Turkish Warrs in Hungaria, Austria, Moravia, Silesia and Bohemia*, a book published in London in 1664 – a coupling warranted, as Katalin Péter points out in her background study in the 1987 edition, by the fact that both works formed part of the propaganda campaign prompted by the renewed Turkish offensive of the years 1663–64. "The author is probably the person who signed himself with the initials O.C.", we read in the background study, which also notes the inconsistencies in the author's political stand, and calls attention to some rather curious assertions of the mysterious O.C.'s. Why, for instance, does he claim that Zrínyi, a Catholic, was a Protestant? Why does he change the date of his birth? Why does he suggest that the inhabitants of Csáktornya, Zrínyi's castle in the Muraköz, followed the practices of the Puritans? And finally, of course, there is the key question: Why this great adulation of Zrínyi in far-off England, a country whose trade with the Ottoman Empire continued to be as intensive as ever, though the English were put out, somewhat, at the news of the new Ottoman conquests in the Mediterranean? In lieu of an answer, we are left with an observation: "Systematic primary research will be needed to arrive at the solid facts".[7]

With so many questions raised by this curious publication, and so few answered, can its reference to Zrínyi as Europe's providential champion carry any real weight?

Fortunately, the sentiment has contemporary corroboration. All of the nineteen works dealing with the Ottoman wars of 1663–1664 published in England speak of Zrínyi in terms of high praise. Indeed, "The cult of Zrínyi in England was both more intense and more widespread than we

---

[5] Bukovszky–Gömöri–Zajkás: 1985/II, 17, p. 11.

[6] Facsimile in *Angol életrajz Zrínyi Miklósról: 1987*, "Count Serini's Birth and Education", pp. 43–111 of *The Conduct and Character ...*, pp. 1–111; "The Life and Actions of George Castriot Sirnamed Scanderbeg, the other Champion of Christendome", pp. 112–146; and "Tamberlain, the great Scourge of the Turks", pp. 147–168.

[7] Péter: 1987, pp. 27, 40–44, 58–59.

have thought until now".[8] In both the Bolton and the John Williams editions of *A New Survey of the Turkish Empire*, Gömöri points out, we find allusions to Zrínyi as Europe's providential champion, and both editions also contain a three-quarter-length engraving of Zrínyi: "This illustration marks the zenith of Miklós Zrínyi's celebration in England"[9] – and certainly, Zrínyi is depicted not just with the insignia of the quintessential statesman, but also the statesman's penetrating gaze, a look that has even today's reader mesmerized. The issue of Zrínyi and his reputation, however, had a context that was wider than the compass of England and The Netherlands: it tied in with the propaganda wars triggered in Venice, the Papal State, the German lands and France by the latest round of Ottoman conquests, and the competing theories of kingship and government still very much in the air at that time.[10]

My own research has led me to associate the writing of *The Conduct and Character of Count Nicholas Serini* with the meeting of the Imperial Diet in Regensburg during the crucial winter of 1663–1664. In the light of the impassioned debates concerning the conduct of the war, and the person of the commander in chief in particular, however, it seems too simplistic to assume that this English biography of Zrínyi should have represented the Ban of Croatia as a key player on the contemporary European political scene spontaneously, so to speak.[11] It would have taken some distinguished, highly-informed person or political group with a very clear idea of the kind of Europe that was wanted to make the claim that Zrínyi personified the policy capable of reversing the continent's unhappy fate.

Who, then, was the mysterious O.C.? What was this vision of Europe that Zrínyi was supposed to represent? And, no less importantly, how objective is this notion of Zrínyi as Europe's providential champion?

Time and again, we read in the secondary sources: "Overnight, his name became a household word thoughout Europe"; he generated "enormous enthusiasm"; he was "renowned all through Europe".[12] So much the more

[8] Gömöri: 1988, p. 65.

[9] *Ibid.*, p. 69.

[10] Jászay: 1990, pp. 298–300. – Perjés: 1989b. – Kéry: 1989. – Bene: 1989; 1992, p. 228; 1993, pp. 650–668.

[11] For a summary of the various views, see in *Angol életrajz Zrínyi Miklósról*: 1987, pp. 18 and 411, note 12. – I made a photocopy of *The Conduct and Character* ... at the time of researching the documentary sources of Zrínyi's ties to the League of the Rhine. That the biography is related to the events in Regensburg is suggested by the reference to *The History of the Turkish War in Hungary* (London, 1664. OSZKK App. H. 933), and several other circumstances: cf. R. Várkonyi: 1975, pp. 58, 86/55.

[12] Széchy: 1896–1902, V, p. 81. – Klaniczay, T.: 1964, p. 778. – Perjés: 1965, p. 354. – Szakály: 1990, p. 275.

reason for asking: How could this great celebrity disappear practically without a trace? Zrínyi the poet and soldier is recognized by most outstanding scholars of the period;[13] but when it comes to studies of the political factors, we look for his name in vain. When he is mentioned in a political context, it is as the "hot-headed Hungarian", the adversary of Montecuccoli and the Emperor Leopold I, the scapegoat whose ego-nationalism was responsible for the Austrians' failure to defeat the Turks in 1663–1664.[14]

The fact that Zrínyi's contemporary political celebrity could fall into oblivion is rooted in the fact that – much as has been written about him as a poet and a soldier – no attempt has ever been made to discover the real nature of his politics. How does Zrínyi the politician stand to Zrínyi the writer and soldier? What kind of political position can we deduce from Zrínyi's poems and writings? What political interests – in Hungary or farther afield – were served by his military exploits?[15]

In Hungary as well as abroad, seventeenth-century Hungarian history has been written, in the past, in one of two mutually exclusive variants: anti-Habsburg and pro-Turkish, or pro-Habsburg and anti-Turkish. Zrínyi cannot be fit into either category without inconsistency: to do so would be to make him out to have been a dreamer as a military man, or faithless as a writer.

In the past thirty years, a whole series of excellent studies based on new sources have shed light on some less-known – or downright unknown – aspects of Zrínyi's world. Continuing the work started by János Arany yet, scholars have placed Zrínyi's literary output in the context of world literature.[16] Others have reconstructed the international repercussions of his victories, and analyzed his theoretical background as a military strategist.[17] In short, the Zrínyi studies of the past few decades have exploded the myth of the lone soldier doing his best to influence his country's immediate political future by just military means. What has emerged is the image of a statesman with an all-embracing political agenda. What he wanted was no less than to reform Hungary. And, it turns out, he had the lion's share in persuading the League of the Rhine to spearhead the international anti-Turkish alliance which finally embarked on an offensive against the Ottoman forces in 1664.[18]

---

[13] Eickhoff: 1973. – Evans: 1979. – Bérenger: 1994, p. 322.
[14] Wagner: 1964, pp. 8, 73, 92–99.
[15] Makkai: 1966, pp. 1312–1313.
[16] Arany: 1859. – Kovács, S. I.: 1985. – Szörényi: 1993.
[17] Sztanó: 1985, pp. 676–681. – Imregh: 1985, pp. 660–675. – Perjés: 1965, pp. 25, 93.
[18] For a summary, see R. Várkonyi: 1984a; 1984b, pp. 341–368; 1987–1988, pp. 131–141.

All this, of course, raises a whole new series of questions. How did Zrínyi, the statesman, come to be known abroad? How can we account for a contemporary English biography vindicating Zrínyi in this capacity? What chain of information was there between war-torn Hungary and the British Isles?

From what we know of the abundant crop of Italian, German and French pamphlets and journals, the courts of Europe as well as the various political groups and factions throughout the continent made very deliberate use of the printed word for propaganda purposes, and operated highly sophisticated news networks.[19]

How can we filter out, from this eclectic multinational crowd, the particular set of people who saw Zrínyi as the man into whose hands Providence had placed the future of Europe? Why did they pick Zrínyi? Which of the possible "futures" facing the contemporary peoples of Europe was he to guarantee, and how? And then, of course, there is *the* question, which both sums up, and follows from the above: Granted the benefit of historical hindsight, what is the essence of Zrínyi's reputation as a statesman of European significance?

What I propose to do in what follows is to suggest some answers, based on a new look at certain unknown – or till now but superficially studied – documents from the manuscript collection in the British Library, the Public Record Office, and the Bodleian Library in Oxford.[20]

THE COORDINATES

We have absolutely precise publication data for *The Conduct and Character of Count Nicholas Serini*: the imprimatur was issued on February 24, 1664, and the book was registered on March 12 of the same year.[21] But when, one wonders, was the notion of Zrínyi as Europe's providential champion born? Given the international implications of the concept, we must seek our clue throughout all of Europe.

By the 1660s, Hungary had been rent into three for over a hundred years, and was of interest to the West primarily as a probable site of any new Ottoman expansion. By the 17th century, however, a qualitative change in

[19] Héjjas: 1987–1988. – Bodó: 1987–1988. – Bukovszky: 1987–1988. – Németh: 1989, pp. 568-570. - G. Etényi: 1995a. – Kovács: 1995.

[20] My thanks to László Péter, Catherine Evans, and James Lapin for their help, and to the FEFA for making this research project possible.

[21] Gömöri: 1988, pp. 68–69.

this interest had set in. It is enough to compare the reports that the various Western residents and ambassadors to Constantinople sent home in the latter half of the 16th century with those written fifty years later and more, or consider the tenor of the negotiations conducted by the Hungarian delegates to the courts of Europe over the same period. In sixteenth-century England, for instance, the Ottoman threat was a part of the public consciousness. When Sultan Suleiman I set siege to the fortress of Szigetvár in 1566, and the garrison of Hungarians and Croatians held out for weeks under the command of Miklós Zrínyi (–1566), public prayers were said for the heroic defenders three times a week in churches throughout Europe. In the light of the considerable international repercussions of the siege of Szigetvár,[22] one is particularly struck by the very different milieu of the Europe of three generations later.

This Europe was definitely Janus-faced. On the one hand, it was a Europe pregnant with the future: great power politics, nation-states, overseas trade, standing armies, absolute governments, binoculars, firearms, banks, the unexpected overcrowding that would attend urbanization, the redrawn world map of the explorers, ports and regular ports of call, the ostentation of courts and kings, a money-based economy, and the information revolution. On the other hand, it was a Europe unable to divest itself of the unresolved problems of its past. It was a Western and Central Europe of partitions and integrations: a Europe of hopes, disappointments, and crises.

In 1645, the Ottoman Empire began military operations against the Venetians in Crete, the maritime republic's most important stronghold; even as the Christian powers of Europe were finally thinking peace, and negotiating an end to the Thirty Years' War, "the Sick Man of the Bosporus" was taking steps that would guarantee Ottoman dominance of the eastern Mediterranean.[23]

The ink was hardly dry on the Peace of Westphalia, it was already clear that the *Pax Optima Rerum* was a dream. Fighting resumed on both the western and eastern fringes of Europe. The Netherlands, the "godchild" of the Peace of Westphalia, attacked England in 1652; the frontier zone between the Christian and the Muslim world from the Ukraine to Croatia

[22] Angyal: 1900, pp. 309–320. – Hubay: 1948, pp. 245–269. – Plan of Sziget: 1566. szept. 15. – "Sziget eleste. Latin vers Zrínyi Miklósról; Szulejmán halála: szept 28., 29., okt. 21., nov. 1" (The Fall of Sziget. Latin verse about Miklós Zrínyi; The Death of Suleiman: Sept. 28, 29, Oct. 21, Nov. 1), SP 70/86. PRO SP 70/85. – Sz. Jónás: 1997, pp. 113–117.
[23] Inalcik: 1973. – Eickhoff: 1973.

was smoldering, and likely at any moment to go up in flames; and the Habsburgs were preparing to compensate themselves for the losses they had suffered by the terms of the Peace of Westphalia. Bohemia and Moravia, which were not included in the peace treaty, were demanding the restoration of their freedom of religion, and Sweden sacked Poland. Transylvania, recognized as a Protestant country by the Peace of Westphalia, could have been an island of stability in the region, though it was under Turkish suzerainty; a grievous political miscalculation, however, brought on a new round of overt Turkish aggression. Louis XIV, "the most Christian monarch", fell out with Rome, and set about gaining a political foothold in Poland and Transylvania, in anticipation of the opportune moment to strike at Leopold I, Holy Roman Emperor and King of Hungary and Bohemia. The French were no less busy on the island of Crete: during the protracted siege of its system of fortifications, French military engineers worked, and French mercenaries fought, for the Turkish and the Christian side alike. A new star, *raison d'état*, eclipsed the *Universitas Christiana*, and all political decisions were now taken by its light.[24]

"All the world is a labyrinth...; the Labyrinth built for the Minotaur in Crete was a joke compared to the bewildering maze that is Europe", declared Comenius in his *Labyrint sveta a ráj srdca* (a work that was first published in 1628, but had a second, definitive, edition in 1663).[25] How, we might ask, could Zrínyi have played a commanding part in such a Europe?

By the time the revised edition of Comenius's *Labyrint* came out in 1663, the crisis in Europe seemed even more profound; but there were also signs of possible ways out. One such sign was the League of the Rhine, called into being in an effort to defuse tensions on the western borders of the Habsburg Empire, and stabilize its relations with France and the German principalities. The other was the role that Restoration England assumed, after the decades of revolution and civil war: protecting trade on the high seas, guaranteeing the balance of power, and safeguarding the interests of Protestantism.[26]

In the early 17th century already, England had shown a special interest in developments in Hungary and Transylvania. The English residents in Constantinople regularly sent home exhaustive reports filled with astute observations. And the King of England recognized the significance of

[24] R. Várkonyi: 1994a, pp. 62 ff. – Haley: 1972. – Forst: 1993.
[25] Comenius: 1628–1631 (Hungarian edition: 1977, pp. 217–218.)
[26] Auerbach: 1887, pp. 117–148. – Raab: 1975, p. 68.

Transylvania in the Treaty of Westminster.[27] György II Rákóczi (1621–1660), the Protestant Prince of Transylvania, received a great deal of English encouragement for the plans he had made with Sweden for Poland, and it was an influential Englishman, Samuel Hartlib, who tried to persuade the English and French governments to go to Rákóczi's rescue in 1658. Educated Englishmen with an interest in politics had the benefit of regular reports sent from Constantinople by the English ambassador, Heneage Finch, Lord Winchilsea, and his extraordinarily able secretary, Paul Rycaut. Kept up-to-date on developments on the mainland through a network of scholarly and church connections – to say nothing of the intelligence coming from the merchants engaged in overseas trade – the literate English public was quite keen to see the pacification of the Ottoman Empire, whose Mediterranean conquests were becoming a source of serious anxiety.[28]

In Hungary – "a country which is more a name than a reality", as Miklós Zrínyi sadly noted – the mounting crisis was threatening the very fabric of society. The leaders of the nation-wide movement to stem the Turkish tide made contact with Johann Philipp von Schönborn (1605–1673), Archbishop Elector of Mainz, and the President of the League of the Rhine. Johann Philipp not only recognized that the League must make common cause with the nations on the eastern fringes of Central Europe, but undertook to spearhead the organization of the international coalition against the Ottoman Empire.

The person in the key position to resolve the crisis, Leopold I, Holy Roman Emperor and King of Hungary and Bohemia, on the other hand, seemed determined to procrastinate. There could be no denying, of course, that in drumming up the international coalition, the League of the Rhine was also strengthening the hand of the German principalities, which were bent on asserting their independence of the Habsburg Emperor. The French, too, were looking for ways to fish in the troubled waters of the war preparations. As for the Hungarians, they were hoping that the war would finally win the country self-determination. Little wonder, thus, that for a disconcertingly long time, the Habsburg government was reluctant to commit itself on the matter of the war against the Ottoman Turks, much to the disappointment of the rest of Europe.

The Hofkriegsrat, which dictated the Habsburg Empire's eastern policy, sought to preserve the status quo *vis-a-vis* the Sublime Porte, and refused to take an unqualified stand throughout the crisis-ridden years anteced-

---

[27] Smith: 1907. – Roe: 1740. – Angyal: 1900, pp. 378 ff. - Gál: 1976, pp. 223–238.
[28] PRO SP 97/17. – Kvacsala: 1892, pp. 805–807. – Holorenschaw: 1939. – Matar: 1993, pp. 203–215.

ent to 1664.[29] In 1658, for instance, Leopold failed to keep the promise that had been the condition of his election as Holy Roman Emperor, namely, that he would send troops to help Transylvania fend off the Turkish offensive: even in 1660, the most he hazarded at a critical juncture of the conflict was to amass his troops along the Transylvanian border; he never did cross into Transylvania, and allowed Várad to fall into Turkish hands. By 1662, Prince Lobkowitz, the President of the Hofkriegsrat, thought war with the Turks to be a realistic possibility, and Montecuccoli actually set off for Transylvania. For all that, Duke Porcia, the President of the Geheimsrat, and the strongest supporter of the traditional Habsburg priorities, made a secret agreement with the Porte (a move that put Montecuccoli in an impossible position), and, dropping Prince János Kemény, threw his weight behind Mihály Apafi, who was duly elected Prince of Transylvania. Porcia was satisfied that he had resolved the immediate crisis; he was, however, soon disillusioned. A new crisis was already brewing on the country's northwestern frontier.

Miklós Zrínyi had a new fortress, Zrínyiújvár, built along the banks of the Mura River.[30] We have detailed information as to how and why the fortress was built, and a great deal of conjecture as to why the Porte was so absolutely against it.[31] The fortress would greatly impede the planned campaign against Venice. With the Ottoman assault on Crete deadlocked at Candia, the central fortress of the island's system of fortifications, it was decided to resort to the old plan of marching against Venice overland, through Friuli, and attack it from the rear. Accordingly, the Porte demanded that the Habsburg Emperor allow the Turkish troops transit through the south of Royal Hungary, Carinthia and Craina. Zrínyi's new castle was not only a violation of the Ottoman–Habsburg peace agreement, but also defied this latest compact, located as it was in the transit zone. Johann Goes and Simon Reninger, the two imperial legates who had mediated the Porte's application for transit, reported back time and again: if the Emperor does not have the fortress razed, Zrínyiújvár will be regarded as *casus belli*.

Duke Porcia, though he had tried to keep the fortress from being completed, did not believe that the Porte would go to war over it; confident of

---

[29] Nehring: 1986, pp. 36–40. – Hiller: 1993, p. 155.

[30] Miklós Zrínyi to János Rottal, Légrád (no year), Aug. 1. MOL P-507. 507. Nádasdy-család levéltára. Levelezés A (Nádasdy family archives, Correspondence A), V.19. cs. No. 688. fol. 141.

[31] Széchy: 1896–1902, vol. IV, pp. 159–160. – Klaniczay, T.: 1964, pp. 702–705. – Perjés: 1965, pp. 309–312.

peace in the east, he sent a substantial part of the army of Royal Hungary off to Spain. It was not the only wrong-headed decision made at the Habsburg court. A whole series of erratic moves – the demobilization of certain divisions, placing restrictions on the Protestants' freedom to practice their religion, the refusal to deal with the just complaints of those suffering religious discrimination – totally undermined what little confidence Leopold's Hungarian subjects still had in the court. Hungary could no longer be ruled from Vienna, and the social disintegration was beginning to take its toll on the country's international reputation: Hungary was very near losing the moral prestige won through centuries of resistance to Ottoman expansion.

When the Ottoman armies started marching, the Habsburg government was totally taken by surprise.[32] In early 1663, by the time the court got wind of the confidential letter that Prince Mihály Apafi sent Palatine Wesselényi, to the effect that the grand vizier, Ahmed Köprülü, was preparing to take Zrínyiújvár and occupy Royal Hungary,[33] all Europe was buzzing with news of the Turkish offensive. In the spring of 1663 already, the English ambassador to the Sublime Porte, Count Winchilsea, dispatched a message from Pera that the Ottoman offensive was inevitable, and on April 10, sent a detailed account of the size of the army involved. Winchilsea's missive, entitled "The Number of the Grand Sig[nors] Army leavied against the Emperour Anno 1663", related that Ahmed Köprülü was marching against Hungary at the head of an army of 209,000 men, Tartars and the troops of the pasha of Buda and the pasha of Temesvár included.[34] On April 17, Simon Reninger, the imperial legate, reported that the time for negotiations was up: on April 18, the sultan would hand the grand vizier the flag of the prophet. By the time the sea of Ottoman troops crossing the bridge at Eszék slowed down to a trickle, the grand vizier had entered Buda. Reninger, who had made the trip with him in an unrelenting downpour, sent the following message to Vienna: The time for stalling was over; negotiations, presents, the tried and true methods of buying off the invader were all to no avail; there was not a chance of peace; they would have to prepare for war.[35]

---

[32] R. Várkonyi: 1994a, p. 104. – Bene: 1992, pp. 233–242.

[33] Palatine Ferenc Wesselényi to János Rottal, Jan. 23, 1663. MOL Kamarai lt. E-199. Wesselényi lt. Fasc. 8.

[34] Winchilsea's report of April 10, 1663 reached London on June 20. PRO SP 97/18, 21. – Contradictory reports on the strength of the army discussed, with an estimated strength of 150,000 suggested in Perjés: 1990, pp. 42–43.

[35] Simon Reninger's reports to the emperor, Nándorfehérvár, June 14, 1663, and Eszék-Buda, July 10, 1663. Wien, ÖstA, MEA, Rtg, Fasc. 217.

By the summer of 1663, it was generally taken for a fact – and would be echoed in *Le Mars à la mode de ce temps*, a work subsequently attributed to Giovanni Sagredo, the Venetian envoy to Vienna – that the Grand Vizier Ahmed Köprülü, "the head of the dragon", was bent on conquering all of Europe – thus satisfying the fond ambition of his father, the Grand Vizier Mohammed Köprülü.[36] Zrínyi and the League of the Rhine wanted to wage an offensive war. The Emperor Leopold, however, only asked for help to defend his lands, and it was with a view to mustering a defensive alliance that Count Peter Strozzi set out for Paris, and then went on to Madrid, while Baron Windischgrätz waited on the kings of Sweden and Denmark, and Count Rudolf Sinzendorf appealed to the Estates of The Netherlands, and sought an audience with the King of England. The imperial legates sent to Pope Alexander VII, the King of Poland and the Czar of Russia were also commissioned to just ask for help to defend the borders of Christendom.[37]

Even arranging for the defense of the country the Hofkriegsrat put off too long. Palatine Wesselényi had to order the *levée en masse* in defiance of Leopold's explicit command to the contrary. The siege of Érsekújvár was well under way by the time the court, at the insistence of György Lippay, Archbishop of Esztergom, finally appointed Zrínyi commander in chief of the Hungarian armed forces. After reviewing his troops in Vat on September 8, Zrínyi set about the painstaking task of organizing the Hungarian army. In the meanwhile, the first set of auxiliaries arrived from abroad. It was, however, too late to reverse the course of events. Érsekújvár surrendered, the Turkish and Tartar troops made repeated forays into Moravia, and ravaged Silesia and Bohemia, looting and burning dozens of villages, and taking hundreds of civilian prisoners. The wave of panic reached Vienna along with the flood of refugees; and the court removed to Linz for reasons of security. On October 31, the League of the Rhine, meeting in Regensburg, announced its plans for a winter campaign; not long after,

[36] OSZKK App. H. 971. – Hungarian translation by Réka Tóth, *Ezen idők módja szerint való Mars*, vol. III of the *Zrínyi könyvtár*. Budapest, 1989, pp. 334, 524. For a critical analysis, and the suggestion of Giovanni Sagredo's authorship, see Bene: 1989, pp. 388–389, 524–525. – For evidence that 1672, the date of publication, was not the year of the book's writing, there is the reference to the ongoing Turkish war: "I dare say that this year yet, there will be Christian flags flying on the ramparts of Esztergom, Székesfehérvár and Buda". Bene: 1989, pp. 377, 533/145.

[37] Jeucourt's reports of Sept. 6 and Nov. 5, 1663. Archives of the French Foreign Ministry, Tome d'Autriche 18. 418., 431. My thanks to Domokos Kosáry, who allowed me to use his microfilm of the documents. The copies made by Sándor Molnár (OSZKK Fol. Gall.75, vols I–II) have been translated and published by Bíró: 1989, pp. 77, 85. – Sbrik: 1912, p. 49.

the armies of the League arrived in Hungary. Zrínyi and General Hohen-lohe, the commander of the army of the League of the Rhine, set about preparing for the massive campaign. On December 23, the Emperor Leo-pold arrived in Regensburg. The assembled Imperial Diet expected that he would finally bring the months of negotiations to a head, and author-ize the winter campaign. Even the starting date had been set: January 14, 1664. The *Kurzer und warhafter Bericht* reporting on the campaign would subsequently conclude that its only aim had been to forestall a Turkish offensive, but certainly, few people thought so at the time.[38]

Instead of bringing the expected decision, on January 18 the Emperor Leopold issued an ordinance. We have every intention, the ordinance read, to protect Hungary with the strongest of armies, but the inclement weather, the shortage of food and fodder, and the shortage of fighting men obliges us to reconsider whether or not to pit our weak forces, come spring, against the might of the enemy. The edict then went on to entrust the Geheimsrat with the government of Royal Hungary, and placed Cisdanubia, Trans-danubia, and Upper Hungary under the authority of royal commission-ers. With this, the Palatine was relieved of his office, and Zrínyi was effec-tively terminated as commander in chief.[39]

The reason for Leopold's surprising decision was his hope that peace with the Turks might be restored. The ray of hope was sparked by Hans Christoph Pucheim, commander of the fortress of Komárom and vice-pre-sident of the Hofkriegsrat, who had reported to the Emperor intelligence received from Turkish prisoners taken during a raid on Moravia.[40]

The prisoners claimed that the grand vizier's Hungarian campaign was only meant to frighten the Habsburgs into acceding to more favorable terms of peace. His real plan, the prisoners insisted, was to send a part of his army against Venice *via* Dalmatia, and use the rest to launch an attack on the Principality of Moscow.[41]

Pucheim's memorandum, dated at Komárom on December 31, coun-seled caution by its very title: "Relation und parere". The document re-views in detail the chances of success in a war against the Turks. He notes that the catastrophes of 1663, too, could have been avoided, had they con-fined themselves to securing the zone this side of the Rába River. He begs

[38] *Kurzer und wahrhafter Bericht*, App. H. 912. Cited in Perjés: 1989b, pp. 58, 91.

[39] Emperor Leopold to Palatine Wesselényi, Regensburg, Jan. 18, 1664. ÖstA, MEA, Militaria, Fasc. 15.

[40] *Relation und parere des Grafen von Pucheim, wegn des Jüngsten Türckenkriegs und der Tartaren Einfalls in Mähren, wie solche zu verhüetten gewesen; und wie dergleichn weitern gefahrn vorzubringen.* Comorn, 31. Decembris 1663. ÖstA, KA, AFA 1663. Fasc. 9. No. 12.

[41] Kraus: 1994, pp. 575–576.

the Emperor not to act in haste. With due circumspection, they might be able to postpone the outbreak of hostilities. If not – and this seemed to be the more likely – they would have to opt for the simplest, safest, and cheapest solution. Pucheim left no doubt in his royal reader's mind that the Habsburg army was woefully unprepared for war. There was not enough ammunition. No provisions had been made for feeding the army. The troops were undisciplined, apathetic, and in a general state of utter disarray. It would not take much to make them turn and flee in panic. As for the Hungarians, they were unreliable and hard to control; they seemed to have grown more sullen, but there was no way to fight the Turks without them. Pucheim had done his homework, and adduced examples from the Fifteen Years' War as to how an effective army should function. But he spoke from experience when he gave instances of the pitiful reality of their own situation. He noted, for example, that there was not enough gunpowder in Komárom, but that there was no way to have some brought from Vienna, since there was a law against transporting gunpowder to Hungary. The imperial troops, he wrote, had not an iota of warlike spirit in them. In the absence of thorough preparations, Leopold would be jeopardizing his whole empire in going to war. Still, it was not too late to start preparing. If they set to it immediately, they could think in terms of initiating hostilities in late March or early April. But only after having provided for a reliable intelligence network, and having made the appropriate preparations; for a hungry and undisciplined army had no hope of success. All in all, the most they could aim for is to try to take Esztergom.

By the time the Emperor Leopold received Pucheim's "Relation", and issued what amounted to the cancellation of the war, the troops led by Zrínyi and Hohenlohe had already set out on the winter campaign.

The Conduct and Character of Count Nicholas Serini was probably written at this dramatic juncture. We have several dates to substantiate this dating. The last pieces of information given in Part I come from letters dated February 2 and February 4 in Győr and Pozsony, respectively. The last identifiable event described by their author is the taking of Pécs on January 29.[42] The author of the letters also knows of the plan to burn the bridge at Eszék: "Whence he intends to cut off a Bridge of theirs that cost 300,000 Rix-dollars the Building". On the basis of the information received from Pozsony, however, the author of *The Conduct and Character* mistakenly attributes the burning of the bridge to the Turks.[43] Our last clue as to the time of the biography's writing is the correction at the foot of the last page

---

[42] *The Conduct and Character* ..., pp. 39–42, 48–51.
[43] *Ibid.*, pp. 38–39.

of the book: "Since these sheets past the Press, news came that it was Seges, not Zigeth that Count Serini hath lately taken."[44] The declaration of Regensburg included in Part II of the book was made after February 12. The author, obviously, had lost no time getting the book to press.

It took three to four weeks at the time for news to travel from Vienna to London. It is highly likely, therefore, that the volume was compiled in great haste, perhaps in Regensburg, perhaps in The Netherlands, with each of the chapters being written by someone else, though in the same spirit, and then the completed manuscript was taken to London for printing. All the more astonishing, that a work prepared in such an incredible rush should have a leitmotif that is so well thought-out and so surprisingly original. The writer of the chapter entitled "Count Serini's Birth and Education" summed up Zrínyi's significance in an image symbolic of the interrelatedness of the two halves – as he saw it – of the European continent: Zrínyi, the Central European, "singly undertakes the despondencies of the West behind him, and the threatenings of the East before him".[45] A concept of this sort would take time to develop, a careful reflection on events, and a vision of Europe as an organic whole. A unique vision, one might say; or is it something that we shall find traces of in the contemporary propaganda?

NEWS AND INFORMATION

The notion of Zrínyi as the providential champion of Europe emerged in a political milieu defined by the revolution in communications that had taken place in the course of the Fifteen Years' War, and the Thirty Years' War. A network now linked all of Europe from Constantinople to Paris, and from the Bosporus to the Atlantic. The transmission of news and information became routine, structured and institutionalized. From 1610 on, there were the *avisi*, copied by hand or printed; and there were the journals and weeklies that sprang up, one after the other, in Augsburg, Strassburg, London, Amsterdam, Florence and Rome. The surfeit of news and information became a part of everyday life and politics.[46]

In the 1650s and 1660s, news of every kind and quality travelled to and from the royal courts of Europe, and to and from council chambers, embassies, battle fields, merchant houses, banks, book stores, coffee houses,

[44] *Ibid.*, 168. – *Angol életrajz Zrínyi Miklósról:* 1987, pp. 405–406/87.
[45] *The Conduct and Character ...*, p. 111.
[46] Eisenstein: 1993. – Shaaber: 1932. – Köpeczi : 1976.

salons and marketplaces. Comenius was one of the first to recognize the significance of newspapers, and suggested that reading them be made a part of the regular school curriculum. Without information, he maintained, people had no clear sense of direction, and could work against their own best interest; their craving for news, on the other hand, made them easy for "newsmongers" to manipulate. "They're trouble if you have them, and there's trouble if you don't",[47] is his diagnosis of the net effects of the new information networks.

The news networks, we find, were built on the sophisticated system of diplomatic and trade contacts, and around financial centers, and centers of government and military administration. The intelligentsia was one of the groups with a stake in their development. But news was also good business, and all presses and publishing houses were private ventures. The information networks of Zrínyi's time had three main hubs: Constantinople, Venice and Amsterdam. The European ambassadors, residents and agents accredited to the Sublime Porte constituted the chief information exchange of Christendom, and sent reports not just to their governments, but to their national embassies in other European capitals. One great drawback was that there was no press in the Ottoman Empire. Newspapers were brought in by the trading ships, with Pera, a veritable hive of travelling newsmen and informants, as the entrepot for both the incoming and the outgoing news. Venice, Vienna, and Cracow were the closest places for printing the information originating with the diplomats and trade attachés of Constantinople.

Venice, with its old and established news networks, cosmopolitan diplomatic corps, prosperous merchants, polished bureaucrats, vibrant cultural life, and busy ports was the military headquarters of the maritime war, and was the information center *par excellence*.[48] Amsterdam was the open city of the new Europe, its financial capital, and the place of international rendezvous. It was through Amsterdam that the latest journals and diplomatic news from England reached continental capitals such as Paris, and Amsterdam was the route that news of the continent took back to London. The gathering and disseminating of facts of current interest was becoming the new obsession of thrill-seekers, but it was also seen as a

[47] Comenius: 1628–1631 (1977), pp. 121–123.
[48] Jászay: 1990, pp. 282–284. – Bene: 1993, pp. 650 ff. – For the issues of propaganda, publicity, and public opinion in the seventeenth century, see the studies of the students attending the special seminar at the Department of Medieval and Early Modern Studies at the Arts Faculty of the Eötvös Loránd University (ELTE BTK): Lukács: 1995; G. Etényi: 1995b; Csapodi: 1995.

civic/moral obligation. The English politician and man of letters, Samuel Hartlib, for example, took time to start up and operate the General News Agency in London.[49]

Printed newsletters, pamphlets, and the various *Relatios*, *Zeitungs*, and *Gazettes* were all so many business ventures, with the news agencies vying with one another for the latest news item, and the broadest readership. Wars now had for an adjunct that "other war": to be the first to know the most, and get into print the latest and most authoritative news; sway the decision-makers; make seem like the cause of humanity the particular aspirations of courts and power groupings; and foster and steer public opinion, that budding and somewhat elusive entity. Confidential communications, intelligence reports, royal decrees, accounts of clandestine consultations, and private letters, both real and fictitious, were served up to the public with no time lost, and with as little discretion. Every major city of Europe had its contingent of unscrupulous pen-wielding mercenaries who specialized in disseminating bogus "news" items. Being the first to know of something had been valued for some time; what was at a premium now was the accuracy of the information.

Embassies could no longer rely solely on their diplomatic contacts, and employed a staff of "correspondents". Diplomatic reports now included the news contained in the local newspapers: the informant would either copy passages of a news item, or would simply append a copy of the paper to his report. Embassy accounts show that substantial monies were spent on whatever newsletters, journals, and weeklies reached the capital in question. It could happen that a news item that an embassy secretary read in a local paper would be included in the report sent to his home capital, and would appear in print there; it would crop up again, translated into the respective languages, in journals throughout Europe; then, for its final printed metamorphosis, it would find its way into some contemporary diary or book.[50]

Pamphlets became the new secret weapon of political warfare, with the inexhaustible stores of (mis)information and propaganda serving as the ammunition. The contemporary pamphlets were infinitely varied, their form, content and genre depending on the purpose – and the readership – that they were meant to serve. There was a growing rift between elite journalism and the popular press. Those writing in the former genre aimed to please the fair sex, too: they counted on the ladies of the literary salons

[49] Althaus: 1884. – Carter: 1964. – Wood: 1925. – Benna: 1965. – Köpeczi: 1976. – Vocelka: 1981. – Van der Wee: 1995.
[50] Bleyer: 1900, pp. 221–227. – Bene: 1992, pp. 226–227. – G. Etényi: 1995a, pp. 65–68.

to form their readership, as well as the patrons of the London coffee houses.[51]

The new means of disseminating information put the old traditions of visual culture to new use, and radically transformed them in the process. This was the age of "talking" pictures, as well as of "centered" tableaux, a telling arrangement where the importance of the key event was brought home to the viewer by its prominent location in the center of the frame, and much smaller pictures of the happenings leading up to it (and/or the denouement) were arranged in a circle (or concentric circles) around it. Illustrated pamphlets recounting the siege of a castle, the events of a battle, an execution or a royal wedding served to inform even the illiterate. People could buy their own copies at bookstores or at postal stations, or "read" the copy nailed to the doors of the town hall. "Talking" maps – where the geographic information was supplemented by illustrations of the events of significance associated with each particular place – were another source of information. Kings and queens, Turkish pashas and mercenary captains rubbed elbows on the market stalls and on the shelves of bookstores, which were piled high with caricatures, panegyrics, military reports, accounts of portents and predictions of the future. A picture of an important figure would be passed around an entire neighborhood. Zrínyi was perhaps the first Hungarian whose features – at least as the graphic artist pictured them – would suddenly become familiar throughout Europe.[52]

Depictions of heroes and other outstanding personages were always schematic, and followed a strict iconography. Very little came through of the personality of the "portrayed" subject.[53] The topoi that served as the idiom of these representations were essentially normative, and mediated value judgements which Christianity had adopted from Antiquity. The mythological topoi of the humanists were rule-bound, and conveyed a world of well-defined meaning. "Mars", "Hercules", and "Phoenix", for instance, conveyed – besides all their mythological connotations – a positive value judgement throughout the 17th century, and were a recurrent convention of prose, poetry, painting and the other graphic arts. Their purport was understood in every corner of Europe.[54]

Stylistically speaking, *The Conduct and Character of Count Nicholas Serini* had very little in common with the newsletters and popular panegyrics of the time; its author (or authors) refrained from using any of the stand-

[51] Pepys: 1961, pp. 165, 167, 179–180.
[52] Cennerné Wilhelm: 1987, pp. 369–390. – Gömöri: 1988, pp. 84, 95.
[53] Tarnai: 1975. – Borzsák: 1984. – Klaniczay, T.: 1985.
[54] Király: 1961. – Bene: 1989, pp. 388–403.

ard topoi. Instead, the significance of Zrínyi's heroism and military prowess was brought home to the reader in terms of the future of Europe, an altogether singular frame of reference.

Singular in every sense of the word, if we consider the implications, particularly in light of Hungary's far from rosy international reputation by the early 1660s. Not that the diplomatic corps residing in Vienna did not try to get objective information to send to their governments (they employed special Hungarian informants, and regularly attended the sessions of the Diet).[55] But news from Hungary in the 17th century was erratic, and dealt mostly with battles, sieges and Diets. There was no resolving the country's religious conflicts, in-fighting consumed the energies of the Hungarian political elite, the Protestants were easily swayed by the Turkish promises of religious freedom – these were the recurring themes of the reports about Hungary. But there were also details about the economy: Hungary had rich copper mines, rivers teeming with delectable fish, countless grazing sheep, an abundance of wool, and an established trade network linking the towns with the highlands.

The reports sent home by Alvise Molin, the Venetian ambassador to Vienna, can be considered typical from the point of view of the contemporary picture of Hungary. Molin himself noted that he often spoke with Zrínyi; for all that, his comments of September 27, 1661 on the Hungarian aristocracy are far from flattering. If we said that they would gladly allow the Turks as far as the door of the Emperor's chamber, Molin wrote, we would still be a long way from what the Hungarian aristocracy really think and want. Their unruliness has made their country poor and powerless, though it is a land blessed with a staggering wealth of natural resources. But the enmity they harbor for one another is stronger than their devotion to the common weal. They are content to let their country decline, as long as they themselves make a profit.[56]

Montecuccoli, in a pamphlet about the campaign of 1662, blamed its failure on the disorderliness and cowardice of the Hungarians. (The rebuttal would come in a pamphlet of Zrínyi's, a spirited testimonial to the show of Hungarian mettle during the Turkish wars.) Even the author of *A Short Relation of the Rise and Progress of the Turkish Warrs* ... maintained that the fall of Érsekújvár was the work of a traitor, and "a shame on all Hungarians".[57]

[55] Fiedler: 1866. – Heckenast: 1983. – Hiller: 1992.
[56] Fiedler: 1866, II, pp. 78–79.
[57] *A Short Relation of the Rise and Progress of the Turkish Warrs in Hungaria, Austria, Moravia, Silesia and Bohemia*, London, 1663, App. H. 2067; cf. Péter: 1987, pp. 35 ff. – G. Etényi: 1995b. – *Le Mars à la mode de ce temps* (Hung. edition: 1989): pp. 343, 350.

The French propaganda, on the other hand, emphasized the responsibility of the Habsburg government. The Order of the Golden Fleece, after all, was conferred on Palatine Wesselényi in recognition of Hungary's valiant stand against the Ottoman Empire. Molin himself was keenly aware of Hungary's and Transylvania's desperate plight, and noted with some disapproval the imperial court's hedging on the Turkish question, and its mistrust of the Hungarians. He himself had to meet in secret with the highest dignitaries of Royal Hungary, who were determined to fight the Turks in an all-out war.

The author of *Le Mars à la mode de ce temps* – presumably Giovanni Sagredo, the Venetian envoy to Vienna in 1664 – was just as hard on both sides. He castigated Count Ádám Forgách, the captain of the fortress of Érsekújvár, spoke contemptuously of Palatine Wesselényi, and then had some very hard words for Duke Porcia. All over Europe – he wrote – people thought that Leopold's all-powerful councillor was doing Christendom irreparable harm: ancient as he was, when it came to politics, he was a greenhorn. Montecuccoli Sagredo saw as being interested mainly in making a fortune; as for Sinzendorf, the President of the Geheimsrat, and Lobkowitz, the President of the Hofkriegsrat, they were busy bringing charges of embezzlement against one another. (We must keep in mind, of course, that Venice's interest would have been served by Leopold's marching against the Turks forthwith; the Venetians accredited to Vienna were, in part, rationalizing their inability to effect this by painting as dark a picture as possible of the people responsible for the delay.) So poor was Hungary's reputation, Sagredo wrote, that no one would lift a finger for it: "In vain the good old palatine's lamentation at the graveside of a despised and scorned Pannonia, in vain the attempts to inspire respect for Hungary's decaying corpse; it is not healing herbs that are needed to bring her to life, but a strong hand and finely honed steel, and action by generals and statesmen bordering on the miraculous".[58]

Zrínyi himself had a poor opinion of his compatriots, and was very much aware of Hungary's bad name abroad: "It is we ourselves, with our indolence, who have given Europe cause for the disgrace we are in; it is we who detest each other more than any nation on earth". Citing Tacitus, he noted that the Romans, when they suffered a decline in reputation, "would not rest until they had reestablished their good name". Zrínyi, for his part, was determined to reestablish Hungary's. The key, as he saw it, was publicity. The Croatian chancellery at Csáktornya operated with a

[58] Quoted in Jászay: 1990, pp. 294–296.

network of informants which kept Zrínyi abreast of developments throughout Europe, just as the Ban's spy network kept him updated on whatever
was newsworthy in the lands under Ottoman control. There was also a
regular flow of information to and from the leaders of the reunification
movement in Royal Hungary: Palatine Wesselényi, Archbishop Lippay,
Chief Justice Nádasdy, Péter Zrínyi and István Vittnyédy, all of whom
thought it of the utmost importance to keep the world informed of the
events in Hungary. Zrínyi himself was a great believer in the power of
propaganda, and made the most of his opportunities to speak for the country.[59] The notion of Zrínyi as Europe's providential champion, however,
could not have originated in Hungary.

Zrínyi was by no means unknown in Western Europe by the mid-17th
century. The victorious border skirmishes he led with his brother Péter
had fired the imagination of all Europe; by the late 1640s, news of his military exploits appeared together with the big news of the decade, the Ottoman Empire's war with Venice for Crete.

In 1655, Zrínyi addressed the Diet meeting in Pozsony to elect the new
palatine, and expounded his views on government, and on the relative
roles of the king and the dignitaries of the realm. He must have caused
quite a stir, for the speech figures in the reports of all the ambassadors
accredited to Vienna. It was, perhaps, the first time that Zrínyi the politician was heard of outside the country; it was clear that he would be a
personality of considerable weight if it ever came to a showdown with
the Turks.

By the 1660s, we find Zrínyi's name cropping up in the European journals in connection with two new themes. The first was Zrínyiújvár:
Zrínyiújvár was *casus belli*. The Sublime Porte was ready to go to war if it
was not razed. Portraits of Zrínyi appeared in the papers along with pictures of the fortress, as well as inventories of the Ban's military exploits.
In May of 1662, Giovanni Chiaromanni, the Florentine ambassador to Vienna, sent home detailed reports on Zrínyiújvár on three separate occasions. The Porte insisted that it be demolished, he related. The next time
he included information received from the Florentine resident in Constantinople: The fortress had to be demolished because it was built on land
belonging to the Sultan. The Turkish garrison in Kanizsa had already been
put on alert: the fortress was to be attacked. Chiaromanni's third report
was an account of a personal interview with Zrínyi: They had had lunch

[59] Zrínyi's letter to an unidentified correspondent, Csáktornya, May 2, 1663. – *Aphorismák*, in: *Zrínyi Miklós összes művei*: 1958, I, pp. 467–468, II, p. 328. – Bene: 1992, pp. 227–229.

together, and the Ban had spoken at length about Zrínyiújvár – and explicitly declared that he had no intention whatsoever of razing it.[60]

The international press of the early 1660s also yields repeated references to the political movement headed by Zrínyi. Palatine Wesselényi, Archbishop Lippay, and Chief Justice Nádasdy are names that crop up again and again in the news items dealing with Hungary, along with brief reports on Zrínyi's latest engagement of the Turks along the country's borders. Absolutely no one, however, thought to connect the Hungarian scene to the direction being taken by great power politics. The Peace of Olivia, the attempts at coordinated action being made by the League of the Rhine, and the Ottoman war preparations were all related but indirectly to the crisis in Hungary. True, the Geheimsrat was beginning to take some note of the Hungarian councillors' evaluation of their own situation, in a memorandum the latter presented to Leopold in Graz the autumn of 1660, and the *Opinio* they submitted to Duke Porcia at the January 1661 sitting of the privy council. In particular, the Geheimsrat appreciated that the Hungarian lords temporal and lords spiritual had finally agreed among themselves. But there was no special mention of Zrínyi.[61]

All the more emphatic was the notice taken of Zrínyi's political prestige by Chiaromanni, the Florentine ambassador, an expert on Hungary. Reporting on the sittings of the Diet of 1662, he notes that the Estates assembled in Pozsony wished to elect a national leader (*capo nationale*), and that most of them wanted to see Count Miklós Zrínyi, Ban of Croatia, in that capacity. The hawks in the Diet, wrote Chiaromanni, were not so much the aristocracy as the nobility, and the Palatine and Zrínyi egged them on. There was no telling whether they simply wanted to go to the aid of Transylvania, or wanted to forestall the grand vizier's offensive, and wage an all-out war. Their arguments, the Florentine ambassador notes, were the perennial ones: without help, Transylvania would succumb, and then Royal Hungary, too, would fall prey to the barbarians.[62] Johann Philipp, Archbishop Elector of Mainz, received detailed reports from Pozsony to the same effect from his chargé d'affaires, Wilderich von Waldendorf, who

---

[60] *Recht-Eigentlicher Abriss der Neu-aufgebauten Ungarischen Gräntz-Vestung* / Neu-Serinwar ..., N.p., n.d., App. H. 373. – Vienna, May 6 and 24, 1662; Pozsony, May 31, 1662. AStF, Mediceo del Principato 4404. The reports of the ambassador to Vienna, Giovanni Chiaromanni, to Bali Gondi, Tuscany's minister of state for foreign affairs. (Based on István Hiller's research.)

[61] Molin, Jan. 1 and 15, 1661. – Pribram: 1901, pp. 189–191.

[62] Chiaromanni to Bali Gondi, Pozsony, May 31, 1662. AStF, Mediceo del Principato 4404.

added the observation that the nobility's faith in Zrínyi had a great deal to do with their despairing of Montecuccoli's leadership.[63]

From all of the above, we can draw the guarded conclusion that, beginning with the years 1660–61, Zrínyi was the object of growing international attention in diplomatic reports, newspapers and pamphlets. His military successes were duly recognized; but I have found no trace of his being discussed as a politician of European stature.

The year 1663 – when the Emperor Leopold finally appointed Zrínyi Commander-in-Chief of the Hungarian forces – brought a qualitative change, though no one has yet counted the exact number of newsletters, pamphlets, *Relatios*, *Zeitungs*, and *Gazettes* reporting on the military operations in Hungary, and Zrínyi's successes.[64] Certainly all the *Zeitungs* and pamphlets appearing in the German-speaking lands kept up a running commentary of Zrínyi's engagements, and reported his every move.[65] The weighty political issues raised by the Turkish invasion of the autumn of 1663 were also discussed. A great deal was written about the conflicts between the Habsburg court and the Hungarians, and about how astutely the Ottoman propaganda exploited the Hungarian Protestants' grievances, and tried to win them to the Turkish side with promises of religious liberty. The Palatine was ill, the papers reported, and unfit for military leadership. And there appeared the first historicist interpretation of Zrínyi's victories over the invading Turks: the heritage of Szigetvár, and the example of the Miklós Zrínyi of yore, the story of whose heroic stand came out in a new edition, with a ballad highlighting the similarities between the two Zrínyis appended.[66]

The news of Ahmed Köprülü's campaign gave rise to all kinds of rumors, for instance that Zrínyi was negotiating with the Turks.[67] Report-

---

[63] Wilderich von Waldendorf to Johann Philipp, Pozsony, May 10 and Aug. 16, 1662. ÖStA, MEA, Rtga Fasc. 211, fol. 59–60, 81.

[64] Péter: 1987, p. 35. – G. Etényi: 1995a, pp. 65–67.

[65] Zrínyiújvár, Aug. 13, 1663. App. H. 875. – Vízvár, Oct. 10, App. H. 865. – Mura menti győzelem, Nov. 27, App. H. 878. Cf. G. Etényi: 1995a, pp. 123–126.

[66] *Etzliche, zu fernerem Nachdenken movirte Politische und Historische Discursen...*, Wittenberg, 1663. App. H. 2063. – *Jährige Relation Von dem tapffren Ritter, dem Alten Grafen Niclas von Serin, wie derselbe Anno 1566. vom Türkischen Käyser Solymanno in der Vestung Sigeth hart belagert, erschlagen und der Ort erobert worden*. Neu auffgelegt Anno 1663. App. H. 2065.

[67] "Verdacht der Minister gegen Nikolaus Zrinyi und seinen Bruder Peter, dass sie mit Türken Verbindung und Nikolaus nach dem Beispiele Bethlen Gabors sich zum Könige machen will. N. möchte nicht an ihre Untreue glauben, weiss aber, dass sie unzufrieden mit dem Wiener Hofe." Franz Paul Lisola, Vienna, July 21, 1663. Cited in: Levinson: 1913, p. 362.

ing on November 21, 1663, Jeucourt, the French ambassador to Vienna, noted that Zrínyi was alleged to have declared that the nobility would fain elect Louis XIV King of Hungary.[68] It was a false allegation: we have found absolutely no hint of any such thing in any of the relevant contemporary sources, including the correspondence of the aristocracy and fortress commanders belonging to Zrínyi's movement. On the other hand, allegations of this sort could damage Zrínyi's reputation abroad in certain circles.

By late autumn of 1663, Zrínyi, the Commander-in-Chief of the Hungarian forces fated to try to stem the Turkish tide, was a pet subject of the international press. But, though his every move was reported, no paper or newsletter spoke even of his victories – let alone of Zrínyi himself – as being of significance for all of Europe. Even the French and Italian propagandists confined themselves to traditional military reporting, and analyzed events in terms of the perennial Habsburg–Hungarian–Ottoman conflicts. Zrínyi was hailed as "hero", "fearless Mars", and "the champion of Christendom", particularly by the propagandists of the German princes, but there is no suggestion that his actions, however heroic, would affect the fate of Europe. We can, thus, rule out the court propagandists as possible sources of the core concept of *The Conduct and Character of Count Nicholas Serini*.

Research has shown that certain details of *The Conduct and Character of Count Nicholas Serini* are taken, more or less verbatim, from *A Short Relation of the Rise and Progress of the Turkish Warrs ...* (published in 1663), and *A New Survey of the Turkish Empire* (published early in 1664), and that all three books are the work of the same printer.[69] Another thing that the three publications have in common is an uncommon fixation on all of Central Europe, which, for the anonymous author (or authors) always includes Moravia, Bohemia and Silesia.

Considered in terms of the sheer number of pages, *A Short Relation of the Rise and Progress of the Turkish Warrs in Hungaria, Austria, Moravia, Silesia and Bohemia* which was in the bookstores in the first weeks of 1664 deals with Moravia in the greatest detail, describing a vast number of local happenings in the form of eyewitness reports.[70]

---

[68] Jeucourt, Vienna, Nov. 21, 1663. Tome d'Autriche t. 18. 441.

[69] About *A Short Relation ...*, see *Angol életrajz Zrínyi Miklósról:* 1987, pp. 433–435. – About *A New Survey ...*, see Bukovszky: 1987–1988, pp. 207–211. – Gömöri: 1988, pp. 69–70.

[70] *A Short Relation of the Rise and Progress of the Turkish Warrs in Hungaria, Austria, Moravia, Silesia and Bohemia.* London, 1663. App. H. 2067. – Cf. Péter: 1987, p. 42.

The work is one of the most exhaustive of the contemporary accounts of the wasting of Moravia on September 3, 1663.[71] It tells of the comet, and of how the Jesuits of Olomouc interpreted it as a portent that Moravia was in peril. We also learn of an another omen of destruction: a piglet born, a mile from Selmecbánya, with a clump of feathers growing out of its head. The omens, the anonymous author suggests, were warranted: Moravia was overrun by a horde of 15,000 Tartars on horseback, and 40,000 Turks. They looted and burned over sixty castles and villages, slaughtered the children and those too old to march, and enslaved thousands of young men and women. A great many people fled toward Vienna, where the drawbridge collapsed under the weight of the crowds, carts and horses. The author quotes one of the refugees, who saw elderly gentlefolk being stripped along the highway and hacked to death, and saw Mapagelo Brokowisto and Ostrowa go up in flames. A mile from Prague, another eyewitness recounts, a troop of Tartars broke into a cloister, and took all the valuables, and also some of the nuns with them. An English count boarding at the cloister barely managed to escape by jumping out the window. (The "English count" was probably a bit of poetic license, introduced to bring home a point, as was the reference to "Dutch horse traders" in connection with how the value of the Christian captives was determined at the slave market.)[72]

Recounted with deep feeling, the sufferings of Moravia figure also in another contemporary publication, *A Brief Accompt of the Turks Late Expedition*.[73] "Silesia is wasted, Moravia is made desolate ...", we read again in *The Conduct and Character of Count Nicholas Serini*.[74] Moravia's tribulations are, however, not the only common strand in all the contemporary English works that speak of Zrínyi. The meeting of the Imperial Diet at Regensburg is another common leitmotif: it is to this that we shall now turn.

---

[71] Hungarian edition, with bibliography: Kraus: 1994, pp. 568–569, 703/681. – For the organization of the defence, see the decisions taken by the estates of Lower Saxony on Sept. 27, 1663, the recommendations of the Elector John George II, and the order of conscription: Leipzig, Oct. 10, 1663, ÖStA, MEA, Militaria, 36. Fasc. 15.

[72] *Angol életrajz Zrínyi Miklósról:* 1987, pp. 346–347.

[73] *A Brief Accompt of the Turks Late Expedition, against the Kingdome of Hungary, Transylvania, and the Hereditary Countries of the Emperour.* By Richard Hodgkinson and Thomas Mab. London, 1663. App. H. 866., 19.

[74] *The Conduct and Character ...,* p. 27.

The letter in which Johann Philipp von Schönborn, Archbishop Elector of Mainz, draws a parallel between Zrínyi and George Castriot was sent from Regensburg to Csáktornya on January 22, 1664. Writing in his capacity as president of the League of the Rhine four days after the Emperor Leopold cancelled the winter campaign, Johann Philipp was, more than likely, replying to Zrínyi and Hohenlohe's letter of January 11.[75] The original letter, though it may yet come to light, was among the documents that disappeared along with the Zrínyi library; the Augustinian Mark Forstall, Zrínyi's Irish-born secretary, was likely to have been familiar with it, and so, probably, was the Paulist János Kéry, another one of Zrínyi's supporters.

It is the draft of the letter that has come down to us, preserved in the archives of the Archbishopric of Mainz. In it, Johann Philipp emphasizes Zrínyi's excellent soldierly virtues and capacity for military leadership, and expresses his hope that, uniting his forces with those of the alliance, he will, like a latter-day Castriot, triumph over the Sultan's army, to the immense benefit of Christendom.[76]

Of all the sources dating to a time prior to the winter campaign, this letter is, to the best of my knowledge, the only one to contain the Zrínyi-Castriot parallel. It seems plausible, thus, to trace to Johann Philipp's letter the third chapter of *The Conduct and Character of Count Nicholas Serini*, namely, the chapter entitled "The Life and Actions of George Castriot Sirnamed Scanderbeg, the other Champion of Christendome". All the more so as it is evident that the volume was written and compiled before the conclusion of the winter campaign. It stands to reason, therefore, for us to ask whether it might not have been Johann Philipp von Schönborn, Archbishop Elector of Mainz (and/or his circle) who first spoke of Zrínyi as the providential champion of Europe.

In the winter of 1664, all Europe was in Regensburg. Besides the Emperor Leopold and Johann Philipp, there were present Duke Porcia, the Bishop of Strassburg, the Duke of Lotharingia, and practically every one of the electors. Several countries had sent their diplomatic representatives.

---

[75] R. Várkonyi: 1975, pp. 54–55. Zrínyi to Johann Philipp, Csáktornya, Jan. 11, 1664. ÖStA, MEA, Rtg, Fasc. 219. T. 7. No. 142.

[76] "Totus sane orbis Christianus aliquod prisci Castriotae instar in Vestra Excellentia veneratur." Johann Philipp to Zrínyi, Regensburg, Jan. 22, 1664. ÖStA, MEA, Rtg, Fasc. 219. fol. 21-22.

Among them were the imperial diplomat Franz von Lisola; Caraffa, the papal legate; Abbot Robert Gravel, the French envoy; Count Archinto, the Spanish envoy; Antonio Negri, the Venetian representative; and the Chevalier Giovanni Chiaromanni, the Viennese resident of the Duke of Tuscany.[77] György Szelepcsényi, Chancellor to the King of Hungary, was in Regensburg, and other Hungarian delegates were on their way: the Jesuit Imre Kiss, the envoy of Princess Zsófia Báthori, György II Rákóczi's widow; Palatine Wesselényi's envoy; the Lutheran magistrate Mihály Bory; and the delegates of the Hungarian towns and counties. The merchant István Moro, Zrínyi's Venetian agent, was there already, and Wasenhofen, his military engineer, was due to arrive. Péter Zrínyi and Ferenc Frangepán arrived with news of the success of the winter campaign (written up and ready to go to press) on, or a few days before, February 12.[78]

The first weeks of 1664 had been a time of extraordinary tension in Regensburg, a time of drawn-out and inconclusive negotiations, tight-fisted offers of financial support for the war against the Turks, and even more reluctant offers of men – a time, in short, of overall uncertainty, and impatience to know the Ottoman plans. Spain and Denmark had refused outright to give any help; the Pope and the Italian states were willing to contribute money, but for the moment, no men; as for Louis XIV, he had yet to give Leopold his answer. England and The Netherlands, it seemed, were staunchly determined to maintain their neutrality. It is noteworthy, however, that just over a year earlier, Sir William Swann, the English resident in Hamburg, had seen fit to enquire – in the light of the instructions London had sent Winchilsea in Constantinople – whether England was not planning to break with the Sublime Porte on account of the Algerian pirate raids.[79] And though Swann's job was to keep an eye on commercial affairs, his reports of January and February of 1664 contain detailed news of the Regensburg Diet.

Everyone in Regensburg knew that Zrínyi's campaign was about to get under way. On January 2 already, Jeucourt was reporting from Vienna that he had had word from Graz that Zrínyi's offensive was imminent, and that Count Hohenlohe was to join up with the Ban's substantial forces. Chiaromanni's report of January 15 makes clear that news of the Sultan's

[77] R. Várkonyi: 1975, p. 33. – Bene: 1992, pp. 227 ff.
[78] Chiaromanni reported Péter Zrínyi's arrival in Regensburg on Feb. 12. AStF MP 4404. Cf. Bene: 1992, p. 231.
[79] "... Wishes to know whether England will break with the Porte in Consequence to acts of Piracy committed by Algerians." Sir William Swann to Williamson, Hamburg, Jan. 2/12, 1663. PRO, SP 82/10. fol. 163.

planned march on Vienna had already reached Regensburg: half of the Ottoman army was to march up along the Danube, and lay waste to Moravia, Silesia, and Bohemia; the other half was to head straight for Zrínyiújvár, and attack Vienna from the south after taking the fortress and ravaging Styria.[80]

All this played against the background of another sign from the heavens, a comet first sighted, to the consternation of all Europe, over Styria and Carinthia. German, and bilingual Dutch–English pamphlets reported on its course, noting that it had been sighted over Radkersburg and Csáktornya (!) between two and three in the morning since January 12, 1664, and over Silesia and Moravia since January 17.[81]

On January 16 already, Jeucourt reported from Vienna that Zrínyi had deployed his troops, but, from the evidence available to date, it seems that it was not until January 22 that news reached Regensburg that the winter campaign was actually on its way. We know from Chiaromanni that subsequently, there was absolutely no further news for another week; no news was good news, he noted.

Details of the first series of successful clashes along the Drava started coming in on February 5, and by February 12, Péter Zrínyi and his young brother-in-law, Ferenc Frangepán had arrived in Regensburg. Sir William Swann included their glad tidings in his report back to London: "That fieldmarshal Count Nicolaus Zrinyi has taken Fünfkirchen", he wrote, his use of the town's German name betraying that he was working from German-language propaganda material. He added that the spoils of war were considerable, and that Zrínyi "has also occupied Szeged". Zrínyi had taken *Segesd*, but it was the name of the better-known market town that had stuck in Swann's mind.[82] Soon, Wasenhofen, Zrínyi's military engineer, arrived in Regensburg, and the campaign's journal was passed around town. The Florentine Giovanni Chiaromanni, too, managed to get hold of it, and copied it to append to his report of February 26, along with a letter

[80] Chiaromanni to Bali Gondi, Regensburg, Jan. 15, 1664. AStF MP 4404. – Swann to Williamson, Lübeck, Jan. 22 / Feb. 3, 1664. PRO, SP 82/10 fol. 166.

[81] *Abbildung des Neuen Comet und Wunder Stern*, [Nürnberg], and printed in London, translated from the Low-Dutch as: *Delineation Of a Marvellous New Blazing Star, Which appeared to Austria, chiefly about Radkelsburg and Czakenthurn, seen several mornings betwixt two and three of the Clock, from 12th of January, 1664 to the amazement of the Beholders*. In the translation from the High-Dutch, the last three words of the title read: "to the terrour of the Beholders". In: Harms: 1985, vol. II, pp. 399, 401. – Cf. Kraus: 1994, p. 583.

[82] Swann to Williamson, Feb. 16 and 23, 1664. PRO, SP 82/10. fol. 168–169. – Winchilsea to Henry Bennet, Pera, March 8, 1664. PRO, SP 97/18. fol. 67–68.

of Zrínyi's addressed to the Hofkriegsrat in Graz, and dated February 11 at Babócsa. It must be left to future scholars to examine the correlations between this journal, and the two other journal-like accounts of the winter campaign that have come down to us: Zrínyi's and Hohenlohe's.[83] What concerns us is how the various interest groups tried to get news of the winter campaign as quickly as possible, in what form they passed this news on, and to what purpose. In the German-speaking lands, the lands within the League of the Rhine, the campaign was, naturally, seen as Zrínyi and Hohenlohe's joint victory.[84]

It would be hard to overestimate the impact of the winter campaign. It was the first time that the Christian forces had won a victory over the Ottoman armies in over fifty years. Zrínyi and Hohenlohe's triumph breathed new life into the cause of the anti-Turkish alliance. The Emperor Leopold and his court quickly forgot that they had stripped Zrínyi of his position as Commander-in-Chief of the Hungarian forces. Count Peter Strozzi, dispatched by the Emperor to Paris in haste, was able to report back that Louis XIV had decided in favor of offering aid to the alliance.[85]

Thanksgiving processions and banquets, however, did not yet make for unanimity. The most crucial of the points of disagreement (which we need not go into here) was the question of who should be Commander-in-Chief. The Swedish Wrangel? The French Turenne? Frederick William, Elector of Brandenburg, announced that he was joining the alliance, had taken steps to win the support of the King of France, and was offering his

[83] *Relation*, was massen durch Herrn Grafen *Serini* die Oerter in Nieder-Hungarn *Berzenche, Koppan, Seges, Babocza* und *Fünfkirchen* den Türcken aberobert. M. Januaris A. 1664. App. H. 929. – *Feldungs-Journal...* 1664. App. H. 904. – *Kurzer und warhaffter Bericht ...* 1664. App. 912. – *Relation*, Kurtze jedoch warhafft-verfasste, der sehr notablen und weit über ein hundert Jahr von den Christen wider den Erbfeind tentirter Entreprise und Anschlags, Welche Ihre Hochgräfliche Excellenz Herr Graf Wolff Julius zu Hohenlohe und Gleichen etc. Anno 1664 von dem 10., 20. Januarii bis auf den 6., 16. Februarii vorgenommen und glücklich effectuirt. – *Relation*, Ausführliche und aller Umständen recht gründliche, vom Srinischen Feldzug in der Nider-Hungarischen Türkey, welcher gewähret vom 20./1 bis 18/2 App. H. 895. Cf. G. Etényi: 1995a, pp. 67–68.

[84] It was only on Feb. 6 that Jeucourt in Vienna was able to report Zrínyi's successes at Babócsa, Sziget, and Pécs, and was obliged to note on Feb. 13 that he still had no confirmation of the news he had sent on Feb. 6; the reason: Zrínyi had pushed so far into enemy territory that he found it difficult to get information out. Jeucourt from Vienna to Paris, Feb. 13, 1664. Bíró: 1989, pp. 99–101.

[85] Lisola, Regensburg, Jan. 15 – Feb. 12, 1664. – Levinson: 1913, pp. 389–393. – Pachner: 1740. – Intercessions-Schreiben, Allerunterhänigstes (13. April aus Regensburg). In: Schauroth: 1751. B. II. 19. – Jeucourt's reports: Vienna, Jan. 2 – Feb. 13, 1664. Bíró: 1989, pp. 95–102.

services as Commander-in-Chief.[86] Montecuccoli, for his part, naturally felt that he was entitled to the position. Pucheim, on the other hand, declared him unfit for the job, suggested the appointment of a foreign general, and wanted to see Zrínyi take charge of the border defense. One fascinating contribution to the debate made in writing, and attributed to Zrínyi, is the memorandum entitled *La verita Consigliera del Conte Nicolo di Sdrino sopra gl'emergenti della presente guerra Fra Sacra Maesta Cesarea et il Gran Turco.*[87] The memorandum gives a character analysis of each of the possible candidates, and rejects every one on political grounds; then, it boldly suggests that the Emperor Leopold himself should fill the position of Commander-in-Chief. The relevant parts of this piece of writing would find their way into the second chapter of *The Conduct and Character of Count Nicholas Serini*, under the title "Count Serini's Birth and Education".[88] The suggestion, it goes without saying, was only a formal solution to the problem. The Commander-in-Chief who would actually conduct the war in the field had yet to be found.

Johann Philipp, Archbishop Elector of Mainz and president of the League of the Rhine, saw Zrínyi as the man they were looking for; his first priority, however, was to avoid a rift in the alliance. For all that, he spoke of Zrínyi in two of the letters addressed to Hohenlohe, mentioning that he was doing his best with the Emperor and his ministers to win him recognition commensurate with his deserts.[89]

Based on the documentary evidence, Johann Philipp was the first to use the Zrínyi–Castriot parallel; nevertheless, the delicacy of his position, the infinite tact needed to keep together the international coalition make it very unlikely that he had any direct influence on the framing of the "Zrínyi as Europe's providential champion" concept. In its subject matter, spirit and particulars, *The Conduct and Character of Count Nicholas Serini* points in a direction very different from the world of the Archbishop of Mainz. It took a sovereign individual (or group of individuals) detached from the clamor of day-to-day politics to make pronouncements of such weight in the pressured days of the Regensburg Diet.

---

[86] Frederick William, Elector of Brandenburg to Johann Philipp, Köln an der Spree, Jan. 23, 1664. – ÖStA, MEA, Rtg, Fasc. 219. fol. 4.

[87] Szelestei: 1980, pp. 185–198. An exact dating has been suggested by Bene: 1992, pp. 236–237.

[88] *The Conduct and Character ...*, pp. 48–50.

[89] Johann Philipp to Hohenlohe, Regensburg, Feb. 5 and 26, 1664. ÖStA, MEA, Rtg, Fasc. 219.

"The Locusts of the East (the Turks) shall suffer miserie likewise, for a great foul (which was the wingd Venetian Lion, but now Count Serini) will flye among them and make great havock among them."[90] I came across this odd prediction paging through *The Herauld of Regensburg. Proclaiming to the gathered members of the Empire by their Opper-head,*[91] a 135-page quarto manuscript in the Sloane Collection of the British Library.

The frontispiece indicates that the MS was copied from the title page of a published book. Under the title, the anonymous copyist wrote the following three questions: "I. From whence this Turky-warr arose? II. How to be appeased after the will of God III. Being not appeased, what at last may be expected?"[92] The reader is promised wondrous new revelations concerning the great judgement of "Lord Zebaoth" on this "Turky-warr". The title page also tells us why the author (or authors, or publisher) behind the initials "C.H.L.P.J.G." saw fit to present the writing to the public: "To awaken the drowsie and sleepy / To stirre up the awakned unto animositie / To convince the Impenitent [?]."[93] Finally, the frontispiece gives the date of publication: "In the yeere [*sic*] of our Lord 1664."

The text, as the title suggests, is an admixture of the concrete and the occult, and operates on three distinct, though related planes. The first is a review of the Turkish wars, from 1657 – the year of György II Rákóczi's Polish campaign – to May 24, 1663, the day the Grand Vizier Ahmed Köprülü launched the offensive that threatened to annihilate Hungary, Transylvania and Austria. The second plane relates to certain "revelations" made, between 1616 and September of 1655, by three Central European visionaries: Christopher Kotter of Silesia, Christiana Poniatovska of Bohemia, and Nicolas Drabicius of Moravia. Prophecies were a typical genre of the times; *The Herauld of Regensburg* makes use of excerpts from *Lux in Tenebris* (1657), and *Historia Revelationum* (1659), two collections, published by Comenius, of revelations made by the threesome.

(Robert Codrington's abridged English translation of these two prophecy compilations was likewise published in 1664;[94] Codrington mentions

---

[90] *The Herauld of Regensburg,* 264. The text is an abridgement of revelation CXXXVIII of *Lux in Tenebris,* 120–123. – Cf. John, *Revel· iions* 9.

[91] *The Herauld of Regensburg.* C.H.L.!·!.G. In the yeere [*sic*] of our Lord 1664. BL Sloane Ms. 2541.

[92] *The Herauld of Regensburg,* fol. 1.

[93] *Ibid.*

[94] *The Prophecies of Christopher Kotterus, Christiana Poniatovia, Nicholas Drabicius.* Translated into English by R. Codrington. London, 1664. App. H. 885. – Péter: 1987, pp. 32, 38.

Comenius in the title of his book, and makes several other explicit references to him. The reason for publishing the prophecies just then, Codrington tells us, was the ongoing Turkish war, an event which Drabicius had foretold several years earlier. It is worth noting that Codrington's reference to the Ottoman offensive is practically a verbatim quote of the introductory lines of the 1663 bilingual edition of Busbequius's *Exclamatio*: back in 1572, Busbequius "like a prophet, had foretold the predicament the Holy Roman Empire finds itself in today".[95])

The Herauld of Regensburg interprets Zrínyi's military exploits in terms of a vision Kotter had on September 24, 1624, when he saw the "Locusts of the East" (an allusion to *Revelations* 9), i.e. "the Turks" (as *The Herauld* hastens to make clear), arrested and destroyed by "a great fowl", i.e. "Count Serini", the champion who had risen to take the place of the "winged Venetian Lion". It was, of course, an angel who had revealed all this to Kotter, and so the notion of Zrínyi as the bane of the Turks had angelic authority. The apropos of the explication could have been the winter campaign, or it could have been the proposed all-out war. Either would date the notion to late 1663, early 1664.

The third plane is the tense and conflicted days of the Diet of Regensburg, the time between late winter of 1663 and the last days of January, 1664. The ominous comet, at any event, is already in the skies: "By the terrible blazing starrs and other celstiall signes...".[96]

The Herauld of Regensburg is conspicuously well-informed about the latest happenings in Transylvania, and devotes an extraordinary amount of space to the Rákóczis. "This Turkish warr originally is caused by prince Rakoczy", we are told; Rákóczi's Polish campaign so provoked the Porte that the Turks launched a punitive expedition against him; the Holy Roman Emperor, on the other hand, refused to go to his aid. Indeed, when the Transylvanian estates elected a new Prince after Rákóczi died – a Prince, to boot, who allied himself with the Emperor – even then the Holy Roman Emperor stood by and watched the Ottoman armies lay waste to Transylvania.[97]

[95] Augerii Gislenii Busbequii trium caesarum legati Exclamatio sive de Re Militari contra Turcam instituenda Consilium Aug. Gisl. von Busbek Dreyer Keysere Legatens bewegliche Aufmahnung ... Neben einem vor albereit 140. Jahren heraus gegebenen Anschlag eines Zugs wider die Türken, dem günstigen Leser zu Lien hiebey gedrukt in diesem nunmehro zu End laufenden 1663-sten Jahre. *Vorbericht.* App. Hung. 2062. 1.

[96] *The Herauld of Regensburg*, 44.

[97] *Ibid.*, fol. 11–11/v.

Like a latter-day Jonah, *The Herauld of Regensburg* prays and adjures the "German Nineveh", "Regensburg, that Babylon" to repent of its sins, and has some very harsh words for the Emperor. It decries at length the religious conflicts that divide Christian from Christian, and pleads for the restoration of religious liberty, so that those who had fled from the religious persecutions might return to Bohemia, Moravia, Silesia and Austria. Catholics and Protestants should live as subjects of the common Lord of all, Christ the King. The Protestant estates should pray, lest the Protestant princes themselves goad the Turks into attacking them.[98]

The Herauld of Regensburg was probably a translation from the German original: *Regenspurgischer Heerholdt / Aussruffend an die aldabey ihrem Ober=Haupt versamlete Reichs-Glieder*, Im Jahr Christi 1664,[99] C(hristian) H(oburg) L(üneburger) P(redigern) J(esu) G(otte).[100] The German version of *The Herauld of Regensburg* was likely to have found its way into Transylvania.[101]

It is surprising to find that *The Conduct and Character of Count Nicholas Serini* gives the same reasons for the beginning of the Turkish wars – i.e. Rákóczi's Polish campaign, and the emperor's failure to go to his aid – as *The Herauld of Regensburg*: The grand vizier "made way to his present Enterprizes by inroads into *Transylvania*, (against *Ragotski*, who without his privity had engaged in the Polish War) which the Emperour neither assisting effectually, nor yet deserting the Turk, observing his underhand dealing, having setled *Abafti* in that Principality".[102]

Another salient similarity is the focus, in both works, on the free exercise of religion, and the special attention paid to Turkish religious practices. One of the revelations in *The Herauld of Regensburg* is an exhortation to translate the Bible into Turkish. An entire chapter of the book is a call for cooperation between Catholics and Protestants, with some strong criticism for the religious policies of the German principalities. The chapter in the Zrínyi biography entitled "Count Serini's Birth and Education", in turn, emphasizes that Christians could learn from the Mohammedans' devotion to their religious rites, and notes that while the Turks never wage war for reasons of religion, Zrínyi has appealed to the religious sentiment

---

[98] *Ibid.*, fol. 14, 21, 25, 45, etc.

[99] Cf. *Ungarische Drucke ...*: 1993, H. 810, pp. 274–275. – "I. Woher dieser Türcken-Krieg entstanden. II. Wie er nach dem Willes Gottes zustillen. III. Was endlich (da er nicht gestillet) zuerwarten." *Ungarische Drucke ...*: 1993, H. 810, p. 274.

[100] *Ungarische Drucke ...*: 1993, H. 810, p. 275: Németh's and Gömöri's reading.

[101] Kvacsala: 1892, pp. 809–810.

[102] *The Conduct and Character ...*, p. 19.

of all the Christian denominations in the effort to achieve their cooperation.[103]

The three-quarter-length engraving of Zrínyi in both the Bolton and
the John Williams editions of *A New Survey of the Turkish Empire* shows
him as not just a military commander – dressed in full armor and holding
a baton (or scepter?) – but a statesman. This is the point of the four icons
in the four corners of the portrait: two rulers on the top – the Habsburg
Emperor and the King of France; and two military leaders on the bottom –
Tamerlane, and George Castriot, "Scanderbeg". The latter, obviously, are
an allusion to the last two chapters of *The Conduct and Character of Count
Nicholas Serini*, where the picture appeared (though with a difference, as
we shall see) with the same legend as in *A New Survey...*: "The true Effi-
gies of Count Nicolaj Serini / Generalissimo of the Christian Army in Hungary". The portrait in *A New Survey ...*, however, contains an element that
is unique to the known Zrínyi iconography: the shrouded figure of a deceased forebear (Zrínyi's great-great-grandfather, obviously), from whose
mouth issue the following words: "Avenge thy country and my Blood!" –
a sentiment hardly in keeping with the humanist thinking traditionally
associated with the Christian hero. The vengeful ghost, with its passion-
ate rhetoric and touch of the occult, is, on the other hand, very much in
keeping with the fiery injunctions of *The Herauld of Regensburg*.

The Herauld of Regensburg differs from *The Conduct and Character of Count
Nicholas Serini* in respect of genre, focus, mode of argumentation, and style.
The extravagant emotionality of the former seems to have little in com-
mon with the latter's dispassionate objectivity. There is between the two
works, however, an inescapable point of intersection: the person of
Comenius.

It was, as we have seen, Comenius who published the revelations of
the three visionaries with Samuel Hartlib's support.[104] Robert Codrington,
too, mentioned Comenius in his English translation of the threesome's
prophecies. And it was a pupil of Comenius's, the Swiss preacher Jacob
Redinger, who made the following entry in his journal in 1664: "The
electress of Heidelberg gave me six thalers, and I let her have the *Regenspurgischer Heerholdt*".[105]

---

[103] *Ibid.*, p. 62.
[104] Kvacsala: 1892, p. 807.
[105] *Ibid.*, p. 809. – Cf. Németh: 1995.

Redinger had studied with Comenius in Amsterdam. In 1656, the Bishop of the Bohemian–Moravian Brethren found sanctuary in The Netherlands, and lived there the last fifteen years of his life. Thence he watched the Turkish war unfold, and came to revise his earlier views on the Turkish question. During the Thirty Years' War, Comenius had counted on Ottoman support for the Protestant countries in their conflict with the Habsburgs. He had also been keenly interested in the religious traditions of Islam, and, in his search for points of agreement among the various religions, had thoroughly studied Muslim religious practices. Comenius had high regard for the Turkish custom of regular prayers, and, as one of the leading figures of the movement to convert the Turks, insisted on the importance of having the Bible translated into Turkish. Indeed, work on the translation actually started, thanks to the backing of Samuel Hartlib, Robert Boyle, and the Royal Society.[106]

It was as a member of the movement to convert the Turks – which, incidentally, had numerous highly-placed supporters in England – that Jacob Redinger visited the Turkish army camped under Érsekújvár in early autumn of 1663, and then travelled around Transylvania, enjoying Prince Apafi's hospitality. Apafi had his court chaplain, Mihály Tofeus, help Redinger get to Eperjes, and meet with Nicolas Drabicius.

Comenius was much moved by Transylvania's misfortunes. As for Moravia, his heart went out to his native land at the news of the unspeakable destruction wrought by the Turkish and Tartar armies. His *Letzte Posaun über Deutschland*, a pamphlet written in 1663, is a telling indication of his state of mind: the Turkish onslaught, he writes, is God's judgement on a world ensnared in sin; let all Christendom take heed, repent, and reform.

Comenius was obsessed by the need – and the obligation – to influence the European public. Correct and timely information, he believed, would help people preserve their sense of judgement. A well-informed society was likely to be stable, while lack of information could easily lead to mass hysteria. Comenius, like the mysterious O.C. of *The Conduct and Character of Count Nicholas Serini*, wanted to give the reader the entire picture, convinced that there was not a soul who would not wish to know what had happened in the past and what was going on at the moment.

---

[106] Matar: 1993. – Kvacsala: 1892, p. 807.

Comenius scholars are wont to find the reformer's fascination with prophecies and revelations the most incongruous element of his complex cognitive system.[107] Even at the time, Comenius had to overcome a great many setbacks and opposition to be able to publish the prophecies of the three Central European visionaries – Kotter of Silesia, Poniatovska of Bohemia, and Drabicius of Moravia.

Prophecies and revelations, however, were an organic part of both the elite and the popular culture of Europe in the 16th and 17th centuries. Rooted in the traditions of Antiquity, divination enjoyed a veritable revival with the spread of printed almanacs, and the paradigm shift that ushered in the modern era. Astrology, for instance, was considered an integral part of contemporary "science". It was only natural, therefore, that *The Conduct and Character of Count Nicholas Serini* should tie the date of Zrínyi's birth to the auspicious constellation registered by "the busie Astrologer", and that the *Lacrymae Hungaricae*, a collection of elegies written at the news of Zrínyi's death and printed in London, should have taken over this propitious date.[108]

Prophecies and revelations were particularly rampant and popular in times of war and natural catastrophe. They satisfied a genuine need, preparing society for the worst, making suggestions as to what to believe and how to conduct oneself. They were also a safety valve, a release for social tensions, and a form of political prognosis, a way of habituating people to the inevitable.

Comenius himself saw his three favorite prophets proved wrong time and time again; he was also very well aware of Drabicius's personal shortcomings. For all that, he revised the threesome's revelations for publication – or had them revised – on several occasions, and saw to their printing.[109] Most of the costs involved were borne by Samuel Hartlib. Typical of their association is Comenius's letter to Hartlib of September 9, 1654, in which he suggests that the latter wait with the publication of the prophecies until they were fulfilled.[110]

Samuel Hartlib was born in Elblag, Silesia, of an English mother. The family moved to London, where Hartlib became a successful merchant, and a central figure of the Baconian Philosophical College. The young scientist Robert Boyle was a member of the scholarly society, as was John

---

[107] Pánek: 1991. – Szőnyi: 1981.

[108] Warburg: 1986. – *The Conduct and Character* ..., pp. 43, 97, 409–410. – Bene: 1987, p. 355.

[109] Kvacsala: 1889, pp. 745–765. – Dukkon: 1988. – Pánek: 1991, p. 54. – Szőnyi: 1981.

[110] BL Ms. 648.

Pell, and several of the founders of the Royal Society. One of Hartlib's great preoccupations was educational reform, and it was to him that Milton dedicated his *On Education*.[111]

Comenius went to London at Hartlib's invitation, and made the close acquaintance of the "Baconian Reformers" in the course of 1641–1642. It was at this time that he met the Bohemian graphic artist Václav Hollar. (Hollar, as we shall see, would draw the map of *A Prospect of Hungary, and Transylvania*, one of the books dealing with Zrínyi's exploits that would appear in 1664.) He also met John Dury (Dureus), another apostle of educational reform, whose other great purpose was to effect the reconciliation of Lutherans and Calvinists. Dury's acquaintance with Transylvanian Protestantism dated back to his friendship with the ambassadors of Prince Gábor Bethlen (1580–1629), and he had remained in lively contact with the Protestants of the Principality through the good offices of Henrik Bisterfeld, Ludovicus Piscator, Johann Henrik Alsted and a succession of Protestant pastors.[112] It was this circle of reformers, particularly Hartlib (who had considerable influence with Cromwell), who tried to further the cause of György II Rákóczi's diplomatic initiatives, fostered Comenius's plans for Moravia, and financed the publication of his works. During the Turkish wars of 1663–1664, Hartlib and his circle, along with Comenius, played an active part in an intellectual network that spanned several of the countries of Europe.

The Hungarians living in London were introduced to Hartlib and his circle by Comenius.[113] Pál Jászberényi was a senior when he first met Comenius in Sárospatak; both had studied with Ferenc Szedrei and Ferenc Száki. The Swedish mathematician Megalinus, likewise a member of Hartlib's circle, had probably met Comenius through his Swedish patron, Le Geer. Comenius, who had taken upon himself the responsibility of the Rákóczis' diplomatic representation, was regularly kept abreast of developments in Hungary. His informants in Eperjes were Illés Ladivér and his pupil, the philosopher János Bayer, as well as Jónás Mednyánszky, the agent of the Prince of Transylvania, who was in constant contact with Zrínyi through the Sopron lawyer, István Vittnyédy. Eperjes was an important source of news for the Palatine Wesselényi as well: his secretary, István Gyöngyösi, who was privy to the plans of Zrínyi's reunification movement, had been Comenius's pupil. News from Royal Hungary

[111] Clucas: 1991, pp. 33–55. – Milton: 1975, pp. 61–63.
[112] Turnbull: 1947. Cf. Makkai: 1958. – Pánek: 1991, pp. 39–40, 83.
[113] Péter: 1987, p. 58. – Bene: 1992, p. 228.

reached Comenius through his son-in-law, Daniel Ernst Jablonszky (Figulus), who lived in Danzig, and there was also János Windisch, the courier who, during the crucial early 1660s, reported to Comenius every month.[114]

Between 1661 and 1665, there were about twenty young Hungarians studying in London, several of them on grants from the Dutch Reformed Church in England. The Hungarian students attending university in England or The Netherlands paid regular visits to Comenius; and we know that János Nadányi, the author of *Florus Hungaricus*, also paid his respects.[115]

Besides these "back home" connections, Comenius had contacts in practically every corner of Europe: in Sweden, France, Switzerland, and the German principalities in particular, especially the Lutheran parts. As for Constantinople, he is likely to have got news at least from a German gentleman by the name of Warner, who had gone to live there with the purpose of working on a Turkish translation of the Bible.[116]

The question, of course, is whether Comenius (then living in Amsterdam) or his circle of English reformers had any direct contact with Zrínyi. One of the officers who took part in the winter campaign hailed from the British Isles: a Scotsman of gentle birth called Andrew Melvill, the scion of a family that had seen better days. He served with the Waldeck regiment in Hohenlohe's army, and would publish his memoirs. In it, he tells how he fought alongside Zrínyi at Szigetvár and Pécs, but to date, there is absolutely no indication that he ever sent reports from the field.[117]

We know that Zrínyi had agents working for him in Venice, that he had contacts in Regensburg, and that news from the British Isles reached Csáktornya through Mark Forstall's correspondence with his brother in Ireland, if no other way.[118] To date, however, we have no concrete proof that Zrínyi and his circle had direct ties to Comenius, or his adherents in Amsterdam or London. All we have, besides Miklós Bethlen's well-known trip to England and the possibility of indirect contact through Vittnyédy, are some fragmentary data suggesting the need for further research. One such fragment is what we might call "the Dutch connection".

---

[114] Kvacsala: 1892, pp. 801–803. – Bán: 1976, p. 166. – Klaniczay, T.: 1964, p. 652.

[115] Kathona: 1975, p. 222. – Herepei: 1971, pp. 395–403.

[116] Based on Hartlib's letter to Boyle: Kvacsala: 1892, p. 804.

[117] *Mémoires de Monsieur Le Chevalier de Melvill, General Major des Troupes de S.A.S.M. le Duc de Cell et Gr. Bailiff du Comte de Giforn*. Amsterdam, 1704.

[118] Fodor, Veronika, "Ír szerzetesek kapcsolatai Magyarországgal. Forstall Márk pályafutása" (Irish Monks and Hungary. The Career of Mark Forstall), MS, Major paper.

The Conduct and Character of Count Nicholas Serini contains a great many Dutch references. Judging by the "Translated out of Dutch" on the title page of *A Brief Accompt of the Turks Late Expedition*, the connection, in the case of that contemporary book, is altogether direct. It seems only reasonable, in the light of all this, to turn to examine the 1663–1664 issues of one of the most authoritative newspapers of the time, the *Hollandtze Mercurius*.[119]

Of the letters written by Zrínyi published in the *Hollandtze Mercurius*, there is a fragment dated February 4, 1664, in which Zrínyi asks the unknown addressee to "pray fervently for us".[120] We should note that of all the known letters of Zrínyi's, there is not one in which he ever asked for someone's prayers.[121] This can, however, be related to the phrase "So prayeth" at the end of the chapter addressed to the reader in the English biography.[122] It is to be noted that in Comenius's circle those corresponding with one another sometimes used their initials only to sign their letters in which instances of the above concluding formula can also be found.[123] On the other hand, if we examine the context of the letter (written by Zrínyi or just in his name), we shall see that the same issue speaks of Drabicius's prophecy, the comet, the decisions made at Regensburg, and other items of news which figure also in *The Conduct and Character of Count Nicholas Serini*.[124]

Comenius, living in Amsterdam as he did, could easily have obtained from the *Hollandtze Mercurius* his information concerning the events along the Drava. Evidence of his personal involvement is the speed with which he completed his assessment of Zrínyi's significance in his *De progressibus*

---

[119] *"Hollandtze Mercurius*. Vervatende de voornaemste geschiedenissen, vor-gevallen in't gantze Jaer 1663, in *Christenryck*. Harlem, 1664. – Péter: 1987, pp. 49, 51, 55. – Bene: 1992, p. 226. – Fischer–Fülöp: 1988.

[120] "Bidt ijvrich voor ons", *Hollandtze Mercurius*, February, No. 35. – Fischer–Fülöp: 1988, pp. 193–194.

[121] The version of the letter (dated Jan. 24) appended by the Venetian Antonio Negri to his report of Feb. 12 reads: "Let *them* (my italics) pray well for us". The assumption that it got to the *Hollandtze Mercurius* via Negri is yet to be substantiated. Bene: 1992, pp. 226–227. – Chiaromanni, who was punctual to a fault, reported on Feb. 5 that the first news of Zrínyi had reached Regensburg: he had reviewed his troops on Jan. 21; and then a courier brought the news that he had taken "Koppány and Berzence". FStA, MP 4404

[122] Cf. *Angol életrajz Zrínyi Miklósról*: 1987, p. 391. – Gömöri: 1988, p. 69.

[123] John Pell closes his letter to Samuel Hartlib with "I pray you", July 17–27, 1656. Patera: 1892, p. 186.

[124] *Hollandtze Mercurius*, 1664. 32–36. – The letter from Pozsony of Feb. 4 published in: *Angol életrajz Zrínyi Miklósról*: 1987, is said to have been taken from the *Hollandtze Mercurius* by Bene: 1992, p. 227.

Zerinianis adversus Turcas in Hungaria inferiori... (Anno 1664, in Januario et Februar) Meditatiuncula ductu revelationis. 146. The manuscript copy signed "Johannes Amos Comenius, Amsterdami, 1664"[125] is by no means unknown to Zrínyi scholars.[126] The text is a commentary on Drabicius's prophecy of September 20, 1652, as well as a report on the Turkish wars of the year 1663, up to and including the winter campaign.[127]

The prophecy in question reflected Drabicius's outrage at the cold reception György II Rákóczi had given him. Because the House of Rákóczi had failed to do God's will – we read his prediction in *De progressibus Zerinianis ...* – its members would be sorely tried, and Jehovah would accomplish His work without them. There follows an oblique reference to Zrínyi, as well as several cryptic pronouncements regarding the future.

Commentating the prophecy, Comenius points out that since György II Rákóczi had proved unworthy, Zrínyi had been called upon to fulfill God's plan. A series of substantiating details follows: Zrínyi had had Zrínyiújvár built not far from Kanizsa; and he had harassed the Turks with border raids and assorted ruses. They retaliated by attacking Royal Hungary in 1663, taking Érsekújvár, Léva, Nógrád and sundry other places. Here, too, as in the English reports that appeared in print in 1663, and in *The Conduct and Character of Count Nicholas Serini*, we next hear of the Tartar raids on Moravia.[128] But – Comenius continues – as soon as the Tartars withdrew to their winter camps, Count Zrínyi, "acting with marvellous speed", pressed deep into Turkish territory "with an army of thirty thousand Croatian, Hungarian and German soldiers", massacred the Turks and the Tartars, destroyed the bridge over the Drava that had been built at great expense, sacked and burned the towns between the Danube and the Drava, and returned home, laden with spoils – having "proven the power of the prophecy that no one in human memory ever troubled the waters of the East" as had he.[129]

---

[125] Bodleian Library, Oxford, Rawlinson D 399.

[126] Bán: 1976, p. 164. – Klaniczay, T.: 1964, pp. 777–778. – Gömöri: 1988, p. 91, note 9.

[127] This, essentially, is the text published in Comenius, Johannes Amos, *Lux e Tenebris, novis radiis acuta ...*, MDCLXV. App. H. 2086.

[128] "Moraviam vero, imisso, Tartarorum exercitu foede vastarent." *De progressibus Zerinianis adversus Turcas*; cf. *Lux e Tenebris*, 140.

[129] "Sed illis reversis, et per hyberna distributis, Comes Zerini collecto celeritate mira ex Croatis, Hungaris, auxiliaribusq[ue] Germanis ad triginta millia exercitu, hyemis, et glaciei ope profunde in Turciam irrupit, obvios ubiq[ue] Turcas, et Tartaros mactavit ad Esecum usq[ue], per Germanica milliari ultra 20. ubi pontem anno superiori a Turcis ingentibus impensis super Dravum flumen, et vicinas paludes stratum, duorum milliarum Longitudine destruxit, ac exussit, domumq[ue] revertens permultas urbes, et arces

141

It was only natural that Comenius should have been keenly interested in the progress of Zrínyi's offensive. Hungary's geo-political position being what it was, he had assigned it a central role in his plans for Central Europe: "Because of the country's central location, you Hungarians are the most qualified to unite East, West, and North."[130] Nor is it surprising to see Comenius mention, along with the Turkish raids on Hungary, the incursions into his native Moravia. What is striking is that Zrínyi emerges from Comenius's account as a charismatic individual of supra-national significance, capable of repulsing the Turks, and thus clearing the way to a new balance of power in Central Europe.

What role can we assume Comenius and his circle to have played in the publication of the contemporary works on Zrínyi? The map in *A Prospect of Hungary, and Transylvania* provides us with another clue. What appears to be the first edition of the book[131] ends its account of Zrínyi's military movements with the burning of the bridge at Eszék: "He [Zrínyi] returned home". The book lists the kings of Hungary and the princes of Transylvania, gives descriptions of Hungary's and Transylvania's neighbors – Bohemia, Austria, Croatia, Dalmatia, Moravia and Silesia – and speaks of the Imperial Diet meeting in Regensburg. The verbose title page calls the reader's particular attention to the map.

Indeed, as we shall see, it is no ordinary map, drawn by no ordinary artist. At the very bottom, in tiny letters, there are the words: "Wencelaus Hollar fecit 1664". Hollar was one of the outstanding graphic artists of the time. The minuscule "signature" allows us to decipher the monogram at the end of the legend: "A new map of the Kingdom of Hungaria with other bordering countries ... in diuers places corrected and augmented by [W]encelaus [H]ollar ... 1664".[132]

Comenius, as we have seen, had met Hollar over twenty years earlier in England, and the map certainly squares with his conception of Central Europe. It is, as far as we know, one of the first maps of Central Europe as a region. Hungary, and Zrínyiújvár, are presented in the broad international framework of the area between Salzburg, Ragusa, Cracow and the

---

occupavit, totumq[ue] inter Dravum, et Danubium tractum vastavit, et sic demum ingentibus cum spoliis domum se recipiendo, vim oraculi verificavit, et aquas Orientis ita, ut ille, post hominum memoriam turbavit nemo." Comenius, *De progressibus Zerinianis adversus Turcas*, 5. – Cf. *Lux e Tenebris*, 272.

[130] *Sermo Secretus*. Cf. R. Várkonyi: 1994b, p. 70.

[131] App. Hung. 893. – A copy registered in Oxford on Aug. 30, 1664, and another one registered May 2, 1665 is attributed to Samuel Clarke by Gömöri: 1988, pp. 83, 93.

[132] Apponyi: 1927, p. 120. – *Angol életrajz Zrínyi Miklósról*: 1987, p. 47.

Iron Gate. As for the cartouche, it suggests that the artist was familiar with Zrínyi's suggestion that the Emperor himself assume the role of Commander-in-Chief of the joint Christian forces, or at least familiar with the decision of the Regensburg Diet. For on the right, the Emperor Leopold is depicted in full armor – a sign that he himself has personally undertaken the conduct of the war. War is the theme of the figure on the left as well: a gallant Hungarian soldier with a drawn sword.

Based on all of the above, the most we can say is that the notion of Zrínyi as Europe's providential champion probably originated with Comenius's circle, a network encompassing England, The Netherlands, Sweden, Transylvania, and the German principalities. *The Conduct and Character of Count Nicholas Serini* reveals a thorough familiarity with how matters stood in Hungary, Moravia, Silesia, indeed, in all of Central Europe, and shows a good understanding of the problems of England and The Netherlands.[133] Within the conceptual framework of the book, George Castriot, "Scanderbeg", symbolizes "contacts and action". Tamerlane is likewise of symbolic significance: a Turkoman Mongol, he was the "insider" who turned against the Sultan's unbridled power; he was also an excellent commander, for all his ruthlessness. In this sense, the chapter entitled "Tamberlain, the great Scourge of the Turks" is the acknowledgment of some commendable Turkish qualities; primarily, however, it provides a parallel – and a foil – to the image of Zrínyi as Europe's providential champion.

"ORBIS EUROPAE JUBAR"

Zrínyi represented the interests of Europe in that the containment of the Ottoman Empire was an all-European interest. Neither half of the proposition, however, seemed obvious at the time. Zrínyi, as we know, conjured up the example and policies of Charles V in his works precisely because the emperor *had* seen the Turkish onslaught as a danger not just to Hungary, but to all of Europe. The documents of the Regensburg negotiations show that it was in the winter of 1663–1664 that the realization finally began to dawn on Europe's politicians that an offensive war against the Ottoman Empire was not just a helping hand to Hungary, but in the vital interest of Europe as a whole.

---

[133] For the Dutch and English sources of Comenius's ideas, see: Polišenský: 1953. Cf. Makkai: 1958, p. 968.

La verita Consigliera ... pointed out that if the Turkish armies were not routed presently, they would soon be storming the gates of Vienna. *The Conduct and Character of Count Nicholas Serini* makes much the same point: "Once the great Turk dines in Vienna, he will sup in Paris". *The Herauld of Regensburg* speaks of the Turks overrunning Vienna, and threatening the foundations of Christendom. The Venetian envoys to the English government saw the Ottoman expansion in the Balkans as destructive of Christian civilization, and Sinzendorf, the imperial ambassador, likewise spoke of the "Mohammedan ambition to destroy Christendom".[134]

All three works plead for cooperation among the princes of Europe. Let them set aside their grievances, and rid themselves of their "sins": the sins of indecisiveness, turbulence of spirit, indifference, and the fostering of religious discord. Of the numerous pamphlets urging cooperation in the face of the Turkish threat, all point to the conflicts among the powers of Europe as the cause of the impending catastrophe. *The Conduct and Character of Count Nicholas Serini*, in the chapter on "Count Serini's Birth and Education", paints a vivid panorama of these conflicts, and – putting the words of criticism in Zrínyi's mouth – notes that the grand vizier's attack was well-timed: "The greatest Politicians now extant, as he observed, being more imployed in balancing the Interest of *Europe* upon the several late great alterations, than in raising such banks that might stop this general inundation upon the face of the Western world ...".[135]

Reviewing the preconditions of effective joint action, *La verita Consigliera* ... comes to much the same conclusion as *The Conduct and Character of Count Nicholas Serini*. The first precondition is England's and The Netherlands' participation. For the war in Hungary is the same war as the war against Venice, and cannot be won without the help of the superb English navy. "If the wildfire burning in Hungary", writes Zrínyi, "which lays a pall of smoke over Germany, and brings tears to the eyes of our Italian neighbors, looks like too distant and paltry a spark through the telescopes of France, England, and The Netherlands, let them, for God's sake, cast a glance at the Mediterranean, and tell me the meaning of that mass of arms which, with a fleet of over seventy pirate ships, wreaks havoc on these seas. Are they Turks, or are they not? Unless the factious and indolent Christian swords smite the enemy in these regions a wholehearted blow with all their might, they had best prepare to be shattered by the furious assault

---

[134] Szelestei: 1980, p. 193. – *The Conduct and Character* ..., p. 106. – *The Herauld of Regensburg*, 19–20, 25–26, 114–115. – Dec. 11/12, 1663, and Nov. 27, 1663. PRO SP 84/168. fol. 115, 213.

[135] *The Conduct and Character* ..., p. 101.

of these ships and this tremendous multitude ... If the hearts of the rulers of today be not consumed by a thirst for uncommon glory, let them at least be roused by a judicious will to self-preservation. ... And if they do want to save their lives, let them strive to join forces, and join forces without delay, for make no mistake, their common enemy, if he finds them disunited, will annihilate them one by one."[136]

The purview of *The Conduct and Character of Count Nicholas Serini* was not confined to the Hungarian scene; its author was very much aware of the plight of hard-pressed Candia and Dalmatia. Ascribing the observation to Zrínyi, he notes that England's domestic troubles did not excuse it from going to its fellow Christians' aid. It is in this context that we must understand two pronouncements of the Zrínyi biography which, otherwise, are more than incongruous. One is that the grand vizier had allegedly declared that if he ever were to change religions, he would choose the religion of the King of England, and his God. The other is that the Turks could be inspired to benevolence and moral rectitude if they came into regular contact with more cultured and more civilized nations.[137] Both these elements are borrowed from the schemes to convert the Turks to Christianity, and were introduced into the Zrínyi biography with a view, perhaps, of persuading the maritime nations to join the anti-Turkish alliance. The Ottoman Empire, the author might have reasoned, would prove a more cooperative trading partner, once the Christian alliance had broken its military might.

It has been said to have been characteristic of the cult of Zrínyi in England that "the attention of the English public turned to Central Europe".[138] True enough; but the statement needs amplification. From *The Conduct and Character of Count Nicholas Serini*, as well as the other books we have been considering, Central Europe emerges as a very special region. Special in that the peoples of the region attached singular importance to religion, religious toleration, culture and education. They had a keen awareness of the need to institute these values in the political sphere, and had a fond attachment to those who had attempted to do so. In Transylvania, Gábor Bethlen lived on as the Prince who had succeeded; in Bohemia and Moravia, Frederick V (1619–1620) was remembered as the man who had ventured to try. Codrington dedicated his English edition of the three Central European prophets' revelations to Prince Rupert, the son of the exiled

[136] Szelestei: 1980, p. 198.
[137] *Angol életrajz Zrínyi Miklósról:* 1987, pp. 82, 103.
[138] Gömöri: 1988, pp. 66–67.

Protestant King of Bohemia. Rupert, who was the grandson of the King of England, and had inherited the titles Duke of Cumberland and Count Palatine of Rhine, would likely not dismiss lightly opinions associated with that champion of religious toleration, Comenius.[139]

The Conduct and Character of Count Nicholas Serini is amazingly well-informed of Transylvanian events, and views them as illustrative of the need for Christian cooperation. We learn, for instance, that Zrínyi "hath contrived many suspitious Letters to withdraw *Abafti* [Apafi] from the Visier, and the Visier from him."[140]

Zrínyi, the providential champion of Europe, emerges as a master not just of the art of war, but also of the arts of peace. He is a statesman who understands the prerequisites of peace, and is capable of establishing its conditions. "This is he who hath set bounds to the fears of *Europe*, and the hopes of *Asia*; Who coops that ambition in a Province, that aims at a World: Who fils up the gap of *Christendome* with his great self, and singly undertakes the despondencies of the West behind him, and the threatnings of the East before him."[141]

A comparison of the cognitive content of *The Conduct and Character of Count Nicholas Serini* with the ideas expressed in Zrínyi's prose works will reveal some close similarities. We find analogous thoughts in his *Mátyás király életéről való elmélkedések* (Meditations on the Life of King Matthias), for instance; and what seem to be practically verbatim "borrowings" in Part II of his *Vitéz hadnagy* (Lieutenant Courageous) and his *Aphorismák* (Aphorisms).[142] We know that parts of Comenius's *Gentis felicitas* also show a strong likeness to sections of Zrínyi's *Vitéz hadnagy*.[143]

The Conduct and Character of Count Nicholas Serini takes an altogether unambiguous stand for the necessity of launching an offensive war, "it having been the great defect of *Christendome* hitherto, to stand upon the defensive: whereas the great Turk seldom troubles himself with Embassies, treaties, but appears always the first in the Field, enjoying this advantage, that he makes other Countries the stage of War ..."[144] In its cen-

---

[139] "Many of these Phrophecies were very much desired by the late King of Bohemia & were presented to him by the learned Comenius". In: *The Prophecies of Christopher Kotterus, Christiana Poniatovia, Nicholas Drabicius*. Translated into English by R. Codrington. London, 1664, p. 3. – Cf. Péter: 1987, pp. 38–39.

[140] *The Conduct and Character ...*, p. 74.

[141] *Ibid.*, pp. 110–111.

[142] Péter: 1987, pp. 57–58.

[143] Makkai: 1958, p. 971.

[144] *The Conduct and Character ...*, p. 65.

tral idea as much as in points of detail, the book reads very much like Comenius's doctrine of one, interconnected Europe.[145]

Comenius, we know, spoke of the need for peace in Europe in several of his writings. Zrínyi and his circle seemed to echo this sentiment when they pointed out, again and again, that there would be no peace as long as the Turks were in Hungary. The only purpose of the offensive war was to drive the Turks out of the country, so that finally, peace might be restored. *The Conduct and Character of Count Nicholas Serini* repeatedly makes the point that Zrínyi was a master not only of the rules of war, but also of the rules of peace, and refers to Grotius, whose works were familiar to the Hungarian politicians in both Comenius's and Zrínyi's movement.

From all of the above we can quite safely conclude that the notion of Zrínyi as an Atlas who had shouldered the cause of European peace must have originated in Comenius's circle, a heterogeneous group of English scientists, German and Swiss clergymen, Transylvanian students, Silesian, Bohemian and Moravian informants and of Hungarian expatriates living in London, united by their commitment to the idea of the peaceful coexistence of the peoples of Europe.

"Orbis Europae Jubar"–"Europe's Shining Star": it is the introductory thought of *The Conduct and Character of Count Nicholas Serini* – and of our study – that was given poetic formulation by Pál Jászberényi in one of the verses in the *Lacrymae Hungaricae*, the anthology of poems published in England in memoriam Zrínyi by the disciples of Comenius.[146]

His death was a blow to all of Europe. Indicative of the void he left behind him is the letter of March 13, 1665 written to Mark Forstall by Laurencius Rebek, an Augustinian monk living in Laibach: "I received a letter from Salzburg about the deceased Count Miklós, which tells of a nobleman come to Salzburg from Paris, France, who said that he had seen my lord the Count Miklós in Paris, and had spoken to the men in his entourage. I've had similar reports from others as well, people who had come from Venice. From all this a lot of people believe that he did not really die, but that they probably killed one of his servants, so that he himself might escape, and continue the work he had set himself".[147]

***

[145] *Ibid.,* pp. 91–92, 97–98, 123.
[146] Kathona: 1975, p. 220. – Bene: 1987, p. 358. – Borián: 1995, pp. 14–16.
[147] Öst. Staatsregistratur. Karton 17. Rep. N. Fasc. 14. Pars 1. fol. 188.

A great deal of research still needs to be done to clarify the origins of the notion of Zrínyi as Europe's providential champion – and of Zrínyi's English biography as such. We can summarize our own conclusions as follows:

The concept of Zrínyi as Europe's providential champion originated with Comenius's circle. Zrínyi himself rose to a challenge facing all of Europe, and offered both theoretical and concrete solutions in terms consistent with the values and interests of Hungary and the peoples of the region. That is why many people saw him as the personification of the European statesman, the statesman committed to peace and unity, one who was able to express the needs of the times in terms of universal values, and had the courage to fight for its dreams.

The appearance of *The Conduct and Character of Count Nicholas Serini*, along with several other of the English publications that we have considered above, was closely tied to the organization of the anti-Turkish league, the possibility of Zrínyi's appointment as its Commander-in-Chief, and the prospect of a new, post-Ottoman balance of power in Central Europe, particularly in the region including Hungary, Moravia, Bohemia, and Transylvania. Comenius and Zrínyi, as will be evident by now, were urging Europe to espouse the same political alternative. It was to this alternative that the mysterious O.C. was referring in the introduction to *The Conduct and Character of Count Nicholas Serini* when he called Zrínyi "the Heroe, upon whom Providence hath devolved the Fate of *Europe* ...".

The Reconquest of Buda
and Public Opinion

ℰꙨ ꙨᏕ

At the very end of the last century, Ignác Acsády (1845–1906) summarized the historiographical consensus that had by then emerged on the contemporary local reactions to the recapture of Buda:

"All of civilized Europe celebrated the glad news of the redemption of Buda with overwhelming enthusiasm... In Hungary, too, thanksgiving services were held, in the fortresses there were salvoes of rejoicing, and the *Te Deum* was sung in a number of churches. And yet the hearts of the masses did not skip a beat on hearing that the ancient castle of King Mátyás was no longer under the yoke of the crescent moon. What celebration there was, was official, Hungarian society at large was little moved by the news of this historical turning point... For glorious as the recapture of Buda was, and a great boon to posterity, the generation that lived through it could hardly rejoice in it... For much as they had longed to be freed from the Turkish yoke, the liberation took such a form that the scant population that was left could not but look back and consider the past to have been an ideal state as compared to the horrendous present, and people longed in sorrow for the happier days of yore."[1]

To this date, historians have been unable to contest the validity of this summary, and even the most recent works – mine included – have reiterated Acsády's conclusions.[2] If anything, today the picture appears bleaker still, and the contrast between Europe, rejoicing, and Hungary, struck dumb, yet more harsh.

Research done in the last fifty years has shown that European public opinion – a new development of the seventeenth century – fed on a veri-

---

"The reconquest of Buda in contemporary Hungarian political thought and public opinion." *Acta Historica Acad. Sci. Hung.* 34 (1985) pp. 3–15.

[1]   Acsády: 1898, pp. 454, 458.

[2]   Károlyi–Wellmann: 1936, p. 385. – R. Várkonyi: 1985a, p. 224 and ff. – *Magyarország története 1526–1686:* 1985, III/2, p. 1629 and ff. – Nagy: 1986a, p. 381 and ff. – Nagy: 1986b, p. 55 and ff.

table cornucopia of pamphlets, treatises, reports, and illustrated papers all dealing with the Turkish wars in Hungary.[3] The Baroque world – the courts of the absolute monarchs, of princes, and of aristocrats, as well as the emancipated bourgeoisie of the Dutch, Italian, English and German towns – have left behind a mass of representative works of art testifying to a self-aware participation in what was recognized as the greatest event of the century. Of all these contemporary coins, odes, paintings, dramas, tapestries, and musical compositions, not one is by a Hungarian artist. Nor do we find any Hungarians among those who commissioned these works. As for the works of art, they are spectacular expressions of the ideology presumed to be behind the Turkish wars, and the apotheoses of foreign military leaders, of heroes exiled from their far-off homes, of distant lands and empires.[4] To date, no evidence has been found of any contemporary Hungarian-language work – military report, poem, hymn of praise, marching song or play – referring to the siege of Buda.[5]

Why in the chorus of victors celebrating their triumph over the Ottomans in Europe was the voice of Hungary not to be heard? Two major circumstances have been emphasized by way of an answer.

Hungary was a battlefield, and hardly fit for celebration. The horrors of war swept away all other thoughts. What have come down to us are plaintive records of a country laid waste by one army after another, looted and plundered.

The second circumstance researchers have pointed to is the country's dividedness at the time, and its backwardness in matters of politics and culture as compared to the rest of Europe.[6]

In the light of the most recent research results, however, the above are seen to provide but a part of the answer, and to stand in need of some revision. My own findings show that there is a great deal more that we must pay attention to: our national consciousness leaves something to be desired when it comes to an understanding of the interrelations of the Hungarian and the western European culture of those times.

My own investigations were grounded in the fact that in the summer of 1686, all of Hungary was an embattled front: beyond the extensive en-

---

[3] *Buda és Pest 1686. évi visszafoglalásának egykorú irodalma* (The contemporary literature of the reconquest of Buda and Pest in 1686). Budapest, 1936, and *Buda és Pest grafikus ábrázolásai a visszafoglalás korában 1683–1718* (The graphic representation of Buda and Pest at the time of their reconquest 1683–1718). Budapest, 1937. Both are offprints from vol. VI of *Fővárosi Könyvtár Évkönyve* (Municipal Library Yearbook), Budapest, 1936.

[4] *A magyarországi művészet története:* 1970, p. 159 and ff.

[5] *A magyar irodalom története:* 1964, , II, p. 327 and ff.

[6] Recently summarized together with literature by Iványi: 1991.

virons of Buda and Pest, there were troops stationed in Transylvania, east of the Tisza, and around Eger, Szeged and Eszék, and the courier service between them, as indeed the postal service, were networks extending to practically every point in the country. The Hungarian army numbered about twenty thousand, and the whole country worked to supply Buda. Every county had its quota of ammunition, food, salt, fodder, tools and firewood to provide and deliver. Inhabitants from a number of places were ordered up to Buda to dig trenches, carry the wounded, and pile munitions. Along the Danube and the Vág, there were villages engaged in nothing but weaving gabions; around Lőcse, people were making fuse and rope by the ton at the Treasury's orders; thousands of shingles, staves, and stakes were requisitioned, as well as hundreds of barrels of gunpowder, flour, and wine. Miners were ordered in from Lower Hungary to lay and explode mines under the besieged camp. Those with lighter injuries were removed from Buda to locations both near and far. In May, Kecskemét and Kőrös in the Turkish occupied area were ordered by Abdurrahman in Buda to provide four ox-drawn carts each, every one laden with rations for fifty, and received Turkish safe-conduct from "well-fortified Buda"; but at the same time, they had to provision the besieging Christian armies as well.[7] During the siege, thus, the country was full of people coming and going: a number of national fairs were held during these months, one of the biggest on August 15, the feast of the Assumption. The population knew all too well what was happening in Buda, and there can be no doubt that there was a great deal of talk about it at the markets, around the mills, inns and churches, in the fortresses and in the manor houses, or wherever people were put up for the night.

But how can we know what they said? Their words have faded, and little has been left to us by the miserly centuries. Still, I was amazed to see how much of this evanescent material has, in fact, come down to us.

It was an old practice in Hungary for the fortress captains to keep each other informed, and to keep informants in the Turkish areas. We also know that it was part of the duty of the toll and tax collectors, and of those running the salt and food depots, to report to the authorities the opinions they heard expressed. The letters written in the period by the county and town authorities, by scholars, and in general by the nobility also served

---

[7]   May 29, 1686 and August–September 1686. Published by Hornyik: 1861, II, pp. 460–461. – On the hardships of war transport because of the national burdens see Ferenc Nagy Lessenyei to Ádám Batthyány, Captain-General of Transdanubia, Nemti, July 16, 1686. MOL Batthyány Archives Miss 33090.

more than just to pass the time: they substituted for newspapers, which were then as yet unknown in Hungary.

Countless letters written during the months Buda was being fought for contain accounts beginning: "A few people have arrived from Buda and say...", "We heard from Buda", "A man coming from Buda saw with his own eyes..." Or, as we read in a letter of August 24, written by Ferenc Tassi, an officer from Szolnok: "Soldiers arrived at nightfall from Buda, Petneházi's soldiers, who assert that some sort of janissaries have managed to enter Buda Castle."[8]

We have here a fine example of the natural curiosity with which people receive the news the "travelled" man is so eager to impart; the self-importance of those in charge, and the willingness of the "eyewitness" to tell his tale. Such material is of great value for the multifaceted picture it gives us of things as they were then.

Information travelled at times quickly, at times slowly. News of the explosion of the gunpowder magazine (July 22) took a whole week to reach Tokaj. Word of the offensive launched by the relief forces on Wednesday, August 14, reached the Tisza within four days.[9] Groundless rumours abounded, as did blatant exaggerations. As early as August 4, in Nyírbátor they were convinced that "Buda has been redeemed from the infidel with blood, and Christianity is now restored".[10] We know that Vienna, too, was all astir with groundless news of a similar sort, thanks to the zeal of Maximilian Emmanuel and his war correspondents.[11] For all that, information was surprisingly accurate as far as the essence of the matter was concerned. People were careful to name their sources: deserters from the castle, captured spies, or the wounded. We often read: the account was told by someone who had "seen it with his own eyes". As for what it was like inside besieged Buda Castle, we have a report of July 20: A man freshly come from Buda "can speak of nothing but the great bombardment; those inside Buda have but two places to shoot from; bombs have destroyed even the stone walls of a part of King Mátyás's palace; the population has grown weary; a horse's liver sells for one gold piece; there is said to be great famine among them; more than two hundred people have fled from

[8] Francis Tassi to the councillor of the Chamber of Szepes, Aug. 24, 1686. MOL E 254 Representationes et instantiae 1686 N 93.

[9] György Szenczy to the Chamber, Tokaj, July 23 (1686). – Ferenc Tassi to the Chamber of Szepes, Szolnok, August 18, 1686. MOL E 254 Representationes et instantiae 1686 N 93.

[10] Stephanus Bekes to Administrator of the Chamber Mihály Fischer in Kassa, Bátor, Aug. 4, 1686. MOL E 254 Representationes et instantiae 1686 N 93.

[11] Károlyi–Wellmann: 1936, p. 353.

the castle; there's not a sixth as many infields left in the castle as before." Another witness reported that "of a hundred men in the relief forces, ten have no weapons to speak of".[12]

The account of the explosion of the gunpowder magazine was spread by one of István Csáky's men just come from Buda:

"Two leading artillerymen escaped from Buda, and reported everything: where the Turks were hemmed in, where their Council chamber stood, and also when the next Privy Council was to be held. A bomb was thrown where the gunpowder was stored; the building caught fire, and spat its walls into the Danube. As for the Turkish lords, they were rent to pieces. The Turks took fright inside the walls, and thought our troops were beginning a siege. For protection, some five hundred janissaries jumped into a trench. Guessing what they were about, our troops quickly dug a mine under them, and blew them sky high. Through God's mercy, it's hoped Buda will soon be retaken."[13]

Should the names of the Hungarian heroes ever be inscribed on the walls of Buda Castle, they shall include in the list a son of the famous Keczer family, János Keczer, only because of a report made on August 18 of what a man just arrived from Buda had to say: "He saw with his own eyes a detail of 12–13 men fight with the Turkish army, though like Lieutenant Petneházy, six of them were buried under Buda, János Keczer among them."[14]

The names of the great commanders had become household words: "the Prince of Lorraine", "Prince Carolus", "the Bavarian", "the Turkish Emperor", and most frequently along the Tisza, Petneházy. People had no trouble using the terminology of the war: "mines", "divan", "artillerymen". They liked to be exact as to dates and figures:

"On the fourteenth, as on Wednesday, around twelve thousand Turks set out on a raid, and fought well; under their cover, they wanted to send in to Buda about four thousand janissaries interspersed among four thousand Turkish cavalry, and twelve howitzers; but His Majesty's troops noticed them, and though not much harm befell the cavalry, the four thousand janissaries fell to a man."[15]

---

[12] Francis Tassi to the councillor of the Chamber of Szepes, Szolnok, July 20, 1868, MOL E 254 Representationes et instantiae 1686 N 93.

[13] György Szenczy to the Chamber, Tokaj, July 31, 1686. MOL E 254 Representationes et instantiae 1686 N 93.

[14] Francis Tassi to the councillor of the Chamber of Szepes, Szolnok, Aug. 18, 1686. MOL E 254 Representationes et instantiae 1686 N 93.

[15] MOL E 254 Representationes et instantiae 1686 N 93.

All the above has preserved for us the immediacy of the dialect of the times; but what do they really tell us of what the still silent survivors really thought? A great many details show the anxiety they felt: people were certain that the relief forces of the Sultan were already on their resistless way; and everyone seemed to know the Sultan's orders to the Ottoman army encamped under Buda: either they relieve the city, or die to a man in the attempt. My own research shows that while the tone might vary by geographic or political regions, or by the educational level of those expressing the opinions recorded, all in all, most people dreaded the thought of a Turkish victory, and desired the victory of the Christian armies. They cherished the hope that the forces of Christendom – naturally the Hungarians among them – would soon reoccupy Buda. Let us listen to a three hundred years old news item expressive of these hopes: "While he was in Buda, as on July 28, His Majesty's troops laid fine siege, so that the Bavarian's troops entered King Mátyás' dwellings, along with the Hungarians."[16]

The above will suffice to show that the siege of Buda was a nationwide experience: the entire country was talking about it. The question is how far all this verbalized experience can come to shape public opinion. And even more importantly, in what way?

It is something of a scholarly commonplace that the experiences of an age – either direct or indirect – are organized into public opinion according to a generally accepted value system. This value system takes shape over time through the complex interaction of tradition and the actual needs of the community, and finds expression in the works of politicians and men of letters, of artists, theoreticians, and historians, its measure being the educational level of the period, its means the patterns of association typical of the age, and more universal political and ethical topoi.[17]

On the eve of the reconquest of Buda, Hungarian society had such a well-defined value system by which to measure the ensuing events.

There is disagreement both among contemporary and present-day historians as to the dates given for the beginning of the end of Ottoman rule in Europe. The siege of Candia, the Treaty of Westphalia, and the wars against the Turks that broke out in 1657 first in Transylvania, then in the

---

[16] Francis Tassi to the councillor of the Chamber of Szepes, Szolnok, Aug. 3, 1686. MOL E 254 Representationes et instantiae 1686 N 93. No. 119. Cf. Notes 10–11. "The Germans are attacking Buda hard ... the Turks inside are defending it heroically" – Mátyás Baló to Prince Apafi from the Turkish camp in Eszék, July 27, 1686. MOL P 1389. Apafi collection box 4.

[17] Literature offers extensive material related to contemporary European public opinion: Köpeczi: 1976.

Kingdom of Hungary, then in Poland, and lastly in Russia are the various dates proposed to mark the initial steps to the wholesale attack that 1683 initiated. And the Hungarian wars against the Turks in 1663–1664 are generally considered to have been the dress-rehearsal for the years 1683–1699.[18]

This latter fact is important from our point of view because of the great historical significance universally attributed to the reconquest of Buda in all the various works – literature and the plastic arts, political philosophy, pamphlets, and recruiting songs – in which the Hungarian politicians prepared, organized, and coordinated the international cooperation needed for the 1663–1664 war effort. The siege of Buda was never in fact undertaken at the time, but the plans had called for it, and Montecuccoli had even got hold of a map of Buda Castle.[19]

The war was started after long and careful preparation by the Kingdom of Hungary and the Principality of Transylvania, and included attempts to win international support for a movement to push the Turks out of Europe, and to restore Hungary's integrity.[20] This period of political activity coincided with a time of intellectual ferment in Hungary. A great many outstanding literary works and works of art were created in the period from 1648 to 1664: epics, pamphlets, paintings, engravings, lyric poetry, marching songs, political treatises. All these various genres, however, reflected one and the same conceptual system, and had a common programme and view of history. Generally speaking, each and every work created or commissioned by the members of the movement was a coherent and amplified reiteration of the century-old hope and expectation, nay, demand, which had received its classic, laconic formulation in the poem written by the writer-preacher, Péter Bornemisza, in the mid-1550s: "I wonder when I can return again to dear old Buda!"[21]

For Buda was more than just the castle; Buda was the country, the capital of the unified kingdom of yore – this was the essence of a number of passages in the *Adriai tengernek Syrenaia* (The siren of the Adriatic) written by the leader of the movement, Miklós Zrínyi, Ban of Croatia, in 1651. The epigrams, but especially the epic, *Obsidio Sigetiana*, a tale of the siege of Szigetvár in 1566, are particularly significant in this respect, as we shall see.[22] Lord Chief Justice Ferenc Nádasdy had the battles of the Fifteen Years'

[18] Summarized in R. Várkonyi: 1986a.
[19] Wagner: 1964, p. 493.
[20] R. Várkonyi: 1975.
[21] Bornemisza: *"Siralmas énnéköm"* (It is painful to me). In: *A magyar irodalom története:* 1984, I, p. 375.
[22] Zrínyi: 1651 (1980).

Turkish War painted on the walls of the great hall of his castle in Sárvár, with the fresco of the siege of Buda predominating.[23] A three-part epic poem *A Marssal társolkodó Murányi Venus* (The Venus of Murány conspiring with Mars) which appeared in 1664 with Palatine Wesselényi's support and was addressed to people at all levels of society referred to Buda as the seat of King István the Saint.[24] The idea was, of course, blatantly anachronistic. Its source, however, we discover in a text written at the beginning of the century by the great Hungarian humanist and historian, István Szamosközy (cca 1570–after 1607): "Grant us, O Lord, that our royal Buda, our Buda Castle of fair renown among the nations ... the bastion of our country ... once the castle of István the Saint, might once again be the court of our dear Hungarian crown."[25]

His contemporaries could not think of Buda without at the same time thinking of the great kings of medieval Hungary. A hundred years after the Battle of Mohács, in the 1630s, the knights stationed in the border fortresses of Lower Hungary still referred to Buda Castle as "King Mátyás' palace".[26] Zrínyi, too, makes the same association in a political treatise entitled "Mátyás király életéről szóló elmélkedések" (Reflections on the life of King Mátyás): had Hungary had good rulers, "we would not be lamenting our many calamities; our country would be intact, and Buda the centre if not of all Christendom, at least of Hungary."[27]

In this train of thought, the association is to the foundation of the Hungarian state, to the Hungarian crown, and to the country's former integrity. Like the Crown, Buda, too, is a symbol of the integral nation. This is how Transylvania comes into the picture in this view of history: "He squandered away Transylvania, one of the loveliest gems in our crown," wrote Zrínyi, and his works leave no doubt that for him, too, Buda stands for the old Hungary, the Hungary that must be won back.[28]

---

[23] *A magyarországi művészet története:* 1970, p. 275 – Garas: 1953. Mausoleum Potentissimorum ac Gloriosissimorum Regni Apostolici Regum et Primorum Militantis Ungariae Ducum... Nürnberg 1664. – Cf. Rózsa: 1970, pp. 466–478.

[24] Gyöngyösi: 1664, I/96. – Cf. R. Várkonyi: 1987a.

[25] István Szamosközy: "Budához" (To Buda). (Transl. by László Geréb). In: *Janus Pannonius. Magyarországi humanisták:* 1982, pp. 495–496.

[26] János Nagy Gyöngyössi to István Pálffy, Captain General of Lower Hungary, Szögyén, Sept. 6, 1635. Bratislava, Central State Archives. The Archives of the Pálffy family Arm VIII. Lad, II. Fasc 1 fol 384.

[27] Miklós Zrínyi: "Mátyás király életéről való elmélkedések" (Thoughts about the life of King Mátyás). In: *Zrínyi Miklós összes művei:* 1958, I, p. 592.

[28] Miklós Zrínyi: "Az török áfium ellen való orvosság" (Antidote to Turkish opium). In: *Zrínyi Miklós összes művei*, 1958, I, pp. 643 and 648.

The plans for the recapture of Buda, the symbol of the unified Hungary of the Middle Ages, took shape in the 1650s and 1660s in an emotional synthesis of past and future. The past was a Hungary ceaselessly at war with the Turks; the future was the vision of a Hungary enjoying, after a century and a half, the fruits of a much deserved peace.

While the Turks ruled Hungary, peace was impossible, for there was no security in negotiations. "We cannot trust the Turkish Sultan, / For he's not a man of his sworn word; / He failed to yield Buda to the King's son, / But, perfidious, kept it for himself",[29] is the way Zrínyi put the story of the taking of Buda in the *Obsidio Sigetiana*, expressing his conviction that Hungary's politicians had no choice left but to shake off the Turkish yoke with force of arms. All the works written in this period emphasize the battles the forefathers waged against the Turks. The stories, tales of extraordinary valour told in exaggerated, graphic terms, are, of course, of suspect historicity. The paragons of Hungarian chivalry are the heroes of Szigetvár, János Hunyadi, Pál Kinizsi, the champions of the past battles against the Turks, but more interestingly from our point of view, László the Saint, the eleventh-century chevalier-king, also appears as a model, as one who could have led an alliance against the Turks. The engravings present scenes of Turkish heads rolled far from gory torsos. On the pages of the *Murányi Venus*, Wesselényi is the scourge of the Turks. And Zrínyi, in *Az török áfium ellen való orvosság* (An antidote to Turkish opium), has this to say about the forefather of Lord Chief Justice Nádasdy: "For Tamás Nádasdi would have held Buda against Sultan Suleiman, had foreign powers not compelled him to surrender."[30] And shortly after Zrínyi's death, the anonymous "Cantio alia de Nicola Zrényi" mourned Zrínyi as the "stalwart besieger" of a number of Turkish strongholds – Kanizsa, Sziget – and also added Buda for emphasis, although Zrínyi had never in fact fought there.[31]

Greek mythology was another source of the value system that permitted the reconquest of Buda to become a metaphor for banishing the Turks in political thinking of the decades between 1648 and 1664. Mythological symbolism was, as is known, a powerful tool of evaluation and persuasion for the European mind from the Renaissance on.

[29] Zrínyi: 1651 (1980), V/32.

[30] *Zrínyi Miklós összes művei*, 1958, II, p. 648.

[31] Cantio alia de Nicolao Zrényi. In: *Régi Magyar Költők Tára* 10: 1981, p. 277. – Miklós Zrínyi: "Vitéz hadnagy, Szent László beszéd" (Valiant lieutenant, The speech made on the day of László the Saint). In: *Zrínyi könyvtár*: 1985, I, pp. 114, 115–116, 453–454, 457. – Cp. "Budai török is futott, mint por széltűl" (The Turks of Buda ran like the wind too). Zrínyi: 1651 (1980), IV/18.

In Hungary, the symbolism of antiquity had been used by those seeking to unite the country against the Turks right from the beginning. Miklós Oláh, later Archbishop of Esztergom, wrote his *Hungaria* and *Athila* in 1536 and 1537 to encourage the European powers to ally against the Turks. In Oláh's "history", the chief of the Huns is the embodiment of the strong, centralizing, absolute ruler, a chief whom Mars himself has armed and who offers sacrifice to Mars, and whose soldiers "revered Jupiter, Mars, Mercury and Venus as their gods".[32] By the mid-seventeenth century, the Hungarians preparing to drive out the Turks were making use of every element in the storehouse of European symbolism. In *Obsidio Sigetiana* we find "belligerent, angry Mars", Cupid and Venus mourning over Adonis;[33] and in the *Mauzoleum*, a collection of copper prints of Hungary's kings, we have Nádasdy's introduction citing examples from the Trojan wars.[34] In contemporary sources we are likely to find the Huns, the conquering Magyars, the chieftains and István the Saint wearing the garb of antique ideals. *A Marssal társolkodó Murányi Venus* is the apogee of this approach: it follows the traditions of antiquity as much in its construction as in its didacticism and personifications.[35] Zrínyi is the true follower of Mars, Pallas and Venus; in the songs the encamped soldiers sing, in presenting him as the exemplar, he is the "Hungarian Mars", "Mars Zrínyi", the "chivalric Mars". Venus, too, weeps in the dirge sung for a knight who fought against the Turks and died in 1663.[36] Taken out of context, all this might seem at best curiosities. Considered as organic parts of the European mentality with its humanist traditions, however, they take on a wealth of meaning. We know that it was an age when the graphic and the verbal forms of

[32] Miklós Oláh: "Athila". In: *Humanista történetírók:* 1977, pp. 335–336. – Cf. János Sylvester: "Elégia a török ellen indítandó háborúról" (Elegy on the war againt the Turks) (Transl. by Győző Csorba). In: *Janus Pannonius. Magyarországi humanisták:* 1982, p. 344 and ff.

[33] Zrínyi: 1651 (1980), I/1, IV/46, – IV/60, –VII/67, – IX/2–3, XII/2–4 (Venus bemoans Adonis): 8, – 25, – XIV/4, 72, XV/12.

[34] Translated into Hungarian by Márton Csernatoni: A hun és magyar vitézek verses históriája (The history in verse of the Hun and Hungarian soldiers). Kund: "His head is like that of Pallas / his hands are the ones of Mars wielding weapons, "Szent István: Szentelt Hector" (István the Saint: Consecrated Hector). *Régi Magyar Költők Tára* 10: 1981, pp. 121, 146, etc.

[35] Zrínyi: 1651 (1980).

[36] "Anno 1664." – "Zrínyi Miklós keserves halálárul való ének" (Song on the painful death of Miklós Zrínyi), pp. 267, 269; Zsigmond Petkó: "Cantio Militaris", p. 305; Miklós Pázmány, p. 567; "Szánnyad Kovács Györgyöt, szerelmetes Venus" (Take pity on György Kovács, lovely Venus): Kovács György éneke (The song of György Kovács), p. 236. All of them in: *Régi Magyar Költők Tára* 10: 1981.

expression had not yet become clearly distinguished. Warburg, Gombrich, Chastel, Bahtyin, Panofsky and others have shown that people still expressed their abstract thoughts through a system of conventional signs: emblems and symbols. In poetic and prose writings abstract thoughts are given graphic formulation, or appear as gestures; in the fine arts, on the other hand, the objects and mythological characters represented stand for ideals, and express entire programs.[37]

The essence of what I am driving at is well illustrated by one of the famous paintings of the seventeenth century, commissioned by the Duke of Tuscany in the 1630s. The picture depicts Mars and Venus, with cupids and monsters, a mother with a babe in her arms, and a woman dressed in mourning, amidst books, drawings, and a broken flute. Rubens, who painted the picture – and was also one of the great diplomats and classical scholars of the age – called the painting "The Horrors of War". In a later letter, he explained its symbolism as follows: The principal figure is Mars – writes Rubens – who, leaving open the Temple of Janus (which it was a Roman custom to keep closed in times of peace), advances with his shield and his bloodstained sword, threatening the nations with great devastation and paying little heed to Venus his lady, who strives with caresses and embraces to restrain him, she being accompanied by her Cupids and her lovegods. On the other side Mars is drawn on by the Fury Alecto, holding a torch in her hand. Nearby are monsters, representing Pestilence and Famine, the inseparable companions of war; on the ground lies a woman with a broken flute, signifying harmony, which is incompatible with the discord of war; there is also a Mother with her babe in her arms, denoting that fecundity, generation and charity are trampled underfoot by war, which corrupts and destroys all things. In addition there is an architect, lying with his instruments in his hand, to show that what is built for the commodity and ornament of a city is laid in ruins and overthrown by the violence of arms. I believe, if I remember aright, that you will also find on the ground, beneath the feet of Mars, a book and some drawings on paper, to show that he tramples on literature and the other arts.[38]

Rubens's explication rests on deep-rooted traditions. To elucidate it, let me just quote Ficino's comments on Venus as depicted in Botticelli's "Mars and Venus": Venus is nothing less than humanity, love, fertility, rebirth – everything. Venus is the ideal in virtue of which human contacts are pos-

---

[37] Warburg: 1920. – Gombrich: 1975. – Chastel: 1978. – Panofsky: 1970. – Bahtyn: 1982.
[38] Magurn: 1955, pp. 408–409, quoted by Gombrich: 1975, pp. 126–127.

sible. "Mars and Venus" is an allegory expressing the victory of the human spirit, of humanity, over raw force. Venus represents beauty personified, the fecundity of the spirit, man's being born again of the spirit.[39]

To turn again to Hungary, we know that the figures of antiquity were familiar to educated Hungarians from Venetian, Belgian, and French tapestries, from their readings, from sermons and from their school studies.[40] But it would be a great mistake to look for direct influences even in the case of graphic symbols, to see, for instance, Rubens's picture of war-ravaged Europe as the inspiration for the many contemporary paintings we have of war-torn Hungary.

In speaking of the woman in mourning in "The Horrors of War", Rubens has this to say: That lugubrious Matron clad in black and with her veil torn, despoiled of her jewels and every other ornament, is unhappy Europe, afflicted for so many years by rapine, outrage and misery, which, as they are so harmful to all, need not be specified. Her attribute is that globe held by a putto or genius and surmounted by a crest which denotes the Christian orb.[41]

And now let us listen to the description of war-torn Hungary given by Gyöngyösi, the author of *A Marssal társolkodó Murányi Venus*. "Where black mourning, in torn rags, / With shoulder-length hair wind-torn /, Walks dismayed, with sorrowing face, / Multiplying clouds with her lamentation / Here all around there's dread horror, / Tearful captivity and cries of pain, / Terrible devastation and despair, / And the heart-rending torture of poverty."[42]

The similarities only show that Hungarian artists, too, relied on the common international system of symbols for topoi. For Hungarian society, the century and a half of Turkish occupation was, all things considered, a period of permanent war. In one of the arguments advanced by Hungarian politicians for the liberation of the country, we read the following: since the Battle of Mohács, when the Sultan occupied two-thirds of the country, "Mars, the god of war, has been constantly burning the flame of war."[43] In the system of references of the times, only a war waged to drive out the Turks could bring peace. It is in this sense that we must read the last lines of Zrínyi's dedication to his *Obsidio Sigetiana*: "In galea Martis

[39] Boskovits: 1963. References to the analyses of Warburg and Gombrich; see pp. 34–38 and 68.

[40] László: 1980, pp. 25–65.

[41] Magurn: 1955, pp. 408–409, quoted by Gombrich: 1975, pp. 126–127.

[42] Gyöngyösi: 1664, I/177.

[43] Kibédi Varga: 1983. – Opinio 1661 MOL P 125 The documents of Palatine Pál 91/9321.

nidum fecere columbae, / Apparet Marti quam sit amica Venus" (The doves have made their nest in Mars's helmet, showing how much Venus loves Mars).[44]

Finally, we must note that an essential element of the ideas related to the recapture of Buda – as one of the best paintings of the period, the "Cloaked Madonna" also illustrates – was that the Turks would be driven out with the help of the Habsburg emperor.[45] In fact, Emperor Leopold was chosen King of Hungary in 1655 on condition that in the course of his reign the Turks would be driven out of the country.

The political hopes of the 1650s were just about destroyed by the events of the two decades between 1664 and 1684. The Habsburgs managed to alienate every stratum of Hungarian society with the Peace of Vasvár, the execution of Nádasdy and his followers, their suspension of the Hungarian constitution, their persecution of the Protestants, Thököly's exclusion from the international anti-Turkish alliance, and finally, their total disregard of Palatine Esterházy after 1684. Nevertheless, the Pope's mediation, a realistic evaluation of the country's situation, and the changes they thought to discover in the Habsburg court's policy in late 1685 and early 1686 rekindled the hopes of Hungary's leaders. The conditions outlined in the course of the Transylvanian–Habsburg talks, and the agreement signed in the summer of 1686 in preparation for the siege of Buda all indicate that for all their disappointments and all their reservations, and in spite of the horrendous war losses and sufferings of the year 1685, the Hungarian politicians still hoped that Hungary would be taking part in the war against the Turks as a coequal power. The reconquest of Buda would bring salvation; the country, restored to its former unity, would, as a sovereign state, enjoy the blessings of peace.[46]

It was with such hopes that the Palatine – following the protocol of the times – wrote to Emperor Leopold, the Pope, and the rulers of Europe on hearing the news of Buda's liberation. This was the spirit in which the aristocracy and the higher clergy, the nobility and the soldiers – even those who had seen the burned-out ruins – informed whoever they passed on the news to: the Prince of Transylvania, the faithful assembled in the churches, their families, their comrades.[47]

[44] Zrínyi: 1651 (1980).

[45] Galavics: 1975, 1976.

[46] The standpoint and instructions of the Transylvanian Prince and the Estates to the envoys of the Principality in Vienna 16 March, 1686. OL P-1239. The documents of Mihály Apafi Box 4. – Gergely: 1886, p. 300.

[47] László Csáky to Mihály Apafi, Prince of Transylvania "In Buda September 4. 1686". In: *Diplomatarium Alvincziarum:* 1870–1887, II.

It was with faith in this kind of future that the town of Sopron celebrated the victory in Buda: "On September 9 we gave thanks to the Lord in every church, and the burghers marched in arms to the Main Square. When the cannons were heard from the bastions, they shot salvos in the square. The magistrates and the Council were invited to dine at the Town Hall, and drank to the health of His Majesty. In front of the Town Hall, the young people danced in the square, and finally they were let into the Hall itself, to continue their dance there. All this they did, so that in their old age people might look back and say: When Buda was won, I was young yet, but I, too, danced in the square then, and even inside the Town Hall."[48]

Public opinion in the rest of Europe after the reconquest of Buda was increasingly influenced by the political slogans of the growing conflict between the Habsburgs and the French. The pamphleteers discussed in terms of "nationhood", "economic interests", "freedom of conscience", and "natural right" the question of who in fact reoccupied Buda, and who should rule in Hungary, and spoke of the wars of 1663–1664, and of Zrínyi.[49] The Habsburg propaganda machine expressed dynastic interests in an extreme form. The entire arsenal of contemporary publicity techniques was mustered: the baroque magnificence of the court was flaunted, treatises on government were written, pamphlets were published, and the glory of the Emperor was communicated to every social stratum in the appropriate terms. Emperor Leopold was the subject of coins, woodcuts, paintings, Latin school dramas, and German and Spanish plays: he was the triumphant general, the Jupiter who had banished the infidel with thunderbolts, he was Hercules, and winged Perseus who had liberated enchained Hungaria. Leopold was "Mars orientalis occidentalis", "the bastion of Christendom". His glory dimmed all else, and even the generals who had led the battle felt he had appropriated their due, and it was partly by way of protest that marvellous works like the Lotharingian tapestries were made (between 1700 and 1714), or the paintings in Schleissheim of 1710 commemorating Maximilian Emmanuel's battles against the Turks.[50]

In this system of thought, Hungary was branded the "enemy of Christendom". No one remembered her battles against the Turks, the decades of effort to remain a state. The first regulations of November 5, 1686, determining the future of reconquered Buda – specifying that only Germans and Catholics could buy a house in the castle area – were followed by a

---

[48] Quoted by Bárdos: 1984, p. 329.
[49] Köpeczi: 1976.
[50] Rózsa: 1965, pp. 17–23.

whole series of ordinances destructive of Hungary's statehood, and the country was engulfed in the horrors of protracted warfare. Hungarians found no way to relate their personal experiences of the siege of Buda to the circumstances they found themselves in, and to the alien value system behind it all. And so the reconquest of Buda entered public consciousness in terms of the traditional values, those formulated in the 1650s and 1660s, and was seen to be a piece of unfinished business. Bishop Balázs Jaklin, speaking at the funeral of Colonel Mihály Czobor, who had also fought for Buda, made reference to the Hungarian Mars. The *Mauzoleum* was translated anew, and copies were made of Zrínyi's works. The second edition of the *Murányi Venus* appeared in 1702, the pictures of Hungary in mourning and Mars holding the flashing blade of his sword having acquired a new relevance. And everyone in Hungary and the rest of Europe understood the allusion when Ferenc II Rákóczi referred to "The nation conspiring with Mars" in the "Recrudescunt" introducing his proclamation to the peoples of the world.

Nor were pieces of the news anonymously spread of the siege of Buda entirely lost. Research has shown that some of the stories found their way into Mihály Cserei's *Historia*. Mátyás Bél, too, made use of the first, contemporary formulation of the story of the siege, and retold it in detail in his treatise on Hungarian government.

All in all, September 2, 1686, ushered in a new era for Hungary. The centuries of struggle to safeguard and renew the nation's sovereignty have since left a "reconquest of Buda" motif to every age. Historical works, poems, works of art, and music like Kodály's *Te Deum of Buda Castle* leave no doubt that Hungarian history is one, incessant, reconquest of Buda.

Alternatives in Hungary
Recaptured from the Turks
℘   ℭ

My paper is going to deal with the connections of the challenges presented in the era of the victory at Zenta and the political movements in the Kingdom of Hungary and the Principality of Transylvania.

This is a long period, largely covering the last third of the European power reshuffle. It appears to be divided by the two wars affecting the whole continent. But in the process of the reshuffle of power relations there are no clearly marked dividing lines. The Peace of Westphalia in 1648 made it possible for Christendom to unite its material and spiritual power, and push back the frontier of the Ottoman Empire from the middle of Hungary to the threshold of the Balkans. And it was owing to the deranged power relations that the War of the Spanish Succession broke out, in order to achieve the main purpose of modern Europe, the balance of power.

The unity of the period is well represented by the reports of the English ambassador to Constantinople. As a representative mediating the negotiations between the countries of the Holy League and the Ottoman power, William Paget stated that after the victory of Prince Eugene of Savoy the Turks were no longer reluctant to make peace, but they could end the protracted war only if Emperor Leopold showed compliance and guaranteed sufficient liberties. And the wars came to be concluded only by the peace treaties of the 1710s.

I am sketching out two problems in my paper: the consequences of the Peace of Westphalia, and the alternatives after 1697.

The Congress of Westphalia produced a decisive change in the Turkish policy of the Kingdom of Hungary. It established universal peace between the Christian countries, and, consequently, created the possibility of their joining arms and turning against the Turks. It was Miklós Zrínyi, Ban of Croatia who gave voice to the opinion that the time had come for the ex-

"Magyarország az új kihívások korában (1648–1711)." *Valóság*, 41 (1998) 6. (Transl. by Kálmán Ruttkay)

165

pulsion of the Turks and the unification of the country. He organized a wide-ranging movement in order to seize the favourable opportunity and start the war against the Turks.

They were realistic in their calculations, and knew that the Domus Austriae was to be the basis of power and only an international confederacy could be efficient in fighting the Turks. At the Diet of Pozsony in 1655 Archduke Leopold was elected King of Hungary with the proviso that in his lifetime he would recapture the Turkish occupied territories. They stated repeatedly that it was a matter of life and death for Hungary to get rid of Ottoman power, since its population was living in a situation which "non pax est, sed bellum, et quidem crudele et atrox". They emphasized that this was the common interest of Europe, since the Ottomans were expanding their power, had attacked Venice, were threatening Carinthia, Moravia, and would soon reach Vienna. By the spring of 1664 it seemed as if Hungarian politics had achieved its aim: an alliance was formed with the League of the Rhine, and an army, about sixty thousand strong, consisting of Imperial, Hungarian and German forces and French auxiliary troops started an offensive war. Political propaganda and international journalism equally emphasized the common interest of Europe, the dynasty and the Hungarian nation. Gottlieb Rinck, historiographer to the Imperial Court wrote: "Ungarn ist die Vormauer vom gantzen Europa gegen die Türcken." In an English work published on the occasion of the winter campaign Zrínyi is called the hero "upon whose success or overthrow the Western world seems to stand or fall." A great number of German newspapers celebrated the battle of Szentgotthárd: Emperor Leopold had achieved the victory of Christendom over the pagans. After this it caused a severe trauma to Hungarian politics that the Hofburg unexpectedly ended the war and concluded the Peace Treaty of Vasvár. In the opinion of the English ambassador to Constantinople the Hofburg had missed a great opportunity: "the Turks are happy, for if the Emperor had not made peace, he could have chased the Grand Vizier as far as Adrianople, since the latter had lost his best officers, and his army was not combatworthy." The opinion of György Lippay, Archbishop of Esztergom was shared by the counties and the towns, by Protestants and Catholics alike: the peace treaty had been concluded without the knowledge of the Hungarians, and an illegal decision had been taken, "sine nobis de nobis." Transylvania was exposed to the revenge of the Turks, at the same time, as János Bethlen, Chancellor of the Principality put it: the peace of Transylvania was connected "with the safety of the rest of Europe."

Ending the Turkish war in this way indicated a new policy of the Habsburgs. This followed equally from the agreements ratified in Westphalia. The stress was laid on the Austrian interests, and the Danube region was brought into focus. It was during the years of the Turkish war that three significant representatives of a more efficient kind of absolutism came into contact with the Hofburg. Joachim Becher was the planner of mercantilist structures increasing the incomes of the state; Mario Spinola stood for the idea of one state – one religion; while Baron Johann Paul Hocher elaborated the legal categories of absolutist power, and insisted intolerantly on the principles of the interest of the state, the "ragione di stato". The Turkish–Habsburg trade agreement concluded after the Peace of Vasvár, the establishment of the Orientalische Handelscompagnie, the Wiener Kommerzkollegium, the standing army, the bureaucracy, the regulated diplomacy, the forms of the monarch's self-expression, and the Baroque pomp of representation all served the formation of a strong great power.

The consequent change in the position of Hungary was called by a contemporary Hungarian writer the situation of a labyrinth. Efforts to find a way out made be the Hungarian estates and Habsburg absolutism are well known: Zrínyi's plan for a confederation, the Wesselényi scheme, the trials, the executions, the suspension of the Hungarian constitution and of the freedom of Protestant worship, Thököly's uprising and the compromise of 1681. The objective analysis of all these, free from the habitual axioms and would greatly exceed the limits of a paper like this. All I can say is that Hungary, badly divided by internal struggles, had become the epicentre of the hectic changes in the international power relations. Simultaneously with their attacks in the West, the French established their new bases ranging from Poland through the Principality to Constantinople. If only in view of their own trading interests in the East and the North, the Protestant countries, England, Holland, Sweden, the German principalities, extended their protection to their Hungarian brethren whose existence was threatened. And how aggressive the Ottoman Empire was, is well shown by the fact that within two decades it gained supremacy over the Eastern basin of the Mediterranean, attacked Poland and, later, Russia, and it occupied a larger territory in Hungary than ever. In possession of Érsekújvár and Várad it isolated Upper Hungary both from Vienna and Transylvania. At the same time the primary aim of Hungarian politics was invariably to get rid of Turkish rule. After 1681 Thököly repeatedly offered his sword to Emperor Leopold, and the inhabitants of Hungary and Transylvania took part in the international alliance formed after Kara Mustafa's siege of Vienna and the long war of reoccupation, suffering losses in human life and material resources largely beyond their means.

Coming to the second point of my paper I will outline the alternatives taking shape after the Turkish war.

It is well known that political responses are elicited by the complexity of historical developments. The views concerning the state and the future of the country were determined by the structure of the society of Hungary, its organization, legal system, mentality, its system of institutions, economic structure and culture together. I can only hint at these structural relations.

Following the defeat at Mohács the country lost its natural increase in population, and suffered enormous losses, material and otherwise. Nevertheless, as a result of the protoindustrial development taking place in Central Europe as well, the conditions for the transformation of the economic structure were given. In the decade of the capture of Buda by the Turks the balance of foreign trade was unquestionably active. The price of cattle, wine, copper, salt, mercury was constantly rising. During the war of reoccupation the ready-made clothes trade was considerable, there were several glassworks, thirty-three paper mills and innumerable saw-mills. The technology used in the ironworks at Csabar built by the Zrínyis in 1651 was the same as at Krajna. In 1692 the first real blast-furnace was built by the Treasury.

The social structure, too, was modified. The nobility was no longer determined by its status only, it was differentiated according to property, profession, culture, education. Layers of persistent merchants emerged, privileged groups were formed or grew stronger, such as that of the heyducks, and the communities of soldier-peasants' settlements and market-towns with a single line of cultivation. The country was throughout a territory ready to admit foreigners; the different ethnic groups formed peculiar economic and social communities. A multitude of Italian, German, Austrian, Bohemian people were tied to Hungary by landed property, commerce, part-ownership in mines, or marriage. Members of the Hungarian political élite – noblemen, burghers, intellectuals – received an up-to-date education at Western universities, and kept abreast of international events. Aristocratic families had palaces in Vienna as well. Young Prince Ferenc Rákóczi who had been awarded the title of Imperial Prince was on as good terms with Villard, French ambassador to Vienna, as was Prince Eugene of Savoy. The Palatine, Duke Pál Esterházy and Samuel Oppenheimer, purveyor by appointment to the Court gained the monopoly of salt in partnership. Landowners' estates producing for the market were well-organized units, complemented by workshops of early industry based not only on the labour of serfs, but also on that of a multitude of paid workers. Apart from works on Hungarian and universal history the writings of

Machiavelli, Bodin, Grotius, Pufendorf and the mercantilists formed the views of this political élite. The works on military theory to be found in Zrínyi's library at Csáktornya, or that of András Szirmay, a squire in the county of Zemplén, were, proportionately and in quality, comparable to those in the world-famous library of the victor of Zenta. Their opinions on how to settle the affairs of the country centred round four great topics which were: military, economic, ecclesiastic problems, and politics, the latter including the control of public administration, legislation, the supervision of the monarch's decisions, and the maintenance of law and order. The Hungarian society of the three component parts of the country was held together by Protestant and Catholic church organizations and schools, and, over and above economic interdependence, a well-working network of information, and common historical experiences. Hungarian culture was made up of the vernacular, the world of the Middle Ages, the Renaissance and the Baroque, the views of the Reformation, and the ideas imported from Western universities. Life in towns, border castles, manor-houses on big estates was adjusted to mechanical clocks. Manifestations of public opinion concerning the siege of Buda show that people were well aware of the changing times.

Three answers emerged to meet the challenges of the changing times, three solutions to settle the affairs of the region for the future.

One answer was the compromise of the dynasty and the Hungarian estates, made at the Diet of Pozsony in 1687. They agreed that while formerly kings had been elected, now the members of the Habsburg dynasty would inherit the throne in succession, but in return the king's charter and oath would guarantee the laws and the Hungarians would be entrusted with making arrangements in the recaptured territories. The estates argued that the decision had been taken "for the preservation of our country" and "in the interest of our welfare and survival", and nine-year-old Joseph I crowned king by hereditary right, received the present of a game of labyrinth.

The second answer was tested by a great number of procedures, plans, protocols of transactions, projects, votums, memorials. These originated in various forums in Hungary, Transylvania and Vienna, but the fundamental principle was common to all: conformity and accommodation to the new situation. A few examples picked out at random: In the Puncta Instantiarium submitted to the King, Count Miklós Bercsényi, quartermaster general of Upper Hungary and "ablegatus primarius" of the community of counties asked for the achievement of an order similar to that of the hereditary provinces, the observance of imperial military "Ordnung"-s, controlling the devaluation, and the freedom of trade. Count

Siegfried Breuer, President of the Hofkammer, thought it was in the interest of the Empire to keep the so-called Hungarian national militia, instituted by the Kingdom. György Széchenyi, Archbishop of Esztergom asked for the same care for injured and invalid Hungarian soldiers as was secured by Prince Eugene of Savoy for the members of the imperial army in the Allgemeines Krankenhaus. As is shown by the protocols of several transactions resulting in an agreement between the Emperor on the one hand and the political élite of the Kingdom of Hungary and Transylvania on the other, in contrast with the general military anarchy, law and order would be the condition which would make it possible for the country to pay the enormous taxes distributed in accordance with modern demands. If churches and schools were confiscated from the Protestants, if there was discrimination against them in the army and in the recaptured territories, this could have unpredictable consequences. The Habsburg Government reckoned with the international power relations, for instance Count Kinsky argued at the negotiations in Ryswick that Savoy, though hostile to the Emperor, should not be omitted from the peace treaty, because otherwise it would fling itself into the arms of France. At the negotiations ending the Turkish war of the Holy League, Paget, the English mediator mentioned earlier in my paper, stated that several laws, and recently Emperor Leopold, had guaranteed the recognition of the statehood of the Principality and he requested, together with the Turkish representative that Transylvania should be included in the peace treaty accordingly. However, the Habsburg–Turkish armistice concluded at Carlowitz in January 1699 made decisions in which the territories of the Kingdom and Transylvania were dealt with as parts of the Empire.

The third solution suggested after 1700 was that state power, even the force of arms should be used to vindicate the fundamental principle of the Peace of Westphalia, that is, to ensure the sovereignty not only of the great powers, but that of the small countries as well. It was, among others, in his instruction given to this envoy sent to the King of Prussia that Ferenc II Rákóczi summed up his opinion concerning the War of the Spanish Succession: "Whether the French or the Habsburgs will win the war, the European balance of power will be upset." It became evident in 1703 that a very large part of the population of the Kingdom and Transylvania were ready to seize the new opportunity of remedying the evils of the country, even if they had to give their blood for their country. Among those taking part in the venture variously called war of independence, discontent, or rebellion, there were, irrespective of their social status or religion, noblemen, serfs, country squires, townsfolk, soldiers of the border fortresses, Catholics and Protestants, speaking Hungarian, German, Slovak,

Ukrainian and Romanian respectively. The leaders of the state organized simultaneously with the armed attack, did not restore the old feudal state. Incidentally, the high dignitaries of the Hungarian estates, the Palatine, the Lord Chief Justice and the Ban of Croatia all remained in Vienna with the king. With Holland as an example, the form of government was defined as a confederacy of the Hungarian estates which included not only the lords spiritual and temporal, the towns and the counties, but the armed forces and the market towns as well. Central institutions were established (Consilium Aulicum, Senatus, Consilium Oeconomicum). A standing army was organized, an income-tax affecting the nobility too was introduced, and the serfs were granted protection by the supreme power. In the course of hectic debates these reforms were incorporated in law by the Diets. Of these I can refer to such as offered an alternative with regard to the future of the country.

The Principality of Transylvania would keep its independent statehood, and the unity of the country would be brought about by the confederacy of the countries under the Hungarian crown. Laws giving equal chances to the Catholic and Protestant churches regulated the equality of denominations, and the liberty of conscience. According to these the denomination which was in the majority was entitled to the local church. There was, however, a significant proviso: the majority were obliged to build a church for the minority. Since the borderlines of denominations often coincided with those of linguistic communities and ethnic groups, and the schools were maintained by the churches this secured equal chances for the development of culture in the vernacular languages. Finally there was a law regulating the country's right to peace. The relations of the Domus Austriae and the country should be arranged with English and Dutch mediation.

Rákóczi emphasized repeatedly that he would enter the War of the Spanish Succession on the side of the French with the proviso that Louis XIV would guarantee the inclusion of the Kingdom and the Principality in the universal peace concluding the war. This aspiration was embraced also by the Maritime Powers forming a great coalition with Austria. They had several reasons for doing so. English and Dutch banks gave loans to the Hofburg accepting the copper and mercury mines of the Kingdom and the Principality as security, and both military and economic considerations were in favour of peace in the country. The freedom of Protestant worship was thought to be rightful both by the masters of the City of London and the common people. However, it was chiefly with an eye to the European balance of power that some English policy-markers thought it desirable that the country's rights to liberty should be secured. The English and Dutch attitude worried the Hofburg very much. E.g. Chancellor Wenzel Wratislav characterized the Hungarian situation in a letter to Archduke Charles fighting in Barcelona as follows: "We have got into a terrible labyrinth."

Apparently there was a way out when Joseph I ascending the throne in 1705 acknowledged the right to international mediation, but the negotiations were broken off shortly after they had been started. In the summer of 1706 George Stepney, English Ambassador to Vienna sent a report from Nagyszombat to Minister Harley, concluding it by saying that since the Habsburg Government would by no means consent to the Principality of Transylvania retaining its independence, "This is laying the Axe to the Root of the Tree and any man who has had the happiness of living under a free Government cannot but be a little concerned to see a poor people (where 5 parts of 6 are of the Reform'd Churches) depriv'd of their Liberties at one Blow, and given up to servitude and future persecutions, notwithstanding a Powerfull Mediation, of the same Profession with themselves, has been pleased to appear in their behalf."

A new turn in the European labyrinth presented itself when, at the time of the election of Charles III as King of Spain, the French were willing to recognize the new Hungarian state only on condition that Joseph I was dethroned: the Diet of Ónod declared the decision of 1687 concerning hereditary monarchy illegal. Even so, and contrary to repeated promises the French alliance did not come about. The government of Louis XIV failed to recognize the importance of the Danube region. Nevertheless Rákóczi established strong connections at different levels with several states opposed to one another, such as Prussia, Russia, Sweden and Poland. And in spite of the military power relations which had been unequal from the beginning and were constantly deteriorating he managed to hold out fighting to the concluding phase of the European war. In August 1710, when after the negotiations at The Hague and Gertruydenberg Rákóczi felt sure that he had the support of Queen Anne and the Duke of Marlborough, he declared that he was going to begin peace negotiations. Queen Anne of England immediately sent a special envoy to Vienna.

It is well known that the ministers of the Hofburg believed that the war in Hungary could be concluded either by force of arms or by a general amnesty granted to the subjects. However, as soon as the English Queen's envoy, Peterborough arrived in Vienna, Prince Eugene of Savoy, President of the War Council changed this attitude. He knew best of all that the twenty to fifty thousand soldiers of the imperial forces engaged in Hungary were badly wanting from the Western and Italian battlefields. Nevertheless, as the minutes of the meetings of the Cabinet Council, the

"Staatskonferenz" in January 1711 and on the 14th of February show, it was chiefly at the request of the English and Dutch allies that he decided for negotiations instead of a military solution or amnesty, and the Emperor sent a representative on behalf of the Habsburg Government to carry on the negotiations begun by the imperial general, János Pálffy. The question how, under what conditions the Peace Treaty of Szatmár was concluded would require another paper. It is certain that this compromise was one local variant in the Danube region of establishing the European balance of power. Supporters of another variant, citing the principles of Grotius, kept emphasizing, even at the negotiations in Utrecht that the independence of the Transylvanian state was a security of peace in the region and the effectiveness of the freedom of conscience and other liberties. Moreover, the rational interests of the Austrian House would also demand the maintenance of an independent Principality of Transylvania. "It is not to be feared that if this principality is restored to its rights the Austrian House will become weaker, and the power relations necessary to secure the European balance will be upset. On the contrary, if it is thus guaranteed that its freedom of conscience and its other political liberties shall be respected, Hungary would contribute a great deal more to meeting the Emperor's economic demands."

Instead of summing up I will mention two works of art. One of these is a painting. It was hidden probably about 1670 and found as late as the 20th century. The picture shows Emperor Leopold clad in steel, wearing the imperial crown, and surrounded by the Hungarian high dignitaries, the Palatine, the Lord Chief Justice, the Ban of Croatia, the Archbishop of Esztergom. Above them a map can be seen guarded by the Blessed Virgin Mary in a blue cloak, and the Holy Crown. For quite a long time even experts were at a loss to interpret it, taking the map to be that of the regularization of the Rába. Now we know that it is the map of recaptured Hungary, and the picture represented the chance missed in the decade of the Peace of Westphalia.

The other work of art is the equestrian statue of Prince Eugene of Savoy standing in front of the royal palace of Buda. In the 1960s it was demanded that it should be removed from its place. An art historian and a historian spoke up for it on behalf of history. The victor of Zenta was able to weather through the past half century, and now his statue stands above the Danube as a grave memento and a new challenge to Europe seeking its identity.

Hungarian Independence
and the European Balance of Power
ℰ)   ℭ℞

During the time of the War of the Spanish Succession, in the summer of 1706, George Stepney (1663–1707) English Ambassador to Vienna sent a report from Nagyszombat, a town in North-West Hungary to Minister Harley (1661–1724) concluding it as follows: since the Habsburg Government will by no means consent to the Principality of Transylvania retaining its independence, "This is laying the Axe to the Root of thê Tree and any man who has had the happiness of living under a free Government cannot but be a little concerned to see a poor people (whereof 5 parts of 6 are of the Reform'd Churches) depriv'd of their Liberties at one Blow, and given up to servitude and future persecutions, notwithstanding a Powerfull Mediation, of the same Profession with themselves, has been pleased to appear in their behalf."[1]

How did the English Ambassador to Vienna come to Nagyszombat, a town held by Ferenc II Rákóczi who was fighting against the Habsburg Empire? How could it happen, that the most eminent English diplomat of the period should have stood up for the independence of the Principality of Transylvania, in opposition to the opinion of Joseph I (1678–1711) the Habsburg Emperor and King of Hungary, an ally of England?

Attention to the English political stance maintained with regard to the Hungarian War of Independence has been paid long since in the literature of the subject, but it has been traced to a purely personal bias of a few diplomats. A thoroughgoing analysis, however, can reveal that more general interests were involved, and it was related to the characteristic tendencies of the three quarters of a century following the Treaty of Westphalia, such as the efforts to establish a balance of power, and the

---

"Hungarian independence and the balance of power." In: *The Fabric of Modern Europe. Studies in Social and Diplomatic History.* Ed. by Attila Pók. Nottingham, 1998. (Transl. by Kálmán Ruttkay).

[1]   George Stepney to Robert Harley, Tirnau (Nagyszombat), July 20, 1706, PRO SP/191. Cf. *Archivum Rákóczianum:* 1872–1877, Section II/III, p. 159.

struggle for stability in Europe. This is a topic of vast scope, with an almost inexhaustible stock of documents. Using the evidence of archival material I have explored in Hungary, Transylvania, Vienna, and, last but not least in England, in the British Library and the Public Record Office, I will present a few aspects of the topic, within the given space of this paper, concentrating on the Principality of Transylvania.[2]

What could be the reason why, in the course of the War of the Spanish Succession, Transylvania had become important enough to engross the attention of England as much as it did?

As is well known, the Treaty of Westphalia was concluded in 1648 with a view to establishing a balance of power in Europe.[3] However, there was a most vulnerable spot in the peace treaty, namely Central Europe. Bohemia was an absolute loser, Poland lived under constant threat, the Eastern region, bordering on the Ottoman Empire, formed a critical zone, ranging from the Ukraine to Croatia, with focuses of social and political tensions, and occasional outbreaks of armed conflicts. What was generally expected of the Treaty of Westphalia all over Europe was that the Christian countries would make up their differences, and uniting their forces would turn against the Turks. But the projectors of the peace treaty had failed to raise the question: what was going to happen to the Eastern regions of Central Europe after the expulsion of the Turks? That is why the inclusion of the Principality of Transylvania in the Treaty of Westphalia was of great significance. This meant not only that the Principality was recognized as an independent state by the international forum of Westphalia, but also that is was regarded as a part of the community of the Christian world, in spite of the fact that the country had lived in the sphere of Ottoman power for a century. And since the principle guiding the projectors of the Treaty of Westphalia was to form a peaceful system of European states that could be resistant to conflicts, Transylvania could be reckoned with as a factor, a stabilizing factor of the international balance of power.[4]

This was supported, besides the geographical, geopolitical and historical conditions of Transylvania by its peculiar ethnic and cultural characteristics as well.

---

[2] Éva Haraszti-Taylor's essay implies the question of how old English diplomatic relations were *vis-à-vis* Hungary; my paper likewise hopes to contribute to the clrification of this problem. Haraszti-Taylor: 1988, pp. 593–599.

[3] Dickmann: 1959a, remains essential reading and should be supplemented with Dickmann: 1959b, in particular part I, *Instructionen*. – Raab: 1975.

[4] R. Várkonyi: 1994a, pp. 187–198.

The territory of Transylvania[5] was twice as large as that of Switzerland, about 70 per cent of it being mountainous region; it had gold, silver, quicksilver and copper mines, and abundant salt deposits. Sometimes it was called "the Scotland of Hungary". Lying in the Eastern borderland of the Central European region it held a most significant position, forming a bridge between the Balkans and Poland, the Eastern world and the countries under Habsburg rule. As early as 1570, the first edition of Ortelius's famous atlas of the world showed the "Principatus Transylvaniae" on a separate page, as an independent country. However, it took a century or so for it to arrive at that stage developing under very grave circumstances. The Principality was formed from the Eastern region of the Kingdom of Hungary at the time of the Turkish conquest. After the disastrous defeat at Mohács (1526) and the death of King Lajos II (1505–1526) of Hungary one faction of the Hungarian Estates chose János Szapolyai (1478–1540) another one Ferdinand Habsburg (1503–1564) as King of Hungary. King János who possessed the Eastern part of the country joined the League of Cognac (1527), France concluded with him the alliance of Fontainebleau (1528), and Sultan Suleiman extended his protectoral power over him (1529). At the same time King János maintained a close contact with Emperor Charles V (1500–1558). The head of the Habsburg Empire recognized Transylvania as a state in its own right, King János's son renounced his royal title and took the title of Prince of Transylvania. Successive Princes of Transylvania all established close links of alliance with West European Christian powers and the neighbouring countries, i.e. Poland and the Romanian Voivodeships as well. Prince Gábor Bethlen (1580–1629) entered the Thirty Years' War as a signatory to the Alliance of the Hague, and concluded the Westminster Pact with Charles I of England (1600–1649), in order to have the independent statehood of the Principality recognized, and included in the universal peace that was to bring the war to a close. What a rich country Transylvania was is well shown, for instance by the Swedish proposal made to Prince Bethlen in 1626 for the joint control of the European copper trade.

So the inclusion of György I Rákóczy's (1593–1648) Principality as an ally of Sweden, in the Treaty of Westphalia meant the recognition of a country with a well-balanced economy, and in contact or alliance with almost all Christian countries, and also as one that had achieved the peaceful co-existence of different religions, nationalities and cultures, a particularly significant feat in Central Europe, considering how mixed the popu-

---

[5]   PRO SP 80/6 fol. 144. – Szekfű :1929 (1933), pp. 226–227. – R. Várkonyi: 1994b.

lation of the region was both from the religious and the ethnic point of view.

In the 16th and 17th centuries it had a population of about 800,000 to 1,000,000. Its society was made up of three layers. The top layer included the aristocracy and the county magnates; the middle one the burghers, craftsmen and members of the lesser nobility; while serfs, miners, daylabourers, carters, shepherds formed the lowest layer. Along the Southern and Eastern borderlines of the Principality the Hungarian tribe of the Székelys performed the duties of defending the frontiers, and they were granted collective liberties. The community of the "Saxons" possessing a self-government of their own was formed by groups coming from different German-speaking regions, and settled by the kings of Hungary in the 12th and 13th centuries. The Romanian shepherds practising transhumance on the slopes of the Carpathians were first mentioned in written documents in the 13th century. The Hungarians were Roman Catholics, Calvinists and Unitarians, the Saxons Lutherans and the Romanians were members of the Greek Orthodox Church. The peaceful co-existence of the population which followed a variety of religions and spoke three different languages was secured by a statute of religious tolerance. In 1568 the Diet of Transylvania was the first in Europe to enact the equal rights of Calvinists, Lutherans, Unitarians and Catholics, their freedom of worship and liberty of conscience.[6] The law securing freedom of worship continued to be in force as can be seen in the tolerant policies of successive Princes. Protection was extended to Jews, support was granted to Romanians belonging to the Greek Orthodox Church, Anabaptist refugees from Moravia, Polish Unitarians, Armenians, Gypsies, so-called "Greek merchants" from the Balkans and Hungarian Protestants driven out of the Kingdom of Hungary. All victims of all kinds of persecution found shelter in Transylvania.

Culturally the country was very open. Students returning from foreign, chiefly German, Dutch and English universities contributed to raising the academic standard of colleges, disseminating Cartesian, also Puritan views; they helped the development of printing and promoted literature. And Isaac Basire (1607–1676) who spent the last years of his life in Durham as canon, had been Professor of Divinity for several years at the Academy of Gyulafehérvár, the capital of the Principality of Transylvania.[7] Between 1657 and 1664 the Turkish wars did great damage and harm to Transylva-

---

[6] R. Várkonyi: 1993, pp. 99–122.
[7] Bitskey: 1993, Futaky: 1993, Gömöri: 1993 – all in: *Régi és új peregrináció*: 1993, II.

nia. Still, rapid economic consolidation was taking place at the same time. The country's incomes were increasing, chiefly from the salt trade, and the English Levant Company, as well as Greek trading companies were active in Transylvania.

When the international anti-Turkish alliance had been formed, and the troops of the Holy League were driving the Ottoman forces back to the Balkans, the Principality also entered the war of liberation. In the first few years of the war this demanded absolute secrecy in negotiating the matter, since Transylvania was still within the zone of Ottoman power. Among the Treaty Papers at the Public Record Office there is a document drawn up in the summer of 1686, stipulating that the Prince of Transylvania joins the anti-Turkish Christian coalition, helping the imperial forces with money and provisions, in return for which Emperor Leopold will guarantee that when a peace treaty is concluded with the Turks, the Principality of Transylvania will be included in it, and the Principality will maintain its independence.[8] However, by the time the Ottoman power was driven back to the Balkans, Transylvania had lost its statehood of one and a half century's standing, and its society had been deprived of its basic material possessions and spiritual assets.

The Hungarians were excluded from the Treaty of Carlowitz concluded by the Habsburg Emperor and the Turkish Sultan in 1699, and Transylvania was turned into a province of the Empire, brought under the control of the imperial central government.[9] Its Prince was interned in Vienna, the country was occupied by a strong imperial army, its trade was monopolized, and heavy taxes were imposed. The Habsburg government deprived the Protestants of their rightful liberties, including their freedom of worship, and confiscated a large part of their possessions, their churches, schools, hospitals, printing presses and foundations.[10] In Transylvania, as well as in the Kingdom of Hungary social and political tensions were gathering rapidly. Under the leadership of Prince Ferenc II Rákóczi (1676–1735) a substantial part of the population of Hungary and the Principality of

[8] PRO SP 103/18 fol. 440–441.

[9] In his reports Sir William Paget, Ambassador to Vienna from 1689 to 1692 and, later, Ambassador to Constantinople, participated as mediator in the protracted Habsburg–Turkish negotiations of the Peace Treaty of Carlowitz and discussed in detail the possibilities for making peace and the preservation of the Principality of Transylvania's independence. On completing his mission he visited Transylvania in 1702 and appears to have established close contacts with Miklós Bethlen, Chancellor of the Principality, and the Calvinists. Cf. British Library Lexington Papers, Add Ms 46 5286. – Gömöri: n.d., pp. 61–68. – R. Várkonyi: 1997, pp. 55–56.

[10] L. and M. Frey: 1998, pp. 432–441.

Transylvania entered the war, in the spring of 1703, siding with France, with the object of obtaining independent statehood which should be included in the articles of the peace treaty to be concluded by means of international mediation and with international guarantees.[11]

It is evident from the relevant, partly unpublished material that the English government had an excellent and rapid information service with regard to Central Europe. As early as the first weeks of 1703, Lord George Stepney sent extremely accurate and detailed reports to London on what was happening in Hungary and Transylvania, and the impressive quantity of documents proves a continuing, unflagging interest. The reason why could be obviously manifold.

First and foremost it could be the War of Spanish Succession. Very early, in June 1703, Lord Stepney prognosticated that the war in Hungary would divert a substantial part of the imperial forces from the Western theatre of war, and indeed, an imperial army, 20 to 50 thousand strong had to be kept in Hungary for a period of eight years.

Also, from the very beginning Stepney was fully aware of the significance of the legitimate Protestant claims to freedom of worship and religious tolerance, which excited the sympathy of the Protestant population of England. For example, when the imperial troops set the college of Nagyenyed on fire, and killed several inhabitants, students and professors who had sought shelter there, a collection was taken up all over England for the rebuilding of the college.[12]

Examining the reasons why English people showed so keen an interest we must not forget that the Habsburg government borrowed high sums of money from Dutch and English banks, offering the copper and quicksilver mines of Hungary and Transylvania as security for the larger part of the loans, and while and where guns were rattling there was not much hope that creditors could recover their money.

It is also evident from the reports of ambassadors that England never viewed the wars in Hungary and Transylvania as isolated, local affairs, but always in a larger context, with reference to other countries of the region, such as Poland, Prusssia, Sweden and Russia. The reports of Sir Robert Sutton, Ambassador to Constantinople made it possible for English government circles to keep track of Turkish policies, with special regard to their misgivings which never came true, that Rákóczi might ask help of the Turks.

[11] Hengelmüller: 1913. – R. Várkonyi: 1980b, pp. 313–336. Reprinted in this volume. – L. and M. Frey: 1982, 1989.
[12] Cf.: BL Ms, 816 m. 22. 105, pp. 122–127.

The most essential motive, however, must have been the idea of the balance of power. It was with the intention to maintain the European balance of power that England entered the war on the side of the Habsburg dynasty, at the price of immense material sacrifices. Daniel Defoe not only summed up the experiences of the past, but indicated a political tendency as well when he declared: "A just Balance of Power is the Life of Peace."[13]

All in all, it appeared to be evident that English politicians were also aware of the fact that the Eastern region of Central Europe was undergoing a dramatic change, and that without pacifying the restless, turbulent population of this area an enduring and stable balance of power could not be achieved, and a secure European peace could not be concluded.

In August 1704, almost simultaneously with the Duke of Marlborough's victory at Höchstädt-Blenheim which determined the further course of the War of the Spanish Succession, Rákóczi was elected Prince of Transylvania at the Diet of Gyulafehérvár.[14] In agreement with the government circles of the Hungarian Transylvanian Confederation and naming the former allies of the Principality, Rákóczi sent his envoys to the various European powers. It is reasonable to ask why Rákóczi insisted on the independence of the Principality of Transylvania. Nothing was wanting in Transylvania, but a good Prince – he said in his *Mémoires*. What is relevant to our topic is that in Rákóczi's political writings the idea of the European balance of power occurs very frequently, chiefly in connection with Transylvania. I am quoting a few extracts from his writings. "We assume that the powers now at war wish nothing so much as peace for their peoples after a bloody war like this, and since they are contemplating the future as well, they want to bring about a stable, lasting and indissoluble peace which succeeding generations may enjoy. However, no peace will be stable enough without the restoration of Transylvania." – "Whether the French or the Habsburgs will win this present war, the European balance of power will be upset."[15] He emphasized several times that the independent statehood of the Principality was the main security for maintaining the liberty of Hungary, and that Transylvania was an important

[13] Defoe: 1700.

[14] Stepney's opinion of this was to be the greatest obstacle to peace: Stepney to Duke to Marlborough, Vienna, Sept. 7, 1704. In: *Archivum Rákóczianum:* 1872–1877, II/I, pp. 419–420.

[15] A memorandum submitted to Charles XII of Sweden by Pál Ráday. Heilsberg, April 1704. In: *Ráday Iratok:* 1955–1961, I, p. 138.

factor in establishing the balance of power, and it was "the bulwark of Europe", in the sense that, together with Hungary, it could counterbalance the rise of a big power, which could threaten the freedom of the whole Europe. Minister Robert Harley (1661–1724) who wrote that "I should be very sorry if the Battle of Hocstet (!) should have the effect to let your court subside in their former insensibility, I hope they will take care of both Peace in Hungary, and war in Italy",[16] instructed Stepney several times, citing the Queen, to press the Imperial Court for peace negotiations, and emphasized that the Duke of Marlborough had similar instructions from the Queen. Incidentally, the Duke of Marlborough himself urged the Court of Vienna repeatedly to make peace with the Hungarians, and summoned Stepney to appear in person and inform him on the situation in Transylvania. In October 1704, preliminary steps were taken for peace negotiations, through English and Dutch mediation. There were shorter and longer breaks in the talks, and progress was very slow. It should be mentioned, however, that in 1705 the Diet of the Hungarian Confederation enacted the freedom of worship, and an Act was also passed to the effect that with the benefit of the country and public welfare in view, peace negotiations would be continued, with England, Holland and other powers acting as mediators.[17] In the summer of 1706 peace negotiations actually started, in Nagyszombat.

As one of the mediators, Stepney discussed matters with the leaders of the Hungarian Confederation several times, and was in permanent contact with Chancellor Johann Wenzel Graf von Wratislaw (1669–1712), head of the Imperial Committee and Prince Eugene of Savoy (1663–1736), head of the Council of War. He made himself thoroughly familiar with the standpoints of both parties. Also, he could see the faults of both. For instance, the Hungarians were overfond of display. The Imperial Court was not sincere in professing a desire for peace, seeing that the military position of Vienna had been consolidated by Marlborough's victories, and Emperor Joseph declared that he would sooner part with his shirt than with Transylvania. Stepney was in agreement with the Hungarian Confederation with regard to the conditions they offered. So much so that Graf von Wratislaw accused him of a pro-Hungarian bias. In spite of this Stepney persisted in his opinion that the Hungarians were justified in their demands

---

[16] Harley to Stepney, Whitehall, Sept. 1/12, 1704. In: *Archivum Rákóczianum*: 1872–1877, II/I, p. 429.

[17] Articuli Inclytorum regni Hungariae Statutuum et ordinum pro Libertate Confoederatorum in Generali Eorundem Conventu ad Oppidum Szécsény praeterito mense Septemb. Annos 1705. In: *A szécsényi országgyűlés 1705-ben*: 1995, p. 441.

when they wished to conclude an internationally guaranteed peace and to see that the freedom of worship and the independence of Transylvania were secured. In his opinion the military circles of the imperial court were to blame for the breakdown of the negotiations.

A letter from Warre, Secretary of State written to George Stepney contains a statement highly characteristic of the English opinion, namely that the breakdown of the negotiations, and the failure to bring about a peace with guarantees because of the militarist circles of the imperial court, would be detrimental to the common cause of Europe. "I cannot however but lament with you, for the private and publick Share you beare in this disappointment, out of your Zeale for the publick Good which cannot but Suffer in the Common Cause of Europe."[18]

At a session of the Council of State Queen Anne sharply rebuked Johann Graf von Gallas (1669–1719), Imperial Ambassador to London in public for the breakdown of the negotiations at Nagyszombat, and all the diplomat could say was: "Surely, the Emperor cannot renounce Transylvania". When the negotiations were broken off Rákóczi thanked the Queen for her help and the English mediation, and asked her to continue to give them her powerful royal support, and to remember them in the universal peace treaty ending the War of the Spanish Succession. Following this, Queen Anne repeatedly assured Rákóczi of her affection and good-will for the Hungarian nation. She was convinced of the nation's peaceful intentions and she would do her utmost to enable the Hungarians to make peace, since that was to be the first step towards concluding the universal peace ending the War of the Spanish Succession.[19] As is well known, the English–Habsburg relations were deteriorating, the national debt had risen dramatically, and the protracted war in which Habsburg participation was inadequate was felt to be an increasingly heavy burden on England. One of the conditions for ending the war was making peace between the Habsburgs and the Hungarians. By 1709 Rákóczi's resources had become almost completely exhausted, imperial troops had marched into Transylvania, and the plague was raging in the armies of both parties.

Marlborough assured Rákóczi as early as 1709 that the Queen, the cabinet and the States-General of Holland were invariably concerned about the cause of Hungary. On the occasion of the conference at The Hague he

[18] Richard Warre, under-Secretary of State to Stepney, Whitehall, July 30, 1706. In: *Archivum Rákóczianum: 1872–1877, II/III*, p. 175.

[19] Queen Anne to Ferenc II Rákóczi. Newmarket, Oct. 6, 1706. In: *Archivum Rákóczianum: 1872–1877, II/III*, pp. 253–254.

received Rákóczi's envoys who submitted a memorandum, to the effect that only an internationally guaranteed peace treaty and the independence of Transylvania could secure tranquillity in the country and the balance of power in Europe. Marlborough decided that the memorandum should be seen by Minister Boyle and the Queen.[20]

In August 1710 the senatorial session of the Hungarian Confederation declared that they would start negotiations, and Rákóczi sent a letter to Anne: "We are standing here, with the flickering candles of liberty", and asked her help.[21] The Queen immediately sent a royal note to Emperor Joseph persuading him to come to an agreement with the Hungarian Confederation on conditions which would benefit the common good. In the autumn Bolingbroke (1678–1751), British Secretary of State instructed Francis Palmes, British Ambassador to Vienna "to smooth the way for the Mediation of the Queen and States", since the Hungarians wished to make peace.[22] The Whig government, about to abdicate, then the Tory government coming into power made a series of decisions between September and December 1710 in the interest of a Habsburg–Hungarian agreement, sending Lord Peterborough (1658–1735) as special envoy to Vienna to promote an agreement with guarantees. When the negotiations started, Rákóczi and his governing body withdrew to Poland, firmly convinced that Peterborough's mission would be successful. In the same year Rákóczi had a pamphlet issued, proclaiming that Hungary and Transylvania had a right to peace. In its theoretical assumptions this is an international work, pivoting as it does on fundamental principles of Grotius. Drafted by Rákóczi's Roman Catholic diplomat, Provost Domokos Brenner, published in Latin and French, and printed in Poland under the title "Letter from a Polish Royal Counsellor", it expounded the view of Hungarian politicians concerning the European balance of power. This pamphlet expresses, most concisely, the still valid essential point in the seventeenth-century interpretations of the concept of peace, namely, that peace, even for smaller nations, can be secured only if it is internationally conceived, and achieved by the co-operation of different countries.[23]

However, by the time Peterborough arrived in Vienna, Prince Eugene had fended off Rákóczi's demand for peace with guarantees by bringing

---

[20] R. Várkonyi: 1983, pp. 202–211.

[21] Fiedler: 1855–1858, p. 126.

[22] St. John (Herny 1st Viscount Bolingbroke) to Palmes, Whitehall, Sept. 26, 1710. *Archivum Rákóczianum*: 1872–1874, II/III. 460.

[23] Lettre d'un Ministre de Pologne à un Seigneur de l'Empire sur les affaires de la Hongrie. 1710 (Mittau). App. Hung. 1506. Cf. Köpeczi: 1970, pp. 296–369.

about an agreement quickly concluded by Count János Pálffy (1663–1751), Commander-in-Chief of the Imperial Forces and General Sándor Károlyi (1669–1743), Commander-in-Chief of the forces of the Confederation. The essential point of this Habsburg–Hungarian agreement, the Peace of Szatmár (May 1, 1711), was that the subjects would return to their allegiance to the sovereign; the monarch and the aristocracy had arrived at a compromise. No foreign mediation was used, and the peace was concluded without international guarantees. The laws of the Confederation were annulled, the efforts to include the cause of Hungary and Transylvania in the universal peace failed; Transylvania was omitted from the Peace of Utrecht.

Europe was deprived of a country which had existed as an independent state for a century and a half, and Central Europe could no longer rely on the experience gained from the functioning of the Principality of Transylvania where religious and ethnic peace had been assured by the law. However, the fact remains that English policies had a large share in effecting the relatively favourable compromise that ended the war of insurrection carried on, from the very beginning, against great odds.

To sum up: knowing as we do now the English political efforts concerning Hungary and the Principality of Transylvania, we have to revise the earlier views on West European policies with regard to Central Europe. Formerly it was generally maintained that these policies were completely subordinated to the Bourbon–Habsburg conflict or contention for power, and it was France alone that gave support to the countries of this region, Poland, Hungary and Transylvania, as enemies of the Habsburgs. By now, however, it has become evident that England acknowledged the claims of Hungary and Transylvania to the freedom and independence of their states, sympathized with the Protestants who insisted on the freedom of worship and conscience, and England appreciated the demands of the population for free trade, culture in the vernacular, and peaceful progress.

Some years ago a Hungarian scholar, József Jankovics found a most peculiar document in the manuscript collection of the British Library. This is an album of hand-painted pictures, entitled *"The True and Exact Dresses and Fashions of all the Nations in Transylvania"*.[24] One thing is certain, that it dates from the turn of the seventeenth and eighteenth centuries. The pictures are of artistic value, with original captions in English, for example,

---

[24] BL Ms, Add MSS 5256. Cf. *Régi erdélyi viseletek:* 1990, 5, pp. 41–49.

"A summer dress of a Saxon Virgin", –"A Wallachian Woman", – "A Jew Merchant",– "Rascian", – "A Hungarian Nobleman", – "Hungarian Girl from Clausenburg", – they are the nations of Transylvania, whose future was decided during the decades between the Peace of Westphalia and the Peace of Utrecht. In Lord George Stepney's words: if Transylvania is deprived of its freedom, this small country lying in the Eastern border district of Central Europe, will be "given up to servitude and persecutions". His words proved to be Cassandra's prophecies.

"Ad pacem universalem".
The International Antecedents
of the Peace of Szatmár
℘ ℭ

When the peace conference of Gertruydenberg had been broken off, in the middle of 1710, Ferenc II Rákóczi, Ruling Prince of the Hungarian Confederation, sent a confidential message to his envoys in Constantinople, informing them that "negotiations will be continued secretly, for a universal peace treaty, and that we shall not be omitted from it has been confirmed recently not only by the French, but the Allies as well."[1] In his capacity as head of a state at war with the Habsburg power, he stated in his proclamation of August 19, 1710, intended for circulation all over the country, that "treating of the peace"[2] would begin soon, mediated and guaranteed by England and Holland, allies of the Emperor Joseph I, on the one hand, and Peter, Czar of Russia, ally of the Hungarian Confederation, on the other.

However, it was without the mediation and guarantee of foreign powers that the Hungarian and Transylvanian war was brought to an end in the spring of 1711, by the agreement known as the peace of Szatmár, signed by two generals, Count János Pálffy, Commander-in-Chief of the Imperial forces in Hungary, and Baron Sándor Károlyi whom Rákóczi had recently deprived of his post of Commander-in-Chief of the military forces of the Hungarian Confederation. Moreover, the case of Hungary and Transylvania was not included in the over-all European settlement, the peace treaties of Utrecht and Rastatt (1712–13, 1714), which terminated the War of the Spanish Succession.[3]

"'Ad Pacem Universalem'. (The international antecedents of the Peace of Szatmár)." *Studia Historica Acad. Sci. Hung.*, 145 (1980), pp. 77–80.

[1] Rákóczi to János Pápai and Ferenc Horváth, Sarud, July 29, 1710. In: *Archivum Rákóczianum*: 1872–1874, III, p. 296.

[2] MOL G. 19. Archives of Rákóczi's War of Independence, 11 3/d, fol. 153. OSZKK, Fol. Hung. 1389, Fasc. 14, fol. 42.

[3] Lukinich: 1925. – Kállay: 1962. – Benda: 1976, pp. 44–50. – Köpeczi: 1971, pp. 301 ff.

What diplomatic actions and political decisions were assessed in Rákóczi's proclamation of August 1710? And what attempts, if any, were made by the various European powers to achieve a new regulation between Hungary, Transylvania and the Habsburg dynasty at the end of the war which had been started in 1703 with the aim of establishing an independent Hungarian state? The present paper is intended to answer these questions.[4]

1. A PLAN FOR AN INTERNATIONAL PEACE CONFERENCE IN HUNGARY

On September 5, 1709, a distinguished Swedish delegation headed by Baron John Augustus Meijerfeldt, general and diplomat, communicated a proposal from King Charles XII to Rákóczi. Nursing his wounds at Turkish-controlled Bender in Bessarabia where he had taken refuge after the battle of Poltava, the King, trusting the Turkish pro-war party and the French aid, was planning to fill the ranks of his remaining Swedish forces with Turkish, Tartar, Cossack, Romanian and Polish troops, and to transfer his headquarters to Hungary, in order to invade Poland and carry on the war against Russia. He asked Rákóczi to grant him protection, permission to march across his territory, and support. In return he offered to guarantee that Hungary would be included in the over-all European peace treaty in due course.[5]

Rákóczi's state had close connections with the Swedes. At the very beginning of the insurrection Protestant, mainly Lutheran groups of the lower nobility and commoners interested in commercial and industrial enterprises had given their ardent support to Rákóczi's diplomatic plan to revive the Swedish alliance of the former Princes of Transylvania György I Rákóczi and György II Rákóczi.[6] Nevertheless, Ferenc II Rákóczi who himself had been elected Prince of Transylvania failed to achieve this, in spite of the fact that his first diplomat Chancellor Pál Ráday had got to the Swedish Court in 1704, following the path trodden by the Protestant lower no-

---

[4] Within the limited scope of this paper we do not intend to give an over-all survey of Rákóczi's diplomacy; only the essential common points of foreign relations are indicated.

[5] Ballagi: 1922, pp. 17–38. – Köpeczi: 1966, pp. 216–217. – *Archivum Rákóczianum*: 1978–1997, III/I, II. *Rákóczi Ferenc fejedelem Emlékiratai*, pp. 410–411.

[6] Szilágyi: 1873b, 1874. – Jonasson: n.d.

188

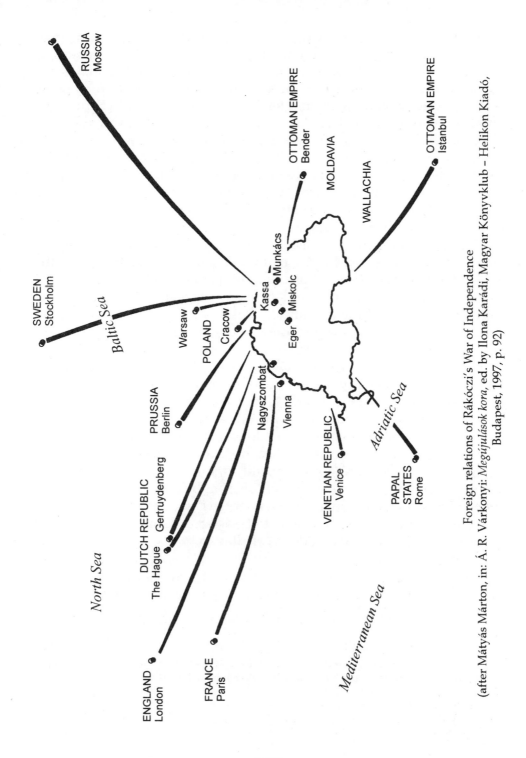

Foreign relations of Rákóczi's War of Independence
(after Mátyás Márton, in: Á. R. Várkonyi: *Megújulások kora*, ed. by Ilona Karádi, Magyar Könyvklub – Helikon Kiadó, Budapest, 1997, p. 92)

bility.[7] Though Charles XII had formed no alliance with the Hungarian and Transylvanian Confederation, he gave support to the Lutherans in the form of scholarships, school foundations and other aids under ecclesiastic auspices.[8] Connections with the Swedish King based on religious grounds were maintained even after Rákóczi had signed, in September 1707, the Warsaw Pact with the Czar Peter who was at war with the Swedes.[9] Under the unstable conditions of power which were characteristic of Europe at that time, it was by no means an exception that fundamental differences and a partial identity of interests should have brought about a heterogeneous system of international relations.[10]

The Swedish proposal was a great trial to the foreign policy of the Hungarian Confederation committed to both sides. General Meijerfeldt's delegation was accompanied by Bishop Daniel Krmann who had been with the Swedish King as envoy of the Hungarian Lutherans at the time of the battle of Poltava, and had escaped with him to Bender.[11] The French had an interest in Rákóczi's war of independence insofar as they had a common enemy. Spiritually and politically Rákóczi was deeply committed to Versailles, and a French-oriented foreign policy of long standing was supported chiefly by an important, though not too large, group of Roman Catholic noblemen and clerics.[12] Rákóczi wished to maintain formal relations with the Ottoman power, but he consistently refused to ask for Turkish military aid.[13] However, from 1708 on, quoting historical examples mainly, a considerable number of his officers and a few Transylvanian noblemen demanded more and more loudly that Constantinople should be asked for help. And since the French, traditionally pro-Swedish in their foreign policy, were considering the utility of involving the Sublime Porte in the war on their own side, the reports sent by László Kökényesdi de Vetés, Rákóczi's ambassador plenipotentiary to Paris, and those of the Marquis Des Alleurs, the French resident at Rákóczi's Court, were intended to support the Swedish and Turkish orientation.[14]

[7] *Ráday Iratok:* 1955–1961 – the mission of 1704: pp. 114–165; the mission of 1705: pp. 248–284. – Benda: 1960.

[8] Majláth: 1880. – Zsilinszky: 1898.

[9] Márki: 1913. – Perényi: 1956. – Váradi Sternberg: 1965. – Artamonov: 1978, pp. 527–531.

[10] Rákóczi's instructions for Nedeczky, Aug. 6, 1707. Nedeczky: 1891, p. 265.

[11] "Kermann Dániel Oroszországi útjának leírása 1708–1709" (A description of Dániel Kermann's trip to Russia, 1708–1709). In: Mencsik–Kluch (eds): 1894. – Szimonidesz: 1940. – Zsilinszky: 1899.

[12] Köpeczi: 1966.

[13] R. Kiss: 1906.

[14] Köpeczi: 1966, pp. 216–217.

However, in the autumn of 1709 Rákóczi was not simply allied to the Czar Peter, but he sent his representative Domokos Brenner, Abbot of Szepes, and Counsellor, to the conference of Marien-Veder, where Russia made an anti-Swedish pact with Poland, Denmark and Prussia.[15] Owing to Protestant relations, the Prussian Royal Court had also been a stable foothold for Hungarian foreign policy from an early date. Jablonski (grandson of Comenius who, in his time, had spent several years at Sárospatak), Court Chaplain to King Frederick who was on good terms with the Habsburg Emperor, maintained, through the medium of an ecclesiastic movement, also utilizing the official diplomatic organizations, an essentially illegal, but exceedingly well-functioning line of diplomatic communication between Rákóczi on the one hand, and influential Dutch and English groups on the other. Spiritual links were tightened through the workshops of early pietism. Professor Francke of Halle and Rákóczi's circle of leading government officials were in constant touch all the time. These multiple connections could be easily used as channels for diplomatic mediation.[16] Not only Ilgen, Minister of the Prussian King, and Baron Wolfgang von Schmettau and Baron Ezechiel von Spanheim, his ambassadors to The Hague and London, respectively, or the Dutch and English ambassadors to Berlin had supported Rákóczi's representatives for several years past, but Adam de Cardonnel, the Duke of Marlborough's all-powerful military and political secretary, the son of a French protestant, also tried to promote the success of Hungarian diplomacy.[17]

In England and Holland the activity of other Hungarian circles, cultural or religious in their origin, had to be taken into account. Both the group of Hungarians around Jakab Bogdány, Court Painter to Queen Anne, and the Hungarian students attending Dutch and English universities were instrumental in propagating information.[18]

Rákóczi's state found staunch supporters also in the Hungarian and Saxon students from Transylvania, taken to London by Paget, English ambassador to Constantinople who, on his return journey, had crossed Transylvania.[19] The Maritime Powers which carried the main burden of the war gave the Habsburg government huge loans on the mineral resources

[15] Benda: 1959. Concerning the alliance of Marien-Veder: Rákóczi to Ráday, Munkács, Dec. 5, 1709. In: *Archivum Rákóczianum:* 1872–1874, I/II, pp. 582–583.
[16] Szalay: 1870, pp. 80–81. – Fabiny: 1976, p. 1101.
[17] Bittner–Gross: 1936. – Churchill: 1968, p. 237. – Kvacsala: 1955.
[18] Országh: 1937. – Esze: 1964. – Jankovics: 1972, pp. 142–143. – Jankovics: 1973.
[19] Trócsányi: 1944. – Tappe: 1960, pp. 534–536.

of Hungary and Transylvania, consequently the interest English and Dutch ecclesiastic circles took in Hungary was becoming saturated with the financial interests of groups of merchants and contractors. As instructed by their respective governments, Lord George Stepney and Jacob Jan Hamel-Bruyninx, the English and Dutch ambassadors to Vienna, had been trying for several years, beginning with 1704, to bring about an agreement between the Habsburg Emperor and the Hungarians. They managed to get a thorough insight into the affairs of Hungary; moreover, they gradually came to understand why people in arms in Hungary and Transylvania, who spoke different languages and belonged to different denominations and social layers, were demanding the right of the state to self-determination. To be sure, there were contrary opinions also, e.g. that of Defoe who wished to deflate the pro-Hungarian enthusiasm of those who sympathized with the Hungarians on religious grounds. As early as 1704, he declared in the *Review* that what was going on in Hungary was not a war of religion, but a war of independence, waged against England's ally, the Emperor, who had defended Europe against the Turks. Though in his articles Defoe criticized Rákóczi's policy, suggesting that it was likely to bring back the Turkish threat to Europe, he examined the Hungarian affairs in detail and in their different aspects, and the emotional response evoked in the public was not wholly hostile. As a result of a variety of causes the position, then, was that there were, even in the English government, people who, desiring to bring about a peace treaty as soon as possible, recognized Rákóczi's state, at least indirectly, and thought that his demand of autonomy as understood at that time was reasonable. The Dutch States-General were also for a settlement with Rákóczi as head of a recognized state, and were willing to act as official mediators. As a result of this, the Habsburg government agreed in 1705 that England and Holland should act as mediators in the peace talks with the Hungarian Confederation recognized as a body politic, and in keeping with the internationally accepted diplomatic rules. Although the talks were broken off in the summer of 1706, the Hungarian Confederation continued to keep in close touch with influential Prussian, English and Dutch political groups.[20] The cultural and commercial relations established by the treaty of Westminster, which Gábor Bethlen had concluded between England and Transylvania long before, were still profitable.

---

[20] *Archivum Rákóczianum II. Angol diplomácia iratok II. Rákóczi Ferenc korára:* I–III, 1872–1877. – *Weensche gezantschapsberichten van 1670 tot 1720:* 1934. Here I express my gratitude to Dr. Károly Körpüly who helped me with the translation of passages from this work in

Considering the diplomatic aspect of the position in which the Hungarian Confederation was to make a decision in the autumn of 1709, it should be noted that, after the Warsaw Pact, Russia was taking a new political line. Since the French Court showed little interest in the alliance offered by the Czar Peter, he sought to join the Grand Alliance, hoping that by doing so he could assert his legitimate claim to a larger share in controlling European politics. The Maritime Powers, aware of the increasingly disadvantageous economic consequences of the war, tended to relax their traditionally rigid policy of isolationism, and thinking of Russian sail-cloth, tar, flax and other commodities, they were considering the possibility of making peace without any more delay.[21]

The aggressive plan of the King of Sweden was such as concerned all European powers. If Charles XII could achieve what he wanted the war would be prolonged, the focus of military activity would be transferred to the area of Central and East-Europe, and the end of the nine years' struggle involving practically all European countries, big and small, a struggle rightly called a "world war" in recent studies, would be pushed far into the unpredictable future.

Early in the autumn of 1709, the position of Rákóczi's state, whether considered from within or without, could have easily supplied weighty arguments in favour of accepting the Swedish plan. In Transylvania the Imperial forces had come into power; in the North-West of Hungary the troops of the Emperor Joseph I had captured the district of the mining towns, a district fundamentally important for the Hungarian Confederation, economically as well as socially. Also, the Habsburg government had scored a series of splendid diplomatic successes. They had managed to get Stepney, the pro-Hungarian English ambassador to Vienna recalled by his government, and, neutralizing Prussian support, they had refused the armistice offered by the Hungarian Confederation in the autumn of 1708. They had prevented Rákóczi's diplomatic manoeuvres, getting the Pope to declare openly for the Emperor. Profiting from the new political line of Russia, they were doing their utmost to isolate the Hungarian Confederation also from East Europe, winning over for that purpose the Dutch

Dutch. – Cseh: 1893. – Kovács: 1908. – Kr[opf]: 1907, pp. 269–270. – Márki: 1922–1923. – Szekfű: 1929 (1983), p. 219. – Gál: 1976. – The offer of mediation made by the English Queen and the Dutch States-General was read out at the diet of Szécsény. See Köpeczi–R. Várkonyi: 1973, p. 145. – The relevant articles of the *Weekly Review* are included in Köpeczi: 1970, pp. 75–187.
    [21] Artamonov: 1978, p. 529.

ambassador in Vienna. When in the summer of 1709, complying with the terms of the first Hague peace conference, Rákóczi accepted the English decision that prior to an overall European peace treaty an agreement should be concluded between the Habsburg power and the Hungarians, and he wrote letters to Count Lamberg, the Emperor's First Minister, and the Dutch ambassador, Hamel-Bruyninx, the latter, forgetting the earlier decision of his government, adopted the view of the Imperial Court, according to which rebels rising against the crowned sovereign could ask for pardon only and not claim, as a body politic, an international peace treaty mediated and guaranteed by foreign powers. As is clear from the bitter tone of Rákóczi's letters and the statements made by his leading government officials about that time, they knew very well that the considerable political capital they had managed to amass gradually with the Maritime Powers was suddenly dwindling, and that they had to reckon with the dangers of political isolation. On the other hand, the Turkish envoy brought a message for Rákóczi from the Sublime Porte early in 1709, with a tentative offer of help. Since Charles XII continued, even after Poltava, to be a potentially important military factor, the French reckoned with him by all means. In a report of June 4, 1709 Kökényesdi informed the politicians of the Hungarian Confederation that the French Foreign Minister Torcy, returning from the Hague conference in a state of great agitation, answered his question whether there was to be peace or war, saying "la guerre, Monsieur ...". And since the French had made attempts earlier to involve the Turks in the war on their own side, both Kökényesdi and the Marquis Des Alleurs suggested, following the definite instructions of Louis XIV, that Rákóczi and his cabinet should accept the Swedish plan.[22]

Essentially it was a question of war or peace that Rákóczi and his leading politicians had to consider if they wished to give an adequate answer to Charles XII, and before taking their decision they studied and discussed it carefully at several meetings between September 5 and October 27, 1709. Why did they decline the plan of Charles XII who was intent on lighting new fires of war? Why did they seek to neutralize the Swedish initiative, taking the diplomatic steps to be outlined below, implicitly refusing the Turkish offer of help as well? Moreover, why did they reject the French

---

[22] Kökényesdi's report, Paris, June 4, 1709, in: Fiedler: 1855–1858, I, p. 133. As early as the end of 1705 and the beginning of 1706 Torcy made secret peace proposals, offering Marlborough two million livres provided that the latter was ready to make peace. Churchill: 1968, pp. 498–499. The proposals of Kökényesdi and Des Alleurs and the instructions of Louis XIV are included in Köpeczi: 1966, pp. 216–217, 262. Torcy's opinion of the Hague peace conference of 1709 is quoted in Márki: 1910, pp. 26–27.

proposal? Within the narrow scope of this paper it is impossible to give a thorough analysis of the underlying social and political causes. What can be indicated is that Rákóczi and his politicians examined the situation of the country very carefully. They took into account the military superiority of the Imperial forces, the secret attempts of the French to make peace, also the famine and plague following in the wake of the bad harvest of the year 1708/1709, when they said that "fixing their eyes on the things to come", they wished to make an end to the clatter of arms by concluding a good peace.[23]

Rákóczi informed the Czar of Meijerfeldt's errand without delay, suggesting that "if his Majesty had no objection, *we should send somebody to the Swedish King*, to sound him *whether he would not be inclined to make peace*". These lines were written in Munkács castle, Rákóczi's residence in North-East-Hungary, on September 5, that is, immediately after the Swedish delegation had been received, and were included in the instructions sent to Councillor Sándor Nedeczky, the Hungarian envoy delegated to the Russian Foreign Minister Golovkin. The words here quoted in italics were written in a cipher in the letter of instructions which informed the Russian Court of news from the Sublime Porte, in the spirit of co-operation inherent in the Warsaw Pact. There was, however, a special purpose of all this. While there was the reassuring information, based on the report of Gáspár Pápay, Hungarian resident in Constantinople, that the Czar did not have to reckon with the threat of an immediate Turkish attack, it was suggested that it would be advisable for him to send someone to the Sublime Porte directly, to counteract the plan of a Swedish attack.[24]

The scheme of a Swedish–Russian peace was something that Rákóczi and his inner circle of leading politicians had been contemplating before. In the spring of 1709 they reckoned with the consequences of the Hague conference, and after Poltava they were convinced that the war had reached a stage in which preparations should be made for an over-all peace. Earlier he had suggested to the Czar to make peace through the mediation of the French. Now he came back to this idea, specially emphasizing that a Swedish–Russian peace treaty mediated by the French would make it possible for the Czar to emerge as a leading figure on the European stage of international politics. It would be possible and, as Rákóczi thought, ad-

---

[23] Ráday's draft and Rákóczi's instructions. Oct. 1709. Ráday Levéltár, Ráday Pál iratai (Papers of Pál Ráday) IV d/2–5, Nos 1–2, fol. 1–12.

[24] Rákóczi's instructions for Nedeczky, Munkács, Sept. 5, 1709. In: *Archivum Rákóczianum:* 1872–1874, I/II, p. 537.

visable, too, for Peter I to take on himself the work of promoting an over-all peace.[25]

In terms of the current practice of handling foreign affairs Rákóczi's proposal of September 5 was nothing more than a tentative offer made largely to sound the Czar. Before it could take a more definite form and could be proposed through the regular diplomatic channels, a number of difficulties had to be overcome. It was necessary to know what the Czar would reply, considering that by that time the Swedish King had rejected two earlier peace offers made by him. In Poland the pro-Swedish King Stanislaus Leszczynski was opposed by the increasing party of Augustus II, King of Saxony, who was calling the Polish people to arms against the Swedes, which meant that the anti-Swedish schemes hatching in Poland had also to be reckoned with, particularly at a time when the Czar's troops were pursuing the routed Swedish army on Polish soil.[26] At the same time it was the party of pro-French Polish noblemen that had embraced the cause of the Hungarian Confederation from the very beginning. Moreover, there was the greatest question: was the French court going to change its attitude, as a result of the new situation in East-Europe?

In September 1709, Polish, Hungarian and Russian couriers were arriving at Munkács, one after the other.[27] Rákóczi ordered Domokos Brenner, his diplomat mediating French–Russian relations, to go from Dantzig to Lublin, since the Czar was expected to arrive there. On Sunday, September 15, the Hungarian ambassador Sándor Nedeczky gave a sumptuous banquet in Lublin, in honour of the Czar. The lady sitting at the head of the table was Rákóczi's wife, Princess Charlotte Amelia of Hessen-Rheinfels who, using her family connections, was performing diplomatic tasks in Poland. Seated on her left was the Czar, and next to him Sieniawska, agent of the pro-French Polish party, wife of the Great Hetman. Those present included some of the most important leading figures of Russia, such as Prince Dolgorukij, First Minister, Prince Golovkin, Counsellor, in charge of foreign affairs, General Safirov, the Czar's confident, and, what is particularly important, Mentchikov, an expert on French affairs.[28]

---

[25] Perényi: 1964. – Markó: 1970. – Rákóczi's instructions for Nedeczky, Munkács, Sept. 5, 1709. In: *Archivum Rákóczianum: 1872–1874*, I/II, p. 536.

[26] The open letter of Augustus II, King of Poland, against Charles XII, King of Sweden, Dresden, Aug. 8, 1709, MOL P 512. Papers of the Nedeczky family, packet no. 7, pall: 30, fol. 1–8. Cf. Bercsényi to Rákóczi, Rahó, Sept. 20, 1709. In: *Archivum Rákóczianum: 1872–1877*, III, pp. 337, 339.

[27] Extract from Sándor Nedeczky's unpublished diary, MTAKKt Ms 4958.

[28] Thaly: 1866, p. 217.

On October 12, following the "business dinner" of Lublin, Rákóczi had talks with Sieniawska in Zvadka on the Polish –Hungarian border, in the presence of the French representative Des Alleurs and Miklós Bercsényi, Generalissimo and Rákóczi's Deputy.[29] Later on Rákóczi held an important council at Huszt, not very far from Munkács. This council had been arranged by Chancellor Pál Ráday and it had two aims. One was to inform the various political groups about the steps taken by the Hungarian and Transylvanian Confederation in the field of foreign affairs, and the other was to discuss the plan of the Swedish–Russian peace, duly considering all of its possible consequences, and to draft accordingly the instructions for the envoys to be sent to Prussian, English and Dutch government circles.[30]

It is reasonable to ask how far the English and Dutch governments could be concerned in the Swedish–Russian peace, and what interest the Prussian Court could have in it. At that time it was well known all over Europe that Marlborough, the triumphant general of the War of the Spanish Succession, was very uneasy about the Swedish King. Now he could have felt that he was right in his misgivings which he had expressed to Heinsius, the Grand Pensionary of the Dutch Council of State as early as 1706, saying that this inscrutable and unpredictable monarch was going to cause a great deal of trouble in Europe.[31] If the Swedish King should let the invading Turks loose on the countries about to make peace, this would upset their calculations. Europe could not as yet estimate the actual power of Constantinople, and the Prussian Court was as much afraid of Turkish interference, as it was anxious for the Swedes, sharing their Protestant interests.

It is clear that in the international situation, as things stood after Poltava, Rákóczi judged the momentary chances correctly. However, it could be asked whether he had the power and the possibility to turn the situation to the advantage of Hungary. For it was only with the purpose of ending the war in Hungary as soon as possible that he insisted on bringing about the Swedish–Russian peace, and that he wanted to secure for it the mediation of France. The settlement of the Hungarian affairs he contemplated should have been an international agreement between the Habsburg and

[29] *Ibid.*, p. 219.
[30] Márki: 1910, III, pp. 58–59.
[31] "I am very much afraid, that this march of the Sweeds [*sic!*] into Saxe will create a great deal of trouble ... Whenever the States of England write to the King of Sweden, there must be care taken that there be no threats in the letter, for the King of Sweden is of a very particular humor." Quoted in Churchill: 1968, pp. 549–550.

the Hungarian states, mediated and guaranteed by England, Holland and Russia, and included in the over-all European peace treaty.

The Council of Huszt was attended by delegates of different factions of the Hungarian and Transylvanian Confederation representing a variety of opinions with regard to foreign affairs: noblemen and commoners who were members of the Senate, Transylvanian councillors, and the Marquis Des Alleurs. No evidence has been produced so far to prove whether Des Alleurs and the pro-Turkish Transylvanian faction were still supporting the plan of a Swedish attack. What is, however, unquestionable, is that the new, more subtle diplomatic policy was perfectly in keeping with the peculiar interests of those backing Ráday, i.e. Protestant members of the lower nobility, and Lutheran entrepreneurs who all supported the idea of a strong central power. They deemed it advisable to maintain relations both with the Czar and the Swedish King; at the same time they endeavoured to bring Rákóczi's state into closer contact with Holland, England and the Prussian Court as well. This group included a young diplomat called János Mihály Klement, formerly a student at the Universities of Frankfurt an der Oder and Halle, who was also present at the council of Huszt. Having been sent on an errand to Berlin, London and The Hague in the spring of 1709, he could speak from experience concerning the political attitude of the Maritime Powers towards Hungary.[32]

Considering the logical order of the events alone, there can be no doubt that the Council of Huszt held between October 14 and 26, 1709, decided on the course of a co-ordinated diplomatic action with regard to the relations of Hungary and Transylvania with several European powers. Domokos Brenner was ordered in the capacity of envoy extraordinary to leave Warsaw immediately and go to the Czar.[33] A courier was dispatched with Rákóczi's instructions dated October 21, for Kökényesdi, his resident in France, and Count Henrik János Tournon, his agent in Venice who was a mediator of French connections and an expert on Savoy.[34]

On October 24 Klement left, in the company of Ádám Mányoki, Rákóczi's Court Painter, for Prussia, England and Holland. Apart from

[32] Szalay: 1870, pp. 4–5. – *Ráday Iratok:* 1955–1961, II, pp. 52–53 and 472–473. – Klement's Memorandum, in Fiedler: 1855–1858, II, pp. 6–7.

[33] Bercsényi's draft of the intstructions for Brenner, Verecke, Oct. 14, 1709. In: *Archivum Rákóczianum:* 1875–1882, II/VIII, pp. 137–144. Rákóczi's letter to the Czar and his credentials and instructions for Brenner, Verecke, Oct. 14, 1709. In: *Archivum Rákóczianum:* 1872–1874, I/II, pp. 557–559, and Huszt, Oct. 21, 1709. In: Fiedler: 1871, pp. 487–488.

[34] Rákóczi to Kökényesdi and Tournon, Huszt, Oct. 21, 1709; both included in Fiedler: 1871, pp. 486–489. – For the significance of Savoy in the War of the Spanish Succession, see Churchill: 1968, pp. 547–548.

the instructions concerning his own errand, he was carrying instructions and propaganda material for János Körtvélyessy and István Dobozi jr., who had set out in the summer of 1709 to make a round of the Protestant countries on behalf of the Calvinists and Lutherans of Hungary and Transylvania.[35] Finally, at the end of October 1709, Chancellor Pál Ráday left for Bender on a most delicate mission. Namely, he was to sound the Swedish King and see how he responded to the project of peace Rákóczi was offering instead of armed support; also, he was to find out what line of conduct the Sublime Porte was taking towards Sweden, and he was to make the necessary preparations for the conceptual and logical pattern underlying Rákóczi's co-ordinated diplomatic action.[36]

Brenner's task was to tell the Czar that, if he did not object to French mediation, Rákóczi would do his utmost to secure it. The peace with Sweden concluded in this manner would serve as a basis of a Russian–French alliance planned already earlier which, in its turn, would make it possible for Russia not only to participate in bringing about an over-all European peace treaty, but also to be included in it. The Warsaw Pact of 1707 stipulated not only that the signatory parties would give each other armed assistance, but also that neither of them would conclude a peace treaty injurious to the interests of the other. While offering to obtain French mediation in order to promote a Swedish–Russian peace, Rákóczi asked of the Czar no more than that he should act as a mediator and guarantor in the peace negotiations between the Habsburg government and the Hungarians.[37]

What Klement was to achieve was that Holland and England should take the initiative again and, together with Prussia, should insist on bringing about a Habsburg–Hungarian agreement which was to be included in the over-all European peace treaty, and that they should accept Russia as another mediator. As Rákóczi declared in letters separately written to Marlborough and Hamel-Bruyninx, he was willing to make peace on fair conditions. Klement, too, was to dwell on this point, laying due emphasis on it. At the same time he was to make it clear that if they were not granted the necessary diplomatic assistance they had no alternative but to throw themselves into the arms of the Turks.[38] Since a pro-Turkish policy had

[35] Esze: 1961. – *Ráday Iratok:* 1955–1961, II, pp. 472–473. – Hopp: 1973, p. 734.

[36] Ráday's draft of a letter to Körtvélyessy, Huszt, Oct. 21, 1709, Ráday Levéltár, Ráday Pál iratai d/2-17-32. – Benda: 1954. – Negotiatio Benderiana Ráday Levéltár, Ráday Pál iratai IV-d/2-5.

[37] *Archivum Rákóczianum:* 1875–1882, II/VIII, pp. 140, 142.

[38] Instructio pro Klement... Munkács, Oct. 8, 1709, Fiedler: 1855–1858, II, pp. 70–73. –

never been a serious consideration with Rákóczi, this argument was merely a trick of diplomacy, in fact a threat, or, more bluntly speaking, blackmail. Without reckoning with such moves which were generally characteristic of the diplomacy of the age, it would be impossible to understand the instructions sent to Versailles.

Kökényesdi was to make the French Court unmistakably understand that the Hungarian Confederation was in a critical situation. He was instructed not to be sparing of reproaches. All this was meant to bring the essential points into focus. On the evidence of Poltava it was now clear that the Marquis Bonnac, the French ambassador to Poland, and the Marquis Des Alleurs had taken a one-sided view of the King's interests when they had refused the advances made by Russia. With a view to establishing more favourable relations with Russia, it was to be desired that Louis XIV should, at long last, send an efficient ambassador to the Czar's Court. Last but not least Kökényesdi was to see that the French did not fail or forget to put the case of Hungary and Transylvania on the agenda of the negotiations preliminary to concluding an over-all peace treaty.[39]

In all the instructions the central idea, then, was that the war in Hungary should be ended by a treaty between the Habsburg state and the Hungarian state guaranteed by foreign powers, and that this settlement should be included in the over-all European peace treaty. French mediation would link Russian–Swedish negotiations with the War of the Spanish Succession, and with Russia acting as a mediator beside Prussia, England and Holland, the Hungarian–Habsburg settlement would be drawn into the sphere of interest of the Northern conflict. Since France had promised earlier to include Hungary and Transylvania in the "universal peace", a similar commitment of Russia and the Maritime Powers would give great assurance to all the social layers intent on preserving in Hungary and Transylvania the achievements of the war and those of organizing the state. The plan of ending the war as soon as possible, through the mediation of and with a guarantee from France, Russia, England and Holland, was as much approved by the Roman Catholic members of the aristocracy and lower nobility as by the group standing for the idea of a central power and representing the interests of the Protestant members of the lower nobility, the Protestant commoners and the armed forces, a body of people who had already obtained considerable support from powerful English,

---

Rákóczi to Hamel-Bruyninx, Munkács, Nov. 2, 1709, and to Klement, in: Fiedler: 1855–1858, II, pp. 73–75. – Rákóczi to Marlborough, Huszt, Oct. 20, 1709, in: Fiedler: 1871, p. 483.
[39] Rákóczi's instructions for Kökényesdi, Huszt, Oct. 21, 1709, in: Fiedler: 1871, pp. 486–487.

Swedish, Prussian and Dutch circles in their efforts to achieve cultural autonomy in the spirit of toleration in religious matters. This was a large-scale scheme. It reflected Rákóczi's opinion expressed in a letter to Tournon to the effect that the Hungarian Confederation was in a favourable position as far as foreign affairs were concerned.

Were Rákóczi and his leading politicians realistic in judging their prospects in the field of foreign affairs favourable in spite of the well-known circumstances? Ambassadors' reports generally present facts in more rosy colours than they really are. The Hungarians did not sufficiently reckon with French politics, whereas the cardinal question of the whole undertaking was whether Versailles was willing to act as mediator.[40] In October 1709 there were still a great number of uncertain points. The geographical distance between Bender, Moscow, Warsaw, Danzig, Constantinople, Berlin, The Hague, London and Versailles was very great. This could, in fact, appear enormous, considering the time-consuming and expensive diplomatic technique of the period, and the very limited scope of official activity and the scanty financial means of the Hungarian envoys. It was doubtful whether the very first move could be made, that is, whether it was possible to bring about a Russian–Swedish settlement through French mediation. The over-all peace treaty to end the War of the Spanish Succession was as yet in the distant future. And between the first move and the last there was a series of very difficult questions. How was the French Court going to decide? What would be the issue of the struggle between the war and peace parties at the Sublime Porte? Was there a change to get the English and Dutch mediation and guarantee accepted in Vienna?

In the autumn of 1709 there was a favourable turn in French politics. Surely, the reason why Versailles changed its attitude towards the Swedish-Russian question was the defeat at Malplaquet, not Rákóczi's proposal.[41] While trying to initiate peace talks with the English and Dutch governments, France was taking a new line of conduct in Eastern Europe as well, as was shown by the facts that Bonnac was relieved of his office, and Des Alleurs was transferred from Hungary to Constantinople. Before taking up his new post, however, he was to go to Bender where the Court of the Swedish King was at the time.[42] But he was not to leave before receiving a favourable answer from Ráday.

---

[40] Rákóczi to Tournon, Huszt, Oct. 21, 1709. In: Fiedler: 1871, pp. 488–489.
[41] For Des Alleurs's dismissal and appointment to Constantinople, see the letters of Louis XIV to Rákóczi and Des Alleurs, Nov. 7, 1709, quoted in Köpeczi: 1966, pp. 217, 231.
[42] Rákóczi's letter, Dec. 4, 1709. In: *Archivum Rákóczianum:* 1872–1874, I/II, p. 575.

As all envoys going on delicate errands, Ráday had his real task disguised. The ostensible aim of his mission was to intervene with the Serdar, the Turkish representative in Bender, on behalf of the Transylvanian troops that had been driven to Moldavia. In Rákóczi's name he was to ask that they should be exempted from taxation, that their right to self-government should be recognized, and that they should not be handed over to foreign powers. While this could sound reassuringly to the Transylvanian politicians sheltering in Hungary, it was at the same time a most plausible pretext for Ráday's real task.

Ráday met with great difficulties in performing his actual task. Even as late as December 19, he informed Rákóczi that the Swedish King was carrying on secret negotiations with the Sublime Porte. It took some time before he managed to forward the proposal to the King, through State Secretary Müllern. The answer was far from encouraging. The King thought highly of Rákóczi; he deemed his wish to be included in an overall peace reasonable, and was immediately sending instructions for his ambassador to England accordingly, but as to making peace with the Czar, he did not think it feasible. Meanwhile Rákóczi, in his official capacity of Prince of Transylvania, had sent credentials to Ráday, but the Swedish King was as yet not inclined to recognize him as Prince of Transylvania.[43]

At the same time Rákóczi's residents at the Sublime Porte, and his envoy extraordinary János Pápai, carrying an alternative proposal first to the pashas of the border regions, then to Constantinople, failed to find out the Sultan's intentions.[44] The possibility of a Habsburg counter-move had not been reckoned with either. Without formally accepting Russian mediation, the Emperor Joseph used the Czar's ambassador to Vienna, who set out for Rákóczi's camp on November 13, 1709, to carry his proposal for peace talks, but his conditions were unacceptable. As to the Russian Court, there the whole scheme very nearly collapsed, because Rákóczi had taken into his service remains of the Swedish and Polish armies headed by Potocki, Palatine of Kiev.[45]

However, early in February 1710 Ráday returned with favourable news. It appeared that the Turks had renewed the Russian peace, and the time

[43] Instructions for Ráday, Oct. 1709; his letters to Rákóczi. Bender, Dec. 9, 1709, and Suchova, Jan. 13, 1710, Ráday Levéltár, Ráday Pál iratai IV d/2–5, Nos 1, 9, 16. Rákóczi to Charles XII, Szentmártonkáta, Jan. 18, 1710. In: Fiedler: 1871, p. 496. Bercsényi to Ráday, Kassa, Jan. 19, 1710, and Bercsényi to Nedeczky, Ungvár, Feb. 14, 1710. In: *Archivum Rákóczianum*: 1875–1882, II/VIII, pp. 144–145, 184. Cf. Ráday: 1866, p. 404.

[44] Bercsényi to Nedeczky, Jan. 31, 1710. In: *Archivum Rákóczianum*: 1875–1882, II/VIII, p. 169. Rákóczi to Bercsényi, Feb. 10, 1710. In: *Archivum Rákóczianum*: 1872–1874, III, p. 19.

[45] Köpeczi: 1966, p. 217.

seemed to have come for the "solemnis" declaration of the French mediation of peace. On February 14, 1710, Bercsényi, commissioned by Rákóczi to conduct diplomatic affairs with Russia, could inform Nedeczky with no small satisfaction that the French King "was resolved (as never before) to announce through his solemnly authorized envoy, his readiness to mediate a peace between the Swedish King and His Majesty the Czar". Nedeczky was instructed to pay his respects to Foreign Minister Golovkin and remind him of all that Bercsényi had told him long before, "occasione secretioris tractatus", with regard to the ways of increasing the Czar's dignity and honour. "Now all these ways will be open to him, and the French will enter into a bond with him, cum securitate pacis universalis."[46]

At the beginning of 1710 Ráday was again sent to Moldavia, ostensibly to pay his respects to the new voivode, in reality, to be on the spot, ready to go to Des Alleurs as soon as the Swedish King accepted Rákóczi's offer of mediation besides that of the French. On an equally secret errand Péter Dániel, Rákóczi's trusted man, was staying at Jassy, in order to gain the goodwill of the Romanian voivodes, to keep an eye on the Turks, and to inform Rákóczi systematically.[47]

At the middle of April 1710 Des Alleurs sent word to Rákóczi concerning the Swedish King's official line of conduct, to the effect that the King was prepared to make peace, to send his representatives to the negotiations, and that, recognizing the Czar's title of Emperor, he was going to insist that Russia should be included in the over-all peace treaty.[48]

Where the peace talks should be held was a moot point. Warsaw, Kamenicze, Bender and Moscow were proposed. However, Rákóczi suggested to Ráday, through Bercsényi, as early as the spring of 1710 that, in his opinion, the peace talks ought to be held in Hungary as the most suitable place, since the Swedish King might be reluctant to send his representatives either to Warsaw or to Moscow, while the Czar might object to

---

[46] *Archivum Rákóczianum:* 1875–1882, II/VIII, pp. 179, 182–183, 186. Cf. Bercsényi's draft of a letter to Des Alleurs, Kassa, March 4, 1710, *ibid.*, p. 198. Rákóczi to Louis XIV, Jászberény, Feb. 24, 1710, in: Fiedler: 1871, p. 496. The Hungarian representative accompanying Des Alleurs was Canon Joseph Fray. Josephus F[ray] to Rákóczi, Kassa, April 19, 1710, MOL G 15, Fasc. 203, fol. 35–36.

[47] *Archivum Rákóczianum:* 1875–1882, II/VIII, pp. 199–200.

[48] Bercsényi's letter to Golovkin, Kassa, April 26, 1710. In: *Archivum Rákóczianum:* 1875–1882, II/VIII, pp. 245–248. Cf. Fiedler: 1855–1858, II, p. 610. Josephus F[ray] to Rákóczi, Kassa, April 19, 1710, MOL G 15, Fasc. 203, fol. 35–36. Bercsényi to Nedeczky, Kassa, April 25, 1710. In: *Archivum Rákóczianum:* 1875–1882, II/VIII, p. 241. Bercsényi to Sieniawska, Kassa, April 25, 1710, *ibid.*, pp. 244–245.

Bender; and Kamenicze, situated on Turkish-controlled territory, was unsuitable, because the Sublime Porte would hinder rather than promote the success of the talks. In his capacity as Prince of Transylvania, Rákóczi would participate in the talks as a mediator. A few months later, when Bercsényi was obliged to repeat in detail his instructions given in April 1710, he emphasized that "the peace could be treated of here; the mediator, that is to say, France and the two powers could concur most conveniently ad lucrum tertium sine praejudicione partis alterutrius". In the opinion of Hungarian politicians the preparations for the Swedish–Russian negotiations were important with regard to the over-all European peace and the Hungarian peace alike. In the summer of 1710 Bercsényi wrote that "by concluding this peace treaty His Majesty the Czar would not only retain all·the glory of his fighting against the Swedes, but, by entering into a good and constant bond with the French King, he would both have his share in the universal peace and secure his title of Emperor, and his glory and memory in his capacity as the true protector of Hungary would live for ever".[49]

The negotiations were, however, making no progress between April and the end of July 1710. Rákóczi and his circle believed that the Czar's reply was delayed by a deplorable blunder of Hungarian diplomacy. Namely, Des Alleurs gave his letter for the Czar to Canon József Fray, the Hungarian representative in his company, but contrary to Rákóczi's orders, the latter went to Sieniawska first, and then to King Augustus.[50] It is, however, probable that the reason why the French King was in no hurry to send his envoy to the Czar concerning the Swedish–Russian peace talks was the same as made the Czar adopt an expectant attitude, i.e. that a peace conference had begun in March 1710 at Gertruydenberg, near The Hague. This meant that both the plan of a Swedish–Russian peace mediated by the French, and the question of settling affairs between the Habsburg Court and the Hungarians were to be considered in a larger, international context.

[49] Bercsényi to Ráday [March 10, 1710?], and Bercsényi to Nedeczky, Hernádnémeti, Aug. 11, 1710 and Barkó, July 28, 1710. In: *Archivum Rákóczianum:* 1875–1882,VIII, pp. 201, 270, 282–283.

[50] *Archivum Rákóczianum:* 1872–1874, I/III, pp. 103–104, 136. Péter Dániel's letter to Rákóczi, Jassy, Nov. 29, 1710, MOL G 15, Fasc. 225, pall. 14, fol. 8–10.

2. HUNGARY, TRANSYLVANIA AND THE PEACE CONFERENCE
OF GERTRUYDENBERG

"Since the Peace with the French is almost certain ... we can have a better reason to trust, next to God, in the confederates (who encourage us)", István Dobozi jr. wrote from Berlin to Pál Ráday, on December 26, 1709.[51] At the turn of the years 1709 and 1710 it became known at Rákóczi's Court that international negotiations preliminary to a general peace ending the War of the Spanish Succession were to begin soon. Also, they were informed that at a general session of the Dutch Confederation in January 1710 the possibility of the eagerly expected ending of war and the preparations for concluding a peace treaty had been discussed.[52] Throughout the war Hungarian politicians had always attached great importance to negotiations aimed at an over-all European peace treaty. When the peace conference of Gertruydenberg began, Rákóczi was so firmly convinced of its beneficial effects to be felt in every corner of Europe that, instructing his envoy to Turkey he emphasized that one reason why it was not advisable for the Sublime Porte to enter on new military ventures was that "the universal peace-making conference is in session".[53]

Ending a war by concluding an over-all peace treaty, with an eye to the interests of all countries, settling European power relations in the form of an international agreement, was a principle that had emerged from the ideas and practice of politics as early as the seventeenth century. Before that time, the principles underlying a peace treaty had been determined by the conflict of the momentary and prospective interests of the victorious and the losing parties. However, as a result of economic and social changes, as well as technological and cultural progress, wars in seventeenth-century Europe assumed a different character, and consequently also the concept of peace changed.[54]

The new technique of concluding a peace was worked out, with respect to the international interests of the bourgeoisie engaged in business, by Grotius who was the first to consider the new, universal criteria of war and peace. The aim of a war was a peace concluded in due time and with

[51] István Dobozi, jr. to Ráday, Berlin, Dec. 26, 1709, Ráday Levéltár, Ráday Pál iratai A 16d 2–17, No. 42.

[52] Report from The Hague, Jan. 30, 1710, MOL G 15, Fasc. 203, fol. 5.

[53] Rákóczi to János Pápai, Kisír, March 25, 1710. In: *Archivum Rákóczianum:* 1872–1874, I/III, p. 80.

[54] Pach: 1968. – For the changing concept of war see Roberts: 1956. – For the controversy following and a bibliography, see Parker: 1976, pp. 195 ff.

the necessary guarantees. This meant not only that the spirit of peace was to be kept alive during a war, and that it was more advisable to conclude a peace at a given moment, even at some price, than to fight to the last, unless compelled to do so; it meant also that, even in times of peace, mankind should be intent on warding off the afflictions of wars, in keeping with the law of nature and the general consensus of peoples. For there was no other safeguard against war than a peace concluded with due foresight. Consequently, Grotius insisted that the activity of the military leaders should not be extended to the sphere of politics, and he placed the task of ending a war into the hands of the body politic, the civil political power, or, to use his phrase, the supreme power. He emphasized that a general was not in the position to conclude a peace treaty.[55]

It was, of course, difficult, and took long for Europe to master in practice the new technique of making peace. When wars were fought with a view to laying the foundations of future development, and the objectives were such as trade bases, ports, areas supplying raw materials and manpower and securing markets, cultural autonomy and state interests, it was necessary that peace talks should consider the feasibility of a long-term settlement producing stable conditions. Therefore, wars tended to be protracted, and the path leading to the conclusion of a peace treaty became longer on account of all the secret diplomatic transactions, preliminary agreements and separate peaces preceding it. It was during the negotiations of the Peace of Westphalia that the principle of the balance of power, a concept expressing the conditions of a satisfactory political co-existence, first emerged as an aim to be attained.[56] For a long time afterwards it could be observed as a manifest tendency that those responsible for concluding a peace treaty were directed not by the spirit of unreasonable retaliation, but by the intention to harmonize conflicting interests, in order to establish a lasting settlement on the basis of political co-existence. In 1652 Cromwell called upon Prince György II Rákóczi for nothing less than the joint defence of the internal peace of the Christian world. Spinola and Leibniz suggested that safe co-existence was to be achieved by uniting the interests of different religions and peoples, though their idea of the co-existence of different countries was conceived quite as mechanically as some other ideas in other spheres of contemporary thinking. It is, however, significant that conscious efforts were made to use peace treaties as a means to eliminate the causes of new conflicts as well, and even if the short and restless periods of peace were repeatedly interrupted by new wars, it had

[55] Grotius: 1646, 3. XXII/7, XXV/2–7.
[56] Braubach–Resgen: 1962, 1965, 1975. – Marczali: 1920. – Gajzágó: 1941, pp. 246–247.

been proved by a great number of practical examples by the beginning of the nineteenth century that minor countries could not be omitted from a general consideration of the balance of power in Europe.[57]

The particulars indicated above, which it would be easy to expound in detail and illustrate by many examples, suggest that the politicians of the Hungarian Confederation were not provincially narrow-minded people, misguided by phantasies, and that all that happened at the various conferences leading up to the Peace of Utrecht could be traced to certain antecedents. The idea of a European balance was the star of Bethlehem showing from afar the way out of the maze of secret diplomacy and entangled interests of power.

From the mid-seventeenth century onwards copies of *De Jure Belli et Pacis* could be found in the libraries of many Hungarian politicians, and by the end of the seventeenth century the ideas of Grotius had permeated various schools of European political thought in so many ways and so thoroughly that we are as yet unable to tell through what channels his principles were actually transmitted to those attending West-European universities, or to Rákóczi, for that matter, whose library gave evidence of extensive French culture. As early as 1706 Ráday introduced some ideas of Grotius into the system of arguments current in the political writings produced in the service of the Hungarian Confederation.[58] Also, there are a great number of data to prove that in the contemporary practice of making peace on an international basis Hungarian politicians found a model worth not only following but studying as well. The Peace of Westphalia recognizing Holland and Switzerland as independent states and considering the interests of Transylvania was a case in point, and they paid special attention to all peace treaties concluded by various countries which were guaranteed by third parties.[59] It was, then, a general opinion, a theoretically sound and practically feasible principle that Rákóczi emphasized repeatedly when he said that they were to persist in maintaining the unity of the body politic until the conclusion of the general European peace treaty, or, as Ráday put it, the war was to be prolonged "ad universalem pacem".[60]

---

[57] Cromwell to George II Rákóczi, London, 31 May, 1655. Bodleian L. Rawlinson A. 261 f. 46, cf. Milton: 1975, pp. 132–134. – Already Bacon recognized, as early as 1624, that the balance of power is a criterion of political co-existence, but he did not give a definition of the concept. Gajzágó: 1941, pp. 246–247. – For the appearance and currency of the concept see Acsády: 1899. – Bibó: 1934, pp. 37–38.

[58] "Explosio". *Ráday Iratok:* 1955–1961, I, p. 648.

[59] Braubach – Resgen: 1975, III, p. 431. – Lánczy: 1882.

[60] *Ráday Iratok:* 1955–1961, I, p. 295.

Hence it naturally followed that Rákóczi sent representatives to the peace conference of Gertruydenberg, fully convinced that as a participant in the War of the Spanish Succession he was entitled to be present there. By "presence" he meant that his envoys were to co-operate with the representatives of France and the Sea Powers, respectively, and to use the medium of political journalism in order to influence European public opinion in favour of the Hungarian cause.

By February 25, 1710, it had been decided that Rákóczi's envoys to be sent to The Hague were Domokos Brenner who was to join the French plenipotentiary, and János Klement who was to keep in touch with the representatives of the Maritime Powers, in order to supply information and lend their help when the question of the Hungarian and Transylvanian Confederation came up. Rákóczi and his inner circle of politicians appear to have been convinced that, as far as the case of Hungary was concerned, it was the Maritime Powers, not France that would play the decisive part at the talks preliminary to the international peace conference. In a letter preserved in an abstract only, Rákóczi stated this conviction of his unmistakably: "As regards the universal peace, it will be sufficient to send Brenner to The Hague to Clement, pro directore, since if the French King has to abandon his grandson, he cannot help us either. If his own interest does not urge him to intervene with the allies, nothing will be effected." As in the case of the Russian–Swedish peace talks it was Ráday and his circle, standing for the idea of central power, who supported Rákóczi's policy, now it was Clement, another member of the same group, who was given a crucially important task on the occasion of the peace conference of Gertruydenberg. Rákóczi took special care in specifying the respective duties of the two envoys. Brenner "should be director negotionis attached to the French ministers", while "Clement should negotiate with the allies ... this must be made quite clear to Brenner himself".[61]

It is reasonable to ask why Rákóczi could not believe that France would speak up for Hungary and Transylvania at the peace conference. After all, there was the constantly recurring stipulation that these two countries should not be omitted from over-all negotiations, and this could be traced back to Rákóczi's statement made as early as 1701 that he was willing to take up arms only on condition that France was going to include Hungary also in the peace treaty to be concluded. And there was the decision of Louis XIV communicated to Des Alleurs by Torcy on May 14, 1705, to

[61] For the mission of Clement and Brenner see Rákóczi's letters, Jászberény, Feb. 24, 1710; March 31, 1710, place not indicated; Kisír, April 3, 1710; Eger, April 7, 1710. In: *Archivum Rákóczianum:* 1872–1874, I/III, pp. 51, 81, 85, 87–88.

the effect that His Majesty "has charged me to instruct you to recognize Prince Rákóczi as Prince of Transylvania. Also, to tell him from His Majesty that he will not fail to do his utmost to secure the acceptance of his [i.e. Rákóczi's] envoys – that is, of those who will be sent in this capacity to the over-all peace negotiations, adding that these envoys may be commissioned to represent the Kingdom of Hungary as well". To be sure, the royal decision concluded with the statement that while the House of Austria was in possession of the crown, and the form of government of the Kingdom was unsettled, it would be difficult "to receive the representatives of the Hungarian nation at the peace talks".[62] Since that time, however, the members of the Confederation had proclaimed and codified at the Diet of Ónod that they refused to regard the Emperor Joseph I as their king, and emphasizing that they were simply following the glorious examples of the mighty republics of Portugal and the Dutch States-General, had sent copies of their manifesto to the French and Russian Courts and the ambassadors of England and Holland.[63] Nevertheless, what Rákóczi and his inner circle wanted even in the spring of 1710 was not more than that the Maritime Powers and France, taking their cue from the Hungarian representatives, should submit the case of Hungary and Transylvania to the peace conference, similarly to all other countries involved in the War of the Spanish Succession. But France had not included Hungary in any of her peace projects so far and was, as she always had been, very much annoyed with the Maritime Powers for their mediating activities. This is very well brought out by Le Noble's famous pamphlet published in August 1706, after the breakdown of the Habsburg–Hungarian peace negotiations mediated by the English and Dutch which attacked, among others, the mediation undertaken by the Maritime Powers.[64] Kökényesdi himself objected to the pro-English and pro-Dutch leanings of the Hungarian Confederation. This may perhaps have been the reason why Rákóczi dismissed him in the spring of 1710, commissioning Brenner at the same time.[65] However, it is well known that before receiving the summons to return, and without being familiar with Rákóczi's stipulations intended

[62] Köpeczi: 1966, pp. 93, 97–98.
[63] Sir Philip Meadows, English ambassador to Vienna, forwarded Rákóczi's statement and letter with the following note: "I have received what goes with this, from Rákoczi & Assemblies held in Transylvania and Hungary with the resolutions taken in them to throw off absolutely all allegiance and future intercourse with this court." *Archivum Rákóczianum: 1872–1874*, I/III, p. 325.
[64] Köpeczi: 1966, p. 362.
[65] Rákóczi to Bercsényi, Jászberény, Feb. 24, 1710. In: *Archivum Rákóczianum: 1872–1874*, I/III, pp. 50–51.

for the peace conference of Gertruydenberg, Kökényesdi had prepared a peace project on behalf of Rákóczi which he handed over to Torcy. This was the project received by Marshal Huxelles and Abbé Polignac, the two French representatives at the peace conference of Gertruydenberg.[66] This memorandum and proposal was essentially different from the one sent by Rákóczi and his circle of leading politicians to the representatives of the Maritime Powers.

There may have been several reasons why the case of Hungary and Transylvania was omitted from the French peace project of 1710. A copy of the project has been preserved in the archives of the Nedeczky family.[67] It was probably through Nedeczky that Rákóczi and his circle were informed about its content. The project written in Latin has the following gloss from Nedeczky: "These items have been sanctioned by the French King; but I do not like that there is no mention made of Hungary; they must have wicked designs on us."[68] The reference to the royal sanction may indicate that this was a piece of information that had leaked out and had come to Rákóczi's knowledge before the conference. This can explain, in part, the fact that Brenner who had been charged with a task of practical diplomacy (and who was compelled by the protracted Russian–Swedish talks to stay most of the time in Danzig) served Rákóczi's aims chiefly by expounding the Hungarian view in political tracts.[69]

To our present knowledge it was the Prussian–English–Dutch line of the diplomacy of the Hungarian and Transylvanian Confederation that did substantial work at The Hague in the spring of 1710. The figure in the foreground was Klement, but there were many persons, from Jablonski to Cardonnel, who had paved the way for Klement and Körtvélyessy before they were received by the Duke of Marlborough and Heinsius in the presence of Schmettau and Lord Townshend, the Prussian and English ambassadors.[70] As a result of a decision taken here with regard to the diplomatic sensibility of the Habsburg state, it was not Klement but Körtvé-

[66] Fiedler: 1855–1858, I, pp. 156–164.

[67] Pacis projecta, MOL P 512. Packet No. 7, pall. 35, No. 1683, fol. 1.

[68] The handwriting has been identified by Kálmán Benda to whom I express my gratitude.

[69] Lemaire sent to France on March 15, 1710, provided with a great number of documents, did not get farther than Danzig at the time of the peace talks. *Archivum Rákóczianum: 1872–1874*, I/III, p. 71.

[70] Klement's "Relatio" to Rákóczi, July 1710, and his Memorandum to the Emperor Charles III, 1715. In: Fiedler: 1855–1858, II, pp. 116–118. – Angyal: 1900, p. 901. – Marczali: 1882, pp. 162–163.

lyessy, acting under the pseudonyms 'Berensdorf' or 'Birnsdorf' and ostensibly as a representative of the Lutherans, who was sent to London where he was given a hearing by the cabinet and was well received in ecclesiastic circles, and where he managed, through Boyle, Secretary of State, to submit the political memorandum of the Hungarians in ecclesiastic disguise to the Queen.[71]

What did Hungarian politicians expect from the peace conference of Gertruydenberg? Certainly not the conclusion of a Habsburg–Hungarian peace treaty. It would seem that in judging power relations they were sufficiently realistic and, being familiar with current diplomatic conventions, and considering the foreign policy of the Hungarian Confederation in the light of its failures and successes alike, they insisted on one point only, namely that the Habsburg–Hungarian settlement should be included in the over-all European peace treaty.

The Maritime Powers had declared, as early as the spring of 1709, that the first step towards ending the War of the Spanish Succession would be to silence the clatter of arms in Hungary and Transylvania, under safe conditions, that is, by means of a peace treaty signed by the parties concerned in their capacity of states, and guaranteed internationally. On the other hand, representatives of the Habsburg state power who took into account the aims of the dynasty and the interests of the court aristocracy tied up with millions of acres of landed property had been, from the very beginning, opposed to any attempt to treat the case of the Hungarian war otherwise than an internal affair of the Empire, a conflict between the sovereign and his subjects, a conflict to be settled by force of arms, or pardon and submission, respectively. Therefore the inclusion of Hungary and Transylvania in an over-all European peace treaty negotiated and guaranteed internationally was to be prevented by all means, since this would be tantamount to recognizing Hungary and Transylvania as states. As Rákóczi and his circle had concluded from practical experience that the House of Austria would "by no means allow the nation to get into" an overall peace, their chief aim in the spring of 1710 was to convince the Maritime Powers and European public opinion that they had a legitimate claim to an international peace settlement.[72]

---

[71] Spanheim's reports, London, May 23, June 3, 9, 20, 1710, quoted in Marczali: 1882, pp. 162–163.
[72] Rákóczi's instructions for Nedeczky, Aug. 6, 1707. In: Nedeczky: 1891, p. 254.

Both in the instructions issued by Rákóczi and in the memorandum submitted to English and Dutch circles, the central problem is the political independence of Hungary and Transylvania viewed in close connection with the international situation in contemporary Europe and outlined against a historical background.[73] Attention is drawn both to the similarities in the past history and position of Hungary and Transylvania on the one hand, and England, Portugal and Holland, on the other. Earlier data briefly indicating the fact of Hungarian political independence are given. It is pointed out that the independence of Transylvania was recognized not only by the Peace of Westphalia, but several times by the Emperor Leopold as well. As is emphasized, a peace treaty internationally concluded and guaranteed was desirable not for Hungary alone, but for all Christian Europe. These writings contain an idea which was far ahead of the times, namely, that one reason why it was necessary to secure the conditions of political freedom in Hungary as a state, even though within the Habsburg Empire, was that in this case Hungary would not have to bother about her liberty any longer.[74] This was a general, all-European concern. Profiting from the conditions of political self-determination, Hungary and Transylvania would become important factors in the European balance of power. England and Holland, together with the Czar should, therefore, manage to bring the Habsburg–Hungarian war to an end by negotiating an international treaty which should be included in the over-all peace. This point was pressed the more as not long before Hamel-Bruyninx had refused to act as mediator. The final argument was that otherwise they would be compelled to appeal to the Turks for help.[75]

The conditions suggested by Rákóczi and his politicians gave evidence of political flexibility. They were prepared to accept the Habsburg King, but with the proviso that in regulating the dynasty's hereditary right of succession to the throne the English model was observed. Freedom of religion was to be secured for the Protestants in keeping with the tolerant

[73] Instructions for Körtvélyessy and István Dobozi, jr., Sept. 16, 1709, and undated, Ráday Levéltár, Ráday Pál iratai 1/d/2. Besides these they had to take over Rákóczi's Memorandum and instructions for David Ancillon, Prussian Court Chaplain, sent on July 8, 1709. Klement's Memorandum to Marlborough, The Hague, March 28, 1710. Klement's Memorandum to the Prussian Ministe. Ilgen, Feb. 1710. All published in Fiedler: 1855–1858, II, pp. 95–100, 88–90, 52–62. Cf. Rákóczi's letter to Jablonsky (1660–1741), March 31, 1709. *Ibid.*, pp. 31–34.

[74] Aretin: 1978, pp. 521–526.

[75] The idea of European balance had emerged in the political writings of the Hungarian Confederation long before. Cf. *Ráday Iratok:* 1955–1961, I, pp. 123, 154.

laws passed at the Diet of Szécsény. It was in the interest of the country that it should have an independent army recruited from the native population and commanded by natives of Hungary. Finally, the Emperor should grant a general amnesty. With regard to Transylvania Rákóczi had changed his mind. The Habsburg government regarded Transylvania as a family inheritance, a "province" of the dynasty, while the royalist Hungarian aristocrats thought of it as an organic part of Hungary in medieval terms. This meant that the position of Transylvania within the Habsburg Empire was most ambiguous. In principle, Transylvania was a part of the Holy Crown, and as such formed a unity with Hungary; in reality it was severed from Hungary and integrated with the Habsburg Empire, whereas Rákóczi and his circle had insisted from the first moment of the war that Transylvania was a separate state. As early as March 1706, the diet of Transylvania had proclaimed that they did not recognize the Habsburg Emperor and King Joseph I as their sovereign, at the same time closely linking the Principality to Hungary by means of a treaty. During the earlier talks Rákóczi had insisted on his personal sovereign power not as a descendant of former Princes of Transylvania, but as a legally elected Prince, head of the independent state of Transylvania. Now Klement was instructed to inform the English and Dutch statesmen that Rákóczi did not regard Transylvania as a country where he himself would wish to rule. On appropriate conditions he was prepared to retire to an estate to be assigned to him in Hungary or elsewhere in the Empire. The reason why he was insisting on his title of Prince was that he wished to conclude the peace not in his private capacity, but as a head of state; otherwise, he wanted to secure the independence of the Transylvanian state on the same terms as that of the Hungarian state.[76]

The members of Rákóczi's government took care to present the case of Hungary to responsible quarters adequately documented, supported by a list of authentic historical facts and up-to-date arguments. Already István Dobozi had urgently asked for a copy of János Bethlen's *History of Transylvania* and other documents of earlier dates concerning the Habsburg–Hungarian agreement.[77] Klement took with him two political tracts by Ráday to get them printed. When, at the time of Des Alleurs's mission to

---

[76] Klement's Memorandum to Minister Ilgen. Fiedler: 1855–1858, II, p. 89. His Memorandum to Marlborough, *ibid.*, pp. 98–99. The case of Transylvania in this connection is stated in detail in Rákóczi's instructions for Ancillon, *ibid.*, pp. 54 ff. Kökényesdi's Memorandum and peace proposal are in contrast with the former.

[77] Dobozi to Ráday, Berlin, Aug. 2 and Dec. 26, 1709, Ráday Levéltár, Ráday Pál iratai A. I./d. 2–17. Nos 40, 42.

Bender, the French military engineer Lemaire (who had been active in Hungary for a long time) was dispatched by Rákóczi to France via Danzig, he was supplied with several documents relating to the negotiations of 1704 and 1705/1706. The three numbers of the Hungarian newspaper *Mercurius* (printed in Latin for the information of foreign countries) which came out between January and March 1710, were sent off to Bender in rapid succession. And, as has been proved by recent research, Brenner was responsible for the final wording of the pamphlet called *Lettre d'un Ministre de Pologne ŕ un Seigneur de l'Empire sur les affaires de la Hongrie.*[78] It was very much to the point that he borrowed arguments from *De Jure Belli et Pacis*, to support the policy of the Hungarian Confederation. "The opinion of this great man is beyond dispute, since it is founded on conclusions drawn from history, ecclesiastic and secular, and the customs of all peoples that have lived since Creation."[79] This pamphlet includes documents which prove that in the agreement of 1686 the Emperor Leopold had approved the status of Transylvania as an independent state, and that in 1706, recognizing Hungary as a sovereign power, the Emperor Joseph had thought it acceptable and legitimate to conclude a peace treaty with Rákóczi as a head of state.

The practical action Rákóczi and his politicians were taking in order to open Habsburg–Hungarian negotiations had been co-ordinated with the peace conference of Gertruydenberg. Simultaneously with the peace conference the Czar did start mediating, in keeping with Prince Rákóczi's intentions. After a ceremonious reception and talks at Munkács between May 16 and 18, 1710, Baron Urbich, Russian ambassador to Vienna took over Rákóczi's peace proposal and left for Vienna, accompanied by the representative of the Hungarian Confederation, to begin his mediating activity as instructed by the Czar.[80] The Habsburg Court refused the Czar's mediation in a most spectacular form, but was not disinclined to enter into

[78] OSZKK App. Hung. 1506. – Cf. Esze: 1961, pp. 482–484. – Benda: 1984, pp. 23–38.

[79] "Les sentiments de ce grand Homme sont à couvert de toute contestation, étant fondés sur les temoignages de l'histoire sacrée et profane et les coutumes de tous les peuples, depuis la creation du monde." A letter from a Polish royal councillor to a nobleman of the Empire concerning the affairs of Hungary, transl. K. Benda, in: Köpeczi: 1970, p. 297.

[80] Mihály Okolicsányi's letter to Bercsényi, Homonna, April 29, 1710, OL G 15, Fasc. 203, fol. 38–39. Bercsényi to Urbich, Kassa, May 6, 1710, Projectum Domino Urbik datum, draft, Nagymihály, May 13, 1710, Rákóczi to the Czar Peter I, Nagymihály, May 14, 1710. In: *Archivum Rákóczianum:* 1875–1882, I/VIII, pp. 256–257, 259–260. Rákóczi to Bercsényi, Szeged, May 2, 1710. In: *Ibid.*, III, pp. 106–107. Rákóczi's instructions for György Ottlyk, Szeged, April 23, May 1, 1710.

talks on its own terms. Whether Rákóczi should consider this as a possible starting-point and take the first steps towards peace negotiations depended, in his opinion, on what results the peace conference of Gertruydenberg would yield for him and what support he could expect from the English and Dutch governments.[81]

As is well known, on July 20 the conference broke off suddenly. Probably because it had become evident that the Grand Alliance was divided by a serious conflict of interests and France, perceiving the signs of this internal disintegration, and considering her successes in Savoy and the change of government to be expected in England, demanded more than was reasonable in her military position. On the other hand the diplomatic actions of the Habsburg power were determined by the situation on the battlefield. A general opinion was expressed by a Hungarian officer who served in the Imperial army besieging Douai and who wrote that "as there had been rumours of a peace throughout the winter, so they continued at the beginning of this campaign, nevertheless, the army here being strong enough will pay no heed to the peace negotiations, but besetting the town of Douai we hope to take it within eight days ... we have driven out the French from here so much so that they have not many good forts left".[82] It is worth noting that Count Sinzendorf, the Imperial ambassador to The Hague, would have liked to re-cement the Grand Alliance by emphasizing the necessity of ending the war in the North. At the same time Prince Eugene of Savoy who was in charge of the diplomatic activities insisted that the military advantage of the Imperial forces over the French should be used, the sooner the better.[83] To be sure, it was reasonable that all over Europe there should be more attention paid to the signs of the impending English cabinet crisis than to the news from the battlefields. Reckoning with the influence of the war, and with that of the Dutch who were becoming restive because of the heavy taxes, the Duke of Marlborough, then at the peak of his military glory, had to contemplate the chances of an agreement. Even if formal negotiations had been broken off, secret diplomatic activities continued in the interest of a peace.

[81] Bercsényi to Nedeczky, Barkó, July 28, 1710. In: *Archivum Rákóczianum:* 1875–1882, II/VIII, p. 271.

[82] Pál Baranyai's letter to Nedeczky, Ex castris ad Due, June 5, 1710, MOL P 512, Fasc. 7, pall. 36, fol. 5–6.

[83] Braubach: 1962. – A duplicate copy of the new Habsburg–English–Dutch treaty concluded on March 31, 1710 at The Hague was among the papers in the archives of Sándor Nedeczky, MOL P 512, Fasc. 7, pall. 38, fol. 1–3.

Though we do not wish to exaggerate the importance of the diplomatic action taken by the Hungarian Confederation, it had been, naturally within contemporary limits, an action worth our notice because it has not been noticed so far; still, it cannot be emphasized often enough that the results of the conference of Gertruydenberg favourable for the Hungarian Confederation, were due to the changes in international power relations, particularly to the increasing influence of English and Dutch political groups which were demanding that the war should be ended as soon as possible. Rákóczi's diplomacy simply anticipated the issue of events, by means of flexible proposals, over-all schemes, and, perhaps not least, by insisting on the European balance of power and by referring emphatically to the Turkish peril, thus drawing the attention of the Maritime Powers again to Hungary and Transylvania. A thorough analysis could point out several mistakes in the execution of this diplomatic action. Clumsy management and the lack of zeal in some of the persons involved in the action were a serious drawback to the efficiency of the vulnerable diplomatic machinery. Nevertheless, it is beyond doubt that this time the Maritime Powers did not shelve Rákóczi's proposals, turning a deaf ear to them as they had done the year before. Moreover, the Duke of Marlborough and the Grand Pensionary Heinsius declared that it was wrong and unreasonable of Hamel-Bruyninx to have sent in the autumn of 1709 an insulting answer to Rákóczi, flatly refusing the latter's request for mediating peace talks.[84] They thought it desirable to have peace negotiations between the Habsburg power and the Hungarians as soon as possible. They promised to take the initiative and undertake the task of mediating, pointing out, however, what Minister Boyle emphasized in particular, namely, that the Imperial government was not likely to consent to this easily. They did not object to the Czar's intervening on behalf of the Hungarians, and maintained that if the Czar should send troops to Hungary this would not injure the interests of England and Holland.[85] They held out the prospect of including the agreement of Hungary and Transylvania with the Austrian government in the over-all peace treaty. Speaking for the Dutch States-General, Heinsius said that though it had not been possible to consider the case of Hungary among the pre-conditions of an over-all peace, he "wanted to include the Hungarians in the peace treaty". Queen Anne and the Duke of Marlborough also made it understood that they were willing

---

[84] *Weensche gezantschapsberichten...*: 1934, II, pp. 443–445, 457. – Angyal: 1900, pp. 900–901.

[85] Extracts from Spanheim's reports, London, May 23, June 3, 1710, in: Marczali: 1882, p. 162.

to include Rákóczi and the Hungarian Confederation in the over-all peace, but France was to solicit this from the Allies. And finally, Rákóczi should send his representatives to the English and Dutch governments.[86]

Simultaneously, and obviously reckoning with the consequences of the intense diplomatic activity of the Habsburg government, France took the decisive step in the question of mediating the Russian–Swedish peace. When Baluze, agent of King Louis XIV in Poland, went to the Czar on July 24, 1710 and made in the King's name an offer to mediate he stipulated that one of the items of the peace treaty should be the obligation undertaken by both powers to respect the liberty of Hungary. It is probable, though there is no primary evidence to prove that this was the time when a radical change had taken place with the result that while France had omitted Hungary and Transylvania from her former over-all peace projects, from now on she was willing to include them.[87]

Having gathered information from various sources, such as the report of Clement who had been summoned home, and not least, his verbal account, Rákóczi and his circle of leading politicians were convinced that the English and Dutch declarations, holding out as they did the promise of mediating and including the case of Hungary in the over-all peace, secured favourable conditions for the satisfactory termination of the war in Hungary.[88] In their reports envoys tend to present their errands more successful than they really are, if only because they want to extol their own merits. It is therefore probable that Rákóczi and his leading politicians overrated to some extent the results of the conference of Gertruydenberg, still, they had good reason to begin preparations for sending their representatives to the English and Dutch governments. The change at the Sublime Porte, that the pugnacious Köprülü Numan had been appointed Commander-in-Chief was, in their opinion, a favourable circumstance, since they believed that although the internal troubles in Sweden and the growing Russian influence in the Romanian principalities would ultimately prevent the Sultan from going to war, the news of Turkish military preparations would increase the internal tension between the Habsburg government and the Maritime Powers.[89]

---

[86] Extracts from Körtvélyessy's letter to Heinsius, written under the pseudonym Berendorf, in: Marczali: 1882, p. 162. – Klement's report, in: Fiedler: 1855–1858, II, pp. 109–122.

[87] Köpeczi: 1971, pp. 301 ff.

[88] Rákóczi to Bercsényi, Sarud, July 27, 1710, Poroszló, July 31, 1710, to János Pápai and Ferenc Horváth, Sarud, July 29, 1710. In: *Archivum Rákóczianum:* 1872–1874, I/III, pp. 142, 144–145, 296.

[89] Cernovodeanu: 1976, pp. 1078–1079.

However, the situation in Hungary and Transylvania had become very grave. There was not enough food, because large tracts of land had been left uncultivated, owing to the plague, the floods and labour shortage, and the harvest was particularly bad that year. As Rákóczi and his inner circle had decided for a defensive war, all grain was stored in the granaries of towns and castles in the fortified North-Eastern area of the country. The Imperial troops were starving and deserted in bands.[90] Seeing the international successes of the Hungarian Confederation, the well-informed Habsburg government suddenly changed its policy. It took a definite line of action in order to make an end to the war in Hungary as soon as possible, and in keeping with the interests of the dynasty. It offered personal privileges to the aristocracy, freedom from taxation to the lower nobility, a general amnesty to the soldiers, freedom of religion to the Protestants, so that the war in Hungary could be terminated without international interference, merely by an act of grace of the monarch. On August 7, 1710, the Hungarian and Turkish affairs in the Aulic Council were placed in Count Karl Locher's charge who was a member of the Council of War and a typical representative of the group of loyal Austrian aristocrats around Prince Eugene of Savoy, possessing large estates in Hungary. Marshal Count Heister was dismissed and in his place Marshal Count János Pálffy was appointed Commander-in-Chief of the Imperial forces in Hungary, on September 27, 1710.[91] Although the Hungarian Confederation had lost its most important stronghold in the West, the castle of Érsekújvár, and its dwindling territory overcrowded with refugees, noblemen and peasants, was much exposed to Imperial propaganda, and symptoms of panic were appearing, its social and military power was still considerable.[92]

It was under such circumstances that Rákóczi summoned a few members of the Senate, and the session of this incomplete Senate opening on August 10, ended with a military parade ten days later, on August 20, the day of King István the Saint.[93] It was decided that steps would be taken with a view to starting peace talks, as suggested by Rákóczi, but since the intention and the opposition of Vienna could be foretold, the Hungarian Confederation as a state organization and a political factor was to be sustained until the negotiations of the over-all peace. All troops were con-

---

[90] Lukinich: 1925, pp. 17–18, 266–268.
[91] Vienna, Sept. 26, 1710, *ibid.*, pp. 216–217.
[92] As in the past scholars' opinions are still largely divided concerning this problem.
[93] Rákóczi to Károlyi, Köröm, Aug. 21, 1710. In: *Archivum Rákóczianum: 1872–1874*, I/III, pp. 151–152, 305–306.

centrated along the defence line of the river Tisza and a few bases of operation, Munkács in particular, and preparations were made to uphold the institution of the state embodied in the Prince's Court and the Senate, even if these were to be transferred to the neighbour country, Poland.

It was, then, a decision of the state power that was made public in the proclamation of August 19 quoted in the introduction of this paper. The Prince informed the country that he was going to start peace negotiations soon, and hoped that the war would be ended by a peace treaty internationally guaranteed and implicitly recognizing Hungary as a state. He made a brief survey of the earlier peace talks with the Habsburg Court. He recalled what the English and Dutch mediators had said on the occasion of the peace talks of 1706, namely, that "it was the House of Austria, not ourselves, that caused those peace negotiations to fail". The proclamation contained information also about Urbich's attempts made in Vienna. It stated that the Emperor Joseph I wished to end the war not by regular negotiations, but by an Imperial decision "de nobis sine nobis", and "wanted us and the nation to surrender ad Gratiam et Disgratiam". In a style characteristic of the age the proclamation suggested that the international situation was favourable and that Hungary and Transylvania had the chance of ending the war by a satisfactory peace. "Her Majesty of England and the Dutch potentates wish to maintain their former mediating activity and to co-operate in resuming and efficiently continuing our earlier peace negotiations." That the Czar could be expected to mediate was suggested in rather vague terms, for obvious reasons. By way of conclusion this scholarly proclamation wished it to be generally known that "foreign powers are favourably inclined towards our cause". No one should think that "any private ambition or particular interest can be an obstacle to the peace negotiations".[94]

Acting in the spirit of the proclamation Rákóczi and his circle took diplomatic steps with a view to making arrangements for the peace talks. Klement was dispatched to the Maritime Powers with the terms of an agreement. In his letters written at Szerencs on August 30, 1710, Rákóczi turned to Queen Anne and the Dutch States-General in his capacity as Head of State. He expressed his gratitude for the mediation they had offered, and asked them for further intervention, so that he might conclude a peace securing the liberty of his country which was in a critical situation.[95]

[94] Rákóczi's proclamation, Aug. 19, 1710, *ibid.*
[95] Rákóczi to Queen Anne, Szerencs, Aug. 30, 1710, in: Fiedler: 1855–1858, II, pp. 126 ff. Rákóczi's letter to the Dutch States-General, Szerencs, Aug. 30, 1710, *ibid.*, pp. 128 ff.

As has been proved by recent research, it was equally in August that the great pamphlet, printed in Latin and French, appeared which used Grotius's arguments and historical documents to support the rightful claim of Hungary and Transylvania to political independence and a fair peace. It included a verbatim reprint of an Imperial document of 1706 which, in the context of new developments, had become topical again. "We, Joseph etc. ... have been informed by the ambassadors ordinary and extraordinary of the Queen of Great Britain and of the confederate States-General of the United Provinces of the Netherlands that the confederate Hungarians and Transylvanians desire to make an end to the war by a favourable peace."[96]

*

In this paper we have examined two significant diplomatic actions of Ferenc II Rákóczi, the plan for a Swedish–Russian peace, and his diplomatic contribution to the peace conference of Gertruydenberg which had led up to the decision he made in August 1710. Whether he judged the potentialities of the international situation realistically, or deluded himself with false hopes, the fact remains that in the autumn of 1710 the Maritime Powers took the initiative with a view to a Habsburg–Hungarian agreement. This opened a new chapter in the history of the international aspects of the peace of Szatmár which have been hardly noticed so far. Concluding this paper we can indicate only a few main points of this chapter.

One of the last actions of the Whig cabinet of England before its resignation was to initiate peace negotiations. Minister Boyle informed Palmes, English ambassador to Vienna, that although the Austrian government did not favour the idea of English and Dutch mediation the Queen was resolved to propose it. On September 5, 1710, Queen Anne sent the Emperor Joseph a written note requiring that a peace beneficial to the public weal should be concluded to end the war they had been waging in common, and that he should settle his affairs with Savoy and come to an agreement with the Hungarians. And as soon as the new Tory government came into power, it took energetic measures in the interest of making a satisfactory end to the war in Hungary. On September 26, Henry St. John, Viscount Bolingbroke, now Secretary of State, instructed Palmes, ambassa-

---

[96] "Lettre d'un Ministre de Pologne à un Seigneur de l'Empire sur les affaires de la Hongrie", in: Benda: 1984, pp. 28–30.

dor to Vienna, "to smooth the way for the mediation of the Queen and States", since the Hungarians intended to conclude an armistice. In December 1710, Peterborough was sent as ambassador extraordinary to Vienna with the task to promote a settlement of the affairs of Savoy and an agreement in Hungary. On his way to Vienna, Peterborough met Klement, and later, contacting Rákóczi through Raby, English ambassador to Berlin, he received his terms. As instructed by his government, Hamel-Bruyninx also drew up a memorandum stating the views of the Dutch States-General concerning the peace to be concluded with Hungary and the mediation offered for the purpose.[97] And even though Queen Anne's letter and instructions of September were very cautions in mentioning mediation as one of the criteria of a satisfactory peace, by December both the Maritime Powers and Russia were busily engaged in promoting a mediated peace.

As to the French decision and the deterioration of Turkish–Russian relations and the declaration of war (November 20, 1710) which foreshadowed an open conflict, differences between the Czar's Court and the Habsburg government were becoming increasingly marked. In Vienna Urbich had repeated talks with the ambassadors of the Maritime Powers concerning the Hungarian settlement.

It was chiefly through Raby, English ambassador to Berlin, that Rákóczi kept in touch with the ambassadors of the Maritime Powers in Vienna, and it was through Poland that he was in contact with Urbich. As soon as the decision of the French King arrived in October 1710, and the government of the Hungarian Confederation could get to know officially that Louis XIV was resolved to begin the Swedish–Russian peace negotiations in effect, and to bring together the parties concerned, and that he had declared Prince Rákóczi one of the mediators of the negotiations, a courier was dispatched to the Czar's Court without delay to press for mediating the Habsburg–Hungarian peace negotiations, and to name their terms of agreement. At the same time Bercsényi went to Poland in the capacity of Prince Rákóczi's representative, to carry on talks directly with the Czar.[98]

[97] Minister Boyle to Palmes, Ambassador to Vienna, Whitehall, Aug. 25 and 29, 1710; Queen Anne to the Emperor Joseph, Kensington, Sept. 5, 1710; Henry St. John, Viscount Bolingbroke to Ambassador Palmes, Whitehall, Sept. 26 and Nov. 21, 1710; instructions for Peterborough, London, Dec. 6, 1710. In: *Archivum Rákóczianum*: 1872–1877, II/III, pp. 454–458, 464–466. "But I must acquaint you that as to the Mediation in the affairs of Hungary you are not to offer it directly to the Ministers..." Minister Boyle to Palmes, Whitehall, Sept. 5, 1710, *ibid.*, p. 455.

[98] Sándor Károlyi's report to the Court of Vienna concerning Rákóczi's diplomatic activities, in: Szalay: 1865, II, pp. 490–495.

Rákóczi was perhaps among the first to see the threatening omens of a Turkish–Russian war. Nevertheless, the messages from General Meijerfeldt, the news leaking out from the Swedish–English talks, and, not least, the Czar's policy with regard to Moldavia and Wallachia made him optimistic, and even as late as the end of 1710 and the beginning of 1711, he did not give up the hope of a Swedish–Russian peace, in spite of the fact that French mediation was considered at the Czar's Court more and more as a factor in postponing the conflict with the Turks.[99] In the question of Transylvania Rákóczi and his politicians stuck persistently to their resolution submitted to the Maritime Powers on the occasion of the peace conference of Gertruydenberg. After having made the necessary arrangements for transferring the government institutions to Poland, and after having organized internal military bases, and after having obtained various kinds of guarantee in advance, Rákóczi made the next moves in the cause of peace negotiations.

In the autumn of 1710 Rákóczi initiated an armistice, authorizing, as was the custom in those times, the Commander-in-Chief of his forces, General Sándor Károlyi, to make the necessary arrangements. The proposal was carried to General Pálffy by György Komáromy Csipkés, Chief Justice of Debrecen and Sheriff of the County of Bihar. Pálffy was given to understand that, if the internal unity of the country was preserved and the chief criteria of the independence of the state guaranteed "by foreign protectors", that is to say, by their mediation, they were prepared to carry on what Urbich had begun in the summer of 1710, and conclude a "solemn peace". If necessary, they could wait until the over-all peace or the death of the Emperor who was very ill.[100] Then, in keeping with what the Habsburg Court had demanded at the time of Urbich's first attempt to mediate in Vienna, and what Rákóczi himself had decided to do in the spirit of the English and Dutch replies, having received Pálffy's answer (December 19, 1710), he wrote a letter to Prince Christian Augustus, Archbishop of Esztergom (January 2, 1711), proposed a personal meeting with János Pálffy (January 31), and sent a letter to the Emperor Joseph. Next, he took the opportunity of inspecting his forces at Olcsva to inform them of the peace talks begun in the spirit of his proclamation issued in August 1710. And after having settled military and political questions at the session of the incomplete Senate at Salánk, Rákóczi deputed General István

[99] Artamonov: 1978. – Péter Dániel to Rákóczi, Foxin [Focsani], Jan. 7, 1711, MOL G 15, Fasc. 225, fol. 28–30.
[100] Esze: 1976, pp. 5 ff.

Sennyey, Chancellor of the Senate, to run the affairs of the Hungarian Confederation, and he himself, together with his circle of leading politicians transferred his seat to Poland, close to the Hungarian border. Sándor Károlyi, Commander-in-Chief invested with full powers over all the military forces and the whole country, except Munkács, the provisional political centre and military base, received strict instructions from Rákóczi (in the spirit of the doctrines of Grotius) not to meddle in "matters of policy". That is to say, the right to negotiate and make important decisions was reserved for Rákóczi and his intimate circle of politicians. They controlled the activities of Klement and Brenner, and Rákóczi was preparing to have talks with the Czar personally. How well they timed the publication of political tracts was shown by the fact that the famous pamphlet called *Lettre d'un Ministre de Pologne...* was reprinted early in 1711, and Rákóczi and Bercsényi were each sent a batch of copies for distribution.[101] It is reasonable that after the death of the Emperor (April 17, 1711), an event causing great stir and giving rise to a great deal of speculation, the person of Rákóczi should have gained in international interest. In spite of the grave internal situation that had emerged, Pál Ráday, the Prince's negotiator of peace was optimistic when he returned to Hungary to inform Pálffy, with reference to Peterborough's "solemn mission" that Rákóczi and his leading politicians knew of "the sincere co-operation of the Allies for peace in Hungary", and wished to carry on peace negotiations on regular terms, in keeping with the talks of the English ambassador to Vienna.[102]

Simultaneously, however, there was a feverish military and diplomatic activity directed by Prince Eugene of Savoy, with the purpose of ending the war in Hungary and Transylvania without any international intervention, purely for the benefit of the House of Habsburg and a group of Austrian and Hungarian aristocrats. This was urgent, since it was evident that England was about to make a separate peace with France. And it was important that the peace with Hungary and Transylvania should be an act of grace on the monarch's part, since international mediation and a settlement with Hungary as a state in its own right would badly injure the interests of the dynasty. The first response of the Vienna government to the initiative of the Maritime Powers was a decree of amnesty issued on October 5. This was followed by talks between Prince Eugene of Savoy and the ambassadors of the Maritime Powers in Vienna. Hamel-Bruyninx, re-

---

[101] Bercsényi to Rákóczi, Ilyvó, March 30, 1711. In: *Archivum Rákóczianum:* 1875–1882, I/VI, p. 704.

[102] Rákóczi to Ráday, Kukizov, Apr. 18, 1711. In: *Archivum Rákóczianum:* 1872–1874, I/III, pp. 621–622.

porting the conversation on the occasion of submitting his memorandum to Prince Eugene, recorded the latter's opinion to the effect that the Hungarians had no alternative but to surrender unconditionally, and mediation was unnecessary, since Locher, the Emperor's representative, had already gone to Hungary.[103] Namely, the Court of Vienna had been informed as early as December 1710 that Károlyi, unable to cope with his delicate task, had accepted the Emperor's letter of pardon and had shown allegiance to Pálffy, executing, nevertheless, Rákóczi's commission at the same time, that is, playing a double game, and that he was ready to surrender several fortified castles. The social aspects of this process have been and are still being discussed extensively in Hungarian historiography. Here it is mentioned only insofar as it was instrumental in neutralizing the initiative of the Maritime Powers and in blocking the peace negotiations of Rákóczi and his circle. It is characteristic that the English government had been informed of the separate talks of Károlyi and Pálffy before Rákóczi knew anything about them. On April 19 it was rumoured in London that the peace had been concluded. In fact it was only after this date that Rákóczi dismissed Károlyi from his post of Commander-in-Chief and that the hectic days came when a manifest cleavage took place in the Hungarian Confederation. Károlyi, Pálffy, Locher, a few officers, a few Hungarian and Transylvanian noblemen signed the agreement in its final form, and the fifteen thousand soldiers summoned under the pretext of a military parade, laid down their arms. At the meeting convoked for the formal acceptance of the agreement in the granary of Szatmár surrounded by armed Imperial soldiers, Ráday was allowed to speak only in his private capacity; he could not demand to give an account of Peterborough's negotiations, and he could not execute Prince Rákóczi's commission.[104] The talks carried on by the mediators in Vienna are still to be explored; some of their details are totally unknown. Yet they are probably not negligible. Otherwise it would not have been so urgent for the Empress Regent Eleonora to inform the Imperial ambassadors to The Hague and London directly after the conclusion of the agreement that the "rebellion" in Hungary had been luckily brought to an end.[105]

---

[103] *Weensche gezantschapsberichten...:* 1934, II, pp. 503–504.

[104] *Spectator*, No. 43, April 19, 1711. Rákóczi to Károlyi, Kukizov, April 19, 1711. In: *Archivum Rákóczianum:* 1872–1874, I/III, pp. 624–625. – "Pulay napló" (Pulay's diary), in: Szalay: 1865, II, p. 395. – Summary of Ráday's speech made at the Szatmár meeting, *ibid.*, p. 408.

[105] The Empress Regent Eleonora to Johann Gallas, Imperial Ambassador to London, Vienna, May 9, 1711. In: Kállay: 1962, pp. 3–4.

In the decisive phase of the peace talks Rákóczi and his circle of leading politicians lost all that had consumed such a tremendous amount of their diplomatic energies. Rákóczi declared that the agreement was not a peace, but a defeat by arms; even though several points of it were such as met his original demands. It was, however, built on a shaky foundation. Instead of an agreement concluded between state powers regulating and guaranteeing the relations of Hungary, Transylvania and the Habsburg Empire, and instead of an international system of the balance of powers, it had for its basis a compromise between the dynasty and the Hungarian Estates, something like a domestic bargain. It failed to preserve the social and cultural achievements of the war for the coming era of peace.

The governing body of the Hungarian Confederation, diminished in numbers, held out for three months in Poland and carried on a lively diplomatic activity. After the fall of Munkács, however, Rákóczi dissolved the incomplete Senate; several members of the group supporting the idea of a central power, including Ráday, returned to Hungary, after they had obtained pardon from the Emperor Charles. Still, Rákóczi continued his efforts until the negotiations of the peace of Utrecht. Brenner and Klement were present in Utrecht, and the French envoy brought up the case of Hungary.[106] There was, however, no solid prop to support it; there was no autonomous state organ, no internationally recognized institution of political self-determination, and strictly speaking, there was no country. The result was that while even Savoy was included in the over-all peace at the request of England, the case of Hungary and Transylvania disappeared from the conference table as a result of the incorporation of these two countries into the re-solidifying power system of the Habsburg Empire. Nevertheless it would be impossible to maintain that Hungarian politics was simply not present on the European scene of that period. Its history is an organic part of the history of the international efforts made for international peace, the European balance of power, and good treaties which should prevent wars.

[106] Köpeczi: 1971, pp. 301 ff. – Weber: 1891.

Public Healing and Belief in Witchcraft

$\wp$ $\varOmega$

In the Eastern regions of Central Europe the Saxon high sheriff Andreas Teutsch was the first to suppress witch trials in the 1720s, in the Saxon townships of Transylvania, while the practice of prosecuting and convicting witches in court was continued for a long time in the immediate neighbourhood and in more remote territories. In Hungary the last instance of burning a witch at the stake dates from 1756, and the Constitutio Criminales Theresiana, a highly important decree in the matter of witchcraft initiated by Van Swieten was issued by Queen Maria Theresa in 1768.[1]

There is evidence that doubts and protests had been raised in the Kingdom of Hungary and Transylvania as early as the 17th century. However, no attempt has been made as yet to take stock of the opinions which correspond with what a widow of Kassa, accused of witchcraft and imprisoned in 1686, said: "only people with a diseased imagination can bring forward the charge of witchcraft".[2]

What happened in Hungary during the long period covering more than a century and a half from the emergence of the first doubts to the actual cessation of the persecution of witches?

This question cannot be answered on the grounds generally given to explain the cessation of the trials, such as the spirit of the enlightenment, an early manifestation of rationalism, the breaking up of the feudal system, and the rise of capitalism. And as long as we cannot tell what the criteria of the new rationality prevailing in the 17th and 18th centuries were, and how they operated, the particular causes of the cessation or,

"Connections between the cessation of witch trials and the transformation of the social structure related to hygiene." *Acta Ethnographica Hung.*, 37 (1991/92), 425–477.

[1]   Linzbauer: 1852–1856, I, p. 575, II, pp. 425, 461, 467, 776–785. – Komáromy: 1910, pp. 638–659, 715–717. – Spielmann: 1977, p. 92. – Klaniczay, G.: 1985, pp. 35–38.

[2]   Mrs. Márton Szepesi to the Chamber, n.d., arrived on Sept. 17, 1686. MOL E 254 Representationes et instantiae (1686) No. 122.

conversely, the long continuance of the witch trials will remain a problem to be investigated.[3]

In this paper I am dealing with one particular, and so far largely neglected aspect of the cessation of witch trials in Hungary. Several years ago, when I was doing research on the social history of the civilization of the period, I came to realize how necessary it was to investigate thoroughly the hygienic culture of the population and the medical strategies, as well as the interpersonal relations and tensions of healers of every description. This alone can make us really and truly familiar with the social attitudes towards diseases in the period, the patients' responses to doctoring and the choices they took, as well as the ideas of authorities and communities concerning the structural organization of medical service for the masses.

The vast majority of witches in Hungary were involved in curing the sick.[4]

In the background of the witch trials the healers' rivalry can be noticed, and it is the doctors who worked out the decisions restraining and, later, stopping the persecutions.[5] It is, therefore, reasonable to examine the cases of witchcraft not in isolation, but in the larger context of public hygiene.

The structure of the groups involved in healing in the 16th to 18th centuries in Hungary resembles that of a pyramid. The top of the pyramid was formed by doctors with a university degree, and "physicists", i.e. apothecaries, the middle section was made up of barbers working in the guild system, as well as surgeons and chirurgeons. In the lower and largest part of the pyramid we can see a varied crowd of lay healers that is almost impossible to define. They were responsible for the everyday medical care of the population, shouldering the immense burden of looking after the health of the masses.

This was not peculiar to Hungary. In every agrarian society, or where the inhabitants lived in far-away villages or secluded places in mountain regions, they themselves had to solve their daily health problems.[6] It is,

---

[3] Trevor-Roper: 1967, p. 175. – Henningsen: 1980, pp. 21, 25, 313. – Dömötör: 1981, p. 124. – Szendrey: 1986, pp. 345, 323, 313, 174–175. – Valentinitsch: 1987. Witch trials banned in Europe: Holland: 1610, Geneva: 1632, France: 1670–1682, Prussia: 1728, Sweden: 1763, Poland: 1776. Kosáry: 1980, pp. 167–168 – Seligmann: 1971, p. 185. – Klaniczay, G.: 1985, p. 35.

[4] Ipolyi: 1854, p. 408. – Rómer: 1861. – Tagányi: 1887. – Komáromy: 1910, p. XXXII. – Schram: 1982, pp. 67–76. – Grynaeus: 1988.

[5] Linzbauer: 1852–1856, I, p. 575, II, pp. 425, 461, 467, 726–785. – R. Várkonyi: 1984a. – Klaniczay, G.: 1985. – Kristóf: 1991/92.

[6] Valentinitsch: 1987. – Stoll: 1908–1909.

however, unquestionable that the situation in Hungary shows character-istic features of the historical conditions of the country as well.

The medieval unity of the Hungarian state was broken by the Ottoman conquest at the beginning of the 16th century. The narrow strip that was left of the Kingdom of Hungary stretched from Croatia to Upper Hungary, to the North Eastern Borderlands, and the rulers of the Habsburg dynasty organized their central government from Vienna.

The defendant of the first witch trial known in detail, Klára Botzi, was a typical healer who "the flowers and herbs of the meadows talk to". She was brought into court in Kolozsvár in 1565, when the new state, the Transylvanian principality had been firmly established in what used to be the Eastern region of medieval Hungary.[7] Two thirds, the central part of the former country, were occupied by the Ottomans. Under the three centralized powers, the feudal institution of the medieval Hungarian state lived on, more or less.

Owing to the fast spread of the Reformation, most of the ethnic groups of Transylvania, the townsfolk of the Highlands (the Northern part of Hungary) as well as large crowds of the lesser nobility and the peasantry came under the care of the Protestant churches. A large part of the higher nobility were won back by the Counter-Reformation at and after the turn of the 16th and 17th centuries, and in the Western parts a small number of peasants and burghers became Catholic.

Almost one third of the population was made up of non-Hungarian ethnic groups, Germans, Slovaks and Croats and Romanians, the latter living under the spiritual guidance of the Greek Orthodox Church.

90 per cent of the population lived in the country, in villages, on farms, in castles, fortresses, on small estates, in manors, in mountain regions difficult of access, in herdsmen's huts. The climate being continental, during the long and hard winters and the periods of spring floods the roads were impassable for weeks or months. People, whether in need of immediate aid, or in cases requiring a long treatment would have been helpless without the lay healers.

As can be learned from letters, diaries, records of testimonies, documents of witch trials, papers in county archives, all dating from the 16th to 18th centuries, the Hungarian equivalents of "witch doctor", "volksdoktor", "medicine man"[8] were "healing woman" (*orvosló asszony*),

---

[7] Komáromy: 1910, pp. 2–3. – Schram: 1970, 1982, III, pp. 49–50.
[8] Stone: 1984, p. 65. – Oláh: 1986, pp. 39, 191. "Medicine man": Jilek: 1976, quoted by Oláh: 1986, p. 208.

"woman doctor" (*orvos asszony*), "herb-woman" (*füves asszony*), "learned woman" (*tudós asszony*), "midwife" (*bába*), "seer" (*néző*), "bed-maker" (*ágy-vető*), "smearer" (*kenő*), "wise woman" (*tudós asszony*).[9] In social status they differed widely. Among those involved in healing a noblewoman was as likely to be found as a serf, a landlord's lady as well as a yeoman's wife, a cowherd, a peeress, a barber's widow, an innkeeper's wife, a Protestant minister, a Roman Catholic or Greek Orthodox priest, a shepherd's wife, a schoolmaster, a rich peasant's wife, a countess, a municipal officer, and even the hangman. The circle of lay healers cannot be classified according to marital or social status, financial standing, or education. There were "Vlach women", Turks, Croats, Germans, Greeks and Serbs among them, but the majority were Hungarians. Only 10 per cent of them were men. A large part of the lay healers was made up of country women.[10]

Their activity can be defined by means of the characteristics of folk-loric medicine; their knowledge of good health and ill-health was empiri-cal, based on the experience gathered in the course of several centuries, and, appealing to natural and supernatural powers, they used both ra-tional and "irrational" (ceremonial) therapy, ranging from the use of herbs to incantation.[11]

The fact that the activity of the body of people that can be labelled col-lectively as lay healers was recognized and, as it were, "legitimated" through three centuries, can be explained by the hygienic culture of the period and the real needs of society.

In the 17th century there were university trained doctors in every larger town, but, considering the approximately 4 million inhabitants, this number is insignificantly small; however, the ratio was more favourable in Transylvania.[12] These 100 to 200 doctors were members of an as yet unclassified layer of intellectuals; very often they had to do the work of teachers, diplomats, military engineers, economists, or administrative of-ficials as well.[13] Their professional training generally reached the interna-

[9] Demkó: 1894, pp. 407–410. – Fekete: 1910. – Kapros: 1979. – Tárkány-Szűcs: 1981, pp. 224–225. – Szlatky: 1983. – R. Várkonyi: 1984a, pp. 324–325. – Kristóf: 1991/92, p. 106.

[10] A medicine from a Greek priest: György Erdődy jr. to György Erdődy, Sept. 25, 1705. Erdődy Archives (K: 14). – The widow of a barber: OL P. – 1890. Forgách Archives, Miscel-laneous papers, 1. cs, 1. t. (1615) – A Piarist Friar: Schram: 1970, I, p. 201. "Turkish woman": *ibid.*, p. 229. Noblewoman: Manorial court: Varga: 1958, pp. 369–375. – "Taken to the hang-man to be healed" 1757, the county of Békés, Schram: 1982, p. 162.

[11] Oláh: 1986, p. 39.

[12] Spielmann: 1977, pp. 84–97. – Szlatky: 1983, p. 387.

[13] Takáts: 1980, pp. 183–184.

230

tional standard. As there was no medical school at the only Hungarian university founded in 1635, the doctors got their diplomas abroad. They attended the universities of Padova, Basel, Sweden, the German principalities, the Netherlands, England and France, respectively, depending on their religion and financial means, and acquired knowledge of all description offered by Europe at the time. Owing to the traditional division of labour in matters of public health, the Hungarian doctors of the 16th and 17th centuries were unable to look after the physical well-being of the masses.[14]

Treating wounds, curing "external ailments", ulcers, sprains, broken bones, pulling teeth was the task of barbers, chirurgeons, surgeons and "bath attendants". Their functions and the plan of their training were prescribed by the guild.[15] Hungarian society in the 16th and 17th centuries was a belligerent society. As is shown by the hygienic conditions of the border castles and armies, there were not enough trained barbers and surgeons.[16] In the course of time attending prisoners and giving expert opinion on cases of medical jurisprudence were added to their routine tasks of shaving and cutting hair. Their number, according to a register made at the beginning of the 18th century was appallingly small.[17]

According to time-honoured custom, midwives assisted at childbirth. Childbirth belonged under the category of life, not of illness, and it was a woman's task to attend to it. In the 16th and 17th centuries, traditional healers were particularly concerned in the matters of conception, pregnancy, childbed, and the medical care of babies, and in many of the witch trials the charges were in connection with these activities.[18]

A typical case was that of Orsolya Kanizsay, wife of Palatine Tamás Nádasdy (1498–1562), who conceiving a child after a long period of barrenness, was treated and attended throughout the nine months of her pregnancy by Gáspár Szegedi Körös (before 1530–1562?), in all probability the most gifted doctor of the age; nevertheless, a "German midwife" was called in to assist her at the delivery.[19]

---

[14] Demkó: 1894, pp. 200–202, 223–240, 244–245, 356–358. – Kosáry: 1980, p. 159. – Spielmann: 1979.

[15] Rules for the barbers' guild of Marosvásárhely, Marosvásárhely, April 16, 1628. In: Kovách-Binder: 1981, p. 202.

[16] Héjja: 1936. – Takáts: 1980.

[17] Gortvay: 1953.

[18] Hints: 1939, II, pp. 142–143, 258–259.

[19] Grynaeus: 1988, pp. 293–300. – Antal Sárkány to Tamás Nádasdy, Sárvár, Oct. 7, 1555. Vida: 1988, p. 127.

Count Ádám Batthyány (d. 1659) commandant of the Transdanubian area wanted to take his wife, who had had several miscarriages, to Viennese doctors; his mother, Éva Poppel, widow of Ferenc Batthyány (d. 1625) was very much against it, because – as she wrote – women knew more about women's diseases than the doctors. She herself had efficiently helped many infertile women using the knowledge handed down to her by her mother.[20]

The view lay healers took of health and illness was based on traditional experience. The interaction between lay healers and professional doctors remained essentially unchanged through the 16th to 18th centuries and was evident even when medical science was undergoing tremendous changes.[21]

The lay healers never formulated their theory of healing in current scientific terms. It is, however, easy to find out what scale of values they had in mind. Without as much as indicating the principles underlying the question, I mention two lay healers active at the beginning and the end of the period under discussion respectively, whose theoretical arguments for their healing practice have come down to us. The best educated Transylvanian noble lady of the 18th century, Kata Bethlen (1700–1759) worked on much the same assumptions in her healing practice as Gergely Frankovith, the horseherd turned healer at the beginning of the period discussed. Expounding his knowledge in a book he declared that he intended to "preserve life" with the help of the means of healing to be found in nature, since "God has left and granted us medicines by means of which people can be restored to physical health".[22] Similar ideas were expressed from the pulpit by Roman Catholic, Calvinist, and Lutheran clergymen alike. Péter Pázmány (1570–1637) Archbishop of Esztergom (1616–1637), himself a believer in the efficiency of lay healers who utilized the medicinal power of herbs, gave his congregations veritable lessons in anatomy in his sermons.[23]

The statement made in court by one of the chief defendants of the famous witch trial of 1677 to 1688, Ilona Lénárt Pörpeni, also called "Learned Ilona", shows how old and new therapeutic principles blended. She claimed that she had acquired her medical knowledge in the court of

[20] Éva Poppel to her son, Ádám Batthyány, Pápa, May 14, 1634. MOL P 1314 Missilis, No. 38017.

[21] Hints: 1939, II. – Lindeboom: 1968. – Vekerdi: 1984, p. 199. – Kempler: 1984. – Oláh: 1986.

[22] Szlatky: 1983, p. 122.

[23] Szabó: 1979, pp. 34–35. – Melius: 1578 (1979), p. 93. – Bitskey: 1986, pp. 164–186. – Pázmány Péter művei: 1613, 1636 (1983), pp. 286–287, 907.

Zsuzsanna Lorántffy, wife of Prince György I Rákóczi. The Princess herself "had been a very great shamaness", and there had been a man in her court, "also a very great shaman", and it was from them that she had learned the "art" which, by this time, had come to mean a rational kind of knowledge, the familiarity with medicinal herbs.[24]

One of the reasons why lay healers flourished in 16th- and 17th-century Hungary so conspicuously was that the fees of professional doctors were extraordinarily high. A serious illness and a long treatment meant bankruptcy.

Credit letters and last wills testify that an illness could cost anything up to a hundred thalers in doctor's fees and apothecary's bills.[25] But while medical science was undergoing a change, the therapeutic practice of professional doctors often was hardly different from that of lay healers.

Many people did not trust learned doctors.[26] Self-treatment was practised on a large scale by the whole population. A medicine-chest, a medical book and a herbal were indispensable household articles in the homes of aristocrats, members of the lesser nobility and burghers. Letters from the period are full of advice on treatment and descriptions of different diseases. The pieces of medical advice in almanacs and various herbals, the versified rules of the Regimen Sanitatis Salernitanum were in everybody's mouth. Self-treatment practised by the educated and less educated classes received support and encouragement from many quarters.[27]

The practice of self-treatment is still to be investigated in more detail; a few typical examples must suffice here, together with a sketchy survey of the "social context" of lay healers.

"I am not going to look for another doctor... I always try to take medical advice from this" – Potencia Dersffy wrote in 1555 to Tamás Nádasdy, asking him to return her book of medicines, since it was from this book that she cured her two little sons and her household, whenever something was wrong with them.[28] People often diagnosed their own diseases and asked for medicine by letter, sometimes even specifying what they wanted.

[24] Herner: 1988, p. 56.
[25] MOL E 254 NRA Fasc. 101 No. 12, Fasc. 82. No. 3 – Palatine Wesselényi paid 100 Fts annually to his doctor. Acsády: 1885, p. 163.
[26] Grabner: 1987, p. 75. – Stone: 1984, p. 65.
[27] Szlatky: 1983, pp. 383–440. – Kosáry: 1980, p. 168. The Salerno Scuola was published in German in Hungary in 1634 in the translation of Lucas Seular, a Transylvanian doctor, Brassó; in Hungarian in the translation of György Felvinczi: in Kolozsvár, 1693. The second edition: Lőcse, 1693, the last edition: Kolozsvár, 1776. Cf. Hints: 1939.
[28] Quoted by Szlatky: 1983, p. 402.

István Pálffy, commandant of Érsekújvár "ordered" his bailiff to go to the apothecary with Mátyás Borbély and get the required medicine made up.[29]

Count Kristóf Erdődy sent a medicine prescribed for him to Count György Erdődy, enclosing the doctor's "letter to me". Erzsébet Rákóczi received medicine, somewhat late, when her bailiff had written to the doctor describing "the Countess's ailment" for him.[30] Lay healers practised medicine either for a living, or out of a sense of vocation, or for pleasure. They can be easily divided into distinct groups.

Midwives formed a large group. Their work was, after all, invaluable. It was they who assisted at childbirth in towns and villages, in the halls and rooms of castles and manor-houses. "Trained midwife", "municipal midwife", "sworn midwife", "German midwife", "downtown midwife", "uptown midwife" and other similar compound names were used in the 16th to 18th centuries in Hungary to distinguish their many different kinds. "Midwife Elizabeth" and "Midwife Cathy" are instances not only of how names were given, but also of how, in this particular case, in 1591 in Kolozsvár, a daughter inherited her mother's profession. According to a decree issued by Emperor Ferdinand I, King of Hungary, in 1552, which regulated their duties and supervision, midwives working in the towns and villages of the Austrian hereditary provinces received a salary.[31] Similarly in Hungary, from the 16th century onwards, the free royal boroughs employed salaried midwives, which was a natural concomitant of the internal order of town life, and of the municipal self-government administering all affairs within its competence. In Kassa, in 1580, midwives received a salary, and in accordance with the municipal regulations they were allowed to charge 25 dinars for assisting at a childbirth. In Pozsony, in 1626, two municipal midwives were employed, one "Hungarian midwife" and one "German midwife". In Szeged, in 1734, two "sworn midwives", "trained midwives" were employed by the town. According to a register of midwives prepared in 1747, there was a midwife in every village; in Selmecbánya there were 26, in Debrecen 11, and in Szeged 17.[32]

The "learned women", the "women doctors" who made up the main body of lay healers, rose above the crowd of herb-women and smearers,

[29] Pál Keljó to István Pálffy, Tyrnavia, Jan. 26, 1641. SAS Pálffy Archives (Arm. VIII. Lad 11. Fasc. 2. fol. 990).

[30] Kristóf Erdődy to György Erdődy, Pozsony, Dec. 29, 1691. István Bakos to György Erdődy, Vienna, Nov. 3. SAS Erdődy Archives (Karton 14 and 10).

[31] Komáromy: 1910, pp. 72–73. – Linzbauer: 1852–1856, I, p. 174. – Demkó: 1894, pp. 318, 401–402. – Magyary-Kossa: 1938.

[32] Doctors and Therapeutics, the chapter on training and supervising midwives – Magyary-Kossa: 1938; 1929–1940, III–IV, passim.

owing to their superior knowledge, and consequently acquired a good reputation and a large practice. Gergely Frankovith "although not a man of learning", became the doctor in Sopron.[33] Baron Mihály Károlyi (1585–1626), high sheriff of the county of Szatmár, called the "medical woman of Éradony" to attend his son "little Pete".[34]

When István Pálffy, commandant of Érsekújvár was not feeling well in 1641, he ordered his bailiff to ask for the advice of a famous medical woman. The bailiff wrote back and informed him of the diagnosis made by the learned woman who suspected that there were premonitory symptoms of a stroke and advised him "to give up too much contemplation", and sent the recipe of a bath made of the bark of 5 different trees.[35] Count István Csáky (1603–1662), high sheriff of the county of Kolozs was scolded by his mother, because he did not consult a professional doctor but a "woman doctor" when he had pains in his leg.[36]

The family of Count Miklós Esterházy, who was very proud of his skill in self-treatment, and also kept a doctor, was attended by a healer called Mrs. Pál Jó. When Princess Zsuzsánna Lorántffy was suffering from a woman's disease, she had herself treated by the "medical woman of Pocsaj".[37]

László Rákóczi (1635–1664) and members of his household usually called in a doctor to treat them, and doctors from Eperjes, Késmárk, and Lőcse often visited his castles; he even went to see a doctor in Vienna. He called the doctor from Eperjes when his servants or his wife's maid were ill. However, it also happened that he called the "medical woman of Eperjes" to attend his wife, who had been seen by doctors, too, and he paid one gold coin to the "medical woman of Eperjes, Mrs. Kőműves" for her services.[38]

Who were these "medical women"? It was chiefly in witch trials that they were heard to speak. We get to know only from testimonies, e.g. that Mrs. István Vida gathered and took home bagfuls of herbs, or that András Csepi displayed a keen sense of vocation in treating his patients.[39]

[33] Szlatky: 1983, pp. 397–398.
[34] Károlyi Okmánytár: 1897, IV, pp. 171–172, 189.
[35] András Kis Tholnai Szabó to István Pálffy, Újvár, April 23, 1641. SAS Pálffy Archives (Korrespondencia I).
[36] Anna Wesselényi the orphan, to István Csáky, Almás, Nov. 15, 1631. Deák: 1875, p. 101.
[37] "Without my doctoring you cannot really exist, it seems ... my beloved". Miklós Esterházy to his wife, 1634. Történelmi Tár: 1900, p. 273. – Magyary-Kossa: 1929–1940, I. – Szilágyi: 1875.
[38] The Diary of László Rákóczi, Sept. 2, 3, 4, 8, 1656, in: Horn: 1990, pp. 244–245. – Magyary-Kossa: 1929–1940, III, p. 120.
[39] Schram: 1970, II, pp. 353, 386–396. – Herner: 1988, p. 54. – Rómer: 1861.

Educated ladies coming of aristocratic stock or of the lesser nobility formed an interesting group of lay healers. The landowner's lady was responsible for looking after the health of those in her household and those working on the estate. Everybody was expected to know how to deal with common complaints. When Katalin Varga, a midwife, was called to account in 1758, and the examiners asked her what she used the "means of witchcraft in the box" for, and among them the "balm" (Melissa officinalis), she answered: "I use them just the way other people use them".[40] Every nobleman's house had to have a stock of herbs, infusions and medicines as a matter of course. But there were some women among the aristocrats who felt a calling and had a gift for, or were simply interested in the work, and the knowledge they acquired raised them far above the average. The list of names is interesting: Éva Poppel, wife of Count Ádám Batthyány, commandant of the Transdanubian region; Zsuzsánna Vitéz, wife of the Transylvanian peer Pál Béldi; Judit Vér, wife of the famous Transylvanian statesman Mihály Teleki (1634–1694); Anna Listius who came of an aristocratic family of well-known alchemists, and others. They hired women to collect herbs, and searched the neighbourhood for persons versed in curing diseases. Countess Mária Széchy, widow of Palatine Ferenc Wesselényi (1605–1667), who was confined to Kőszeg by the emperor, was so famous for her skill in healing that people flocked to her for a cure from faraway regions, and she even kept a "medical servant".[41]

The "rank and file" of the lay healers did the medical routine work in the villages. They made up the layer of folkloric healers par excellence, and in the 16th and 17th centuries they became familiar, almost invariably, from the witch trials.

Lastly, mention must be made of the many charlatans, adventurers, ignoramuses, quacks swarming about the lay healers, as indeed about all layers engaged in medical activities. The barbers' guilds protected their members against "all those untaught barbers".[42] For the lay healers there was no protection.

Many of the lay healers earned their living by their activity, i.e. by using their knowledge. Their incomes differed largely. They were given money, food or presents depending on the social status and financial resources of the patient, the kind of the particular illness, and the length of the treatment. It often happened that they left it to the patient's discretion. Midwives employed by towns at the end of 17th century and the

[40] Komáromy: 1910, p. 685.
[41] Acsády: 1885. – R. Várkonyi: 1987, p. 111.
[42] Kovách-Binder: 1981, pp. 117, 201–207. – Héjja: 1936.

beginning of the 18th were well paid. The midwives of Szeged received a yearly salary of 100 forints per head. The earning of "medical women" cannot have been small either. On the other hand, we do not know what those women received who collected herbs for particular healers or noble ladies. The market-town of Kőrös kept a "medical woman" with a regular yearly salary.[43]

In several cases it was the healer who dictated the terms. According to the testimony of a witness at the witch trial in Várad, in 1766, the defendant, Erzsébet Békési had told Mihály Sós, who asked her to treat his sore leg: "I am not going to heal your leg until you pay". The above mentioned András Csepi, a zealous healer who charged moderate fees and consequently had many patients, earned a lot.[44]

"Who taught you to heal and where?" – this question, put by the head of the manorial court to Mrs. István Szabó née Sára Szöllősy accused of witchcraft in 1756, was often asked, and in many different forms throughout more than a century and a half.[45]

A healer, originally a horseherd in Sopron, stated that he had acquired the rudiments of his knowledge from a master barber. András Csepi had learnt the craft from his father, Demeter Csepi, and so had his younger brother and sister, who were also healers. Illiterate peasant women had inherited their knowledge from their mothers and grandmothers according to declarations made at witch trials. Éva Poppel, widow of Ádám Batthyány, said the same: she had learnt curing women's disorders from her mother.

There was, however, an amazingly great number of lay healers who had learnt the craft of their own accord. Those who had taught them were similar persons, mostly old lay healers, herb-women or barbers. A statement of peculiar interest was made, by a certain Ilona Borsi summoned before the manorial court of the domain of Munkács in 1735. She said that she was "half shamaness" by birth; in her childhood two shamans carried her off; she knew that shamans would meet three times a year, and they were flying with her to one of those meetings; she saw the shamans fight, and heard one of the magic steeds speak; she was put to the test whether she could "ride a magic steed". Shamanistic belief was, however, compatible in Ilona Borsi's mind with knowledge acquired in a thoroughly

[43] Komáromy: 1910, p. 697. – Tagányi: 1887, pp. 42, 166. – Rómer: 1861, I, pp. 276, 280, 327.

[44] Komáromy: 1910, p. 696. – Rómer: 1861, I, pp. 228–230.

[45] Schram: 1970, I, p. 322; 1756.

empirical manner. She was three years and a half in service with a doctor, István Borbély, and she would go out gathering herbs with some other women, and that was how she got to know the healing power of herbs and rootcrops.[46] In the witch trial of old Mrs. István Sobrák one witness spoke about a "poor man" who could prepare baths, and "living with a doctor" had acquired his knowledge of herbs from him.[47]

Many people, coming mainly of the upper and middle classes, but peasants, too, got their knowledge from herbals and various medical books and formularies.[48] In all probability it was Countess Kata Bethlen who reached the highest degree of learning a lay healer could reach. She did not inherit her knowledge of healing, nor did she acquire it through self-education, but learnt it from Transylvanian doctors of medicine. One of her tutors, Sámuel Kölesséry (1663–1732) had taken his doctor's degree in Leyden.[49]

However great the quantitative differences in the knowledge of individual lay healers might be, they all had something essential in common, namely that what they knew was based on experience. They inherited the accumulated empirical knowledge of several generations, and developed their diagnostic skills at the bedside of their patients, observing them closely. Their medicines and therapeutic methods have been handed down by folkloric healers. Summing up the results of modern ethnographical and ethnomedical research concerning 20th-century folk medicine, Andor Oláh concluded that "it is not only in respect of the principle of humoral pathology but in other respects as well that Hungarian folk medicine has preserved the characteristic features and conceptual elements of 17th-century medical science".[50] When examining the correlation between belief in witchcraft and public health we should pay special attention to the so-called irrational elements of the lay healers' methods.[51]

While they based their diagnostics on the well-tested experience, traditional knowledge of nature and skills acquired in practice by several generations, their therapeutics included incantations, prayers and magic words also.

The lay healers functioned in a health- and life-conscious society in which highly developed forms of self-treatment were practised as part of

[46] Schram: 1970, I, p. 322. – Lehoczky: 1881, II, pp. 250–251.
[47] Schram: 1982, p. 227. Cf. Oláh: 1986, pp. 210–211.
[48] R. Várkonyi: 1987, pp. 111, 126.
[49] Demkó: 1894, pp. 355, 435. – Spielmann: 1977, pp. 153–158.
[50] Oláh: 1986, p. 49. – Vajkai: 1948. – Grynaeus: 1962, 1974.
[51] Stone: 1984, p. 65. – Grabner: 1987, pp. 76–80.

its culture. Healing had to be done with the full cooperation of the patients. Incantations, prayers and magic words gave comfort to the relatives and the patients too: they often helped, and in some cases even saved the patient's life. Incantation had a therapeutic effect, as it aroused the patient's willingness to cure himself and to cooperate with his doctor which was so indispensable for his recovery.[52]

The texts used in lay healing had practical value and did not altogether lack rational elements. Lay healers did not know anything about sterility, nevertheless they were generally successful in healing wounds, having learnt by experience, e.g. that wounds bandaged with material that had been boiled in bubbling water would not suppurate. They also realized that the length of time used in infusing herbs mattered much. Clocks were to be found, as a matter of course, in the homes of aristocrats, members of the lesser nobility and burghers. There were none in villages or herdsmen's lodgings; indeed, people who lived and worked by the time-table of agriculture could do without them. They were, however, far less dispensable for those who went in for healing. According to an inventory of Countess Anna Erdődy's medicine-chest taken in 1631, there was a "golden watch" ticking among the ointments, oils and pills.[53] Masses of lay healers used other methods of measuring time. Reciting a prayer or an incantation always took the same definite length of time. Surely, it never occurred to them that these served to substitute the clock, this was simply a part of their learning, and they knew that what they were doing was effective.

Examining the role of incantations in healing historically, and considering the psychosomatic aspects of the question as well, we have to bear in mind two further points which are not irrelevant to the witch trials either. First, reciting the text gave the healer time to observe the patient, to try to diagnose his disease, and to suggest a cure for it, if he found it curable at all. Secondly, the patient himself insisted on this ritual. It strengthened his will to be cured and his belief in his recovery. It is hard to draw the line between experience, ritual, custom and reason. The hour appointed for a herbal bath was to be a sacral point of time; specific dates, e.g. St. George's Day, or full moon, were chosen for gathering herbs. This was in keeping with their knowledge of nature and with common sense, since herbs were known to be most effective at particular times of the day and in particular seasons. At the same time, the cosmic effect of the celes-

[52] Pócs: 1984, pp. 109–126.
[53] The medicine-chest of Anna Erdődy (1631): MOL (Ue 96, 13). Cf. Magyary-Kossa: 1929–1940, IV, p. 16.

tial bodies was a very important factor in the medieval world view. The moon was a symbol of change and of the capability for renewal, and was supposed to possess healing power. Its presence in the rites of the art of healing is manifold in the 17th and 18th centuries. The text that Count Ferenc Esterházy, high sheriff of the county of Fejér and captain of Csesznek, copied into his medicine book with his own hand was only one of those to be recited when the moon was new: "God give a good day, new moon, new Friday! Let me have a toothache when I have eaten three kinds of meat: that of a lizard, a snake, or a frog."[54]

Varieties of "healing with excrement" can be found in the medical books of noble families and in the records of witch trials.

In 1751 in Dada, in the county of Szabolcs, the parson asked for medicine for a "charmed" cow, which would not let its calf suck, and what Mrs. Csordás the Lame suggested as a treatment was turned into a charge of witchcraft against her: "she said that the calf should be washed with the cow's midday urine, and all would be well". Schram remarks that "this is regarded as a superstition, but it may have been an ancient process of accustoming a cow to its calf".[55]

The value and effects of metabolic waste products used therapeutically in the 16th and 17th centuries have been clarified by the history of medicine and pharmacology. They contain hormones and bactericidal agents, but their application involves the risk of infection.[56]

Notions of overcoming fear and pain were also associated with them, and were supposed to be capable of reducing the evils of illness, and bringing about regeneration. Going into analytical details, and using a large number of examples, Mihail Bahtyin pointed out that in the folkloric world view corporeality had a deeply rooted symbolic meaning. The lower parts of the body, those in connection with digestion and evacuation were partly the symbols of degradation, and partly those of rebirth and biological regeneration. Rabelais, a physician, was still fully aware of and familiar with the symbolic correspondence of excrement with the procreative power and fertility. "Excrement was regarded also as a kind of material that caused mirth and admonished one to be sober, which was degrading and endearing at the same time, and which combined the grave and birth in a most easily tolerable, unformidable and comic form." More remote connections were indicated as well: "The doctor... had a peculiar relationship with the end-products of metabolism, especially urine, which played an important

---

[54] Thaly: 1885, pp. 94–95. – Oláh: 1986, pp. 182–183.
[55] Schram: 1970, II, p. 407; 1982, p. 77.
[56] Kempler: 1984, pp. 57–58. – Oláh: 1986, p. 171. – Grabner: 1987, pp. 76–79.

role in the medical science of earlier times. The doctor told the fate of the patient from his urine; it was taken to be the decisive factor with regard to the patient's survival or death.[57]

The practitioners of traditional medicine were peculiar personalities. They were hard-working, enterprising and skilful people. It turns out from the trial documents that they were experts in many things. They were efficient and painstaking managers who kept their utensils and houses clean and tidy.[58] One of the witnesses gave a fine character sketch of Mrs. István Vida née Borbála Szabó, who was accused of witchcraft: she was a hard-working and resourceful woman, and she cured many diseases, syphilis among them.[59]

Grand ladies who practised healing with zest belonged to the most educated layer of their times. They promoted the publication of books, they lived in elegant surroundings, managing large households and estates the size of counties, and directing a host of domestic servants. Practitioners of traditional healing were gifted people, above the common run. They had to possess suggestive, psychotherapeutic powers. Without skill in establishing contacts and the ability to make decisions they could not have succeeded; also, they had to know the tricks of diagnosing diseases and those of soothing the patients, and had to meet the manifold demands for pity and sympathy. Medical books in manuscript form prove that the duties of doctors and nurses often overlapped. To soothe a child needed love, an urgent case required a quick decision, and to secure the patient's cooperation demanded special abilities, such as sympathy, determination, the power of persuasion and suggestion. Both the patient and the healer must have faith in themselves.

Lay healers were more or less charismatic personalities. They could be so in different ways. The accusers of Klára Botzi, who was charged with witchcraft, knew from her own statements that she understood the language of herbs and wild flowers. Kata Gyarmati stated in 1709 that "on St. George's Eve 72 herbs spoke to her". "The herbs had spoken" to Mrs. Lukács Csonka, who was sentenced to being burnt in 1681.[60] The ability to converse with herbs was a special gift in the 16th and 17th centuries; it meant that the person who knew the efficient power of flowers and herbs was one of the chosen. Gergely Frankovith, a doctor regarded himself as God's elect. He had had miraculous dreams, the first one at the age of

[57] Bahtyin: 1982, pp. 218–227.
[58] Ipolyi: 1854, p. 408. – Schram: 1982, pp. 76–79.
[59] Schram: 1970, II, p. 287 (1741).
[60] Komáromy: 1910, pp. 2, 135, 226.

seven and a half, and he "saw" the second very important dream at the age of fifteen, and finally when he was thirty-one, it was revealed to him in a dream sent by God that he was to follow the calling of a doctor.[61]

A healer may have obtained his charisma from the person who had instructed him and who may have passed on the secrets of healing on his death-bed. Extraordinary success could also produce charisma. This could be the healer's success in curing a patient whom all people had given up, or in bringing back to life someone who was half-dead, or in curing a sick child whom the barbers could not help; he simply "took it on his lap" and "laid his hands on it" and the child was healed. Some had their charisma from shamans. The confession of Mrs. András Bartha née Erzsébet Batári made under torture is typical: "Nobody taught me the art of shamans, because it is all God's doing in the mother's womb".[62] Charisma could also be obtained by a person who claimed to be supported by supernatural powers, or who passed for a witch.

In Vásárhely in 1730 a sick child's father got hold of an axe and wanted to strike Margit Bíró, who was accused of witchcraft, saying: "If you do not heal my son, you will not leave this place, and I will break your head!" Many similar examples could be cited.[63] The lay healer was defenceless. He or she was exposed to the tantrums of people tortured by pain, and to those of other healers and communities. If he refused to treat a patient, he would be accused, or assaulted. The same could happen, if he did not succeed in curing a patient. Margit Bíró turned out to be an efficient healer in the case mentioned: the child recovered and this "miracle", her peculiar medical skill served to prove that she was a "witch".

Conflict was inherent in the position lay healers worked in. And since warding off and eliminating conflicts was a requisite for the utter cessation of the trials, it is reasonable to ask how under the given circumstances it was possible that while one lay healer was held in high esteem all his life, the other should perish at the stake. Why and when was a healer taken for a witch?

It was necessary for all groups practising medicine to have healing strategies of their own. This alone enabled them to safeguard themselves against illnesses, the desperate relatives of patients, the unexpected consequences of the therapeutic process and against fellow competitors.

[61] Szlatky: 1983, pp. 99–101.
[62] Komáromy: 1910, p. 360.
[63] Schram: 1970, I, pp. 233–236. Similar cases: from 1640 – R. Kiss: 1906, p. 211. – Komáromy: 1910, p. 241; Schram: 1970, II, pp. 385; 1982, III, p. 130.

Qualified doctors of medicine were also exposed to people's fits of violent temper. However, their university degree, their professional status, municipal and royal decrees protected them as a corporate body, and they were not accountable to anybody for the therapeutic treatment they chose.[64] The way barbers tried to prevent internal and external discord helps to understand also the conflicts lay healers were exposed to. Barbers built their therapeutic strategies into the rules of their guild. According to the regulations issued by the Saxon "Universitas" for the "guilds of barbers and surgeons" in the Királyföld region (1562), if a seriously wounded person came to see the barber, the latter was to call in two other master barbers and judge together "if the patient could be healed or would remain crippled". In a case of mortal illness, if the master barber had doubts about the issue, he should call in four or five other master barbers. In cases of serious illness or injury, the regulations issued in 1628 for the barber guildmasters in the county of Máramaros prescribed that a consultation should be held. Penalties and prohibitions imposed by the corporation served to check competition within and without. If a doctor settled in a town neither barbers nor surgeons were allowed to administer a potion without his knowledge. A barber did not have to fight single-handed against untrained wound healers or such as were strangers in his town; his guild protected the medicines he prescribed and the therapeutic processes he applied, as he had proved his expertise at the masters' examination. The guild's independence, its place in feudal society were indicated by its seal and arms and the approbation of the state.[65]

In 1678 Mrs. Mihály Szánthay made a complaint before the town council of Kassa against János Demjén, a barber, because instead of curing her little son's teeth, he damaged the child's mouth completely. In the course of the investigation led by the council, the lawyer defended the barber who had been condemned by the guild also, saying that doctors and barbers could not be called to account and brought into court for their medical activities. This would be very strange, for, "great as their learning was", they could not guarantee certain success. Curing children was a particularly hard and delicate task. If doctors were called to account, it was to be feared that people could no longer find doctors and barbers to heal them and their children.[66]

[64] Weszprémi: 1781, III, pp. 70–72. – Magyary-Kossa: 1929–1940, III, p. 377. – Allendy: 1937.

[65] Kovách–Binder: 1981, pp. 117, 201–207. – "irons to cut the heart and veins" on the coat of arms of the seal of the barbers' guild: the county of Árva to György Erdődy, Pozsony, June 30, 1700. SAS Erdődy Archives, Missiles 26, karton 441.

[66] Mihalik: 1894, pp. 387–391.

Lay healers had no institutions to protect them or regulations specifying their activities, such as doctors or chirurgeons had. It was only the midwives employed by towns or aristocratic families, and famous medical women who were protected to some extent. However strong the cohesive forces and retentive power of a village community might be, its mental balance was precarious. In a feudal society the activity of traditional healers was totally unprotected, and they lived in constant danger. If the patient did not get better, or got worse, or died, but also if he recovered, contrary to expectations, it could easily happen that charges were brought against them. Then it was for them to see that they were properly protected against the charges, each engaging the best lawyer they could find or afford.

Secretiveness was the main therapeutic strategy of lay healers. Many people observed that "witches" liked to wrap themselves in mystery. Frankovith noted: "Whoever wants to perform the duties of a doctor", must be, among others, "secretive".[67] Lay healers did not take the final responsibility: it was not them who healed the patient, but the prayer, the incantation; or it was not them who were to blame, but the rite which usually worked well, on other occasions. Failure was not their fault; it might be the patient's or someone else's; surely, the same rite had worked at other times. If the patient or his relatives blamed the healers, or came forward with a certain demand, the latter would defend themselves in a peculiar way. They made an ostentatious display of their knowledge, tried to intimidate their critics, threatening them with specially horrible menaces. Another well-known strategy they chose for defence was aggression.

The statements familiar from witch trials, such as: "you will certainly regret it", "you'll see, I'll do something you'll never forget" are stereotypes. Healers deliberately tried to scare others, to keep them at a distance, as it were, in order to protect themselves. "They did not dare to hurt her, what's more they all tried to win favour with her, because they were scared" – that is what almost every witness said by way of conclusion when testifying against Örzse Német.[68]

The rational self-protecting methods of lay healers were similar to those of the barbers and learned doctors. If the patient's state was hopeless, they would not even touch him, or they said that they were unable to help; they would perhaps try to do their best, but they declared that they ought to have seen the patient a few days earlier. According to the statements of

[67] Szlatky: 1983, p. 122.
[68] Komáromy: 1910, p. 56. – Schram: 1970, II, p. 35.

244

witnesses coming from the county of Zala, recorded in 1750, Mrs. János Sipos née Orsolya Gombos would not touch and see anyone who was seriously ill. Moreover, she refused to go to a patient like that, unless two or three women joined her.[69]

They tried to convince the patients of the excellence of their medical knowledge in different ways. Giving evidence in the trial of a woman called Katalin, mother of a certain Mrs. Varga brought to court in 1584 in Kolozsvár, Demeter, a barber qouted what her son-in-law had said: "What are you barbers, you are all nothing compared to my mother; for she makes such strong potions that the lumps of iron you put in them will simply vanish in an hour; and when she goes to the field, and picking a herb asks it 'What are you good for?' the herb will speak to her at once."[70]

The husband of Mrs. János Incze arraigned in 1742 in Dés had warned her against "doctoring", telling her to give up healing, considering that on one occasion it was with great difficulty that she could be saved from the flames of the stake: nevertheless she continued "bragging" of her medical knowledge.[71] Healers often compared their knowledge with that of other healers. The reasoning of Mrs. Ádám Batthyány née Éva Poppel is worth noting. She advised her son not to take his wife to the doctors in Vienna, because they would only foul her womb and ruin her health with medicines. "Both the wife of János Draskovich and Thököly's lady had been infertile" like her own daughter-in-law, but she healed them and they both gave birth to a large number of children.[72]

Éva Poppel did not practise healing for a living, and did not have to defend herself against charges, or to make strenuous efforts to secure a clientele for herself. She was convinced that doctors knew very little of women's diseases. She even had an inkling of the essence of hygiene from practical experience. Lay healers accused one another, compared their own knowledge with that of the rest, belittling the latter, and spoke of their successes very much in the manner of the widowed countess. Erzsébet Német who had to appear before the manorial court of the Esterházy family, had followed essentially the same line of argument in order to dissuade a witness, now testifying against her at the trial, from taking her daughter somewhere else "to be doctored": "do not take her anywhere, for I'll cure her, and she won't have any problems".[73] When Mrs. István

---

[69] Schram: 1970, II, p. 653.
[70] Komáromy: 1910, p. 45.
[71] Ibid., p. 507.
[72] Éva Poppel to her son, Ádám Batthyány, Pápa, May 14, 1634. Cf. Note 20.
[73] Schram: 1970, II, p. 159.

Vida found out that the patient was about to go and see a doctor, she asked him not to do so, for "no barber can heal him, only myself".[74]

The lay healers lived in constant rivalry. Competition was typical of all groups engaged in medical activities. The barbers' guild of Sárospatak fined the barber who talked slightingly of another barber's knowledge.[75] Professional prestige and financial interests are natural motive powers for all groups of people who earn their living by the services they perform, their expertise, or creative work. E.g. in 1708 the "balneators" (i.e. practitioners treating diseases by baths) of Pozsony and Vienna made joint efforts to prevent the balneator of Moson from taking his examination.[76] What serious differences the lay healers had, chiefly with the barbers, has been amply documented. It is interesting that many outstanding doctors appreciated and had a clear conception of the work of lay healers, nevertheless it is evident from the witch trials that there were doctors as well among the accusers.

Anna Bencsik, wife of István Borbély Váradi was fined by the barbers' guild of Kolozsvár in 1615 for curing sick people.[77] More than a century later, in 1751, a barber treating the sore leg of a girl said that her leg had been "charmed" by Mrs. Péter Kis, who was accused of witchcraft.[78]

In 1732 Mrs. János Pápai went to see the doctor in Gyula, and when she asked what was wrong with her, the following diagnosis was established: Mrs. Samu, the witch had bound her, and "the doctor said, 'You won't be cured, unless Mrs. János Samu's excrement is gathered, and you bathe in it.' Mrs. Pápai duly gathered the excrement which the doctor used in preparing a bath, and she was cured." We know from the documents of witch trials carefully collected, that the doctor of Gyula was not the only doctor to "accuse" others of witchcraft in the 18th century.[79]

There was keen competition between the lay healers themselves. Instances of simple emulation and "imputations of witchcraft" with fatal consequences were equally frequent.[80] In Komárom Mrs. Máté Kossa and a certain seamstress rivalized with each other desperately. Mrs. Máté Kossa did not dare to take Mrs. Mátyás Karkóczi's child as a patient, because the seamstress had threatened her.[81] Kata Pirka of the county of Sopron

---

[74] *Ibid.*, pp. 386, 388.
[75] Zoványi: 1891, p. 151. – Magyary-Kossa: 1929–1940, III, p. 65. – Takáts: 1961, p. 83.
[76] Magyary-Kossa: 1929–1940, IV.
[77] MOL P 1830. Miscellaneous papers, 1615.
[78] Schram: 1970, II, p. 384 (1751).
[79] Schram: 1970, I, pp. 237, 263; 1982, pp. 311–319 (1734–1737).
[80] Klaniczay: 1985. – Herner: 1988. – Kristóf: 1991/92.
[81] Rómer: 1861, p. 76.

blamed now one, now another of her fellow-midwives for the illness of a woman in childbed saying that they had bewitched her, as can be read in the statements of witnesses made at her trial in 1730.[82] Witnesses said that Éva Székely was a "good housekeeper" and successful healer who cured the sick by herbal baths and strange rituals, but she was constantly at war with the woman doctor of Poroszló, who accused her of witchcraft.[83]

If it were possible to prove that the lay healers accused those people of witchcraft who were "professionally" incompetent and by their bungling brought their trade into disrepute, we could grasp an important element in the self-defence of the really "learned", "trained" lay healers. A midwife or a healer was likely to be suspected of witchcraft when he or she had lost the confidence of the community, and a rival noticing this, took advantage of the opportunity. It is strange that the accused should have been charged with witchcraft for doing exactly what the accuser, too, was practising; and it could happen that both ended up at the same stake.[84]

Professional rivalry was, of course, not the only possible cause of the charges of witchcraft. Witch trials served to "settle" conflicts of a different nature as well. As Gustav Henningsen pointed out, the persecutions were often initiated by people who had financial or social advantages to gain from the trials, and they used the belief in witches as a means of accomplishing their objects.[85]

Prince Gábor Bethlen (1613–1629) initiated the trial of three women of high rank, Kata Török, Kata Ifjju and Anna Báthori, in Transylvania in 1614. Anna Báthori was the sister of Prince Gábor Báthori (1608–1613), who had been murdered in 1613, and the other two women were related to him by marital or other family ties. All the three of them owned castles and lands in key positions from the point of view of the defence of the Principality, and it is very likely that the new prince chose this way to get hold of these castles to consolidate his power and to calm down the people.[86]

Feudal order, in which bearing children was important also with regard to the property and name of a family to be handed down, protected women in many ways. However, the charge of witchcraft was so serious that only pregnant women were excused from punishment. An heir could

[82] Schram: 1970, II, pp. 56–124; 1982, p. 329.
[83] Schram: 1970, I, pp. 158–160.
[84] Klaniczay: 1991/92. – Hódi: 1985, pp. 68–70. (For this I owe thanks to the psychiatrist Dr. Péter Rigó.)
[85] Henningsen: 1980, p. 286.
[86] Nagy: 1988.

acquire an estate, a fortune, or valuables by laying a charge of witchcraft against an ancestor. Also, a husband could get rid of his wife, and if someone had an embarrassing secret which another person smelt out, this was a convenient way to have the latter put to death. Lay healers handled matters of vital importance, such as conception, birth, fertility and undesired pregnancy. It also happened that a medicine made by the healer was the real object in the charge of witchcraft. This can be illustrated by an almost farcical story. In 1696 a fatal conflict took place in the county of Nógrád caused by a particular ointment. As it was made from butter and flowers, "such as women needed", it must have been some kind of cosmetic. Relations between Mariana the healer and the village people had become strained; she owed money to many women. One witness reported the quarrel between Mariana and Mrs. Rojkó from her village verbatim: "hitting each other's hands they cried: you are a witch; and the other retorted: you are a witch". When Mariana was put in the county prison, and it became known that she had hidden the ointment in the stable behind the kitchen garden, the women made an assault on the stable, and the ointment was gone.[87]

If lay healing was so dangerous, why did people undertake it?

The social role and position of lay healers deserve close attention. The system they lived in did not legitimate their existence in terms of social status or professional capacity either.

In France in the second half of the 17th century even respectable middle-class girls found the job of a midwife attractive.[88] In Hungary the midwife was a product of the village. A 17th-century Hungarian midwife could prosper in proportion to her personal abilities; if she was lucky, she managed to get a job in a town, or a confidential post in the "lady's suite" of rooms in a manor-house. However, all midwives were liable to be accused of witchcraft by anyone, and at any time.

No matter what a person, a family, or a community had suffered from, whether it was military expeditions, requisitions, political persecution, maybe an epidemic, a famine, a natural disaster, once the individual or collective mental balance was upset, a rational solution of the problems was no longer feasible. A scapegoat had to be found. The notion in everyday use at the time that served to provide a vent for such feelings and passions was "witch".

There were a number of deviant personalities among the lay healers. Inevitably they were more lonely than other members of their social stra-

---

[87] Schram: 1982, pp. 208–212.
[88] Hints: 1939, II, p. 259. – Gélis: 1977.

tum; many people were jealous of them, and they had several conflicts to face. Their sense of being different and their efforts to find their place produced tensions, and in trying to relieve these they often violated the accepted moral code and the rules of conduct. Particularly those people who were urged by an insatiable craving for knowledge.

If the charge of witchcraft was potentially implicit in the lay healers' therapeutic strategies and the conflicts resulting from their profession, how was it, nevertheless, possible for the majority to avoid the stake? Why do the statistics of witch trials not show a numerically uniform trend; why is the figure almost three times as high after the 1690s as before?

It is the second question that is more relevant to the law abolishing witch trials, but it is hardly understandable without answering the first question.

Some of the witnesses unanimously said of Mrs. András Szabó, a widow, brought into court in Kolozsvár in 1629, that she cured diseases by herbs, "for that was the essence of her life". "She treated little children; she was sent for, or the children were taken to her place." The charge of witchcraft was laid against her by the master of a probably neurotic servant girl, and the witnesses of the prosecution gave a long list of the criteria of "witchcraft" as it was understood in those times. The court submitted her to the ordeal by water, and the council made her take the oath purgatory, and finally she was acquitted, although she did not deny the possibility that she might be an "instrument of the devil". However, she said, she did not know and could not help.[89]

About two thirds of the known witch trials were concluded by the acquittal of the defendants or a relatively light sentence. It is, however, clear from the documents of the trials that people were condemned to the stake or acquitted not necessarily according as their "crimes" were more or less grave, and the statements of the witnesses more or less damning.

Looking for the reasons of acquittal, we can notice that the activity of lay healers was tolerated. The bye-laws of villages, towns and market towns show that local authorities intended to secure a stable equilibrium necessary for the functioning of the different, larger or smaller units of society. The health of the population was a question of vital importance, and the task of attending to it indispensable. The changes taking place in the 16th and 17th centuries were accompanied by a crisis in the protection of the health of the masses. The sickly poor, the crowds of disabled and

[89] Komáromy: 1910, p. 93.

249

wounded soldiers, beggars on the highways were a scandalous burden, and a source of unpredictable dangers.[90] It took a very long time and required strenuous efforts all over Europe to find a way out of these difficulties.

There are some sporadic data on the very moderate endeavours made in 17th-century Hungary to organize the preservation of public health. The institutions of the "town barber" and "town midwife" meant that midwives were obliged to attend to the poor. In Eperjes the barber treated the poor and the beggars in the local hospital at the expense of the town. Landlords, ecclesiastical and secular high dignitaries founded several smaller hospitals and almshouses providing for sick, aged serfs, on a very humble scale. Measures were taken to organize the medical care of soldiers in the border fortresses and in the army.[91]

In the last analysis acquitting the lay healers accused of witchcraft means that the community was aware of the fact that they could not do without the healers. The communities knew their midwives and healers. They tried to settle differences between healers and patients. The statements made by witnesses deserve closer examination. Besides damning testimonies there were statements made in favour of the defendants, praising them and denying the charges. The public opinion of a turbulent village or town, an embittered patient, sorrow-stricken relatives had to be pacified. They had to be compensated for injuries whether imaginary or firmly believed to be real. These matters could be handled in many different ways. It often happened that defendants were acquitted, after having bound themselves in writing to discontinue their healing practice, and so redeemed themselves. Were the ill-considered rituals of the ordeal by water followed by the stake? We do not know for sure, even in those cases when the charge was "proved beyond doubt". Sometimes a healer was obliged to leave the village, for the sake of public peace. At a time when it was quite common to perish at the stake, and blood was shed abundantly to legitimate the rule of those in power, the manner of "handling" the conflicts of lay healers, the witch trials that were concluded by acquittal or a relatively light sentence, indicated a degree of tolerance.

This kind of tolerance was a public necessity. Its theoretical grounds had been laid in the second half of the 16th century.

---

[90] For the inadequate medical service for the soldiers in the Fifteen Years' War, see Takáts: 1980, pp. 186–187. – Héjja: 1936, pp. 40–47.

[91] For the organization of a health service, see Kyr Paulus: Sanitatis Studium, 1551, in: Spielmann–Huttmann: 1968, pp. 61–69.

The first theory of repudiating all kinds of witch belief was formulated by Bishop Péter Melius. In his book which ran into two editions (1562, 1570), he pointed out that witchcraft was the work of the devil and Satan was not powerful enough to bewitch God's favourites, appearing in human shape; what many people called "bewitchment", was simply an illness which had its remedies. Casting an evil eye on babies was nothing but "malicious claptrap". By formulating his views on health, and by publishing his principal work, *Herbarium* (Herbal), Melius outlined a policy for the partial acquittance of lay healers. His *Herbarium*, published in 1578 "about the names of trees, and herbs, their nature and their use... compiled from the books of doctors" was essentially a popular book on medicine. It contained the description of various plants, indicating their curative effects, and gave directions for their application. This was, typically, a work that could be used as a handbook by non-professionals as well.[92] Its significance, among others, was that by describing the curative effects of herbs, roots and flowers with scientific accuracy it lifted a great deal of the stock in the lay healers' arsenal into the sphere of science, removing it from the category of superstition. At the same time it supplied the laity with the means of healing free from the stain of superstition. Notes following the formulas, such as "probatum est", or, "has been tested (= tried)" are proofs of empirical knowledge, and, indirectly, can be regarded as implicit negations of the belief in witches. Writing about the fleabane (Conyza minor), Melius added: "Midwives tell a lie when they say that with the help of this herb and the St. John's Wort (Hypericum) they can chase away witches and the horrors of the night. But that is a monstrous falsehood. It is God's spirit that chases away Satan and horrors like these, by means of true belief." Describing the honesty (Lunaria), Melius remarked that it was effective in healing wounds and checking the flow of blood in menstruation, adding: "a herb held in superstitious esteem by midwives".[93] In this way the honesty lost its magic sense, and "superstition" was de- or revaluated. It came to be included in the category of the understandable. "A herb tried out several time" gave rational meaning to something that had been, according to public opinion, an irrational phenomenon. The efficiency of baths, infusions and ointments was no longer due to the devil's power, or somebody's being a witch, but to the natural curative effect of herbs and roots. The principle serving to explain the natural curative effect of plants was that God had created the

[92] Melius: 1578 (1979). – Szabó: 1979, pp. 28–29, 51.
[93] Melius: 1578 (1979), pp. 109, 282, 312. – Szlatky: 1983, p. 331. Cf.: Makkai: 1988.

herbs for the benefit of mankind. Seen from the point of view of lay healers, two essential elements of the belief in witches were modified by Melius: 1. treating diseases by herbs was not a superstition, but God's work, consequently no witchcraft; 2. the ritual, the irrational element in curing diseases was a manifestation of Satan, consequently it was not to be tolerated. This view determined the technique of the struggle against the belief in witchcraft for a long period.

Péter Bornemisza's *Diabolic Temptations* explained the healing effect of herbs similarly: "As God enjoined us to eat bread, drink wine and take medicine supplied by herbs..."[94] Gergely Frankovith, a lay healer affirmed his experiences of healing by herbs as follows: it is God who "granted medicinal power to a great variety of created things... That is why you should fear God when you pick your herbs".[95] A similar vindication of the practice of those who used herbs in treating diseases can be read in a book on the therapeutic use of various plants and flowers, compiled, similarly for non-professionals, by Lukács Pécsi, a Catholic priest and doctor "particularly excellent in botany", published in 1591, at Nagyszombat.[96] Pázmány, too, accepted the lore of healing by herbs – that is to say, lay healing – freeing it, as it were, from superstition, saying: "It was not for his own benefit, or for the sake of the angels or brute beasts that God created the green herbs on the mountain tops, but – Herbam servituti hominis – for the good of humans."[97]

Distinguishing traditional healing from superstitions identified with witchcraft, and counteracting accusations evidently contributed in the long run to the acquittal or defence of the traditional healers brought into court. At the same time, these served to confirm the view that the ritual of lay healers was the work of the devil. Those who separated treating diseases by natural, herbal remedies as a God-ordained activity from superstitions, pursued their point also by describing in detail what they regarded as superstitions. For example Péter Bornemisza recorded that in 1577 one of his preachers exorcized the devil from a witchy rustic woman who had been possessed, and sent him the magic prayers which the woman "had learnt from her grandmother and a papist priest". This is how these eight beautiful archaic prayers got into the *Diabolic Temptations*, actually, they were magic formulas for curing the gout, headache, colic, croup, sprains, tapeworms and stab-wounds.[98]

[94] Bornemisza: 1578 (1977), p. 57.
[95] Szlatky: 1983, pp. 115, 121–122.
[96] Weszprémi: 1781, pp. 623–647.
[97] *Pázmány Péter művei*: 1613, 1636 (1983), pp. 286–287.
[98] Bornemisza: 1578 (1977), pp. 31–37.

Sermons directed against the belief in witches were, at the same time, a means of spreading witch fantasies. The story told by Péter Alvinczi in a sermon, of an Argentine woman who called in another midwife to attend her delivery instead of the one thought to be a witch appeared in a number of local variants in Hungarian witch trials.[99] The sermons of Alexis János Kecskeméti against superstitions must have taken may examples from general custom, but they also transmitted stories to the public. Indeed, they kindled the imagination of the audiences. Kecskeméti asserted that "by tying and untying, weighing and reading, writing slips, with the purpose of conferring the degree of medical doctor on themselves (!) these sorcering midwives ... commit a grave sin against God".[100] The person who "picks herbs to heal by reciting the Lord's prayer commits a sin, ... it is also a sin ... to recite the Credo while we are preparing a plaster to be used in curing a colic, the gout, or a fever". He described in graphic detail how a witch could change into a cat or a wolf, adding, however, that this was merely an instance of credulous belief. He also narrated that witches held their meetings during the first days of the month of Whitsuntide, on a high hill where they went flying on broomsticks; but this was nothing but a dream, a prank of the devil. In reality it could not happen.[101] How did the listeners react to this, and what did it mean to them? Maybe they retained only the story itself. Sermons would deserve a thorough analysis also, because some healing processes of classical antiquity, branded as "pagan lore" were transmitted to the masses through them. For example Kecskeméti quoted the beautiful magic formula from Ovid's *Metamorphoses*: "Nubila pello – I am bringing clouds". Holding an episcopal visitation in 1651, Bishop Christian Barth took down a somewhat similar incantation for conjuring up clouds. In the documents of witch trials still extant the first instance of the cloud formula recorded among the charges dates from 1654.[102]

It is obvious that though Melius and his followers took a long step forward, they could not and did not manage to stop witch trials, or even to reduce their number. They did, however, free the treatment of diseases by natural remedies from the label of superstition, and by doing so they encouraged lay healers. They also changed the notion of superstition. It is enough to compare Erasmus' opinion with Bacon's about superstition to

[99] Alvinczi: 1633, I, p. 474.
[100] Kecskeméti: 1621, p. 89.
[101] *Ibid.,* p. 90.
[102] *Ibid.,* p. 89. – Fabó: 1905. – Schram: 1970, I, p. 450 (1654), p. 490 (1711), p. 193 (1716), p. 257 (1739), p. 343 (1758).

see that the great task of the 17th century was to separate science from magic. "Enlightening people" could not be effective alone. Especially if the ritual, magic elements of lay healing were judged to be "witchcraft" and the work of the devil from the pulpits. The negative examples "popularized" this way became a matter of common knowledge. The lay healer was supplied with new means which he could use for his own ends in his conflicts with patients who took offence, their desperate relatives, or his furious rivals.

Stopping witch trials was a complicated task; there were so many circumstances to be taken into account, and it demanded co-ordinated, well-timed measures on the part of the sovereign power. This is proved by the attempt of Prince Gábor Bethlen.

In 1615 the Prince extended the protection of the state to a lay healer in Transylvania, Anna Bencsik, mentioned earlier. She was attacked by the barbers' guild in Kolozsvár. Gábor Bethlen issued a diploma dated 1615 in which he declared that Anna Bencsik was authorized to heal people suffering from different illnesses, wounds and ailments, and "the knowledge she has in healing she shall be free to use in the future". Healing should not be a privilege.[103] This view, however, was untenable. After all, healing is a privilege, the privilege of knowledge and vocation. The majority of traditional healers were illiterate. The school system did not make it possible to train women even at an elementary level, and in an agrarian society the demands of agricultural labour always took priority over the schooling of young peasant boys. The significance of the diploma issued to Anna Bencsik consisted in the fact that the social acceptance and recognition of a lay healer indicated a genuine demand.

Gábor Bethlen ruled with the methods of early absolutism; he introduced reforms in many fields of government from foreign affairs to economy. Some of his measures prove that he was interested in public health, too. For example he issued a decree regulating the activity of barbers: "if a person had no knowledge of internal diseases, he must not set up as a doctor, for if he should cause anybody's death, he, too must die".[104] The Prince was fully aware of the problems of maintaining the health of the population. This is well illustrated by some details of the famous, or infamous witch trial.

In traditional historiography three lawsuits carried on against three aristocratic women in 1614, 1618 and 1621, respectively, were bracketed un-

---

[103] MOL P 1830. Miscellaneous papers, 1615.
[104] Szilágyi: 1875–1898, VIII, p. 351.

der the heading of "witch trials". However, each of them was of an essentially different order. The first one, as we have pointed out, was a political trial, to consolidate the power of Bethlen who succeeded Gábor Báthori (1608–1613) on the throne. The second trial was a retribution initiated by a jealous husband rather than anything else. The third one was a typical witch trial commenced on a charge of healing and bewitchment. The reason why these three trials were bracketed was twofold. On the one hand, the principal defendant in all three trials was Anna Báthori. The evident features of her personality have not been clarified as yet. We do not know whether she practised the art of healing similarly to other women of her social class, but it is a fact that several other herb women, "seers" and "smearing women" were arrested with her in 1621. On the other hand, the three trials were all judged uniformly to be witch trials due to a misinterpretation of Gábor Bethlen's law of 1614.[105]

Bethlen convoked the diet of Medgyes at the beginning of 1614 to consolidate his power and the internal order of the country. Nothing was said about witches in the Prince's proposals. Among a number of rigorous measures intended to restore public safety and the security of property, he suggested that the Estates should see that "all people holding harmful and strange notions" were rooted out. Keeping this in mind the Estates included in the second article of the laws of 1614 that "seers, soothsayers, charmers, practitioners of devilish lore, as well as persons who, defying the strict commandments of God, follow such people, ask them to tell their fortune or use charms" should be punished. Similar laws decreeing the punishment of sorcerers and charmers had been imposed by Hungarian kings as early as before 1526. Bethlen ordered "peasants to be punished according to ancient custom", while cases of the nobility came under the jurisdiction of their own institutions.[106] In other words, this was not the introduction of a new law, but the revival, in modified form, of one dating from the old Hungarian kingdom. Although the sins listed – sorcery, fortune telling, the use of charms – could easily pass for witchcraft as it was understood in those times, they had other aspects as well in the given political situation. At the beginning of 1614 Bethlen emphasized repeatedly that internal peace was to be restored. With this in view he wanted to suppress all gossiping, guessing, whispering meant to prophesy changes and to interpret signs, in relation to his own deeds as well which ruffled public feeling. Those who were punishable under the terms of this law included the "seer", the clairvoyant capable of identifying the person, the

---

[105] *Ibid.,* VI, pp. 412–413.
[106] *Ibid.,* VI, p. 413.

witch who caused an illness. That is to say, people who "unmasked" witches were responsible for sparking off conflicts. Not even Bethlen's contemporaries regarded his law of 1614 as one conceived for the purposes of persecuting witches. It was never mentioned in the verdicts. Using "charms" occurred as a punishable offence in other similar laws as well which were concerned with trespassers, murderers, receivers of stolen goods and "thieves", i.e. smugglers.

What gave occasion for the trial of 1621 was the illness of the princess-consort Zsuzsanna Károlyi, who had been suffering from severe depression for years past. It may have been the death of their children, her own frail health, and, finally, the disease attacking her that brought about in her that state of mind in which rationality gave way to blind hope and wild fantasies. Apart from a fragment of a testimony, some letters written by Bethlen at a time when he was leading a campaign in Upper Hungary are the only known sources that supply valuable information on the case.[107] The letters have a peculiar tone. Bethlen wrote in a way to reassure his wife, avoiding to contradict her. That was, perhaps, the reason why he called Anna Báthori whom his wife hated, "evidently a charmer". The question is not whether or not Gábor Bethlen believed in witches. In a sense, and within certain limits he obviously did. Even Maria Theresa's celebrated law had its Article 4, which assumed the extraordinary possibility of diabolic magic. However, Bethlen's lines written to his wife when she was seriously ill, show that the opinion he held of the mutually overlapping concepts of lay healers, witches and witch trials had been formed in keeping with the logic of his times. He knew the traditional healers well, but he suggested that his wife should call a "head doctor", and should take medicine prescribed by doctors. It is not possible to state with certainty, whether he himself believed what he wrote to his wife; namely, that the witches should be forced by torture to heal her.[108] If we knew more about the princess-consort's illness, it would be easier to answer this question.[109] It is certain that traditional healers frequented the house of the lady when her condition was deteriorating. She herself cherished credulous notions of "charms" and "bewitching". In a society where the hygiene of the masses was in the hands of lay healers and it was never sure how successful the learned doctors' treatment would be; when people had hardly any rational knowledge of the causes of illnesses, and knew only

[107] Nagy: 1988, pp. 170–181, 191.

[108] With an emphasis on Bethlen's superstitious beliefs, quoted by Nagy: 1988, pp. 174–175.

[109] Csetri: 1992, pp. 114–115.

the symptoms, it was inevitable that the characteristic state should have been one of transition, between belief in witches and unbelief. People relied on the "medical women" and "learned women" because there was no one else, and they knew from experience that these women could help, but at the same time they were aware that the reward for the services of these healers could be death at the stake, if they turned out to be "witches". To improve this state of affairs the reform and radical reorganization of the whole system of public hygiene was needed.

In the second half of the 17th century in Transylvania it was the puritans and mainly the Cartesians who began to link theory, medical practice and the decisions taken by the sovereign power, with a view to judging the charges of witchcraft rationally, and serving the cause of public health.

Mátyás Nógrádi, a preacher, later bishop of Debrecen, who had studied in Leyden and Utrecht and had been to England, too, published his work entitled *The Spiritual Touchstone* in 1651, with the object of separating the well-founded charges of witchcraft from the unfounded ones. He classified the charges of witchcraft according as they were evidently unprovable, vague and worthy of attention, respectively.[110] This could supply a number of new arguments for acquitting lay healers. It is to be noted that Maria Theresa's law of a later date (1766) applied the same method, listing, point by point, what did not fall under the head of witchcraft, and defining what "real" diabolic magic was.

János Apáczai Csere (1625–1659), who wrote his *Hungarian Encyclopedia* in the spirit of Descartes (1653), described in detail the anatomy of the human body, the functions of life, digestion, procreation, pregnancy, and delivery on a level with contemporary science, providing lay healers virtually with a new handbook.[111] Intellectually Apáczai was in close contact with Sámuel Enyedi (1627–1671), a doctor, who was the first to perform an autopsy in the Principality, and with János Nadányi (1643–1707). Besides fostering Apáczai's plan to found an Academy of Sciences, Nadányi also contributed to securing one of its prerequisites when he assisted in establishing a botanic garden, in the court of Prince Mihály Apafi (1661–1690). Here were the roots of the large-scale undertaking to free lay healers, in the long run, from the potential charges of witchcraft.

In the 1680s Ferenc Pápai Páriz, (1649–1716) court-physician to Prince Mihály Apafi, began writing a book in Hungarian which was to unite the

[110] Makkai: 1983, 1988.
[111] Spielmann: 1977, pp. 127–135. – Apáczai: 1653 (1977), pp. 226–280.

257

results of traditional and scientific healing. He received encouragement and financial support from the Prince's wife, Anna Bornemisza (?–1688). This was not the first instance of her conferring her patronage upon an undertaking. János Nadányi, the Cartesian professor of Nagyenyed College had translated a Latin work of a French doctor Antoine Mizauld (1520–1578) published in Paris in 1574, with moral and financial support from Anna Bornemisza, who was interested in healing, too. The translation entitled a *Description of Garden Things* was intended for those people "who, owing to their poverty, cannot always call a doctor, or turn to a money-grubbing apothecary, medical doctors and apothecaries' shops being scarce in our country". The consideration of public welfare with reference to a "medical garden" was no longer new at the time; it had been expressed in the Prince's plan to establish an Academy. Works like that generally had the support of ladies, from the very beginning. The first *Ars Medica* giving a scientifically systematized, comprehensive survey of the entire human body was the work of György Lencsés (1530–1593), steward of the household of Erzsébet Bocskai, wife of Kristóf Báthori, Prince of Transylvania (1530–1581). The book was not written for learned doctors, but was intended by its author "for the poor ignorant people, ... so that they too can benefit from it".[112]

Also Ferenc Pápai Páriz's book, written on a level with the best medical works of the age, was intended "for the householders and housewives and the helpless poor who cannot always find a sensible doctor within reach".[113] Pápai included in his work the new medicinal herbs he had got to know in the course of his studies in Basel, and it was from his book that they came into general use in folkloric medicine. Writing the book from 1683 for several years, he made use of the local experiences gained in his own practice. He borrowed things that he found reasonable and useful, and rejected mere beliefs, making a clear distinction between science and superstition based on the knowledge and mentality of the 17th century, taking into consideration the patients' way of thinking and the importance of rituals. His greatest merit was that instead of underestimating traditional therapeutic processes, folkloric medicines and the curative methods used by lay healers, he incorporated them, after a thorough critical sifting, in scientific medicine, and handed them back in this form to the lay healers.[114] In this sense Pápai's book offered a means to make an

[112] Spielmann: 1977, p. 61. In summary: *ibid.*, pp. 48–97.
[113] Pápai Páriz: 1690 (1977), p. 199.
[114] *Ibid.*, p. 22. – Spielmann: 1977, pp. 136–153.

end to witch trials. There had always been an interaction between scientific medicine and lay healing. The hygienic culture of the élite had never been separated by insurmountable walls from the hygienic culture called folkloric; signs of mutual effects and interpenetration could be observed. This was the cultural sphere in which the customs, gestures, courses of action characteristic of all people of the era were easily discernible.[115] In Pápai's work the utilizable empirical knowledge of several centuries was integrated with the science of medicine, while lay healers were offered the results of learned doctoring. This kind of a legitimate solution of the problems of mass hygiene could have led to the establishment of a health service in the provinces and for the poor, the elimination of really superstitious beliefs, the prevention of outbreaks of mass hysteria, and the cessation of charges of witchcraft. Considering that charges of witchcraft were most often brought against lay healers on account of women's or children's diseases, it is particularly laudable that the two supplementary chapters added to the second edition of *Pax Corporis* (1695) dealt with "women's ailments" and "the external and internal ailments of small children", respectively. What Pápai Páriz said concerning the need for prophylactic medicine, the beneficial effects of fresh air, ventilation, walking, adequate nutrition, public sanitation and checking epidemics, was up to date by international standards. What could be the reason why Pápai Páriz never became the Hungarian Van Swieten, and why more than half a century had to pass before witch trials were abolished in Hungary?[116] The question is all the more legitimate as doubts were raised almost simultaneously with the first witch trials in Hungary. These opinions have not been thoroughly examined as yet, and the relevant documents have not been systematically collected either. However, the not too many 17th-century instances can serve virtually as models in an overall survey.[117] Who were

---

[115] Spielmann: 1979, pp. 36–43.
[116] Szállási: 1975. – Spielmann: 1979, p. 46.
[117] The following examples are not meant to be exhaustive: In 1628 two women, charged with witchcraft, refused to come before a court in Transylvania, and the bailiff stood up for them. According to an unknown defendant in 1641: the person who was suspected would pass for a witch. The steward of István Pálffy in Nagyszombat, talking of captured witches quoted the words of one of them: "if her Moravian skirt should burn, a lot of taffeta and cambric will be burnt afterwards". The words of an equally anonymous woman put in the manorial prison of Németújvár in 1651 were indicative of social tensions: "the little witches are caught, while the great ones go unpunished". A girl accused of witchcraft in 1666 claimed: "Bathing a person in water cannot be taken by a tribunal as an evident proof of witchcraft". Another girl charged with witchcraft in Debrecen, in 1677, protested: "I deny any kind of devilish practices; I am not a witch, and if I bathed anyone in a herbal bath, I did no evil by that". In 1653, in the county of Győr, the counsel for the defendant

259

the people who doubted the existence of witchcraft? Defendants, witnesses, counsels for the defence, judges could be found among them. Furthermore, people who had interests involved in the acquittal of the defendant: members of the family, officers of the estate and patients cured by the defendant. Robert Mandrou, a Frenchman, and József Spielmann, a Transylvanian expert on the history of medicine expressed the opinion almost at the same time, according to which the concept of rationality changed from time to time. That is why the rational content of the doubts should be judged very carefully. It is interesting, however, that the quality and the numerical ratio of the doubts, and the social background and the education of the doubters did not essentially differ from those in the 18th century.[118] It is therefore impossible to evade the crucial question: why was it that the flames of the stakes were put out in Hungary only as late as the second half of the reign of Maria Theresa (1740–1780)?

---

argued the same way as the lawyer István Igriczi in the county of Ugocsa in 1689 in the case of Ilona Varga: the charges were unfounded "a pack of silly rumours", nursery tales, and he referred to Article 56 of the law of 1550. In Zagreb the same argument was used in defence of Marijana Fabriczka in 1657, as could be heard in a sermon preached by János Kecskeméti in Debrecen in 1621: the witches' Sabbath was nothing but a dream. In 1671 a lawyer giving reasons for banning witch trials used the old formula but with a new meaning: "since there are no witches, they should not even be mentioned, let alone brought before a court". The wording of a decision made by a manorial court in 1693 was very similar to that of the Queen's decree to be issued half a century later: "in such criminal cases the evidence produced should be as clear as daylight, and no one should be sentenced to be burnt at the stake on a mere suspicion". In 1699 three defendants were acquitted in the county of Pest, and the reason given was that the charges were founded on "mere suspicions and superstitions" and childish lies, which proved nothing. Sources in the order of the cases quoted: Pálffy Archives (Arm. VIII. Lad. 12. Fl. fol. 1191). – Schram: 1982, p. 281. – Eckhart: 1954, pp. 132, 138. – Komáromy: 1910, pp. 127, 148. – Klaniczay, G.: 1985, pp. 56–57. – Eckhart: 1954, p. 138. – Borosy: 1986, pp. 3446–3447.

[118] As counsel for the defence, the lawyer Ferenc Budaházi argued in 1725 that transformations were but dreams, the accusations were based on hearsay and could not be proved. "Gernyszegh anno 1740 Decembris 30", this was the exact date recorded by somebody whose anonymous comment was added to the minutes of the case of Mrs. Borbála Rozsnyai: "the testimonies were given by half-witted and simple-minded people, and such as were bemused and stupefied with drink, had visionary dreams, or thirsted for revenge". How uncertain the judges had become was well shown by the verdict of the deputy-sherif of the county of Kolozs: on the strength of the witnesses' testimonies "the defendant ought to die, but as the state of witchhood is very obscure, and the human mind can hardly penetrate it, in view of this the defendant shall not be sentenced to death". A characteristic instance is provided by the debate that took place in 1730 when the case of Zsuzsa Szenczy and her two companions was brought before the manorial court of the Archbishop of Esztergom. On the authority of the "Tripartitum" (a Hungarian statute-book published in 1517), I/15, and the Praxis Criminalis, the prosecutor proposed torture to be followed by

It was not in the age of Maria Theresa that the belief in witches and the problems of lay healing were first considered to be problems that the sovereign power was competent to decide and control. It happened, perhaps, during the reign of King Mátyás (1443–1490) for the first time that the King asked for the testimonies in cases of witchcraft as the term was understood at the time.[119] After the few decrees issued in the 16th century, which dealt with the health care of the army, the protection of doctors, and the duties of midwives, Prince Gábor Bethlen used his sovereign power to initiate and supervise witch trials and to acquit defendants.

Somewhat similar methods can be observed in the last large-scale witch trial in the independent Principality of Transylvania. Relatively few witch trials are known to have taken place during the reign of Prince Mihály Apafi (1661–1690), a Cartesian. It is the more surprising to see the legal proceedings taken against Zsuzsanna Vitéz, wife of Pál Béldi, one of Apafi's political opponents, and the more than two dozen lay healing and herb women, "learned women" associated with her. The charge of witchcraft was attributable to the incurable disease of the princess-consort, Anna Bornemisza, who suffered a mental breakdown, caused by grave domestic misfortunes, including the death of probably more than ten children. The trial is important from our point of view because the right to examine and decide the case was reserved for the sovereign power in this instance as well. The Prince set up a special committee to judge the case. The committee consisted of representatives of the Transylvanian Estates, the Hungarian counties, the Székely districts and the Saxon "Universitas" delegated

---

burning at the stake. The defendants denied the charges; their lawyer defended them, supporting his arguments with the authority of János Kithonich's *Directio Methodica* (1619). The prosecutor demanded repeated torture. However, the defendants continued to deny the charges, even after they had been put to the torture. Ultimately, they were not sentenced to death by the tribunal which consisted of the Archbishop's steward, the bailiff and the deputy-sheriff of the county of Komárom. Kristóf: 1991–1992, pp. 96–99. – Schram: 1982, p. 99. – Komáromy: 1910, p. 454. – Kállay: 1985, p. 200.

[119] In 1478 – according to Károly Tagányi – Benedek Kistapolcsányi and Osváth Korlátkövi accused Mrs. Mihály Zerdahelyi and all the women of the Zerdahelyi family of making poison. King Mátyás ordered an inquiry into the case of these women – among whom there were married women, widows, and unmarried women alike; dozens of witnesses were interrogated, and a report was to be made to the King. Tagányi did not call the case a witch trial, nor did Schram include it in the list of trials registered since the middle of the 13th century. Still, it is worth mentioning that the date of this trial coincided with the year of publication of the *Malleus maleficarum,* and the effect of the work of J. Sprenger and H. Kraemer on the witch trials in the Kingdom of Hungary and Transylvania could be felt long afterwards. Tagányi: 1887, No. 2. – Schram: 1982, p. 49. – Spielmann: 1979, p. 42.

by an act of the diet, in 1685, with some more members added the following year. More than two hundred witnesses were interrogated, counsel was heard on both sides, and even after repeated examinations, Chief Justice Péter Alvinczy, an eminent jurist, considered the accusations to be unfounded. In this trial, most probably the longest in the era, dragging on for years and years, only one death-sentence was passed, but whether it was carried out is not known; and the trial was ended, without a conclusion, probably by the death of the princess-consort (1680).[120]

Also Count Lipót Kollonits, president of the Court Chamber, later Archbishop of Esztergom, believed that modernizing public hygiene and stopping witch trials were tasks for the sovereign power, and, relying on several preliminary plans, he worked out a scheme for the establishment of Habsburg administration in Hungary recaptured from the Turks (1686–1689). Although a few decrees partially affecting public hygiene were issued in the 1690s, his comprehensive scheme was never realized. The state continued to persecute witches, putting the law into operation in all its rigour, resorting also to the intimidation of the masses.

In 1696 the Praxis Criminalis, the penal code in force in the Austrian provinces since 1656, was introduced in Hungary as well. Its paragraph 60, "De magia", clearly included lay healers with "venefici, incantatores, stryges" in the category of witches in the general sense of the word. Besides, they were bracketed with common criminals, such as murderers, robbers, highwaymen, and those who were dubbed "evil-doers" for opposing the given political system. At the same time, the Praxis Criminalis (arts. 25, 62) extended the barbers' sphere of activity. It became their task to hold post-mortem examinations, though very often they were not properly qualified for this work.

Barbers were also employed to give expert opinion on procured abortions and the death of infants which gave rise to the charges of witchcraft in a number of cases (II. 66, 67). Extracting confessions by torture became a routine. As stipulated in a special article, doctors were exempted from this. From that time on it was the examiners themselves who recounted the stories of witchcraft in the questions put to the defendants and their witnesses. The decrees issued by the central government between 1683 and 1703 may have been intended to make things better, but ultimately they only served to intensify the charges of witchcraft instead of depriving them of their force.[121]

[120] Herner: 1988. – Szilágyi: 1875–1898, XVIII, pp. 343, 499.
[121] Mayer: 1911 (1980). – Iklódy: 1982.

In the state of Rákóczi (1703–1711) the handling of witch trials by the sovereign power fitted in with the measures taken in the fields of public health, social welfare and medicine. According to the statute-book of the standing army, witches, i.e. lay healers were banned from the camps; at the same time steps were taken to organize the health care of the army on French and Dutch models. All soldiers, from private to high-ranking officer, were entitled to medical service, and, if necessary, the aftercare of invalids. The barber or surgeon who caused the death of a patient, forfeited his life. Those practising the "diabolic art" "should be burnt alive", but only if the charge was "proved". Proving it was the task of the state. Relatively few witch trials have been recorded from these eight years. Since there were two armies – the Emperor's and Rákóczi's – fighting in the country, and the borderlines kept changing all the time, it is impossible to establish the precise number of trials conducted on the territories controlled by the Habsburgs and Rákóczi, respectively. It is certain that the Hungarian state did have a say in the verdicts, and it forbade people to take the law into their own hands.[122] The state power had been concerned in "handling" witch trials for a long time. Connections were found between lay healing and witch trials; the attempts made to reform public hygiene affected the witch trials, too. However, all the attempts failed because of the lack of time and the lack of political stability. At the beginning of the 18th century it became evident that the old system did not work any more. It was not possible to get rid of witches, exterminating them by force of the penal law. The stricter the measures became, the more witches appeared on the scene.

In comparison with earlier figures, the number of witch trials in Hungary trebled between 1690 and 1768.[123] According to András Iklódy the reason for this strange phenomenon was the introduction of the *Praxis*

---

[122] Takáts: 1980. – Hadi Edictum: A War Edict, 1706/45. – Regulamentum Universale: I/1–13 1707. *Ráday Iratok*: 1955–1961, pp. 393–396. An inquiry ordered, by word of mouth, by the Honourable General Pál Orosz, and carried out by the head of the military court. MOL G 16 V 2 h, (Archives of Rákóczi's war of independence). n.d. – Komáromy: 1910, pp. 243–244.

[123] Iklódy: 1982. – Kállay: 1985, p. 199. – On the basis of the summary by Klaniczay, G.: 1985:

	1526–1690	1690–1770
trials:	426	1208
death sentences:	149 (29%)	340 (3.3%)
lighter punishments:	43	181
acquittals:	32	206
not known:	205	501

Criminalis.[124] Other factors suggested by way of explanation include Western influences, the presence of masses of soldiers quartered in the country, and the infiltration of the belief in vampires.[125]

The increasing number of the trials indicated something else as well. It was a symptom of acute crisis. It showed that the methods used, on the whole successfully, to maintain the activity of lay healers and healing the public in general in a state of balance had become ineffective and outdated. What belonged to the past did not work any longer, and there was as yet nothing new to replace it. As is well known, the observations of Lucy Mair on the connections between the techniques of handling diseases and crises on the one hand and witch trials on the other attracted notice in the international discussion of the problems of witchcraft, largely because conclusions of a general character could be drawn from them.[126]

Examining the remarkably increasing number of trials, we have to consider that this was the time when the whole of Hungary came under Habsburg rule, whereas in the 16th and 17th centuries only about one fifth of its territory had been controlled by the Kingdom of Hungary. It was now that the vast, uninhabited or scarcely populated tracts recaptured from the Turks were settled with people who came from the mountain regions of Transylvania and Upper Hungary, and mainly from the densely populated neighbouring and more remote countries.

In the course of eight decades the number of inhabitants doubled, the figure rising from 4 million to 8 or 9 million by 1790.

According to Iklódy, no permanent correlation can be pointed out between the number of inhabitants and the witch trials. However, it is a fact that the majority of witch trials took place in the recaptured areas.

The greater part of the new settlers came from the west. Still, it is not likely that the "fashion of witches" should have been imported by them from the west to the east. The results of the research on Austrian witch trials should put us on our guard. Firstly, the increase in the number of witch trials in Styria about the middle of the 17th century is explained to some extent by the fact that refugees driven out of Hungarian territories by Turkish attacks, as well as some vagabond characters repaired to those parts. Secondly, the ratio of men and women among the defendants was strikingly different in the Habsburg provinces and Hungary (50 : 50%)

[124] Iklódy: 1982. – Demkó: 1894, p. 409.
[125] Klaniczay, G.: 1987, p. 266.
[126] Mair: 1969, pp. 7–9.

(10 : 90%).[127] At the same time, farther to the west of Hungary as anywhere else, the persecution of witches continued in the regions difficult of access, while in the central, more open parts it had ceased.[128]

An examination of the circumstances of public hygiene can reveal some deep-lying inner causes of the increase in the number of witch trials which have not been considered so far.

After the Turkish wars and Rákóczi's war of independence (1699, 1711, 1718), the Habsburg government set up its administration as a result of compromises with the Hungarian Estates, both preserving the old order of things, and promoting the cause of the Empire with a view to achieving unity in religion, administration and economy. In the recaptured areas large estates of several thousand acres came into being. A large number of these were owned by Austrian, Czech and German aristocratic absentee landlords. The competence of the local municipal authorities was restricted, and the towns and counties were compelled to carry out orders issued by the central government. Protestants were not allowed to hold a public office, and were deprived of their colleges, schools and very many of their foundations. The populations were obliged to bear unendurable burdens in the form of taxes, restrictions inseparable from trade monopolies, and the costs of maintaining the soldiers billeted on them. The constant state of war had upset the biological balance of society as early as the previous century, and now (1715), with a large number of young men drafted into the imperial army from areas inhabited by Hungarians, the ratio of men and women became even more unfavourable, showing a majority of women over the men, and the number of unmarried women and widows was high.

New, excessive burdens were loaded on the old system of public health care: conflicts of the new settlers, a multitude of wounded and crippled people, and an unprecedented series of epidemics. At a time when the old system did not function any more, and no new one had been set up as yet, quacks and charlatans flourished under paradisiacal conditions. The

---

[127] Valentinitsch: 1987, p. 300. – Dienst: 1987, p. 20.

	Women (%)	Men (%)	Not known (%)
Hungary	90	10	–
Lower Austria	59.4	34.2	6.4
Upper Austria	20.8	68.8	10.4
Carinthia	40.2	52.8	7
Vienna	41.5	58.5	–
Styria	48	34.3	17.7

[128] Klaniczay, G.: 1991–92, pp. 69–70, 78–81.

neighbourhood of military camps and the recaptured areas were a particularly happy hunting-ground for cheats, impostors and "wonder-working doctors".[129]

The gravely critical state of the country's public hygiene was indicated by the epidemics of the period and the consequences of the inability to cope with them. The plague and the smallpox had often attacked the country before, but no epidemic ever had such terrible consequences as could be compared to those of the plague of 1738–1744, including an outbreak of mass hysteria.

The disease was imported by soldiers fighting in the imperial army against the Turks in alliance with the Russians. It grew to more formidable dimensions than any of the earlier epidemics, not only because the towns kept the first cases secret, making things worse by doing so, but also because it lasted for 6 years, and reached areas which had not been affected before. Whole families died out; and the local daily bills of death reported 20, 40, even 160 cases each. The epidemic spread to the villages, and out of 48,245 patients from 501 Transylvanian parishes 42,622 died. The Council of Governors took severe measures in good time, appointing a commissioner of public health for each particular district. However, it appeared very soon that there were no doctors available, not enough healers, medical servants were often drunk, doctors', apprentices had to be sworn not to rob corpses, and that there was not enough money for medicines, disinfection, isolation hospitals and lime. Poor people did not allow the clothes of the sick to be burnt. There were scandalous scenes and outbreaks of panic; often the army had to intervene. Anyone breaking through the sanitary cordon was to be sentenced to death. The vine dresser who spoke with a plague-stricken person, should pay for it with his life. There were riots which were sometimes put down by force of arms; sometimes a town was blockaded by the military. Mass hysteria was spreading, and it was not too difficult to find scapegoats: the blame could be put upon the Germans, the Serbs, the Armenians, the Hungarians, the Jews, the military, the county officers, the commissioners of public hygiene, the doctors, the surgeons and the lay healers...[130]

The witch trials examined between 1711–1751 show that the charges of witchcraft contained some new elements, and the concept of witchcraft had become practically boundless. A new feature to be found in the belief

[129] Héjja: 1936. – Gortvay: 1953. – Takáts: 1980.

[130] For the reports to the Council of Government from towns and counties, see: Magyary-Kossa: 1929–1940, IV, pp. 271, 286, 288–294, 299–303, 300–303, 310–310/a, 319–323. – Dávid: 1973.

in witchcraft was that now it was absorbing some political views, and political opinions came to influence the verdicts of judges as well. Under the given circumstances of healing, conflicts occurred more frequently, and competition between the lay healers and other groups engaged in medical activities was becoming increasingly desperate.

Still, in these very decades, when an unprecedentedly large number of people were burnt at the stake in Hungary, there were areas where witch trials ceased. In the county of Szepes the last trial was held in 1717, and in the county of Pozsony in 1730. In the county of Nyitra there was only one trial after 1732, in 1745; in the county of Nógrád the stake was used for the last time in 1692, and the last accusation was made in 1754. In the area of the Saxon Universitas the high sheriff, Andreas Teutsch abolished witch trials at the beginning of 1720.[131]

Andreas Teutsch (1669–1730) studied medicine in Holland. In the counties where witch trials had ceased before the queen's decree was issued, there were county head doctors functioning. The counties started employing officially appointed head doctors under the decree issued in 1700 by Duke Pál Esterházy, Palatine of Hungary. All these head doctors without exception had graduated from German or Dutch universities, some of the older ones holding posts in Rákóczi's state, and their activity combined theory and practice. It is very important from our point of view that similarly to Pápai Páriz, they knew and made use of the experiences of the lay healers, and at the same time, they were fighting for far-reaching reforms to reorganize the health service in the whole of Hungary. Their way of thinking was characterized by the early enlightenment and the principles of Pietism. This type of Hungarian doctor was probably best represented by János Dániel Perliczy (1705–1778).

Perliczy, who had graduated from a Dutch university was head doctor of the county of Nógrád in which the lesser nobility was known to have pietist leanings. He knew well that the problem of caring for the health of village people was totally unsolved, and he published two books, following in the steps of his predecessors, intended for lay healers: *Medicina pauperum, or household remedies for the poor,* and *A Guide to the peace of the body.* As early as 1733, he set down rules and regulations for the use of doctors, surgeons, midwives and apothecaries, and had them sanctioned by the general assembly of the county. He also prepared a large-scale work about the hygienic conditions in the country (1742). He maintained that

---

[131] Magyary-Kossa: 1929–1940, IV, pp. 125, 239, 304. Witch trials in the county of Szepes: 1636, 1638, 1639. – Förster: 1910, pp. 242–249 (1618).

the number of doctors and surgeons in the country was appallingly low; part of them were aliens who did not even understand Hungarian. The inhabitants were defenceless, and the medical activities of swindlers and untrained chirurgeons caused irreparable damage. Only those doctors could be expected to be familiar with domestic conditions who were trained in Hungary. He drew up the academic programme and calculated the costs of a medical university to be founded in Pest. After some abortive efforts made in the 17th century the Hungarian diet proposed, as early as 1723, the extension of the University of Nagyszombat by the addition of a medical faculty. Perliczy's memorandum, handed in to the queen in 1751 was discussed and shelved the same year by a committee of the Council of Government.[132] However, it was not in vain that Perliczy made his proposal for a reform embracing practically all problems of public hygiene in Hungary. True, it was only after a delay of two decades, and even then not exactly as he and the other doctors practising in Hungary had expected, that their attempts ultimately met with success.

The early 1740s saw a rare historic instance of the happy coincidence of a cause urgently calling for action, an official power open to reforms and prepared to take decisions, and the appearance of an able, competent personage. Gerard van Swieten (1700–1772) took up his office of "proto-medicus" in Vienna in 1743.[133] The imperial capital was overcome with panic on account of the plague in Hungary and its consequences, the Treasury had run out of funds, and the government was impotent. The young empress, Maria Theresa was scared of the epidemic. She herself and her family had been badly affected by the smallpox. Her counsellors were aware that the problems of public health had a bearing on taxation and also on the strength of the army, and it was the monarch's sacred duty to come to the rescue of poor wretched people.

The decrees moderating the persecution of witches and the law restricting the trials to the utmost, were links of a chain of comprehensive reforms in matters of public health. The more important stages of the process were the following: in 1743 the hygienic conditions of cemeteries were regulated; in 1745–1747 the standardization of medicines was introduced, and a decree regulated the tasks of midwives throughout the country. In 1752 a decree issued by the Queen ordered all counties to employ well-trained doctors who should live in the county town, and should attend to

[132] Magyary–Kossa: 1929–1940, III, p. 304.
[133] Kreuzinger: 1924. – Brechka: 1970. – H. Balázs: 1973. – Klaniczay, G.: 1985.

the poor free of charge. In 1753 the hygienic problems of prisons were regulated, and a decree issued in 1754 ordered that those practising medicine anywhere in the country without a doctor's degree should be imprisoned. In 1755 the "Planum regulations is in re sanitatis" came out and the counties and towns received the Queen's decree condemning various superstitions including the belief in witchcraft. The decree clearly defined the activity of doctors, surgeons (chirurgeons) and midwives. It also ordered that the activity of certain lay groups – lithotomists, herniotomists, tooth pullers (dentifrangibuli) – who had segregated from the barbers should be permitted only if every precaution was taken and they were kept under supervision by the authorities. From the next year on all the sentences of torture and death were to be forwarded to the central authorities for approval, together with the complete minutes of the witch trials. In 1756 a compulsory examination in surgery was prescribed for surgeons. In 1758 a decree was issued with regard to those who were persecuted as magicians and poisoners, and from that date it was no longer the minutes, but the defendants of the witch trials that were to be sent to Vienna, and local authorities were prohibited from dealing with witch trials. In 1765 the aliens among the unqualified healers were expelled from the country, while the natives were imprisoned. In November 1766 the celebrated law, the "Lex caesaroregie ad extirpandam superstitionem ac rationalem judicationem criminalem Magiae, Sortilegii" was enacted. At the beginning of 1768 the "Constitutio Criminalis Theresiana" which codified the law, appeared. In 1769 a decision was made regarding the establishment of the medical faculty. In 1770 the "Generale Normativum Sanitatis" came out which strictly forbade, among others, the activity of healers and midwives who had no diplomas, or had passed no examination. In 1771, at long last, the medical faculty began to function in Nagyszombat.[134]

The law concerning witchcraft, then, was a part of the reform which affected all the problems of public hygiene. It was worthy of the learning and mentality of the man who prepared it. Van Swieten followed in his master's footsteps. Hermann Boerhave (1638–1738) was the revolutionary founder of clinical medicine who hated superstition, but "advocated the superiority of empirical therapeutics following nature as against a set of pedantic dogmas".[135]

---

[134] Linzbauer: 1852–1856, II, pp. 776–785. – Komáromy: 1910, pp. 600–612. – Eckhart: 1954, pp. 138–139. – Fekete: 1970. – Kapronczay: 1985. – Erdős: 1988.
[135] Lindeboom: 1968. – Spielmann: 1969.

As has been suggested earlier, the law which put an end to witch trials was one of the measures taken with a view to a general reform of public hygiene in the country. Wiping out the persecution of witches depended less on the, by no means negligible, force of the law, than a comprehensive organization of public hygiene set up on a scientific basis for the benefit of the masses which could guarantee that there would be no more conflicts producing charges of witchcraft.

What happened, following such measures, to those harassed anonymous outcasts of public hygiene, the lay healers?

Van Swieten, as we have seen, could rely on considerable antecedents in Hungary. In preparing the plan to reform public hygiene in the country he worked together with Hungarian doctors. One of his closest collaborators was István Weszprémi, a doctor (1723–1799) who had studied at Dutch and English universities, but, similarly to his Hungarian colleagues, was thoroughly familiar with the circumstances of public health in Hungary, and he, too, had written a handbook which lay healers could use.

In comparison with the antecedents the law which put an end to the persecution of witches in Hungary had the essential novelty of forming an integral part of a comprehensive reform of public hygiene. In its theoretical assumptions the law observed principles laid down as early as the 16th and 17th centuries, refusing to accept for evidence fanciful, malicious, or misleading stories, the fantasies of people mentally deranged, and the misleading statements of the defendants. It forbade the application of inhuman and ill-advised methods of investigation, such as ordeal by water, pricking, extracting confession by torture, branding people, and the use of antidotes against sorcery. It regulated punishments and suggested reasonable measures; e.g. impostors should pay damages, and the mentally deranged should be taken to hospital. Unless proved by "infallible evidence", charges of diabolic practices should be dismissed. In cases of witchcraft "really and truly proved" the right to decide was reserved for the monarch. Blasphemous fantasts, particularly those whose hands were stained with blood, deserved to be burnt at the stake.

As was clear from the law, lay healers were freed from the threat of the stake. But where was their place now in the new order established for handling the problems of public hygiene, in rural areas, and improving the critical living conditions of village people?

In practice the reform of public hygiene, though prudent and sound in principle, and based in part on Hungarian antecedents, did not work at all, or worked only within very narrow limits. The counties, pleading their alleged or real tax burdens, failed to pay their doctors, or paid them very badly; in the 1770s and 1780s there were counties keeping only one doctor each, or none at all. Provided that these figures are correct, Kassa had three midwives in its employ at the end of the 18th century, exactly the same number as at the end of the 17th century. An increase in population was not followed by a corresponding increase in the number of doctors. When in 1768, the county of Békés was called upon by the Council of Government to employ a county medical officer, they answered that it was impossible, since there was no doctor available, and anyway, they could not see the point of doing what was demanded of them, considering that they had had a county surgeon in their employ for fifteen years whom no one ever went to see. No sudden change set in even when the central government took it upon itself, with effect from 1770, to pay the county medical officers and surgeons. The Council of Government wished to appoint superannuated military medical officers to the posts in the counties, but since they did not know the native tongue of the regions concerned, people did not go to see them, even if they cured the patients free of charge. At the same time the posts of county medical officers were not open to Hungarian doctors who belonged to the Protestant or the Jewish faith. Out of the large groups of lay healers only the midwives were acknowledged by the law, on condition that they were trained, examined and supervised by the authorities of the central government. The multitude of midwives active in the villages, even those who were not illiterate had not attained a thorough knowledge even of the subjects taught at elementary schools. Lay healers *en masse* were simply dubbed quacks and ignoramuses, and by the terms of the law, were liable to imprisonment.[136]

However, there were none but the lay healers to look after the health of the masses living in villages and rural areas; they were simply indispensable. The 18th century was the golden age of lay healing in Hungary. It was in this period that Countess Kata Bethlen was active in Transylvania, who, employing a multitude of herb women, attained to such excellence, particularly in curing diseases of the eye, including cataract, that patients flocked to her for a cure, even from far-away places.[137] In the manors of the nobility herbals and pharmaceutical formularies dating from the 16th and 17th centuries continued to be copied diligently, and it was in this century that the enlightened doctors of the era produced perhaps the largest number of medical books for the benefit of lay healers. The work of Pápai Páriz ran into four editions during the 1750s, the great decade of

---

[136] Linzbauer: 1852–1856, II, pp. 574, 646; III, pp. 89–97, 254. – Magyary–Kossa: 1929–1940, IV, pp. 538, 588. – Oláh: 1986, p. 89.

[137] Magyari: 1975.

the reform of public hygiene. *Pax Corporis* survived two centuries, and a "folkloric healer" of Oklád, a Székely settlement in Transylvania is known to have used it in the early 1950s, while for the ethnic groups scattered in Moldavia it has remained a handbook until quite recently.

The 18th-century reform of public hygiene in Hungary put an end to witch trials, but failed to provide an adequate health service for the masses of poor people. In the villages healing was carried on along traditional lines, and people continued to believe in witches.

The Chances of Central Europe

Some Pertinent Thoughts
from *Mátyás Bél's* Notitia Hungariae novae

Readers of Mátyás Bél's[1] *Notitia* will find the following baffling comment in the Preface: "There is much about Hungary that has been distorted and vilified by spiteful outlanders, and much that seems contemptible because of our own indifference: but there is just as much that is obscure, and in danger of oblivion."[2] Enigmatic words indeed, but ones whose meaning will be clear if we just consider how little is known of Mátyás Bél's perception of Central Europe. The fact is that generations of indifference had relegated his insights to obscurity, and it is only relatively recently that scholars have recognized their importance for all of Central Europe. For Bél addressed problems common to all the region in the decades preceding the Age of Enlightenment, and did so with a discernment, thoroughness and empathy that no European thinker writing at the time could match.[3]

By the early eighteenth century, "Central Europe" as a historical category was well defined. It referred to the central segment of Europe, and was a concept that had evolved over hundreds of years. Hundreds of years, with as many problems amassed and pressing one upon the other, and all

"Bél Mátyást olvasva: Közép-Európa esélyeiről." In: *Europica varietas – Hungarica varietas.* Akadémiai Kiadó, Budapest, 1994. (Transl. by Éva Pálmai)

[1] Mátyás Bél (1684–1749), perhaps the greatest of Hungary's eighteenth-century thinkers, studied theology and philosophy at the University of Halle, the intellectual center of Pietism by that time. Much influenced by August Hermann Francke, he returned to teach at Besztercebánya a committed Pietist. In later years, he was dean of the Lutheran grammar school in Pozsony, the country's effective capital city, and wrote and taught extensively. His most outstanding works include: *Hungariae antique et novae prodomus...* (A Preliminary to a Portrait of Hungary, Old and New), Norinbergae, 1723; and *Notitia Hungariae novae historico, geographica, divisa in partes quatuor...* (A Historical and Geographic Description of Today's Hungary, in Four Parts), whose first volume was printed in Vienna in 1735; most of the work, which we shall henceforth refer to as *Notitia*, is still waiting to be published.

[2] *Notitia*, 1984, p. 202.
[3] Wellmann: 1979, p. 381.

of them contributing to the complex meaning of the term. We shall get a sense of this complexity if we consider the meaning of "Central Europe" as a function of three specific time frames.

The first time frame is the period when, from the fifteenth century on, the countries of the Danube region slowly recognized their interdependence in the face of the Ottoman onslaught, and responded by coordinating their defenses. Their common peril resulted in various forms of at least partial cooperation, at least some of the time.

The second time frame has to do with the beginnings of the "two Europes" syndrome: the time when the winners of the race to explore the New World grew rich, Western Europe saw the emergence of nation-states, and the countries and peoples of the Danube region fell behind. The new dichotomy was expressed by the Peace of Westphalia and its contemporary commentators, who saw clearly how far short the terms of the treaty fell of its intent. Europe, it was recognized, would retain its identity only if it was able to provide for long-term peace through a balance of power. Central Europe carried no small weight in this balance. The Peace of Westphalia, however, did not deal with what would become of the region once the Ottoman armies were forced out of Europe.

The third time frame is the age of Mátyás Bél. The countries of Central Europe had no choice but to try to cope with their accumulated problems themselves. There was the danger of isolation to deal with; there were the issues of poverty, of the old feudal social structure, and of the slow, uneven development of the middle class. And there was the problem of the coexistence in the states of the region of peoples at very different stages of national development, the vast majority of them living in blocks of mixed populations divided along religious, linguistic and ethnic lines. With the region split into spheres of influence, it was not clear that the small nations of the region would ever form states of their own.

Mátyás Bél's own thinking was decisively influenced by the state (1703–1711) set up by Ferenc II Rákóczi:[4] the attempt to form Hungary, Bohemia, Silesia, Moravia, Croatia, the Principality of Transylvania and other countries of the region into a confederation, with legal guarantees of reli-

---

[4] Ferenc II Rákóczi (1676–1735), Prince of Transylvania and a Prince of the Holy Roman Empire, allied himself with France in the War of the Spanish Succession to wrest Hungary's constitutional liberties from the Habsburgs. With widespread support from all segments of society, he acquired control over much of the Kingdom of Hungary (defeating the armies of Leopold I, Holy Roman Emperor and King of Hungary), and of the Principality of Transylvania, and set up a complete system of government institutions.

gious freedom to provide the preconditions of peaceful coexistence, and an organized information network to avert the threat of isolation from the international community, and the danger of inadequate communication between the confederation's various parts.

Recent research has shown that Bél's circle included people who had been members of the Rákóczi government (Chancellor Pál Ráday, for instance, and Privy Councillor Zsigmond Jánoky), or had had a hand in working out its various reform programs (the physician Károly Moller, for example, the entrepreneur Pál Lányi, and György Bucholtz the Younger). Indeed, as both Hungarian and Slovak researchers have demonstrated, Mátyás Bél's writings, much as they bear the stamp of the Pietist reformers at the University of Halle, were a summation to which a wide circle of Hungarian thinkers and scholars had contributed.

It is part of Bél's monumental achievement that his works incorporate the latest in the international scholarship of the time. And it is a measure of his scholarly stature that in his lifetime yet he earned the esteem of the academies of Europe.[5] All this makes it particularly relevant that his works suggest solutions to problems that Central Europe faces today. I should like to call attention to three of these "solutions" — or imperatives, if you will: to be well-informed; to live and let live; and to recognize the ecological fragility of the region.

THE NEED TO BE WELL-INFORMED

Comenius, in his *Labyrinth* of 1623, tells of a virtual community which newsmongers could manipulate at will. When these people were told some "good" news, they rejoiced, though they had no real reason for doing so; when they got some "bad" news, they panicked, again without cause. The newsmongers could simply play on their emotions, and the community was prone to religious and/or political hysteria. Comenius's solution: make people proficient in acquiring accurate information on their own. That is why he wanted students to learn to read foreign newspapers in school, as part of the regular curriculum.

Newspapers were appearing regularly in the seventeenth century in Western Europe and in the German-speaking lands. The eastern half of the continent, by comparison, was about a century behind, so that in Hungary, for instance, the news-hungry literate classes had to make do with

---

[5] Haan: 1879. – Wellmann: 1979. – Mészáros: 1987.

the network of newsletters that crisscrossed the country. The publication of a national newspaper was at the top of the list of the Rákóczi government's reforms — being considered a measure particularly conducive to the population's peace of mind — but they got no further than the publication of a newspaper for the information of foreign readers. Mátyás Bél, it is clear, was himself only too well aware of the need to remedy the misrepresentations which regularly passed for news of Hungary in the rest of Europe, and was no less mindful of the disorientation of his countrymen, who received no reliable news of what was going on around them.

Outlanders, he writes, "charge that the Hungarians are barbarians for wanting to write and speak in Latin. Be this a real fault or an imaginary one, I will not adduce examples from among us to refute the charge; I will note, however, that in foreign parts, too, there are some scholars versed in literature who would please Cicero and his contemporaries less than would many Hungarians."[6] Mátyás Bél, like Comenius, Pál Ráday, and Rákóczi before him, did not hesitate to point out that not everyone in the West was highly cultured, and that there were people of exceptional erudition in the eastern regions of Europe as well. For instance the nobility of Pozsony county, he noted with satisfaction, were highly accomplished, and set great store by their learning.

One of the most outstanding features of Mátyás Bél's *Notitia* is his awareness that culture and education have certain prerequisites. One such *sine qua non*, as he sees it, is the availability of information. Newspaper reading was made part of the curriculum in Pietist schools, and Mátyás Bél himself required his students to read newspapers regularly. He even started up a newspaper of his own, the short-lived *Nova Posoniensia* (1721–1722).[7]

One function of newspapers, as Bél saw it, was to inform the reading public; the other was to inform and influence the country's decision-makers. For a government measure to be effective in a European country, he believed, it would have to be based on exhaustive and accurate information. Acting in this spirit, prior to framing the religious freedom bill, the Rákóczi government had taken stock of the religious composition of the population, and the ecclesiastical/denominational makeup of the parts of the country under its rule. As for the tax ordinance, that was brought only after a careful study of the history of taxation.

[6] *Notitia*, 1984, pp. 200–201.
[7] Dezsényi: 1948. – Kosáry: 1987, pp. 154–155. – *Notitia*, 1984, p. 227.

Mátyás Bél's *Notitia*, which aimed to reconstruct Hungary's demography, geography, history and economy village by village and town by town, was the most detailed and most meticulous treatment of its kind to that time. One of the leitmotifs of the entire work was the necessity of tolerance and cross-cultural communication in that heterogeneous society.

The peaceful coexistence of all denominations was first put into practice in the Principality of Transylvania. Religious tolerance was an organic part of the Principality's political culture, and had been on the agenda for a century and a half already by the time that Rudolf II was forced to grant Transylvania religious self-determination at the end of the Long War (1593–1606). Not that the conditions of peaceful coexistence had been easily come by: the Catholics, Calvinists, Unitarians and Lutherans of Transylvania had had their share of religious strife; but again and again, the will to tolerance proved the stronger, as shown by the series of sixteenth-century edicts by the princes of Transylvania. Thus, Romanian schools were set up, as was a Romanian press, and when Prince Apafi (1661–1690) invited the Greek Orthodox bishop to sit in the Diet, the prospect of political representation opened up to the Greek Orthodox majority. The Rákóczi government would follow this example. Mátyás Bél, too, must have been familiar with the practice that the largest denomination could take over the village church, provided they themselves would build the minority religion a place of worship.

Religious tolerance in Transylvania was more than just the freedom to follow one's religious convictions. "Freedom of conscience" — to use a contemporary expression—meant also the recognition of each individual's personal value and each community's ethnic identity, and meant also the right to education in one's native language. With the churches controlling not just the pulpits, but the schools and for the most part even the presses, religious tolerance also contributed to the emergence of modern national consciousness.

In all his works, particularly the *Notitia*, Mátyás Bél drew the country's religious and ethnic map with special care. He was totally devoid of religious prejudice: though a Lutheran, he detailed at length the strengths of the Catholic religion, speaking approvingly of the work done by the religious orders, the Jesuit system of education, and the University of Nagyszombat. At the same time, he made no effort to conceal his conviction that determined as the Habsburgs might be to make Catholicism the sole religion, religious pluralism in Hungary was a historical fact. In connection with Gecse, a small village in Veszprém county, he writes: "It is a

277

tiny village belonging to the bishop of Veszprém; it has a mixed population of Catholics, Calvinists and Lutherans, who live together in such harmony that the other two denominations do not separate themselves from the Lutherans, who alone have a local pastor there, but join them for weekday services; so that it is only for the Sunday service that the Catholics and the Calvinists go off to their own congregations."[8]

And he made a point of noting: Nagyszombat "had tolerated the Jews in times past".[9] Reading Mátyás Bél, we find him very much aware of the connections between religion, language and national customs. He tells us, for instance, that the Croats of Pozsony county were "an immigrant people". Obliged to flee from the Ottoman armies, they had been given safe-conduct by Miklós Zrínyi (1620–1664). "When they got to Hungary, they were kindly received.... Gáspár Serédy, who owned large tracts of land at the time, designated land for the refugees to settle, and continued to bear special good will towards this industrious people.... Living among Slovaks as they did, it was amazing how little they changed in their language and ancestral habits.... But now, when they are obliged every Sunday to listen to the sermons of Slovak priests, they are not only learning Slovak, but some of the foreign customs as well."[10]

What was of value for Bél could be described not in terms of national affiliation, but in categories like industry and reliability, and in terms of occupations, skills, customs and culture. The Slovaks, he noted, practiced agriculture and viticulture "with great diligence.... The women take on childbirth with exceptional cheeriness; it is with unparalleled grieving, on the other hand, that they bury their dead." Herdsmen, he tells us, have a life so hard it makes them coarse: on their days off during holidays, "they make a habit of going into town on a drinking spree: they get into drunken brawls, disturb the peace, and fight with their fellows".[11] I doubt that any writer before Mátyás Bél ever gave such invariable attention to how the inhabitants of a country related to one another.

He though it important to note that the lifestyle of the people of Pozsony "unless it was disturbed by factionalism, which some people loved to provoke, ... was particularly suited to developing a sense of community". And he has some fine words about the people of Nagyszombat: "The burghers of the city are not all of one nationality. There are Magyars, Germans and Slovaks in about equal ratios." All three nations differed somewhat in their

[8] Lukács: 1943.
[9] *Notitia*, 1984, p. 254.
[10] *Ibid.*, pp. 235–236.
[11] *Ibid.*, pp. 234–235, 240.

customs: "For the fact is that differences in language will involve differences in conventions, unless constant contact leads to a certain degree of similarity. Here the Hungarians have kept their customs, and the Germans and Slovaks have not given up theirs.... All agree on mutually protecting the rights of their neighbors."[12]

This, obviously, was as Bél thought it *should* be. But he also knew that is was not as it usually *was* — thence his exhaustive review of how newcomers were treated in the various towns and villages. We learn that the early kings of Hungary had extended their protection to the Germans — considered to be the oldest inhabitants of Pozsony county — not only because they were skilled craftsmen, but also because these rulers identified with the policies of King István the Saint. "We need not", he continues, "put up with those selfish people who think Hungary's felicity depends on their driving out all newcomers. Certainly they cannot be familiar with István the Saint's injunction in this regard, and so it might be well to quote it here. This is what it says: `As the newcomers (*advenae*) arrive from the various countries, they bring with them their various languages and customs, as well as their various skills and weapons. All these will enhance the glory of the royal court.... And so I adjure you, my son, to succor them with all good will...'".

Analyzing the preconditions of coexistence, Bél leaves no doubt that what is needed is the willingness of all parties to accommodate to the others. And tact, so as not to overtax the other's tolerance. In this, Bél adopted the traditional values of the middle class. In Pozsony, he tells us, "They allow no one to settle except those from decent freeholder families and possessed of a living, so that they will be a burden on no one, and will be able to pay their taxes".[13]

The inhabitants of Pozsony county, Hungarians, Germans and Slovaks alike "take special care not to provoke the others' antipathy". In Besztercebánya, Bél saw the situation as less than ideal, but noted that economic interests were at the root of much of the national discord. On the other hand, the people of Besztercebánya "were most attentive to strangers".[14] So, he noted, were the burghers of Pozsony, for whom hospitality was not just "entertaining company, but a reciprocal service". The inhabitants of Nagyszombat, too, were "particularly friendly to visitors and strangers".[15]

---

[12] *Ibid.*, pp. 253–254, 257.
[13] *Ibid.*, pp. 230, 237.
[14] *Ibid.*, pp. 227, 277–278.
[15] *Ibid.*, pp. 246, 258.

Time and again, Mátyás Bél gave voice to his conviction that understanding one another's language was a chief prerequisite of the various peoples' ability to live together in peace. In his foreword to Pavel Dolezal's Czech-Slavic grammar, the Lutheran Bél quoted St. Augustine's observation that language could alienate man from his fellow man. "Thus, those who study their own language in such a way as to direct to it the eyes and attention of neighboring peoples deserve to be held in as high an esteem as the ambassadors who go back and forth between the divers disputatious peoples and nations."[16]

Bél himself furthered the cultivation of Hungarian, Slovak and German literature equally. His manuals of spelling and style, and handbooks of grammar all served the native-language education of a mixed population, always with a view to enabling the various language groups to understand one another. The mother tongue would always have priority, but let people learn their neighbors' languages as well. He notes, on the other hand, that it is wrong to oblige young Slovaks to study German in school, if they would rather be learning Hungarian. These same principles informed the plans he worked out in 1718 for the creation of a learned society.

The *Notitia* shows Mátyás Bél to have been an extraordinarily perceptive observer of his fellow men. The harder the times, he notes, the harder people find it to make ends meet, the less tolerant they are of one another, the more fragile the will to peaceful coexistence will prove. Bél, like so many Central European thinkers after him, was deeply preoccupied by the problem of poverty. He notes the new phenomenon of his times: the growing urban poverty. There were more and more beggars. The emerging towns had found no way to provide for the poor, though burghers were a cordial lot, and not just to their friends, but to strangers, too. Particularly in times past, when there had been more money all around.

ENVIRONMENTAL CONCERNS

Mátyás Bél has often been quoted for the beauty of his descriptions of nature. What is of interest from our point of view, however, is how his devotion to nature fits into his conceptual system as a whole. Bél, who was well versed in natural science, shared the organicistic approach that

---

[16] Foreword to Pavel Dolezal's Czech-Slavic grammar of 1746; in: *Notitia*, 1984, pp. 303–304.

was one of the philosophical trends of the age. His descriptions of natural settings reflect both the joy of discovery associated with the Renaissance, and the rationalism of the dawning modern era.

Of the area around Pécs he writes: "To the east, there lie charming meadows and plains as far as the eye can see...; to the west, vineyards climb up the mountain slopes."[17] To the north, "are hills of wondrous beauty.... There is a spring here, whose abundant waters well up healthful and crystal clear... it is one of the few spots on earth that Virgil would have found more beautiful than the Elysian Fields."[18]

Every place he wrote about, Bél called attention to the interdependence of the settlement and its natural setting. He pointed out the significance of the observed regularity that people built castles next to rivers, and used these rivers as part of the castle's system of fortification. Writing of the Csallóköz, he noted how the locals' livelihood, identity and sense of well-being all derived from their natural surroundings. Indeed, he always reflected on the kind of livelihood that the natural conditions of a particular place permitted. In Pozsony, he tells us, "you can grow everything that is needed for a decent living.... The fields are excellent for grain,... and vegetables, too, grow so plentifully that there is enough to ship to Austria up the Danube.... There are facilities aplenty for milling, and nowhere is it done with such expertise. There's not a stream that does not have several waterwheels, let alone the many well-built water-powered mills along the Danube."[19]

Mátyás Bél also had a great deal to say about man's interaction with nature: "Human diligence, too, has compounded the effects of nature's beneficence to the growing crops." Granaries were replacing the old method of storing surplus grain in pits: "With this method, in times of shortage, we have a way of drawing on supplies that are enough not only to ward off famine, but also to check the rising grain prices. The Counts Pálffy, Esterházy, Erdődy, and Illésházy and many other noblemen have been provident enough to adopt this new practice, and have given the rest of Hungary one more thing to emulate."

Bél missed nothing when it came to detecting evidence of man's husbanding of nature: "There are some shady chestnut groves with some very tall old trees; this indicates that forestation is not one of our new customs, but was adopted from our ancestors. For evidence of their fore-

---

[17] *Notitia*, "Comitatus Baranyaiensis descriptio", cited in Tóth: 1982, p. 83.
[18] *Idem*, pp. 84–85.
[19] *Notitia*, 1984, pp. 204, 218.

sight, we have the islands of the Danube, particularly those around Pozsony, which they forested with a great variety of trees." And then there were the well-tended gardens. Of János Pálffy's gardens in Királyfalva he writes: "Of all the kinds of trees native to Hungary and the rest of Europe, it would be hard to find one not growing here." Besztercebánya had a water pipeline coming down from the mountains: wooden pipes carried the fresh spring water into every house. "As for the town's cleanliness and tidiness, it owes a great deal to the Saxons' refined way of life." The town had flush toilets, and had an altogether cared-for look.[20]

But Bél also cautioned of the incipient industrial pollution: with all the smelters and coal furnaces, he observed, the air in Besztercebánya was unhealthy, particularly on overcast and rainy days.

Tampering with nature, he concluded from all that he had seen, was an extreme form of folly. To cite just one of his examples, the story of Szentgyörgy wine. The people of Szentgyörgy themselves ruined their famous wine and its good name when, imitating the wine producers of Tokaj, they tried to make *aszu* without knowing enough about it. Their wine soured. "There were, of course, also the Austrian 'wine breeders', who likewise wanted to make the kind of money that was to be made on *aszu*, and who doctored up new wine with sugar and who knows what other concoctions in the effort to pass it off as such." The outcome: wines from Szentgyörgy lost their good name, "but *aszu*'s reputation for quality did not last much longer, on account of the money-grubbers decried above".[21]

"What I wanted to do", Mátyás Bél tells his readers, "was to present a picture of Hungary which would show at a glance its ancient beauty, and also reveal the shortcomings which later disfigured it."[22] Again and again he puts the question: In a country so rich in natural resources, why is the population so poor? He looks at several reasons: the ignorance which has allowed the spoliation of the natural environment, the ruling classes' disregard for the needs of the people, the essentially feudal forms of land ownership and tenure, and several other causes endemic to Hungary's social structure. Of the region around Lake Balaton he writes: "It is one of the misfortunes of this prosperous region that the goods produced by the growers have no market." The fact that they had no way to market their goods "is the main cause of the poverty that afflicts the people of the vil-

[20] *Ibid.*, pp. 205, 212–214, 274–275.
[21] *Ibid.*, pp. 274, 209.
[22] *Ibid.*, p. 201.

lages".[23] Since the wine growers of the settlements around Pozsony had no market for their produce, they themselves drank the wine, and fell into drunkenness and poverty. Since the tradesmen could not make a decent living in their trade, they turned to logging, and cut down the forests.

Mátyás Bél's holistic way of seeing restores society, history and the environment to the oneness that allows the countless strands of their interrelatedness to shine through. It is as if he were our immediate predecessor, as if he were relaying to us directly the baton of his logic. "It is enough for us to have made a start", he said, "let others cross the finish line".[24] Let us, thus, dare in this frenzied world to commit ourselves to intelligence (in every sense), to tolerance, and to the living world around us. Let us take up the baton passed to us by that real Central European, Mátyás Bél.

[23] *Notitia*, "Comitatus Saladiensis descriptio", cited in Deák: 1984, p. 17. – *Notitia*, 1984, p. 201.

[24] *Notitia*, 1984, p. 212, Preface.

An Undivided Europe?

℘   ℜ

If the Western world wants to bridge the gulf that separates it from Central and Eastern Europe, it will have to know more of these regions' history, a subject of which the average British and American student is blissfully ignorant.[1] Theodore Roosevelt's observation, penned by way of introducing a book on a critical episode of Hungarian history in 1913 – the last year this century that anyone could think of peace as being the natural condition of Europe – is as relevant today as it was over eighty years ago. Indeed, the more talk there is of European unity, the more imperative it seems for people to be made aware of how far Hungarian history has always been an organic part of the story of Europe, and conversely, how consistently Europe has shaped Hungary over the centuries. "Europe" has never stood for just another continent; but whatever its connotation throughout the ages, Europe always defined itself as including the central and eastern parts of the expanse stretching from the Atlantic to the Urals, in sum, as including Hungary.

"EUROPE, THAT BARREN OLD WIDOW"

The epithet dates back to 1858, and is to be found in the preamble of an ordinance extending the provisions of the Austrian Forestry Act of 1852 to Hungary, a verdant and fecund land still, and one that the "barren" old Europe could not afford to do without. Europe, the enervated old widow – it was just one of the many metaphors that had been applied to the continent over the centuries. Though the myth of the ravished princess was one that Herodotus already did not give credence to, he did call the continent "Europe"; and, in an escapade weightier by far than what Zeus had

---

"An undivided Europe?" *Budapest Review of Books*, 6 (1996) 58–66.
[1] Hengelmüller: 1913, pp. XIII–XVII.

involved her in, wed her to permanent change: he inducted her into history.

The Middle Ages spiritualized her, and she became *Universitas Christiana*. The Renaissance crowned her with a diadem of humanism and renewal, the jewels thought most expressive of her essence, and declared her to have been called to a future of dialogue, unity, and peace. When did Europe first stray from this path? The discovery of the New World brought her a boundless surge of self-confidence, but destroyed her old sense of proportion. She became a law unto herself, and exterminated the Indians. Torrents of gold and silver from the New World filled her coffers to overflowing, and yet her streets swarmed with the poor. She considered her own culture to be the only one worthy of the name, and rode roughshod over all other cultures. She was the only part of the world to enjoy all the advantages of science, maritime trade and early industrialization, and yet the Ottoman Empire was able to get a stranglehold on her, hemming her in from the south and east, having seized huge chunks of territory in the Mediterranean, and much of the area east of the Danube. Suffering and carnage were the lot of all the peoples of Europe, who groaned under the weight of a seemingly endless series of religious and dynastic wars, and the conflicts that attended the formation of the first nation-states.

Still, the dialogue that was of her essence continued, and louder than ever. Though the Balkans and the Danube region had come under Ottoman rule, those living there continued to consider Europe "our dear abode". There were well-trodden paths leading from the scorched fringes of Europe to the universities in her western parts, and new avenues of exchanging information were forging a new set of strong links between her severed parts. For instance, Constantinople was one of the places through which news travelled from Transylvania to London, and back.

The sixteenth and seventeenth centuries thought of the future in terms of pairs of alternatives. It is an alternative that we find expressed in an allegorical picture of Rubens, painted during the Thirty Years' War, one which he himself explained in detail. The principal figures of the picture are Mars, the God of War and Venus, the Goddess of Love, and to me they seem to be vying with one another for the attention of that "lugubrious Matron clad in black and with her veil torn, despoiled of her jewels and every other ornament, [...] unhappy Europe, afflicted for so many years by rapine, outrage and misery..."[2] They are competing with one another for her soul. Which of them would rule Europe? Aggression, militarism,

---

[2] Rubens's letter to Justus Sustermans, 1638. Quoted in Gombrich: 1975, p. 127.

permanent warfare, brute force? Or humanism, the spirit of understanding?

In 1648, it seemed that Venus had emerged victorious. After three decades of butchery, the nations of Europe sat down with each other to negotiate peace treaties in Münster and Osnabrück. The Europe that signed the Peace of Westphalia looked to the future with confidence, secure in the belief that she had established a balance of power, the chief guarantor of peace. But it did not take long before the mad dogs of war were once more on the loose. Still, Europe survived the wars waged for the trading posts in the colonies, defeated the Ottoman Empire, and fought its revolutions, preserving all the while her commitment to dialogue, and marching through the centuries of enlightenment and the rise of the middle classes under the proud banner of pluralism.

The dialogue between her disconnected parts continued even when The Wall cleft her in two, and she was divided by ideologies and force of arms. Back in the sixteenth and seventeenth centuries, the struggle against Ottoman rule had also been the expression of the occupied territories' sense of belonging to Christian Europe. The history of this struggle became a parable for those living east of the Iron Curtain, it was a code for the fight for national independence and against Soviet influence.

At the first postwar French–Hungarian conference of historians, held in Budapest in the 1960s, which focused on certain neglected aspects of centuries past, it came as a joyful revelation to realize how much the West and the eastern peripheries of Central Europe had had in common: the figures for births and deaths added up to the same demographic trends, and borders appeared to have had the power to confine neither epidemics, nor eating habits, nor beliefs, nor learning. The impact of certain universities, shown to have been Europe-wide, the cultural trends, the sameness of the metacommunicative message that a particular symbol was understood to convey in the most distant parts of Europe were all evidence of how far the divided regions shared a common history. Researchers presented convincing proof that the "Eastern bloc" of countries within the Ottoman sphere of influence – Hungary among them – was part of a flourishing international trade network. It had implications that went beyond the realm of economic history when it was proven that all three countries under Ottoman rule showed a trade surplus after the lost Battle of Mohács (1526).

Obviously, it bore out the claim that it was Hungary which supplied the meat consumed by the burghers of all the towns in the wide belt stretching from Venice to Augsburg, a claim made by the humanist Miklós Oláh (1493–1568), a friend of Erasmus and secretary to "Mary of Hungary"

287

(1505–1558), Regent of The Netherlands, the widow of Lajos II, King of Hungary and Bohemia (1505–1526), who had been slain at Mohács. But the finding did more than that. The fact that post-Mohács Eastern Europe had a trade surplus with the West called attention to the economic inter-dependence of "East and West" at a time when newspapers there were still extolling the superiority of an autarchic socialist economy, though in fact these economies were already proving inoperative.

These were the years when the concept of Europe proposed by Montes-quieu in the eighteenth century took on a new meaning. What distin-guished Europe, ha had said, was that it had no patience with large em-pires: and he who had ears to hear understood the message. It was in 1959 that Géza Ottlik published his *Iskola a határon* (School at the frontier), perhaps the finest Hungarian formulation of a Europeanness intolerant of empires:

"It was a lovely summer night, with the boat carrying us gently down the Danube. There would soon be a celebration for the four hundredth anniversary of the battle of Mohács. It must seem funny, this celebration of a defeat; still, the victors, the great Ottoman Empire, couldn't very well celebrate, since they'd long ceased to exist. The Tartars had also disap-peared from the face of the earth, without leaving a trace, as had the tough Habsburg Empire, practically before our very eyes. So we took to celebrat-ing by ourselves our great lost battles, which we'd managed to survive."[3]

The book was translated into practically every European language shortly after its appearance.

There never was a time, thus, that the dialogue between the West and Hungary actually came to a halt, any more than it did between any of the other countries within the Soviet sphere of influence. For all that, the post-1989 period has been one of mutual disillusionment. No one found what he had expected to find. When he was finally free to travel to the West, the Polish writer and composer Stefan Kisielewski found himself in a "de-Europeanized, Americanized, materialistic Western Europe, one alienated from Christianity".[4] Not that Westerners have been blind to all this, as the verdict pronounced by the Venetian Cesare Tomasetig, for instance, illus-trates: "Western Europe: lies in a double-breasted suit". Still, as Günter Grass has noted, something decisive happened after 1989: "Western Eu-rope is playing deaf".[5] Still, though Western Europe is no longer the Prom-

---

[3] Ottlik: 1966, pp. 266–267.
[4] Cited in Busek: 1992, p. 14.
[5] Grass: 1992.

ised Land, there is no end to the stream of would-be guest workers, illegal immigrants who cross borders in sealed transport trucks or any way they can, putting their lives on the line no less than those who had had to dodge the Iron Curtain. The periphery of Europe is pressing in upon its center, even as the center is seeking for new opportunities on the periphery. We here in Hungary tend to appraise every step in terms of whether it brings us "closer" to the center, or takes us "farther away" from it. "Getting there", it is assumed, is absolutely imperative, even as it is assumed to be imperative to restore Europe to the oneness that had defined her at the end of the last century.

"AN ORGANIC PART OF EUROPE"

Those with a sense of responsibility for Europe are beginning to probe her past for a portent of her future. One particularly fascinating product of this endeavour is the handsome book by Jean-Baptiste Duroselle, *L'Europe. Histoire de ses peuples.*[6] Printed in 1990, the book was also published in German, English, Spanish, Italian, Danish, Dutch, Portuguese, and Greek simultaneously with the French edition. In it, the author – a Professor Emeritus at the Sorbonne, an expert on nineteenth and twentieth-century international relations, and the author of three hundred articles and thirty-two other books – set himself the splendid task of reconstructing the history of the peoples of the continent from an all-European perspective. It is a beautifully designed and printed volume, with 565 colored illustrations, 43 maps, and a number of chronological tables. The book, obviously, was a great success, for it was also put out as a paperback, without the illustrations, but with a few corrections and an added chapter on the events of 1989 to 1992.[7]

The Hungarian edition,[8] published by Bertelsmann-owned Officina Nova, was translated from an unspecified German version of the French text, a convention that I had believed to have fallen into disuse at the end of the eighteenth century. In format and execution, *Európa népeinek története* is the next thing to a reproduction of the 1990 French original; in respect of the text itself, however, there are points of significant difference. There is, for instance, no sign of the Introduction by the author and the project's

---

[6] Duroselle: *L'Europe. Histoire de ses peuples*, Paris, 1990 (hereafter: *L'Europe*).
[7] Duroselle: *L'Europe. Histoire de ses peuples*, Paris, 1990 (1995) (hereafter: *Paperback*).
[8] Duroselle: *Európa népeinek története*, n.p., n.d. (hereafter: *Európa*).

instigator, Frédéric Delouche; instead – by way of underscoring the significance of the subject, presumably – there is a preface by Otto von Habsburg, member of the Parliament of Europe and President of the Pan-European Union. The concluding chapter of the Hungarian translation is a truncated version of the last chapter of the 1995 paperback edition, and the references to Hungary have suffered considerably from the abridgement. This is all the more deplorable in the light of the fact that the occasional emendations and interpolations that have been inserted here and there in the rest of the Hungarian volume can only be described as substandard, to say the least.

The scholars named in *L'Europe* as project consultants – Professor Karl Dietrich Erdmann (Kiel), Kieth Robbins (Glasgow), Sergio Romano (Rome), and Juan Antonio Sanchez García-Sauco (Madrid) – have a Europe-wide reputation, and are highly regarded by their Hungarian colleagues as well. It is difficult to understand, however, why there was no consultant from one of the countries of East Central Europe, or at least a Hungarian historian specializing in European relations. In quality and elegance of style, of course, the book towers above the current spate of simplistic popular histories. It is so much more painful a disappointment, therefore, to find that even in this book, where the best in modern scholarship is matched with the foremost in printing technology, the history of Europe is the history of the West.

Geographically, naturally, Europe is defined as stretching all the way to the Urals. Austrians, Poles, and Romanians are included in the illustration of her peoples, and Hungarian is mentioned among her languages. Still, for a book that promised an all-European perspective, it treats the nations of East Central Europe as if these countries had no past to speak of.

The word "European" stands for a set of positive values: Christianity, statehood, humanism, scholarship, art, literature, tolerance, culture, the rise of the middle classes, democracy, and environmentalism. "Europe" is the evolution of these values through the centuries, and their triumph, in recent times, over Fascism, and then Bolshevism. Reading Duroselle's book, however, one would think that the countries of East Europe had had no part in any of this.

All things considered, the first and last time that Hungary is discussed in a meaningful way in the entire hefty volume is in the "Europe Under Siege" section, under "The Magyars and Their Incursions" heading of the chapter entitled "The Slavs". The French original gives a short and objective account; the Hungarian edition has a number of additional particulars. "Though they are not Slavs but, like the Finns and the Estonians, belong to the Finno-Ugrian family of languages, this is the place to say a

290

few words about the Magyars as well. Between 900 and 950, this amazing (*étonnant*) people managed to pillage the entire eastern part of continental Europe; they then gave up their nomad ways and settled down to farming, keeping their own language all the while." Here the Hungarian text has some romantic details about the fighting style of the Magyars and the destruction they wrought, with their final defeat at the battle of Lechfeld being mentioned twice within a few lines. The French original dates Vajk's baptism to 985; the Hungarian edition has "corrected" this to 975. Obviously, mistakenly. According to György Györffy, Vajk, Géza's son, was *born* in 975, or later. "... Vajk, who, in 985, at the age of ten, took the name István, succeeded [his father] in 997 ... A remarkable statesman and a pious man whom the Church would canonize, he established 'the Crown of István the Saint', along with a wholly autonomous Church, and, in 1001, had himself crowned with a crown blessed by Pope Sylvester II." Then comes a sentence that is to be found only in the Hungarian edition: "A stable Christian kingdom was the legacy he left behind; Hungary had become an organic part of Europe".[9] And the sequel? For centuries, Hungary figures as but a shadowy figure among the "extras" on the European stage, or not even that: it is as if she had fallen down the trap opening. Not even the Hungarian edition follows up the idea of her being "an organic part of Europe"; apparently, it was just a manner of speaking.

Judging by the French original, humanism, "that uniquely European phenomenon", bypassed Hungary. In the Hungarian translation, the relevant passages have been padded with an interpolation: "Of all the states beyond the Alps, it was, perhaps, the Hungary of Mátyás Hunyadi [Matthias Corvinus], parts of Poland, and what today is Austria that were most touched by its emanations before 1550."[10] In the French original, however, Matthias Corvinus appears only in a chronological table; it is the Jagiellons who figure as the principal political factors of fifteenth-century Central Europe; and Hungary is a blank on the map illustrating – among other things – the centers of humanist learning.

Hungary comes up again in the chapter dealing with the Reformation and its aftermath. Calvinism, which had "pronounced social and democratic aspirations", though "it did not, by any means, condemn capitalism", "spread throughout Scotland, The Netherlands, Bohemia, Hungary, Transylvania [only in the Hungarian edition], and Poland." But Hungary, Bohemia and Poland are also mentioned under the subtitle "The Catholic

---

[9] *L'Europe*, pp. 124–125; *Európa*, pp. 124–125.
[10] *Európa*, p. 207; cf. *L'Europe*, p. 206.

Countries", as places where the majority of the population – in Poland, the vast majority – was Catholic.[11] In subsequent pages, one comes across Hungary only here and there, either as the helpless victim of the enemies of Europeanism, or as their accomplice.

Is it possible that Hungary, this thousand years of tightrope walking between East and West, has simply disappeared from European history? Like a forest cleared, or a hamlet bulldozed to make way for a new highway, or a village razed to accommodate a new hydroelectric dam. Disappeared, like in the story books, into thin air.

EXCLUDED?

It seemed only appropriate that Duroselle's history of Europe – which I first read in the Hungarian edition – should have a separate sub-chapter dealing with how the westward expansion of the Ottoman Empire was finally arrested. Under the heading "Eastern Europe" in the section entitled "Toward a Europe of States (the 14th and 15th centuries)", I learned that after "the national dynasties of Bohemia, Poland and Hungary died out", the "Ottoman Turks crossed the Danube and the Carpathians, and ravaged Hungary". Then, in a rather odd context, a tribute to János Hunyadi: "It is still a matter of debate whether the practice of ringing the church bells at noon really was instituted to commemorate the battle of Nándorfehérvár, or whether it was simply that the mid-fifteenth century was the time when the average European became sophisticated enough to want to know the time with at least a relative accuracy. What is certain is that no one would have believed, when János Hunyadi died after winning the battle in 1456, that his great victory would put an end to Ottoman expansion for three-quarters of a century. That was the moment when Hungary truly became 'the bulwark of Europe'! So let us credit this fine tradition..."[12] For a long time, I was puzzled. If Hunyadi's name came up at all, why was it not in the Index? And then there was the tone: Duroselle is an internationally recognized expert in modern diplomatic history; he would never trivialize another nation's achievements. How could he have written such stuff? Then I discovered that he *didn't*: there is no such passage in the French original; it is an interpolation in the Hungarian edition, specifically meant for Hungarian readers. Its message is pretty bleak: Hang on to your "fine tradition"; but in fact, they started ringing the bells

[11] *L'Europe*, pp. 208–209; *Európa*, pp. 209–210.
[12] *Európa*, p. 171.

at noon because the "average European" had got bright enough to want to know what time it was.

And now for the facts: It was on June 29, 1456 that Pope Calixtus III issued what would later become known as the "Bulla Orationum", a bull ordering that prayers be said in all the churches of Christendom to beseech the Lord's protection against the new assault that the Turks were about to launch, and charging that all church bells, in addition to ringing them morning and evening, as was the custom, be tolled three times "around noon". Three days later, the Ottoman armies laid siege to Nándorfehérvár (Belgrade). On July 22, János Hunyadi and his army relieved the fortress, with the help of the Crusaders recruited by Giovanni da Capistrano. News of the victory reached the major towns of Europe faster than the Papal Bull arrived and could be published, and the bells were rung throughout the Christian world to celebrate the deliverance of Nándorfehérvár. When Calixtus III got word of the victory of the Christian armies on August 6, he himself offered a new interpretation of the Bull: "Let the prayers said during the ringing of the noonday bells be also prayers of thanksgiving". Indeed, as Jenő Szűcs (1928–1988) pointed out, "Connecting the noonday bells with the victory at Nándorfehérvár is, in effect, one of the rare instances of history's revising itself".[13]

As for the "average European" and his sense of time, there were no such things in the 1450s. There was "church time" and "tradesman's time", Biblical time and linear time. The coastal peoples measured time by the tides, the peasantry by the changing of the seasons. Townspeople from London to Prague and from Florence to Kolozsvár (Cluj) had only to look up at the clock tower if they wanted to know what time it was from the thirteenth or fourteenth century on. In the courts of Europe, clocks and watches worn around the neck were coming into vogue, but in the countryside in every corner of Europe for generations yet, the minutes were measured by the time it took to say an Our Father or The Apostle's Creed. There are no borders, no lines of demarcation between Western and Central Europe on any map of the fifteenth-century Europeans' sense of time.[14]

Finally, the notion – applied to 1456 – for Hungary was "the bulwark of Christendom". We first find the concept "bulwark of Europe" in the letters Prince Ferenc II Rákóczi (1676–1735) wrote soliciting the help of the princes of Europe: he spoke of it as a possibility, if the Principality of Transylvania and the Kingdom of Hungary were to regain their autonomy with international guarantees. I doubt, however, that the author of the

[13] Szűcs: 1988, pp. 57–60.
[14] Le Goff: 1960, pp. 417–433. – R. Várkonyi: 1992, pp. 310–320.

above unfortunate interpolation had any such reference in mind. Nor is Rákóczi mentioned anywhere else in the book, in either the French or the Hungarian edition. There is no logical place he could be, actually: Hungary's struggle against the Ottoman Empire from 1526 to the end of the seventeenth century has got excluded from the history of Europe.

The chapter entitled "Europe Faces the Turks"[15] quotes one contemporary opinion after another to the effect that the Ottoman expansion meant no less than that the very fate of Europe was at stake. Duroselle cites Aeneas Silvius Piccolomini, the future Pius II: The fact that the Turks were in Constantinople meant that "they were in Europe, in our country, so to speak, in our own house, on our own land".[16] It is amazing to find that Duroselle, who is so thoroughly at home in this subject, too, reduces the three hundred years of struggle to preserve the Europeanness of Europe in Hungary to three dates and three place names of lost battles: 1526 and Mohács, 1541 and Buda, and 1543 and Esztergom. And yet, at the time, Charles V had called the slain King Lajos II the hero of Christendom: the Western powers of Europe had a just appreciation of what would ensue if the Kingdom of Hungary, one of the main pillars of stability in the region for five hundred years, were to collapse. When Suleiman the Magnificent laid siege to Szigetvár in the summer of 1566, prayers were said in the churches of the Western world three times a week, commending to God's protection each defender of the castle by name, and in the streets of Rome, Brussels and Paris, spry vendors hawked accounts of the determined resistance put up by not just the Hungarians, but also the Moravians, Bohemians, Croats, and other peoples of the region. And the courts of Western Europe were deluged with letters dictated by one Hungarian Palatine, Ban of Croatia and Prince of Transylvania after the other, by diplomats and cardinals, all with the same message: Europe must unite against the Turks in her own interest. There is no mention in Duroselle's history of Europe of the substantial *Türkenhilfe* that the German Electors sent to the defenders of her eastern fringes, monies that made an enormous difference at the time, nor of the administrative help offered by the Hereditary Provinces, or the diplomatic and financial aid given by the papal state. Miklós Zrínyi (1620–1664), Ban of Croatia, military leader and poet, has also disappeared from European history. And yet, in 1664, when he joined forces with the League of the Rhine to organize an international army against the Turks, a biography of his published in London – *The Conduct and Character of Count Nicholas Serini* – characterized him as follows: "The Excel-

---

[15] *L'Europe*, pp. 199–202; *Európa*, pp. 199–202.
[16] *L'Europe*, p. 200; *Európa*, p. 200.

lent Count Serini seems to be the Heroe, upon whom Providence hath devolved the Fate of Europe", and promised the reader a thorough acquaintance with this "Heroe... upon whose success or overthrow the Western world seems to stand or fall".[17]

Duroselle's beautifully presented history of Europe, on the other hand, dismisses a hundred and fifty years of local struggle to keep Europe's eastern periphery European in the following words: "... Ferdinand, the Austrian Habsburg, and Philip II, the Spanish Habsburg ... were the ones who led the relentless fight along the Danube and the Save, as they did in the Mediterranean."[18]

In the "Europe, Romanticism and the Nations" section, there is nothing about the Hungarian Age of Reform, István Széchenyi, the founding of the Academy, or the Diet, which emancipated the serfs and enabled them to acquire property whatever the language they spoke. Then, in the chapter entitled "Nationalism, 'the Hydra of the Revolution'", I came across the heading "Hungary". "In Hungary, nationalism emanated principally from a nobility hostile to the Habsburgs, one determined to re-establish the Crown of King István the Saint. In 1825, the poet Vörösmarty published an epic which contributed to the development of a romantic nationalism. Nationalism took a moderate form under the influence of leading politicians such as Eötvös and Deák, but a violent one under the leadership of the lawyer Lajos Kossuth. A real war ensued."[19] In the Hungarian edition, an editorial comment in parenthesis tells us something every high school student knows: "... The author has given a rather one-sided picture of the revolution and war of independence of 1848–1849, and also their aftermath. This, however, is not the place to refute his statements."[20] An odd disclaimer indeed. I hardly think that Professor Duroselle would have taken exception to an objective and scholarly emendation of his text. Judging from the spirit of the work as a whole, I would think he would have welcomed it. But that's not the real point. One hates to think that what the editors are content to call "rather one-sided" is, in fact, a distorted and disparaging picture of Hungary, and the one that French, Spanish, English, German, Danish, and Portuguese readers will be left with. The chronology in the French edition has a separate entry for the March 15, 1848 "Budapest revolution". The Hungarian edition, on the other hand, couples the event to the Czeh revolution, and then adds insult to

---

[17] See pp. 103ff in the present volume.
[18] *L'Europe*, p. 200.
[19] *L'Europe*, p. 318.
[20] *Európa*, p. 318.

injury: "March 1848: revolution in Prague and Pest; on March 16, Lajos Kossuth (1802–1894) calls for a Hungarian government".[21] No mention of the freedom of the press, representative government, embourgeoisement and modernization, the European values that the revolution was, in fact, about.

At the sight of "Liszt at the Piano", one of the illustrations of the chapter "Romantic Europe", our hearts can finally swell with pride. Josef Danhauser has painted the composer with a bust of Beethoven on his piano, a picture of Byron on the wall, and Paganini and Rossini among his listeners.[22] One cannot help but recall some earlier paragraphs headed "Musical Europe", to the effect that it is Europeans who have given "the world" the gift of musical instruments and the infinite variety of musical genres.[23] As European nationals, we can take pride in Bartók, whose music is regularly heard on the BBC and is broadcast throughout the world. But Bartók's name does not occur in Duroselle's history of Europe. One wishes that at least the Hungarian editors had made it one of their interpolations.

One can only applaud the fact that literature, art and science have such a prominent place in Duroselle's account. Hungary, it appears, has contributed little to the common store of European culture, a silver pouch-plate from the age of migrations being the only example of Hungarian art to find its way into the book. The foreign reader is left to glean some idea of the evolution of Hungarian culture from hints: five tentative dots scattered over historical Hungary on the map of Gothic churches; mention of the "Budapest" university (corrected to "Nagyszombat" in the Hungarian edition; founded: 1635); and a picture of the palace at Fertőd, the "Hungarian Versailles ... where Haydn spent thirty years as organist and choir master", and the only thing marked in and around Hungary on the map of the Enlightenment.[24] But what will steer him to discover what scholars, writers and thinkers over the centuries have contributed to European values in the Carpathian Basin?

Fascinating as the chapter on the "four great innovators" – Leonardo da Vinci, Erasmus, Machiavelli, and Luther[25] – is, the portraits are incomplete.

---

[21] *L'Europe*, p. 310; *Európa*, p. 310.

[22] *L'Europe*, p. 323; *Európa*, p. 323.

[23] *L'Europe*, p. 236.

[24] *Európa*, p. 124, illustration no. 184; p. 177, map 17; p. 236, map 26. In the *Paperback*, see: "Budapest", p. 265.

[25] *L'Europe*, p. 202.

There is, obviously, no way to give a realistic picture of Luther, and of the Reformation as a historical development, without speaking of the religious wars. And we must count it one of the finest achievements of the European spirit that it was able to turn away from religious extremism, and work out a variety of forms of coexistence until freedom of conscience finally triumphed. Duroselle details the milestones along the way: the religious Peace of Augsburg of 1555, the Polish Pax Dissidentum of 1573, the Edict of Nantes of 1598, the Edict of Potsdam of 1685, and, at somewhat greater length, the French Edict of Toleration promulgated in 1787. There is no mention, however, of the Act of Toleration that the Diet at Torda passed in the Principality of Transylvania in 1568, the first time anywhere in Europe that freedom of conscience and of religion was guaranteed to Catholics, Lutherans, Calvinists and Unitarians alike. The Principality of Transylvania was, perhaps, the only place in Europe where all the variants of the Reformation took hold, and where Protestants, Catholics, Greek Orthodox and Greek Catholics lived peacefully together for centuries, side by side with smaller groups such as the Jews, and the Anabaptists of Moravia who had sought and found refuge there.

Hungary looks impressive on the two maps showing the changes in the religious map of Western and Central Europe from the mid-sixteenth to the mid-seventeenth century:[26] it gives the illusion of its old integrity, the lines indicating its tripartite division – the Habsburgs in the west, the Porte in the central part, and the Prince of Transylvania in the east – being barely perceptible. If the maps are to be believed, the spread of Islam came to a standstill along the line of the Save and the Southern and Eastern Carpathians; the Moslems assimilated the Greek Catholics of the Romanian voivodeships (who have disappeared), but never built the minarets that can still be seen in Temesvár, Eger, Pécs, and Székesfehérvár. In 1550, almost ten years after Suleiman had the crosses knocked off the towers of Buda and declared the Church of the Assumption to be a holy place of Islam, the map shows only Anabaptists living in the capital city. The "Bohemian Brethren", on the other hand, are emphatically marked on the 1650 map of Bohemia, whence they had already been forced to flee. Comenius visited the refugees in Upper Hungary, and had protested in their name to all of Europe: Now that Bohemia had been left out of the Peace of Westphalia (1648), the freedom of religion that the signatory powers undertook to guarantee their peoples would never apply to the persecuted Brethren, he wrote.

[26] *Európa*, p. 211, map 24.

I wanted to find Comenius in this handsome history of Europe. I could not. It is not just that Erasmus is left without a successor if Comenius is excluded from among the innovators; an essential chapter of the European experience is lost. For this Bohemian exile was more than an educational reformer; he believed that the free flow of information was the best way for the peoples of Europe to come to a mutual understanding of one another. No one ever wrote so much and so tirelessly about how peace and the equality of all the countries of Europe might be achieved.[27] Today's Europe, searching for its identity, cannot afford to ignore him.

"Europe destroys herself (1914–1945)" is introduced with a dramatic photo of soldiers crossing a makeshift wooden bridge laid in a sea of mud. Behind them, the charred remains of a forest; ahead, the disfigured stumps on the other side.

THE OTHER SIDE

"In truth, there was no Europe left in 1918–1919. Would it be possible to reconstruct it?"[28] Duroselle describes the postwar situation with ruthless precision. Eight and a half million people were dead. "The peace terms had to be negotiated on the basis of an American plan"; President Wilson "was determined to make [the conference] a triumph for what he called the New Diplomacy, and to actively play the role of arbitrator ... What he wanted was a peace that would 'make the world safe for Democracy'". In fact, the peace that was made was but the semblance of peace. A peace dictated by the lust for revenge, it proved the hotbed of new enmities. "Central and Eastern Europe were plunged into famine, misery and disorder ... The dissolution of Austria–Hungary upset the established equilibrium in Europe."[29] The region seethed with overheated nationalism: there were too many large national minorities, there was too much poverty. Duroselle, a specialist in the twentieth century, describes the road leading to the Second World War, giving a detailed analysis of Fascist Germany's plan for the "New Europe" that Hitler proposed to build with his war machinery. What he achieved was a Europe of devastation, concentration camps, gas chambers, towns levelled to the ground, and unburied dead. Duroselle, who showed such extraordinary empathy in describing the tragic Central European repercussions of the Treaty of Versailles, now

[27] Pánek: 1991.
[28] *L'Europe*, p. 357.
[29] *L'Europe*, pp. 356–358; *Európa*, pp. 355–356.

looks at the countries that Germany had made its hinterland with the cool objectivity of an astronomer. He sees that they were all ruthlessly plundered, and that there were differences in the way they fell in line behind Hitler's Germany,[30] but he does not notice that in Central and Eastern Europe, too, there were writers, poets, intellectuals and clergymen who fought the corruption.

"The Resurrection and Hopes of Europe" deals with how postwar Europe tried to deal with the debacle, with poverty, the Cold War, the Soviet threat, and, not least importantly, with the fact that – for all the economic prosperity of the West – she again found herself in a state of crisis. She had lost her leading role in the world, her people were having trouble keeping up with the pace of change. Duroselle reviews the struggle for European unity, the efforts the West is making and the difficulties it faces, and makes clear that the big breakthrough came when the countries of Central and Eastern Europe took their fate into their own hands. He has no illusions. For all that, the Postface to his book is optimistic in tone, and recognizes Hungary's historic role in the events of 1989–1990: "L'ouverture des frontičres inaugurée par les Hongrois, symbolisée per la destruction du mur de Berlin, marque ce besoin qu'ont les humains de se sentir libres."[31]

LOOKING CLOSELY AT OURSELVES

This emphatic statement has been left out of the Hungarian edition. More exactly, it has undergone a mutation. Probably because the editors have replaced the "Postface" with a new section entitled "Europe and the Collapse of Communism", a section based, it seems at first glance, on the French paperback edition. The difference is that the latter deals substantially and at length with Hungary, with what it means to no longer have an Iron Curtain, and with the minority problems of the region, with special reference to Transylvania.[32] Not much of this can be found in the Hungarian edition, which has lopped off large chunks of the entire section. There is, however, a chapter heading that I could find in neither of the French originals: "The Liberation of the Satellite States [!] and German Reunification". But the missing sentence is not under this astonishing heading either. There is a part under "The Collapse of the GDR" that refers to

[30] L'Europe, pp. 373–374; Európa, pp. 373–375.
[31] L'Europe, p. 415.
[32] Paperback, pp. 609–610, 621.

the same events, but without recognizing their historical significance: "More than 24,000 people crossed over into Austria at the opened Hungarian borders, and through Czechoslovakia...".[33] And the Hungarian edition, which ends with the Maastricht Conference (Dec. 9–11, 1991), closes on a tone which does not reflect the optimism of the French original: "If one looks at all the misery in the world, Europe's 'unique position' will seem fragile indeed..."[34]

Frédéric Delouche, the instigator of *L'Europe*, admits that "the project is, by definition, controversial". But perhaps for that very reason, it "will contribute, in one way or another, to our reflecting on the future of Europe".[35] Duroselle's book in the French original has a convincing thesis: the future of the European union lies in our sense of European identity in Europe's past. This past, however, will always be incomplete until we come to understand something of the history of the countries on the eastern edge of Central Europe.

I have tried to show, dispassionately and objectively, that Professor Duroselle does not know, does not understand the extent of Hungary's involvement in Europe's history. I have tried to demonstrate this with due respect and courtesy. I do not know if I have succeeded. On the other hand, I am convinced that had he known more of this involvement, he would not have failed to include János Apáczai Csere, a student of Descartes, who, in 1653, wrote his philosophical dissertation in Hungarian, "at a time when Descartes was the only one in Europe who dared write in the vernacular, all the other scholars and writers writing in Latin".

The quote comes from the writer and poet Dezső Kosztolányi (1885–1936), apropos of *Les Langues dans L'Europe*, the work of the French scholar Antoine Meillet. He made bold to take pen in hand, Kosztolányi tells us, because M. Meillet's "work is an affront to the spiritual community to which I belong, to the language which ten million people speak... His comments about us [...] boil down to the view that we are arrogant nobodies, that everything we have produced in the line of literature is useless, that our language is uncouth and without roots, that it has no past and even less future, that it has been forcibly brought back from the brink of extinction, [...] and that its literature is of no significance."[36] It was on July 16, 1930, exactly sixty-six years to the day I am writing this, that the essay

---

[33] *Európa*, p. 411.

[34] *Európa*, p. 415.

[35] "Acknowledgements" in *L'Europe*, p. 5; *Európa*, p. 5.

[36] Kosztolányi: 1990, pp. 88, 102. I am indebted to István Terts for calling my attention to this source.

appeared in the journal *Nyugat*. The world has changed a great deal since then. For one thing, we have learned that we ourselves are responsible for our shortcomings. The Hungarian edition of Duroselle's history also goes to prove that if we drop out of the history of Europe, we have also ourselves to blame.

Looking closely at ourselves, I think that the superficiality and inconsistency of the Hungarian "translation" is due, essentially, to a loss of respect for scholarship, to the fact that we have come to look down on history. Never, it seems, have the words of the liberal thinker and historian László Szalay (1813–1864) been more apt than they are today: scholarship in Hungary is a matter of life and death.

I study the series of pictures in the last section of the book. Joyous German youngsters with sparklers sitting on the Berlin Wall; a smiling Gorbachev giving a wave in the Chamber of Deputies in East Berlin; Václav Havel smiling at Dubček; Tadeusz Mazowiecki, Poland's first democratically elected prime minister, holding high Walesa's hand on a bright and sunny day; the light of the candles in Wenceslaus Square reflected off solemn but festive faces; Romanian boys showing the V for victory through the hole of a flag denuded of its discredited coat of arms. For Hungary, there's a black-and-white photo of a beflowered coffin, with men and women dressed in black: "Ceremony for the rehabilitation of Imre Nagy, and the other victims of the Hungarian Revolution". In the Hungarian edition, this picture has been replaced with an aerial photo of the funeral service, one in which practically the only thing one can identify with any certainty is the Műcsarnok (Exhibition Hall), its pillars draped in black. Instead of the candlelight vigil on Wenceslaus Square there is the well-known photo of Yeltsin atop a tank, speaking to the crowds; and instead of the Romanian boys, the shelled remains of the cemetery in Dubrovnik.[37]

It is a sad fact but true that historical alternatives unfold in the long term. The rebirth of Europe hinges on our ability to give a contemporary expression to its erstwhile unity.

Since the future must build on the past, Hungary must first of all come to terms with its European heritage, and make it manifest to others. A look through any archive abroad will make it clear how little has been done to exploit this kind of priceless evidence of Hungary's involvement in Europe. The research results that have been arrived at seldom get beyond the country's borders; or if they do, they do so untranslated, and so lie useless, gathering dust on the bookshelves of the world. Just in the

[37] *L'Europe*, and *Európa*, illustrations nos 557 to 563, 610.

past few years several works have appeared which should be made available in a scholarly translation in one of the world languages.

When I looked a year ago, the open shelf of the reading room in the British Library had three books dealing with Hungary. The one was a fat tome in Hungarian, *A magyar történet kútfői* (Hungarian Historical Sources, 1901) by Henrik Marczali. Considered very modern at the time, it has, to say the least, become obsolete. The second was a slim volume published in 1958 by Denis Sinor, a *History of Hungary*. The third was the hefty volume, *Information Hungary*. On the spine, there is the coat of arms the world saw being cut out of the flag in 1956. Of the over a thousand pages, a hundred and fifteen deal with the history of Hungary. In the spirit of 1968, the year it appeared. Next to it on the shelf, the nations of Europe – the English, the French, the Romanians, the Poles – offer their histories to the readers of the world in series of several volumes. Shall we be a people without a history in the European Union? Not just we ourselves, all of Europe will be the losers, whether they know it or not. Europe's full identity depends on an appreciation of Hungary's history, too, no less than that of any other nation's. A scholarly, objective broadcasting of the part we have played in Europe's history is more than our national interest: it is in the interest of European unity.

List of Abbreviations

ABBREVIATIONS FOR ARCHIVES

AFA	Alte Feldakten, Kriegsarchiv, ÖStA
App. Hung.	Sándor Apponyi's Collection in OSZKK
AStF	Archivivo di Stato di Firenze
BL Ms	British Library Ms Collection
Bodleian L	Bodleian Library, Oxford, Rawlinson Ms
HHStA	Haus-, Hof- und Staatsarchiv, ÖStA
KA	Kriegsarchiv, ÖStA
MEA	Mainzer Erzkanzler Archiv HHSTA, ÖStA
MOL	Magyar Országos Levéltár, Hungarian Public Record Office
MOL E 199	Archives of the Wesselényi Family
MOL E 254	Archives of the Hungarian Chamber, Representationes, informationes et instantiae
MOL G 15	Archives of Prince Ferenc II Rákóczi
MOL P 125	Archives of the Dukes Esterházy
MOL P 512	Archives of the Nedeczky Family
MOL P 1314	Archives of the Batthyány Family
MOL P 1389	Archives of Mihály Apafi, Prince of Transylvania
MOL P 1890	Archives of the Forgách Family
MTAKKt	Library of the Hungarian Academy of Sciences, Ms Collection
NRA	Neo-regestrata Acta E 148 Archives of the Hungarian Chamber
ÖstA	Österreichisches Staatsarchiv, Vienna
ÖstA, KA, AFA	Österreichisches Staatsarchiv, Kriegsarchiv, Alte Feldakten
OSZK	National Széchényi Library
OSZKKMs	National Széchényi Library, Ms Collection
PRO	Public Record Office, London
PRO SP	PRO State Papers Germany
Ráday levéltár	Ráday Archives, Budapest
Rtg	Mainzer Erzkanzler Archiv, Reichstagsakten
SAS	State Archiv of Slovakia, Bratislava
Turcica	Turkish diplomacy HHStA

ABBREVIATIONS FOR LITERARY SOURCES

Communicationes	*Communicationes ex Bibliotheca Medicae Hungarica* (Országos Orvostörténeti Könyvtár Közleményei, Budapest)

EkvBK: 1995	*A tudomány szolgálatában. Emlékkönyv Benda Kálmán 80. születésnapjára* (Essays presented to Kálmán Benda on the occasion of his 80th birthday). Ed. by Ferenc Glatz. Budapest.
EkvHBÉ: 1997	*Miscellanea fontium historiae Europae. Emlékkönyv H. Balázs Éva 80. születésnapjára* (Essays presented to Éva H. Balázs on the occasion of her 80th birthday). Ed. by János Kalmár. Budapest.
EkvFL: 1994	*Perlekedő évszázadok. Emlékkönyv Für Lajos 60. születésnapjára* (Essays presented to Lajos Für on the occasion of his 60th birthday). Ed. by Ildikó Horn. Budapest.
EkvRVÁ: 1998	*Emlékkönyv R. Várkonyi Ágnes 70. születésnapjára* (Essays presented to Ágnes R. Várkonyi on the occasion of her 70th birthday). Ed. by Péter Tusor, Zoltán Rihmer, Gábor Thoroczkay. Budapest.
EkvSzGy: 1994	*Nemzeti és társadalmi átalakulás a XIX. században Magyarországon. Emlékkönyv Szabad György 70. születésnapjára* (Essays presented to György Szabad on the occasion of his 70th birthday). Ed. by István Orosz, Ferenc Pölöskei. Budapest.
Károlyi Okmánytár: 1897	*A nagykárolyi gróf Károlyi család oklevéltára,* I–V (Archives of the Károlyi family of Nagykároly, vols I–V). Ed. by Kálmán Géresi. Budapest.
Kemény Önéletírása: 1657 (1980)	(Kemény's Autobiography). In: *Kemény János és Bethlen Miklós művei* (Works by János Kemény and Miklós Bethlen). Commentary and annotation by Éva V. Windisch, Budapest, Szépirodalmi Kiadó.
Kőszeg emlékezete: 1982	*Kőszeg ostromának emlékezete.* Selected., ed. and with an introd. by I. Bariska. Budapest.
Martinuzzi levelei és iratai: 1878–1882	*Fráter György levelezése és egyéb őt illető iratok 1535–1551* (The letters of Friar George and other papers concerning him 1535–1551). Publ. by Á. Károlyi. *Történelmi Tár.*
MHH	*Monumenta Hungariae Historica. Magyar Történeti Emlékek,* I–IV. osztály. Pest, 1857 – Budapest, 1948.
Milton: 1975	*Milton, az angol forradalom tükre. Válogatás prózai írásaiból* (Milton, mirror of the English revolution. A selection of his prose). Selected, introduced and annotated by Miklós Szenczi. Budapest.
Mohács tanulmányok: 1986	*Mohács. Tanulmányok a mohácsi csata 450. évfordulója alkalmából* (Mohács. Studies on the occasion of the 450th anniversary of the Battle of Mohács). Ed. by Lajos Rúzsás and Ferenc Szakály. Budapest.
Pázmány Péter emlékezete: 1987	*Pázmány Péter emlékezete halálának 350. évfordulóján* (In Memoriam Péter Pázmány on the 350th anniversary of his death). Ed. László Lukács, S. J., Ferenc Szabó, S. J. Rome.
Pázmány's collected letters: 1910–1911	*Pázmány Péter bíbornok, esztergomi érsek, Magyarország prímása összegyűjtött levelei* (Collected letters of Cardinal Péter Pázmány Archbishop of Esztergom, Primate of Hungary). Ed. by Ferenc Hanuy. Vol. I (1601–1628), vol. II (1629–1637). Budapest.
Pázmány's works: 1983	*Pázmány Péter – Válogatás műveiből: Prédikációk* (A selection from Péter Pázmány's works: Sermons). Writings selected by Miklós Őry, Ferenc Szabó, Péter Vass. Budapest.

Bibliography

Acsády, Ignác: 1885. *Széchy Mária 1610–1679* (Mária Széchy 1610–1679). Budapest.

Acsády, Ignác: 1897. "Magyarország három részre oszlásának története 1526–1686" (The history of the division of Hungary into three parts, 1526–1686). In: *A magyar nemzet története,* vol. V.

Acsády, Ignác: 1898. "Buda visszafoglalása" (The reconquest of Buda). In: *A magyar nemzet története,* vol. VII.

Acsády, Ignác: 1899. *A karlóczai béke története* (The history of the Treaty of Carlowitz). Budapest.

Allendy, René: 1937. *Paracelse, le médecin maudit.* Paris.

Althaus, F. E.: 1884. *Samuel Hartlib, ein deutschenglisches Characterbild.*

Alvinczi, Péter: 1633. *Postilla. Azaz egymás után következő prédikációk az úrnapi szent evangéliumok szerént, rövid magyarázatokkal és világos tanulságokkal,* I–II (Postilla. Sermons in order according to the gospels of Corpus Christi, with short explanations and clear morals, vols I–II). Kassa.

Angol diplomáciai iratok II. Rákóczi Ferenc korára. See *Archivum Rákóczianum:* 1872–1877.

Angol életrajz Zrínyi Miklósról (English biography of Miklós Zrínyi): 1987. (*Zrínyi könyvtár,* vol. II). Budapest.

Angyal, Dávid: 1900. "Erdély politikai érintkezései Angliával" (Transylvania's political contacts with England). *Századok,* vol. 34, pp. 309–325, 398–420, 495–508, 702–711, 873–904.

Apáczai Csere, János: 1653 (1977): *Magyar Encyclopaedia* (Hungarian encyclopaedia). Utrecht. – (Ed. by József Szigeti, Bucharest).

Apponyi, Alexander: 1927. *Ungarn betreffende im Auslande gedruckte Bücher und Flugschriften.* Gesammelt und beschrieben –. IV.B. München.

Arany, János: 1859. "Zrínyi és Tasso". *Budapesti Szemle,* vols 7, 8.

Archivum Rákóczianum: 1872–1874. – *Archivum Rákóczianum,* Section I: Military and Domestic Affairs. (I. Rákóczi Ferencz Fejedelem leveleskönyvei, levéltárának egykorú lajstromaival, 1703–1712 (Registers of the correspondence of Prince Ferenc II Rákóczi with contemporary lists of his archives, 1703–1712). Ed. by Kálmán Thaly, vols I–III, Budapest.

Archivum Rákóczianum: 1875–1882. – *Archivum Rákóczianum,* Section I: Military and Domestic Affairs. Gróf Bercsényi Miklós főhadvezér és fejedelmi helytartó levelei II. Rákóczi Ferencz fejedelemhez. 1704–1711 (The letters of Generalissimo and Princely Regent Count Miklós Bercsényi to Prince Ferenc II Rákóczi, 1704–1711). Ed. by Kálmán Thaly, vols IV–VIII, Budapest.

Archivum Rákóczianum: 1872–1877. – *Archivum Rákóczianum,* Section II. Diplomacy, *Angol diplomáciai iratok II. Rákóczi Ferenc korára* (English diplomatic papers concerning the age of Ferenc II Rákóczi). Ed. by Ernő Simonyi, vols I–III, Budapest.

Archivum Rákóczianum: 1978–1997. – *Archivum Rákóczianum,* Section III. Authors. Ed. by Béla Köpeczi, Lajos Hopp, and Ágnes R. Várkonyi, vols I–V, Budapest, Akadémiai Kiadó.

305

Archivum Rákóczianum: 1978. – *Archivum Rákóczianum,* Section III/1. II. *Rákóczi Ferenc fejedelem Emlékiratai – Mémoires du Prince François II. Rákóczi sur la guerre de Hongrie depuis 1703 jusqu'a sa fin* (Memoires of Prince Ferenc II Rákóczi). (Hague, 1739.) Ed. by Béla Köpeczi and Ilona Kovács. Budapest, Akadémiai Kiadó.

Aretin, Karl Ottomar: 1978. "Magyarország és I. József császár politikája" (Hungary and the policy of the Emperor Joseph I). *Történelmi Szemle,* vol. 21, nos 3–4, pp. 520–526.

Artamonov, P. A.: 1978. "Magyarország és az orosz-lengyel szövetség (1707–1712)" (Hungary and the Russian–Polish alliance [1707–1712]). *Történelmi Szemle,* vol. 21, nos 3–4, pp. 527–531.

Aubin, Jean: 1995. "La mission de Robert Bransetur (Un arrière-plan diplomatique de la campagne de Hongrie de 1529)." In: *EkvBK,* pp. 47–61.

Auerbach, B.: 1887. *La Ligue du Rhin et le traité de Ratisbonne. La diplomatie française et le cour de Saxe, 1648–1680.* Paris.

Bahtyin, Michail: 1982. *François Rabelais művészete, a középkor és a reneszánsz népi kultúrája* (The art of François Rabelais; the popular culture of the Middle Ages and the Renaissance). Transl. by Csaba Könczöl. Budapest, Európa Könyvkiadó.

Ballagi, Aladár: 1922. *XII. Károly és a svédek átvonulása Magyarországon 1709–1715* (Charles XII and the Swedish march across Hungary 1709–1715). Budapest.

Balogh, Jolán: 1982. *Varadinum – Várad vára* (Várad castle), vols I–II. Budapest, Akadémiai Kiadó.

Bán, Imre: 1976. "Comenius és a magyar szellemi élet" (Comenius and Hungarian intellectual life). In: *Eszmék és stílusok. Irodalmi tanulmányok* (Ideas and styles. Literary studies). Budapest, Akadémiai Kiadó.

Barcza, József: 1980. *Bethlen Gábor, a református fejedelem* (Gábor Bethlen, the Calvinist Prince). Budapest, A magyarországi Református Egyház Kiadója.

Bárdos, Kornél: 1984. *Sopron zenéje a 16–18. században* (The music of Sopron in the 16th–18th centuries). Budapest, Akadémiai Kiadó.

Bárdossy, László: 1943. *Magyar politika a mohácsi vész után* (Hungarian politics after the disaster of Mohács). Budapest, Akadémiai Kiadó.

Bariska, István: 1982. "A protestáns Kőszeg II. Ferdinánd korában" (Protestant Kőszeg in Ferdinand II's time). In: *Somogy megye múltjából* (Facts from the past of the county of Somogy). *(Levéltári Évkönyv 1982.)* Kőszeg.

Barlay, Ö. Szabolcs: 1986. *Romon virág* (Flower on the ruins). Budapest, Gondolat Kiadó.

Barta, Gábor: 1983. *A Sztambulba vezető út (1526–1528)* (The road to Istanbul [1526–1528]). Budapest, Magvető Kiadó.

Barta, Gábor: 1986. "Egy magyar politikus a középkori Magyarország széthullásának éveiben (Werbőczy István kancellár, 1526–1541)" (A Hungarian politician in the years of the disintegration of Hungary – Chancellor István Werbőczy, 1526–1541). In: *Mohács tanulmányok,* pp. 275–322.

Barta, Gábor: 1988. *Vajon kié az ország* (Whose country is it after all?). Budapest, Helikon Kiadó.

Bél, Mátyás: 1984. *Notizia.* – "Notizia" (1735–1743, 1984). In: Bél, M.: *Hungáriából Magyarország felé* (From Hungaria towards Hungary). Selected with an introd. study by Andor Tarnai. Budapest, Szépirodalmi Kiadó.

Bencze, József: 1965. "Két újólag előkerült akta a boszorkányperek idejéből" (Two new documents from the time of the witch trials). *Communicationes,* vol. 34, pp. 9–17.

Benda, Kálmán: 1954. "Ráday Pál politikai iratai" (The political papers of Pál Ráday). *Levéltári Közlemények,* vol. 25, pp. 141–151.

Benda, Kálmán: 1959. "Rákóczi és a Vatikán. Brenner apát küldetése XI. Kelemen pápához 1707–1708" (Rákóczi and the Vatican. The mission of Abbot Brenner to Pope Clement XI, 1707–1708). *Történelmi Szemle,* vol. 2, pp. 8–24.

Benda, Kálmán: 1960. "Le projet d'alliance hungaro–suédo–prussienne de 1704". *Studia Historica Acad. Sci. Hung.*, vol. 25.

Benda, Kálmán: 1973. "Gerard und Gottfried van Swieten und die Schulreform in Ungarn", in: *Gerard van Swieten und seine Zeit.* Ed. by Erna Lesky – Adam Wandruszka. Wien.

Benda, Kálmán: 1975. *Habsburg abszolutizmus és rendi ellenállás a XVI–XVII. században* (Habsburg absolutism and the resistance of the estates in the 16th and 17th centuries). Budapest.

Benda, Kálmán: 1976. "A szatmári béke és az általános külpolitikai helyzet" (The Peace of Szatmár and the general state of foreign affairs). In: *A Rákóczi-szabadságharc vitás kérdései* (Disputable questions of Rákóczi's War of Independence). Vaja–Nyíregyháza, pp. 44–50.

Benda, Kálmán: 1978. "Pázmány Péter politikai pályakezdése" (The early years of Péter Pázmány's political career). *Vigilia,* vol. 43, pp. 225–229.

Benda, Kálmán: 1979. "Egy lengyel királyi tanácsos levele" (A letter from a Polish royal councillor). *Magyar Könyvszemle,* vol. 98, pp. 252–268.

Benda, Kálmán: 1984. "Egy lengyel királyi tanácsos levele. 1710" (A letter from a Polish royal councillor. 1710). Text of a lecture in: *Mályusz Elemér Emlékkönyv* (Memorial volume for Elemér Mályusz). Ed. by Éva Balázs, Erik Fügedi, and Ferenc Maksay. Budapest, pp. 23–38.

Bene, Sándor: 1987. "Lacrymae Hungaricae. A Zrínyi halálára Londonban kiadott gyászversek" (Elegies published in London upon Zrínyi's death). In: *Angol életrajz Zrínyi Miklósról,* p. 355.

Bene, Sándor: 1989. "Zrínyi mint 'Magyar Mars'" (Zrínyi as the 'Hungarian Mars'). In: *Esterházy.*

Bene, Sándor: 1992. "Zrínyi-levelek 1664-ből" (Zrínyi letters from 1664). *Irodalomtörténeti Közlemények,* vol. 96, pp. 225–242.

Bene, Sándor: 1993. "A Zrínyi testvérek az Ismeretlenek Akadémiáján" (The Zrínyi brothers at the Academy of the Unknown). *Irodalomtörténeti Közlemények,* vol. 97, pp. 650–668.

Benna, A. H.: 1965. "Doppelspionage im Türkenjahr 1683". *Mitteilungen des Österreichischen Staatsarchivs,* 17/18, pp. 1–23.

Bérenger, Jean: 1994 (1990). *A History of the Habsburg Empire 1273–1700.* London – New York.

Berindei, M. – Veinstein, G.: 1987. *L'empire ottoman et les pays roumains 1544–1545. Étude et documents.* Cambridge.

Bessenyei, József: 1986. *A Héttorony foglya* (Prisoner of the Jedikula). Budapest, Helikon Kiadó.

Bethlen, Miklós: 1955. *Önéletírása,* I–II (An autobiography, vols I–II). Ed. by Éva V. Windisch. Budapest, Szépirodalmi Kiadó.

Bibó, István: 1934. *A szankciók kérdése a nemzetközi jogban* (The question of punitive sanctions in international law). Szeged.

Bíró, Péter: 1989. *A Francia Külügyi Levéltár Zrínyi Miklósra és az 1663-64. évi hazai eseményekre vonatkozó iratai* (Documents in the Archives of the French Foreign Ministry pertinent to Miklós Zrínyi and the Hungarian events of 1663–1664). *Zrínyi dolgozatok,* vol. IV, pp. 63–76.

Bíró, Vencel: 1914. "Bethlen viszonya Pázmánnyal" (Bethlen's relations with Pázmány). *Erdélyi Múzeum* (Új folyam, 9), pp. 181–194.

Bitskey, István: 1977. "Társadalomszemlélet Pázmány Péter beszédeiben." (Social philosophy in Péter Pázmány's sermons) *Világosság,* vol. 18, pp. 411–417.

Bitskey, István: 1986. *Pázmány Péter* (Péter Pázmány). Budapest.

Bitskey, István: 1993. "Magyarországi diákok Rómában a középkor végén" (Students from Hungary in Rome at the end of the Middle Ages). In: *Régi és új peregrináció.*

Bitskey, István – Kovács, B.: 1975. "A pozsonyi jezsuita kollégium XVII. századi könyvtára és a Pázmány-hagyaték" (The library of the Jesuit College of Pozsony in the 17th century and the Pázmány bequest). *Magyar Könyvszemle*, vol. 91, pp. 25–37.

Bittner, L. – Gross, L.: 1936. *Repertorium der diplomatischen Vertreter aller Länder seit dem Westphälischen Frieden*. Berlin.

Bleyer, Jakab: 1900. "Adalék Zrínyi Miklós udvara jellemzéséhez és Zrínyi-Újvár történetéhez" (A contribution to a picture of Miklós Zrínyi's court, and the history of Zrínyi-Újvár). *Századok*, vol. 34, pp. 221–227.

Bodó, Éva Mária: 1987–1988. "Zrínyi Miklós kiadatlan olasz nyelvű levele XIV. Lajos francia királyhoz" (Bécs, 1664, július 19) (Miklós Zrínyi's unpublished letter in Italian to King Louis XIV of France, Vienna, July 19, 1664). *Irodalomtörténeti Közlemények*, nos 1–2, pp. 203–206.

Bóka, Éva: 1983. "Európa és a törökök (Válogatás a török hatalom megdöntésére született XVI–XVII. századi tervekből)" (Europe and the Turks. A selection of papers dating from the 16th and 17th centuries written with a view to overthrowing Turkish supremacy). *Világtörténet*, Új folyam, 2, pp. 84–104.

Borián, Elréd: 1995. "Órám tisztességes csak légyen utolsó" (Let my last hours be honorable). *Irodalomismeret*, pp. 14–16.

Bornemisza, Péter: 1578 (1977). *Ördögi kísértetekről, avagy röttenetes utálatosságáról ez megfertéztetett világnak* (Diabolical temptations). Sempte. Budapest.

Borosy, András: 1984. *Pest–Pilis–Solt vármegye közgyűlési jegyzőkönyveinek regesztái 1638–1711. II. 1666–1680* (The documents of the meetings of the county Pest–Pilis–Solt 1638–1711. Vol. II. 1666–1680). Budapest, Pest megyei Levéltár kiadása.

Borosy, András: 1985. *Pest–Pilis–Solt vármegye közgyűlési jegyzőkönyveinek regesztái 1638–1711. III. 1681–1697* (The documents of the meetings of the county Pest–Pilis–Solt 1638–1711. Vol. III. 1681–1697). Budapest, Pest megyei Levéltár kiadása.

Borosy, András: 1986. *Pest–Pilis–Solt vármegye közgyűlési jegyzőkönyveinek regesztái 1638–1711. IV. 1698–1702* (The documents of the meetings of the county Pest–Pilis–Solt 1638–1711. Vol. IV. 1698-1702). Budapest, Pest megyei Levéltár kiadása.

Borzsák, István: 1984. *A Nagy Sándor-hagyomány Magyarországon* (The Alexander the Great tradition in Hungary). Budapest, Akadémiai Kiadó.

Boskovits, Miklós: 1963. *Botticelli*. Budapest, Képzőművészeti Alap Kiadó Vállalata.

Braubach, May: 1962. *Die Geheimdiplomatie des Prinzen Eugen von Savoyen. Wissenschaftliche Abhandlungen der Arbeitsgemeinschaft für Forschung des Landes Nordrhein-Westfalen*, vol. 22, Köln–Opladen.

Braubach, M. – Resgen, K. B. (eds): 1962, 1965, 1975. *Acta Pacis Westphalicae*, vols I–III. Münster.

Braudel, Fernand: 1949–1965. *La Méditerranée et le monde méditerranéen sous Philippe II*. Vols I–II. Paris, Armand Colin Editeurs.

Brechka, Frank T.: 1970. *Gerhard Van Swieten and His World, 1700–1772*. The Hague.

Brodarics, István: 1527 (1977). "De conflictu Hungarorum cum Turcis ad Mohács verissima descriptio. Cracovia. – Igaz történet a magyarok és Szulejmán török császár mohácsi ütközetéről" (A true relation of the battle fought by the Hungarians against the Turkish Sultan Suleiman at Mohács). In: *Humanista történetírók*.

Brüsszeli Okmánytár: 1857–1858. *Magyar történelmi okmányok a brüsszeli országos levéltárból és a burgundi könyvtárból* (Bruxelles Archives. Hungarian historical documents from the National Archive of Bruxelles and the Library of Burgundy), vols I–II. Ed. by M. Horváth. Pest.

Bucholtz, F.: 1831–1836. *Geschichte der Regierung Ferdinand des Ersten*, vols I–VIII. Wien.

Buda expugnata: 1686 (1986). *Buda expugnata. An Historical Introduction*. Ed. by István Bariska, Gy. Haraszti and János J. Varga, vols I–II. Budapest.

Bukovszky, Andrea: 1987–1988. "Londoni magyar vonatkozású kiadványok és az 1664. évi Zrínyi-életrajz" (Works dealing with Hungary published in London and the Zrínyi Biography of 1664). *Irodalomtörténeti Közlemények*, nos 1–2.

Busek, Erhard: 1992. "Közép-európai ráébredés" (Awakening in Central Europe). In: Busek, E.: *Az elképzelt Közép-Európa* (The Central Europe of our dreams). Transl. by András Székely. Budapest.

Carter, Charles Howard: 1964. *The Secret Diplomacy of the Habsburgs 1598–1625*. London.

Cennerné Wilhelmb, Gizella: 1987. "A londoni Zrínyi-portré és ikonográfiai rokonsága" (The London Portrait of Zrínyi, and its iconographic correlatives). In: *Angol életrajz Zrínyi Miklósról*, pp. 369–390.

Cernovodeanu, Paul: 1976. "A román vajdaságok és Rákóczi diplomáciai kapcsolatai" (The diplomatic relations of the Romanian voivodeships and Rákóczi). *Századok*, vol. 110, pp. 1078–1079.

Charrière, E.: 1848–1860. *Négociations de la France dans le Levante, 1515–1589*, vols I–IV. Paris.

Chastel, André: 1978. *Fables, Forms, Figures*, vols I–II. Paris.

Churchill, W. S.: 1968. *Marlborough, his Life and Times*, abbr. H. S. Commager. New York.

Clucas, Stephen: 1991. "Samuel Hartlib's Ephemerides, 1635–59, and the pursuit of scientific and philosophical manuscripts: The religious ethos of an intelligencer." *The Seventeenth Century*, pp. 33–55.

Comenius, Johannes Amos: 1628–1631. *Labyrint svéta a ráj srdce*. Leszno. – (Hungarian edition: *A világ útvesztője és a szív paradicsoma*. Introductory study and notes by Ilona Komor. Pozsony, 1977.)

The Conduct and Character of Count Nicholas Serini: 1664. London: Printed for Sam. Speed, at the Rainbow in Fleet-street. (In Hung. in: *Angol életrajz Zrínyi Miklósról*: 1987.)

Csáky, Moritz: 1982. "Karl V., Ungarn, die Türkenfrage und das Reich (Zu Beginn der Regierung Ferdinands als König von Ungarn)." In: Lutz: 1982.

Csapodi, Zoltán: 1995. "A Thököly-felkelés visszhangja a Német-Római Birodalom területén" (The repercussions of the Thököly revolt throughout the Holy Roman Empire). *Aetas*, nos 1–2, pp. 140–170.

Cseh, L.: 1893. "Az angolok és hollandok diplomáciai szereplése II. Rákóczi Ferenc felkelésében" (The diplomatic part played by the English and the Dutch in Ferenc II Rákóczi's insurrection). In: *Year-Book of the Roman Catholic Grammar School in Nyitra, 1892–1893*, Nyitra.

Csetri, Elek: 1992. *Bethlen Gábor életútja* (Life of Gábor Bethlen). Bucharest, Kriterion Kiadó.

Dávid, Zoltán: 1973. "Az 1738. évi pestisjárvány pusztítása" (The devastation of the plague in 1738). *Orvostörténeti Közlemények*, vols 69–70, pp. 75–130.

Deák, András: 1984. *Bél Mátyás élete és munkássága* (The life and work of Mátyás Bél). Budapest.

Deák, Farkas: 1875. *Wesselényi Anna özv. Csáky Istvánné (1584–1649) életrajza és levelezése* (The correspondence and biography of the widow Mrs. István Csáky, née Anna Wesselényi [1584–1649]). Budapest.

Deák, Farkas: 1896. "Rövid észrevételek Kemény János önéletírásából és az erdélyi irodalom egy-két kútforrásából" (Short comments on János Kemény's autobiography and a few sources of Transylvanian literature). In: *Értekezések a történettudományok köréből* (Essays in historical scholarship), vol. 13, no. 5. Budapest.

Defoe, Daniel: 1700. *The Two Great Questions consider'd. I. What the French King will Do, with Respect to the Spanish Monarchy. II. What Measures the English ought to take*. London.

Demény, Lajos: 1977. *A székelyek és Mihály vajda* (The Székelys and Voivode Michael). Bucharest.

Demkó, Kálmán: 1894. *A magyar orvosi rend története* (The history of the Hungarian doctors' order). Budapest.

309

Dezsényi, Béla: 1948. "A Nova Posoniensia és az újságolvasók a XVIII. században" (The *Nova Posoniensis* and the newspaper readers in the 18th century). *Magyar Századok*, pp. 142–143.

Dickmann, Fritz: 1959a. *Der westfälische Frieden*. Münster.

Dickmann, Fritz: 1959b. *Acta Pacis Westphalicae*, Part I, *Instructionen*. Münster,

Dienst, Heide: 1987. "Hexenprozesse auf dem Gebiet der heutigen Bundesländer Vorarlberg, Tirol (mit Südtirol), Salzburg, Nieder- und Oberösterreich sowie des Burgerlandes." In: *Hexen und Zauberer*, pp. 265–285.

Diplomatarium Alvincziarum: 1870–1887. Ed. by Sándor Szilágyi et al., vols I–III. Budapest.

Djuvara, T. G.: 1914. *Cent projets de partage de la Turquie (1281–1913)*. Paris.

Dömötör, Tekla: 1981. *A magyar nép hiedelemvilága* (Hungarian folk beliefs). Budapest.

Dukkon, Ágnes: 1988. "A kalendáriumok művelődéstörténeti jelentőségéről a XVII–XVIII. század fordulóján (The cultural significance of almanachs at the turn of the 17th and 18th centuries)." In: *A megváltozott hagyomány. Tanulmányok a XVII. századról* (Changing traditions. Studies on the 17th and 18th centuries). Ed. by L. Hopp, I. Küllős, and V. Voigt. Budapest.

Duroselle, Jean-Baptiste: 1990. *L'Europe. Histoire de ses peuples*. Librairie académique Perrin et Bertelsmann Lexicon Verlag, Paris, 423 pp.

Duroselle, Jean-Baptiste: [n.d.] *Európa népeinek története*. Transl. by Lajos Adamik and Péter Zalán. Officina Nova, n.p., 424 pp.

Eckhardt, Sándor – Ortutay, Gyula: 1942. "Régi magyar varázslóasszonyok" (Hungarian sorceresses of the past). *Magyarságtudomány*, vol. 1, pp. 564–580.

Eckhart, Ferenc: 1954. *Földesúri büntetőbíráskodás a XVI–XVII. században* (Feudal criminal jurisdiction in the 16th to 17th centuries). Budapest.

Eickhoff, Ekkehard: 1973. *Venedig, Wien und die Osmanen. Umbruch in Südosteuropa 1645–1700*. München.

Eisenstein, E. Elisabeth: 1993 (First ed.: 1983). *The Printing Revolution in Early Modern Europe*. Cambridge.

Erasmus: 1516 (1987): *Institutio Principis Christiani saluberrimis referta praeceptis per – Basileam 1516. – A keresztény fejedelem neveltetése*. Transl. Ferenc Csonka, epilogue by Szabolcs Ö. Barlay. Budapest, Európa Kiadó.

Erasmus: 1530. "Utilissima consultatio de bello Turcis inferenco." In: *Opera Omnia Desideris Erasmi Rotterodami*. Amsterdam – Oxford.

Erasmus's Letters: 1906–1958. *Opus Epistolarum Des. Erasmi Rotterdami*. Ed. by P. S. Allen, H. M. Allen and H. W. Garrod, vols I–XII. Oxford – Bruxelles.

Erdélyi Magyar Szótörténeti Tár (An etymological dictionary of Transylvanian Hungarian): 1975. Collected and ed. by T. Attila Szabó, vol. I. Bucharest.

Erdődy, Gábor: 1994. "Útkereső független Magyarország a változó Európában" (An independent Hungary seeking its ways and means in a changing Europe). In: *EkvSzGy*, pp. 305–318.

Erdős, Ildikó: 1988. *Az orvosi igazgatás formái a XVIII. században, 1724–1792* (Szakdolgozat). (The forms of medical administration in the 18th century, 1724–1792). (Thesis – Eötvös Loránd University, Budapest).

Esterházy, Pál: 1989. *Mars Hungaricus*. Annotated by Emma Iványi, ed. by Gábor Hausner. Budapest, Zrínyi Kiadó.

Esze, Tamás: 1961. "Egy lengyel királyi tanácsos levele" (A letter from a Polish royal councillor). *Magyar Könyvszemle*, pp. 482–485.

Esze, Tamás: 1964. "Almási Benjamin" (Benjamin Almási). *Irodalomtörténeti Közlemények*.

Esze, Tamás: 1976. "A szatmári béke előzményei" (Antecedents of the Treaty of Szatmár). In: *A Rákóczi szabadságharc vitás kérdései* (Disputable questions of Rákóczi's War of Independence). Ed. by Mátyás Molnár. Vaja–Nyíregyháza, pp. 5–15.

Evans, R. J. W.: 1979. *The Making of the Habsburg Monarchy (1550–1700)*. Oxford.

Fabiny, Tibor: 1976. "Rákóczi diplomáciájának valláspolitikai vonatkozása" (Rákóczi's diplomacy examined with regard to his ecclesiastic policy). *Századok*.

Fabó, Bertalan: 1905. "Magyar ráolvasások 1651-ből" (Hungarian incantations from 1651). *Ethnographia*, vol. 16.

Fèbvre, Lucien: 1938 (1953). "Histoire et psychologie, La vie mentale" (Encyclopedie Française 8). In: *Combats pour l'historie*. Paris.

Fekete, József: 1910. "Tudósasszonyok" (Learned women). *Ethnographia*, vol. 21, pp. 291–294.

Fekete, Sándor: 1970. "A bábaoktatás története Magyarországon" (The history of midwife training in Hungary). *Communicationes*, vols 55–56, pp. 175–199.

Fiedler, Josef: 1855–1858. *Actenstücke zur Geschichte Franz Rákóczys und seiner Verbindungen mit dem Auslande*. Wien.

Fiedler, Josef: 1866. *Die Relationen der Botschafter Venedigs über Deutschland und Österreich im Siebzehnten Jahrhundert*. (*Fontes Rerum Austriacarum*, II/XVI. 1–2.) Wien.

Fiedler, Josef: 1871. *Actenstücke zur Geschichte Franz Rákóczy's und seiner Verbindungen mit dem Auslande 1706, 1709 und 1710.* (*Archiv für Österreichische Geschichte*, 43. B.) Wien

Fischer, Éva – Fülöp, Lajos: 1988. "Zrínyi-levelek a 'Hollandtze Mercurius'-ban (1663–1664)" (Zrínyi's letters in the *Hollandtze Mercurius* [1663–1664]). In: *Zrínyi dolgozatok*, pp. 187–209.

Fodor, Pál: 1991. *Magyarország és a török hódítás* (Hungary and the Turkish conquest). Budapest, Argumentum Kiadó.

Fodor, Vera: 1989. *Forstall Márk levelei* (Mark Forstall's letters). Thesis (Eötvös Loránd University, Budapest).

Forst, Robert: 1993. *After the Deluge. Poland-Lithuania and the Second Northern War 1655–1660.* Cambridge.

Förster, Jenő: 1910. "Három boszorkányper a XVII. századból" (Three witch trials from the 17th century). In: *Közlemények Szepes Vármegye múltjából* (Lőcse).

Fraknói (Frankl), Vilmos: 1868–1869–1872. *Pázmány Péter és kora* (Péter Pázmány and his age). Vol. I (1570–1621), vol. II (1622–1631), vol. III (1632–1637). Pest.

Fraknói (Frankl), Vilmos: 1869. "Pázmány Péter spanyol évdíja" (Péter Pázmány's Spanish annuity). *Magyar Sion*, vol. 7, pp. 22–39.

Fraknói (Frankl), Vilmos: 1871. "Pázmány diplomáciai küldetése Rómába, 1632" (Pázmány's diplomatic mission to Rome, 1632). *Új Magyar Sion*, vol. 2, pp. 721–736, 801–813, 881–895.

Fraknói, Vilmos: 1886. *Pázmány Péter 1570–1637. Magyar Történelmi Életrajzok*, 5, Budapest.

Frankl *see* Fraknói

Frankovith, Gergely: 1588. *Hasznos és fölötte szükséges könyv* (A useful and very important book). Monyorókerék.

Frey, Linda – Frey, Marsha: 1982. "Rákóczi and the Maritime Powers: An Uncertain Friendship". In: *From Hunyady to Rákóczi: War and Society in Late Medieval and Early Modern Hungary*. Ed. by J. Bak and B. Király. New York.

Frey, Linda – Frey, Marsha: 1989. *A Question of Empire: Leopold I and the War of the Spanish Succession, 1701–1705.* New York.

Frey, Linda – Frey, Marsha: 1998. "The Confessional Issue in International Politics: The Rákóczi Insurrection". In: *EkvRVÁ*, pp. 432–441.

Futaky, István: 1993. "Magyarországi és erdélyi diákok a kisebb német egyetemeken (16–19. század)" (Students from Hungary and Transylvania at minor German universities [16th to 19th centuries]). In: *Régi és új peregrináció*.

G. Etényi, Nóra: 1995a. "A közvéleményformálás eszközei az 1663–1664. évi háború idején. Egy Zrínyi-kártyajátéktól Esterházy Mars Hungaricusáig" (Ways of shaping of public opinion during the war of 1663–1664. From a Zrínyi card game to Esterházy's *Mars Hungaricus*). *Irodalomismeret*, Nos 1–2.

G. Etényi, Nóra: 1995b. "A 17. századi közvéleményformálás és propaganda Érsekújvár 1663-as ostromának tükrében" (Propaganda and public opinion in the seventeenth century as reflected in the material on the siege of Érsekújvár in 1663). *Aetas*, nos 1–2, pp. 95–139.

Gajzágó, László: 1941. "A nemzetközi jog eredete" (The origin of international law). In: *Notter Antal Emlékkönyv* (Memorial volume in honour of Antal Notter). Budapest.

Gál, István: 1976. "Maksai Péter angol nyelvű Bethlen Gábor életrajza 1629-ből" (Péter Maksai's life of Gábor Bethlen published in English in 1629). *Irodalomtörténeti Közlemények*.

Galavics, Géza (ed.): 1975. *Hagyomány és aktualitás a magyarországi barokk művészetben XVII. század. Magyarországi reneszánsz és barokk* (Traditions and timeliness in Hungarian Baroque art, 17th century. The Renaissance and the Baroque in Hungary). Budapest, Képzőművészeti Kiadó.

Galavics, Géza: 1976. "Török ellenes harc és egykorú világi képzőművészetünk" (The fight against the Turks and contemporary Hungarian secular fine arts). *Művészettörténeti Értesítő*.

Galavics, Géza: 1986. *Kössünk kardot a pogány ellen* (Let's gird our swords against the pagans). Budapest.

Gángó, Gábor – Müller, László: 1988. *Pázmány római követsége* (Pázmány's mission to Rome). Manuscript.

Garas, Klára: 1953. *Magyarországi festészet a XVII. században* (Hungarian painting in the 17th century). Budapest.

Gélis, Jacques: 1977. "Sages-femmes et accoucheurs: l'obstetrique populaire aux XVIᵉ et XVIIᵉ siècles". *Annales E.S.C.*, vol. 32, pp. 927–957.

Gergely, Samu (publ.): 1886. *Adalékok Erdély és a bécsi udvar diplomáciájához a 200 év előtti török háborúk idejében* (Contributions to the diplomacy of Transylvania and the Viennese Court at the time of the Turkish wars 200 years ago). *Történelmi Tár*, pp. 296–332.

Gévay, Anton: 1838–1842. *Urkunden und Actenstücke zur Geschichte der Verhältnisse zwischen Österreich, Ungarn und der Porte im XVI. und XVII. Jahrhunderte*, vols I–III. Wien.

Göllner, Carl: 1971. *Hexenprozesse in Siebenbürgen*. Cluj-Napoca.

Gombrich, Ernst H.: 1975. *Symbolic Images: Studies in the Art of the Renaissance*. London.

Gömöri, György: 1988. "Adalékok az 1663–1664. évi angliai Zrínyi-kultusz történetéhez" (On the English cult of Zrínyi in the years 1663–1664). In: *Zrínyi dolgozatok*, vol. V, pp. 65–91.

Gömöri, György: 1993. "Magyar peregrinusok a XVII. századi Angliában" (Hungarian wandering students in 17th-century England). In: *Régi és új peregrináció*.

Gömöri, György: [n.d.] "Lord Paget magyar pártfogoltjai." In his: *Erdélyiek és angolok. Művelődés és kapcsolattörténeti tanulmányok* (Lord Paget's Hungarian protégés. Transylvanians and English people. Studies in the history of civilisation and relations). Budapest, pp. 61–68.

Gonda, Imre – Niederhauser, Emil: 1977. *A Habsburgok. Egy európai jelenség* (The Habsburgs. An European phenomenon). Budapest, Gondolat Kiadó.

Gooss, R.: 1911. *Österreichische Staatsverträge: Fürstentum Siebenbürgen, 1526–1690*. Wien.

Gortvay, György: 1953. *Az újabb kori magyar orvosi művelődés és egészségügy története* (The history of Hungarian health care and medical culture of modern times). Budapest.

Grabner, Elfriede: 1987. "Volksmedizin-Wesen, Begriffe und Grundzüge". In: *Hexen und Zauberer*, pp. 75–94.

Grass, Günter: 1992. *Mein Traum von Europa*. Göttingen.

Grotius, Hugo: 1646. *De Jure Belli et Pacis*. Amsterdam.

Grynaeus, Tamás: 1962. "Nadály és nadályosok" (Leeches and leechers). *Communicationes* 26, pp. 129–155.

Grynaeus, Tamás: 1974. "Bács megyei gyógyító szokások és hiedelmek" (Healing methods and beliefs in the county Bács). *Cumania*, pp. 229–236.

Grynaeus, Tamás: 1988. "Amíg élek, az emberek javát szolgálom... Szegedi Körös Gáspár orvosdoktor és a Nádasdy család" (As long as I live I serve people... Gáspár Szegedi Körös a doctor and the Nádasdy family). In: Vida (ed.).

Gundmann, A.: 1986. "Die Beschwerden der deutschen Nation auf den Reichstagen der Reformation." In: Lutz – Kohler.

Gunst, Péter: 1976. *V. Károly (Életek és korok)* (Charles V. Lives and Periods). Ed. by Éva H. Balázs. Budapest.

Gyöngyösi, István: 1664. *A Marssal társolkodó Murányi Vénus* (The Venus of Murány conspiring with Mars). Kassa.

Győri, Tibor: 1936. "Az orvostudományi kar története 1770–1935" (The history of the Medical Faculty 1770–1935). In: *A Pázmány Péter Tudományegyetem története* (The history of Péter Pázmány University). Budapest.

H. Balázs, Éva: 1973. "Van Swietens Ideen und die ungarische Gesellschaft." In: *Gerard Van Swieten und seine Zeit*, ed. by Erna Lesky and Adam Wandruszka. Wien–Köln–Graz.

Haan, Lajos: 1879. *Bél Mátyás* (Mátyás Bél). Budapest.

Hajnal, István: 1929. *Esterházy Miklós nádor lemondása* (The resignation of Palatine Miklós Esterházy). Inaugural treatise. Budapest.

Haley, K. H.: 1972. *The Dutch in the Seventeenth Century*. London.

Hantsch, H.: 1959. "Zum ungarisch-türkischen Problem in der allgemeinen Politik Karls V." In: *Festschrift Karl Eder zum siebzigsten Geburtstag*. Innsbruck.

Haraszti-Taylor, Éva: 1988. "Egy brit diplomata Magyarországa a második világháború után" (Sir Alvary Douglas Frederick Gascoigne G.B.E. 1893–1970) (A British diplomat in Hungary after the Second World War: Sir Alvary Douglas Frederick Gascoigne G.B.E. 1893–1970). In: *EkvRVÁ*, pp. 593–599.

Hargittay, Emil: 1980. "Balásfi Tamás és Pázmány Péter politikai nézetei" (The political ideas of Tamás Balásfi and Péter Pázmány). *Irodalomtörténet*, vol. 62, pp. 134–147.

Hargittay, Emil: 1987. "A politikai elmélet Pázmány tevékenységének hátterében" (The political theory in the background of Pázmány's activity). In: *Pázmány Péter emlékezete*, pp. 405–455.

Harms, W. von (ed.): 1985. *Die Sammlung der Herzog August Bibliothek in Wolfenbüttel*. Tübingen.

Hausner, Gábor – Monok, István – Orlovszky, Géza: 1991. *A Bibliotheca Zrínyiana története* (The history of Bibliotheca Zrínyiana). *Zrínyi könyvtár*, vol. IV. Budapest.

Heckenast, Gusztáv: 1983. "Bécsi svéd követjelentések, 1652–1662" (Reports of Swedish Ambassadors from Vienna). *Történelmi Szemle*, vol. 24, pp. 205–222.

Héjja, Pál: 1936. *A tábori egészségügy Buda visszafoglalása korában* (Military health care at the time of the recapture of Buda). Budapest.

Héjjas, Eszter: 1987–1988. "Magyarország 1663–64-ben, francia diplomáciai jelentések tükrében" (Hungary in 1663–64 as reflected in French diplomatic reports). *Irodalomtörténeti Közlemények*, nos 1–2.

Hengelmüller, Ladislaus Baron: 1913. *Hungary's Fight for National Existence or the History of the Great Uprising Led by Francis Rákóczi II, 1703–1711*, preface by Theodore Roosevelt. London.

Henningsen, Gustav: 1980. *The Witches' Advocate. Basque Witchcraft and the Spanish Inquisition (1609–1614)*. Reno, Nevada.

Herczegh, Géza: 1980. "Bethlen Gábor külpolitikai törekvései" (G. Bethlen's foreign policy aims). In: *Bethlen Gábor állama és kora* (Gábor Bethlen's state and times). Ed. by Kálmán Kovács. Budapest.

Herepei, János: 1971. "Az öreg Comenius néhány magyar híve (Magyar diákok Amsterdamban)" (Some Hungarian desciples of the aged Comenius. Hungarian students in Amsterdam). In: Keserű, pp. 395–403.

Hermann, Zsuzsa: 1961. *Az 1515. évi Habsburg–Jagelló szerződés* (The Habsburg–Jagiellon Pact of 151). Budapest.

Hermann, Zsuzsa: 1976. *Jacob Fugger*. Budapest.

Herner, János: 1988. *Rontás és igézés. Politikai boszorkányper Erdélyben 1668–1688* (Bewitching and enchantment. A political witch trial in Transylvania 1668–1688). Budapest.

Hexen und Zauberer. Die grosse Verfolgung – ein europäisches Phänomen in der Steiermark: 1987. Ed. by Helfried Valentinitsch. Graz–Wien.

Hiller, István: 1988. "Magyar nádorválasztás és európai politika (Adalékok a királyi Magyarország XVII. századi spanyol kapcsolatainak történetéhez)" (The election of a palatine in Hungary and European politics [Glosses on the history of the 17th-century Spanish connections of the Kingdom of Hungary]). *Memoria Rerum*, vol. I, pp. 111–148.

Hiller, István: 1992. *Palatin Nicolas Esterházy. Die ungarische Rolle in der Habsburgdiplomatie 1625–1635*. Böhlen Verlag, Wien.

Hiller, István: 1993. "A tolmácsper" (The interpreter's trial). In: *EkvFL*.

Hints, Elek: 1939. *Az orvostudomány fejlődése az emberiség művelődésében* (The development of medical science in human civilization), vols I–IV. Budapest.

Hódi, Sándor: 1985. "A konfliktusokról" (About Conflicts). In: Hódi, S.: *Illúziók nélkül. Tanulmányok, esszék* (Without illusions. Studies and essays). Újvidék.

Holorenschaw, H.: 1939. *The Levellers and the English Revolution*. London.

Hóman, Bálint – Szekfű, Gyula: 1935. *Magyar történet* (Hungarian history), vols I–V. Budapest.

Hopp, Lajos: 1973. "Mányoki Ádám fejedelmi képíró" (Ádám Mányoki, court painter to the Prince). *Irodalomtörténeti Közlemények*.

Hopp, Lajos: 1992. *Az "antemurale" és a "conformitas" humanista eszméje a magyar–lengyel hagyományban* (The humanist ideas of "antemurale" and "conformitas" in the Polish–Hungarian tradition). Budapest.

Hoppál, Mihály – Törő, László: 1975. "Népi gyógyítás Magyarországon" (Folk medicine in Hungary). *Orvostörténeti Közlemények*, Suppl. nos 7–8, pp. 13–176.

Horn, Ildikó (ed.): 1990. *Rákóczi László naplója* (The diary of László Rákóczi). Budapest, Magvető Kiadó.

Hornyik, János: 1861. *Kecskemét város története*, II (The history of the town of Kecskemét), vol. II. Kecskemét.

Horsley, R. A.: 1979. "Who were the witches? The social role of the accused in the European witch trials." *Journal of Interdisciplinary History*, vol. 9, pp. 689–716.

Horváth, M.: 1859. *Adalékok János király külviszonyainak történetéhez* (Contributions to the history of foreign affairs during King John's reign). Pest.

Hubay, Ilona: 1948. *Röplapok, újságlapok, röpiratok 1480–1718* (Flyers, newspapers, and pamphlets 1480–1718). Budapest.

Humanista történetírók (Huminst history writers): 1977. Selected and notes by Péter Kulcsár. Szépirodalmi Kiadó, Budapest.

Iklódy, András: 1982. "A magyarországi boszorkányüldözés történeti alakulása" (Witch hunt in Hungary from a historical perspective). *Ethnographia*, vol. 93, pp. 292–298.

Imregh, Monika: 1985. "Francesco Moneta Rómában kiadott beszámolója Zrínyi Miklós 1663–1664. évi csatájáról" (Francesco Moneta's account, published in Rome, of Miklós Zrínyi's battles of 1663–1664). *Hadtörténelmi Közlemények*, vol. 32, pp. 660–675.

314

Imreh, István: 1983. "A székely falutörvények világa". In: *A törvényhozó székely falu* (The world of Székely village laws). Bucharest.

Inalcik, Halil: 1973. *The Ottoman Empire: The Classical Age 1300–1600*. London.

Ipolyi, Arnold: 1854. *Magyar mythologia* (Hungarian mythology). Pest.

Istvánffy, M.: 1622 (1962). *Historiarum de rebus Ungaricis libri XXXIV (1490–1605)*. Selected and with an introduction by Gy. Székely. Budapest.

Iványi, Emma: 1991. *Esterházy Pál nádor közigazgatási tevékenysége (1681–1713)* (Palatine Pál Esterházy's administrative activity [1681–1713]). Budapest.

Jakó, Zsigmond – Juhász, István: 1979. *Nagyenyedi diákok* (They studied at Nagyenyed). Bucharest.

Jankovics, J.: 1972. *A Pápai Páriz-család angol kapcsolatainak történetéhez, I. Ifjú Pápai Páriz Ferenc londoni levelei* (Contributions to the history of the English connections of the Pápai Páriz family, vol. I. The London letters of Ferenc Pápai Páriz, jr.). (*Irodalomtörténeti Dolgozatok*, vol. 92). Szeged.

Jankovics, J.: 1973. *A Hungarian Traveller in Late 17th Century England. Angol Filológiai Tanulmányok*. Debrecen.

Jászay, Magda: 1990. *Velence és Magyarország* (Venice and Hungary). Budapest.

Jászay, Pál: 1838. "A szőnyi béke" (The peace of Szőny). In: *Tudománytár*, vol. 4, pp. 167–274.

Jászay, Pál: 1846. *A magyar nemzet napjai a mohácsi vész után* (The days of the Hungarian nation after the disaster of Mohács). Pest.

Jilek, W.: 1976. "Native Renaissance: The Survival and Revival of Indigenous Therapeutic Ceremonials among North American Indians". *Transcultural Psychiatric Research Review*, vol. 15, pp. 117–147.

Jonasson, G.: [n.d.] *XII. Károly és II. Rákóczi Ferenc kapcsolatai 1703–1707* (The relations of Charles XII and Ferenc II Rákóczi, 1703–1707) (See an abstract of the book in *Századok*, 1976.)

Jones, Mervyn D.: 1966. *Five Hungarian Writers*. Oxford.

Jovius, P.: 1532 (1982). "Paolo Giovio – Paulus Jovius – Historiarum sui temporis libri XLV. Firenze." In: *Kőszeg emlékezete*.

Juhász, István: 1979. "Diákélet a Bethlen kollégiumban" (Life in the Bethlen College). In: Jakó – Juhász.

Justus Lipsiusnak a polgári társaságnak tudományáról írt hat könyvei (Justus Lipsius' six books on the science of civil society). Transl. by János Laskai 1641. In: *Laskai János válogatott művei, Magyar Justus Lipsius* (Selected works of János Laskai; A Hungarian Justus Lipsius). Ed. by Márton Tarnóc. Budapest, 1970.

Káldy-Nagy, Gyula: 1974. *Szulejmán* (Suleiman). Budapest.

Káldy-Nagy, Gyula: 1986. "A török állam hadseregének kialakulása I. Szulejmán korára" (Formation of the army of the Turkish state in the age of Suleiman I). In: *Mohács tanulmányok*, pp. 163–194.

Kállay, István: 1962. "Adatok a Rákóczi szabadságharc végnapjainak történetéhez" (Data concerning the final phase of Rákóczi's War of Independence). *Levéltári Közlemények*, vol. 32, pp. 138–149.

Kállay, István: 1985. *Úriszéki bíráskodás a XVIII–XIX. században* (Feudal jurisdiction in the 18th to 19th centuries). Budapest.

Kállay, István – Papp, Mrs. Gábor: 1980. *Magyarország*, no. 39.

Kapronczay, Károly: 1985. "A hazai orvosi közigazgatás kialakulása" (The formation of medical administration in Hungary). *Orvosi Hetilap*, vol. 126, no. 26, pp. 1607–1608.

Kapros, Márta: 1979. "A gyermekekre vonatkozó preventív és produktív mágikus szokások az Ipoly-menti néphagyományban" (Preventive and productive magic related to children in folk traditions by the Ipoly river). *Nógrád Megyei Múzeumi Közlemények*, vol. 20, pp. 75–95.

315

Kara, György (ed.): 1987. *Between the Danube and the Caucasus*. Budapest.

Károlyi, Árpád: 1879. "Adalék a nagyváradi béke és az 1536–1538. évek történetéhez" (Contributions to the history of the peace of Nagyvárad and of the years 1536–38). *Századok*, vol. 12, pp. 591–617, 687–732, 790–840.

Károlyi, Árpád: 1880. "A német birodalom nagy hadivállalata Magyarországon 1542-ben" (The great military compaign of the German Empire in Hungary in 1542). *Századok*, vol. 14, pp. 265–299, 357–387, 445–465, 558–589, 621–655.

Károlyi, Árpád – Wellmann, Imre: 1936. *Buda és Pest visszavívása 1686-ban* (The reconquest of Buda and Pest in 1686). Budapest.

Kárpáti, E.: 1942. *V. Károly keleti politikája* (The eastern policy of Charles V). Kolozsvár.

Kathona, Géza: 1975. "Zrínyi Miklós halálára Londonban 1665-ben megjelent gyászversek" (Elegies published for Miklós Zrínyi in London in 1665). *Irodalomtörténeti Közlemények*, no. 1.

Kecskeméti, A. János: 1621. *Az Dániel próféta könyvének az Szentírás szerinti való igaz magyarázatja* (The true interpretation of the Book of the Prophet Daniel according to the Holy Scripture). Debrecen.

Kellenbenz, Hermann: 1960. "Zur Problematik der Ostpolitik Karls V. Die westeuropäischen Verbindungen Joan Zapolyas und Hieronymus Laskis zu Beginn der dreißiger Jahre." In: *Karl V. Der Kaiser und seine Zeit*. Ed. by P. Rassow and F. Schalk. Köln.

Kellenbenz, Hermann: 1982. "Das Römisch-Deutsche Reich im Rahmen der wirtschafts- und finanzpolitischen Erwährungen Karls V. im Spannungsfeld imperialer und dynastischer Interessen." In: Lutz: 1982.

Kempler, Kurt: 1984. *A gyógyszerek története* (The history of the pharmaceuticals). Budapest.

Kéry, János: 1989. "Gyászbeszéd Zrínyi Miklós temetésén 1664. december 21-én" (Funeral Oration for Miklós Zrínyi on Dec. 21, 1664, Nagyszombat). In: *Zrínyi dolgozatok*, vol. VI, pp. 293–326.

Keserű, Bálint (ed.): 1971. *Adattár XVII. századi szellemi mozgalmaink történetéhez* (Data on the intellectual movements of the seventeenth century), vol. III. Budapest–Szeged.

Kibédi Varga, Áron: 1983. "Retorika, poétika, műfajok. Gyöngyösi István költői világa" (Rhetorics, poetry, genres. The poetic world of István Gyöngyösi). *Irodalomtörténet*, pp. 545–591.

Király, Erzsébet: 1961. "Az európai keresztény hős mítosza" (The myth of the Christian hero in Europe). In: *Zrínyi Miklós emlékezete*, pp. 31–37.

Klaniczay, Gábor: 1984a. "Shamanistic elements in Central European witchcraft". In: *Shamanism in Eurasia*. Ed. by Mihály Hoppál. Göttingen, pp. 404–422.

Klaniczay, Gábor: 1984b. "A történeti antropológia tárgya, módszerei és első eredményei" (The subject matter, methods and first results of historical anthropology). In: *Történeti antropológia*, pp. 23–60.

Klaniczay, Gábor: 1985. "Gerard Van Swieten és a babonák elleni harc kezdetei a Habsburg birodalomban" (Gerard Van Swieten and the beginnings of the fight against superstitions in the Habsburg monarchy). In: *A felvilágosodás jegyében. Tanulmányok H. Balázs Éva hetvenedik születésnapjára*, ed. by Gábor Klaniczay, János Poór and Éva Ring. Budapest, pp. 33–69.

Klaniczay, Gábor: 1987. "Decline of witches and rise of vampires in 18th century Hapsburg Monarchy." *Ethnologia Europea*, vol. 17, pp. 165–180.

Klaniczay, Gábor: 1990. "Hungary: The accusations and the universe of popular magic". In: *Early Modern Witchcraft: Centres and Peripheries*. Ed. by Bength Ankarloo and Gustav Henningsen. Oxford, pp. 219–255.

Klaniczay, Gábor: 1991–1992. "Witch-hunting in Hungary: Social or cultural tensions?" *Acta Ethnographica Hung.*, vol. 37, pp. 67–91.

316

Klaniczay, Tibor: 1961. "Pázmány Péter." In: *Reneszánsz és barokk* (Renaissance and Baroque. Studies in old Hungarian literature). Budapest, pp. 340–360.

Klaniczay, Tibor: 1964. *Zrínyi Miklós*. Budapest.

Klaniczay, Tibor (selected and ed.): 1982. *Janus Pannonius – Magyarországi humanisták* (Janus Pannonius. Humanists in Hungary). Budapest.

Klaniczay, Tibor: 1985. "A nagy személyiségek humanista kultusza a XVI. században" (The Humanist cult of great personalities in the 16th century). Ms.

Kohler, Alfred: 1980. *Antihabsburgische Politik in der Epoche Karls V. Die reichsständische Opposition gegen die Wahl Ferdinands I. zum römischen König und gegen die Anerkennung seines Königtums (1524–1534)*. Wien.

Kohler, Alfred: 1982. *Die innerdeutsche und die außerdeutsche Opposition gegen das politische System Karls V*. Wien.

Kohler, Alfred: 1990. *Quellen zur Geschichte Karls V*. Darmstadt.

Komáromy, Andor: 1910. *Magyarországi boszorkányperek oklevéltára* (Documentation of Hungarian witch trials). Budapest.

Komáromy, András: 1894. "A 'bűbájos' Báthory Anna" (Anna Báthory, the "enchantress"). *Századok*, 28, pp. 298–314.

Köpeczi, Béla: 1966. *A Rákóczi szabadságharc és Franciaország* (The Rákóczi War of Independence and France). Budapest.

Köpeczi, Béla (ed.): 1970. *A Rákóczi szabadságharc és Európa* (Rákóczi's War of Independence and Europe). Budapest.

Köpeczi, Béla: 1971. *La France et la Hongrie au debut du XVIIIᵉ siècle*. Budapest.

Köpeczi, Béla: 1976. "*Magyarország a kereszténység ellensége*" – A Thököly felkelés az európai közvéleményben ("Hungary, the enemy of Christianity" – The Thököly uprising in European public opinion). Budapest.

Köpeczi, Béla – R. Várkonyi, Ágnes (eds): 1973. "Csécsy János naplója" (János Csécsy's diary). In: *Rákóczi-Tükör*, vol. II.

Köpeczi, Béla – Tarnai, Andor (eds): 1988. *Laurus Austriaco–Hungarica. Literarische Gattung und Politik in der zweiten Hälfte des 17. Jahrhunderts*. Budapest–Wien.

Kornis, Gyula: 1935. "Pázmány személyisége" (Pázmány's personality). *Budapesti Szemle*, no. 239, pp. 133–161, 286–319.

Kosáry, Domokos: 1946. "Français en Hongrie en 1664." *Revue d'Histoire Comparée*, vol. 24, pp. 24–65.

Kosáry, Domokos: 1978. *Magyar külpolitika Mohács előtt* (Hungarian foreign policy before Mohács). Budapest.

Kosáry, Domokos: 1980. *Művelődés a XVIII. századi Magyarországon* (Culture in Hungary in the 18th century). Budapest.

Kosáry, Domokos: 1987. "Magyarország a XVI–XVII. századi nemzetközi politikában" (Hungary in the international politics of the 16th and 17th centuries). In: *A történelem veszedelmei*, pp. 20–62.

Kosáry, Domokos: 1987. *Culture and Society in Eighteenth-century Hungary*. Budapest.

Kosztolányi, Dezső: 1920. "A magyar próza atyja" (The father of Hungarian prose). *Nyugat*, vol. 13, pp. 911–917.

Kosztolányi, Dezső: 1990. "A magyar nyelv helye a földgolyón, Nyílt levél Antoine Meillet úrhoz, a Collège de France tanárjához" (The place of the Hungarian language on our planet. Open letter to M. Antoine Meillet, Professor at the Collège de France). *Nyugat*, July 16, 1930. In: D. Kosztolányi: *Nyelv és lélek* (Language and soul). Selected and ed. by Pál Réz. Budapest.

Kovách, Géza – Binder, Pál (eds): 1981. *A céhes élet Erdélyben* (The life of guilds in Transylvania). Bucharest, Kriterion Kiadó.

Kovachich, Márton György: 1801. *Supplementum in Vestigia Comitiorum apud Hungaros*. 3. Budae.

Kovács, József László: 1995. "Szenczi Fekete István, egy eleddig névtelen emlékirat Zrínyi téli hadjáratáról" (F. I. Szenczi, A Memorandum, believed until now to be anonymous, of Zrínyi's winter campaign"). *Irodalomismeret*, Nos 1–2.

Kovács, Kálmán: 1908. "Egy magyarbarát angol diplomata a Rákóczi szabadságharc idején" (A pro-Hungarian English diplomat at the time of Rákóczi's War of Independence). In: *Year-Book of the Unitarian College in Kolozsvár*, Kolozsvár.

Kovács, Sándor Iván: 1985. *A lírikus Zrínyi* (Zrínyi, the lyrical poet). Budapest.

Kraus, Georg: 1994. *Erdélyi krónika 1608–1665* (Transylvanian chronicle 1608–1665). Translated, introduced and annotated by Sándor Vogel. Budapest.

Kretschmayr, H.: 1901. *Gritti Lajos. 1480–1534* (Lajos Gritti. 1480–1534). Budapest.

Kreuzinger, V.: 1924. *Gerhard Van Swieten und die Reform der Wiener Universität unter Maria Theresia bis zur Errichtung der Studienhofcommission*. Wien.

Kristóf, Ildikó: 1991–1992. "'Wise women', sinners and the poor: The social background of witch-hunting in a 16th–18th century Calvinist city of Eastern Hungary." *Acta Ethnographica Hung.*, vol. 37, pp. 93–122.

Kr[opf], L[ajos]: 1907. "Defoe Daniel a Rákóczi mozgalomról" (Daniel Defoe on Rákóczi's movement). *Századok*, vol. 41, pp. 269–270.

Kubinyi, András: 1985. "A magyarországi orvos- és gyógyszerésztársadalom a Mohácsot megelőző évtizedekben" (Doctors and pharmacists in Hungary before Mohács). *Orvostörténeti Közlemények*, vols 109–112, pp. 69–76.

Kubinyi, András: 1986. "A magyar állam belpolitikai helyzete Mohács előtt" (The internal political conditions of the Hungarian state before Mohács). In: *Mohács tanulmányok*, pp. 59–99.

Kulcsár, Zsuzsanna: 1964. "A tömeges boszorkányüldözések magyarázatai és okai" (The explanations and reasons of the witch craze in Hungary). *Századok*, vol. 98, pp. 158–175.

Kvacsala, János: 1889. "Egy álpróféta a XVII. században" (A false prophet in the seventeenth century). *Századok*, vol. 23, pp. 745–766.

Kvacsala, János: 1892. "Az angol–magyar érintkezések történetéhez (1620–1670)" (A contribution to the history of English–Hungarian contacts [1620–1670]), *Századok*, vol. 26, pp. 709–719, 793–810.

Kvacsala, János: 1898. "II. Rákóczi Ferenc porosz összeköttetéseinek történetéhez" (Contributions to the history of the Prussian connections of Ferenc II Rákóczi). *Századok*, vol. 32, pp. 577–597.

Lánczy, Gyula: 1882. "Széchenyi Pál érsek és a nemzeti politika" (Archbishop Pál Széchenyi and national politics). *Századok*.

Lanz, Karl: 1844–1846. *Die Correspondenz des Kaisers Karl V*. Vol. 1. Leipzig.

László, Emőke: 1980. *Flamand és francia kárpitok Magyarországon* (Flemish and French tapestries in Hungary). Budapest.

Le Goff, Jacques: 1960 . "Le moyen age: temps de l'église et temps du marchand". *Annales*, vol. 15, pp. 417–433.

Lehoczky, Tivadar: 1881. *Bereg vármegye monográfiája*, I–III (The monography of county Bereg, vols I–III). Ungvár.

Leman, August: 1920. "La mission du Cardinal Pázmány". In: *Urbain VIII et la rivalité de la France et de la maison d'Autriche de 1631 à 1635*. Paris.

Levinson, Artur: 1913. *Nuntiaturberichte vom Kaiserhofe Leopolds I. (1657–1669). (Archiv für österreichische Geschichte)* Wien.

Lhotsky, Alois: 1971. *Das Zeitalter des Hauses Österreich. Die ersten Jahre der Regierung Ferdinands I. in Österreich (1520–1527)*. Wien.

318

Lindeboom, Arie Gerrit: 1968. *Hermann Boerhave. The Man and his Work*. London.

Linzbauer, Xavér Ferenc: 1852–1856. *Codex Sanitario Medicinalis Hungariae*, I–III. Buda.

Linzbauer, Xavér Ferenc: 1868. *A magyar korona országainak nemzetközi egészségügye* (The international health care in the countries of the Hungarian Crown). Pest.

Lukács, K.: 1943. "A Balatonvidék földrajza kétszáz év előtt. (Fordítás a Notitia Hungariae Novae ...-ból) (The geography of the Balaton region two hundred years ago). In: *Magyar Biológiai Kutató Intézet Munkái*, vol. 15, Tihany.

Lukács, László, S. J. (ed.): 1987. *Monumenta – Monumenta Antiquae Hungariae IV (1593–1600)*. (*Monumenta Historica Societatis Iesu*: A partibus eiusdem Societatis edita, vol. 131.) Romae.

Lukács, László, S. J.: 1987. "Jezsuita maradt-e Pázmány mint érsek?" (Did Pázmány as archbishop remain a Jesuit?). In: *Pázmány Péter emlékezete*, pp. 197–267.

Lukács, Zs. Tibor: 1995. "A propaganda és közvélemény kutathatósága a történettudományban – A korabeli propaganda és II. Rákóczi György megítélése" (Propaganda and public opinion as possible subjects of objective historical study: The public image of György II Rákóczi and contemporary propaganda). *Aetas*, nos 1–2, pp. 68–94.

Lukinich, Imre: 1925. *A szatmári béke története és okirattára* (The history of the Peace of Szatmár and its documents). Budapest.

Luttenberger, A.: 1982. "Karl V. Frankreich und der deutsche Reichstag." In: Lutz.

Lutz, H.: 1964. *Christianitas afflicta. Europa, das Reich und die päpstliche Politik im Niedergang der Hegemonie Kaiser Karls V. (1552–1556)*. Göttingen.

Lutz, H. (ed.): 1982. *Das römisch-deutsche Reich im politischen System Karls V*. München – Wien.

Lutz, H. – Kohler, A.: 1986. *Aus der Arbeit an den Reichstagen unter Kaiser Karl V*. Göttingen.

Magurn, Ruth: 1955. *The Letters of P. P. Rubens*. Cambridge.

A magyar irodalom története (The history of Hungarian literature): 1984. Vol. 1. *–1600*; Vol. 2. *1600–1772*. Ed. by Tibor Klaniczay. Budapest.

A magyar nemzet története (The history of the Hungarian nation). Ed. by Sándor Szilágyi. Vols I–VII. Budapest.

Magyar Országgyűlési Emlékek. Monumenta comitialis Regni Hungariae 1526–1606, I–XII (Documents of Hungarian Diets, vols I–X, ed. by V. Fraknói, vols XI–XII, ed. by Á. Károlyi). Budapest.

Magyari, András: 1975. "Bethlen Kata". *Művelődés* (Bucharest), vol. 28.

Magyarország története 1526–1686 (The history of Hungary, 1526–1686). Ed.-in-chief: Pál Zsigmond Pach, vol. III/1–2. Budapest.

Magyarországi palatinusnak gróf Esterházy Miklósnak Rákóczi György erdélyi fejedelemnek írt egy néhány intő leveleinek párja (A few letters of warning written by the Hungarian Palatine Count Miklós Esterházy to György Rákóczi, Prince of Transylvania): 1645. Vienna.

A magyarországi művészet története (The history of art in Hungary): 1970. Ed.-in-chief: Lajos Fülep. Ed. by Dezső Dercsényi, Anna Zádor. Budapest.

Magyary-Kossa, Gyula: 1929–1940. *Magyar orvosi emlékek*, I–IV (Relics of Hungarian medicine, vols I–IV). Budapest.

Magyary-Kossa, Gyula: 1938. "Régi magyar bábákról" (About old Hungarian midwives of the past). *Orvostörténelem*, vol. 2, no. 10, pp. 1–10 (Debrecen).

Mair, Lucy: 1969. *Witchcraft*. London.

Majláth, Béla: 1880. "Egy magyar követség Svédországba 1705-ben" (A Hungarian mission to Sweden in 1705). *Századok*, vol. 23, pp. 785–795.

Makkai, László: 1958."Gentis Felicitas." *Pedagógiai Szemle*, vol. 8, pp. 966–972.

Makkai, László: 1960. "Az abszolutizmus társadalmi bázisának kialakulása az osztrák Habsburgok országaiban" (The formation of the social basis of absolutism in the countries of the Austrian Habsburgs). *Történelmi Szemle*, vol. 3, pp. 193–223.

319

Makkai, László: 1966. "Két könyv Zrínyi Miklósról" (Two books on Miklós Zrínyi). *Századok,* vol. 100, pp. 1310–1312.

Makkai, László: 1983. "A középkori magyar hitvilág problematikájához" (About the problems of medieval Hungarian beliefs). *Ethnographia,* vol. 94, pp. 106–116.

Makkai, László: 1985. "Pázmány Péter politikai szerepe" (The political role of Péter Pázmány). In: *Magyarország története,* vol. III/2.

Makkai, László: 1988. Néhány gondolat a középkori magyar hitvilág problematikájához. Kézirat (Some ideas on the problems of the medieval Hungarian system of beliefs. Manuscript).

Makkai, László – Szász, Zoltán (eds): 1986. *Erdély története,* I–II (The history of Translyvania, vols I–II). Budapest.

Manga, János: 1979. *Palócföld* (Land of the "palóc" people). Budapest.

Mandrou, Robert: 1968. *Magistrats et sorcières en France au XVIIe siècle. Une analyse de psychologie historique.* Paris.

Mandrou, Robert: 1970. "Magas kultúra és népi műveltség a XVII–XVIII. századi Franciaországban" (Elite culture and popular culture in 17th–18th-century France). *Századok,* 104, pp. 118–125.

Marczali, Henrik: 1882. *Regeszták külföldi levéltárakból* (Abstracts from documents in foreign archives). *Történelmi Tár,* pp. 114–138, 149–175, 348–359, 522–542.

Marczali, Henrik: 1920. *A béke könyve* (The book of peace). Budapest.

Márki, Sándor: 1910. *II. Rákóczi Ferenc,* I–III (Ferenc II Rákóczi, vols I–III). Budapest.

Márki, Sándor: 1913. *Nagy Péter czár és II. Rákóczi Ferenc szövetsége 1707-ben* (The alliance of the Czar Peter the Geat and Ferenc II Rákóczi in 1707). Budapest.

Márki, Sándor: 1922–1923. "Marlborough herceg és a kurucok" (The Duke of Marlborough and the "Kuruc" insurgents). *Hadtörténeti Közlemények,* vols 23–24, pp. 181–198.

Markó, Árpád: 1970. *XII. Károly svéd király és Magyarország* (Charles XII, King of Sweden, and Hungary). Budapest–Stockholm, *Acta Sueco–Hungarica,* vol. 3.

Le Mars à la mode de ce temps (Hung. edition: 1989): *Ezen idők módja szerint való Mars,* translated by Réka Tóth, introduced and ed. by Gábor Hausner. *Zrínyi Könyvtár,* vol. III. Budapest.

Matar, Nabil I.: 1993. "The Comenian Legacy in England: The Case for the Conversion of the Muslims". *The Seventeenth Century,* vol. 8, no. 2, pp. 203–215.

Mayer, Theodor: 1911 (1980). *Verwaltungsreform in Ungarn nach der Türkenzeit.* Sigmaringen.

Mednyánszky, Aloysius: 1830. *Petri Pázmány S. R. E. Cardinalis et archiepiscopi strigoniensis legatio romana.* Pestini, VI, 170 pp.

Melius, Péter: 1578 (1979). *Herbárium. Az fáknak, füveknek nevekről, természetekről és hasznairól* (Herbarium. About the names, nature and benefit of trees and herbs). (Ed. and introductory study and notes by Attila Szabó. Bucharest. Published for the 400th anniversary of the first edition of *Herbárium* in Kolozsvár).

Memoria Rerum: 1988. – *Memoria Rerum. Tanulmányok, források. Emlékkönyv* (Studies and documents, presented to Ágnes R. Várkonyi on the occasion of her 60th birthday, I–II). Ed. by Ildikó Horn, vols I–II. Budapest. Ms.

Mencsik, F. – Kluch, J. (eds): 1894. *Monumenta Hungariae Historica Scriptores,* vol. 33. Budapest.

Mészáros, István: 1987. "Pázmány Péter 17. századi katolikus iskolaügyünk újjászervezője" (Péter Pázmány, reorganizer of our Catholic educational affairs in the 17th century). In: *Pázmány Péter emlékezete,* pp. 305–354.

Miklós, Ödön: 1929. "Bethlen Gábor és a holland diplomácia" (Gábor Bethlen and Dutch diplomacy). *Protestáns Szemle.*

Molnár, Gyula: 1969. "Népi gyógyítás emlékei a bihari boszorkányperekben" (The remnants of folk medicine in the witch trials of Bihar). *Orvostörténeti Közlemények*, vols 48–49, pp. 195–205.

Monumenta Zrínyiana: 1991. Consilium Editorum: László Benczédi, Ágnes R. Várkonyi, and Vera Zimányi. Vols I–II redegit: Ágnes R. Várkonyi. Budapest.

Muchembled, Robert: 1973. *Sorcellerie, Culture populaire et Christianisme au XVIe siècle.* Paris.

Nadányi, Joannes: 1660. *De jure pacis.* Leyden.

Nagy, Géza: 1979. *Charles Irénée Castel de Saint-Pierre és örökbéke-tervezete* (Charles Irénée Castel de Saint-Pierre and his plans for perpetual peace). – Abbé de Saint-Pierre: *Az örökbéke-tervezet rövid foglalata* (A short summary of his plans for perpetual peace). Introduced and annotated by Géza Nagy. Bucharest.

Nagy, László: 1978. Erdélyi "boszorkányperek" a politikai hatalom szolgálatában ("Witch trials" in Transylvania to serve the political power). *Századok*, vol. 112, pp. 1097–1141.

Nagy, László: 1983. "Erdély és a tizenötéves háború" (Transylvania and the Fifteen Years' War). *Századok*, vol. 116, pp. 639–688.

Nagy, László: 1986a. *A török világ végnapjai Magyarországon* (The last days of Turkish rule in Hungary). Budapest.

Nagy, László: 1986b. "Buda fölszabadulása a török alól" (Buda's liberation from the Turks). In: *Lotharingiai Károly hadinaplója Buda visszafoglalásáról* (Charles Lorraine's war diary of the reconquest of Buda). Budapest.

Nagy, László: 1988. *Erdélyi boszorkányperek* (Witch trials in Transylvania). Budapest.

Nedeczky, Gábor: 1891. *A Nedeczky-család* (The Nedeczky family). Budapest.

Nehring, Karl: 1986. "Magyarország és a zsitvatoroki szerződés (1605–1609)" (Hungary and the treaty of Zsitvatorok [1605–1609]). *Századok*, vol. 120, pp. 3–50.

Németh, S. Katalin: 1989. "Zrínyi-Újvár és az istenek" (Zrínyiujvár and the gods). *Irodalomtörténeti Közlemények*, nos 5–6, pp. 568–570.

Németh, S. Katalin: 1995. "Comenius elfelejtett propagandistái: Redinger és Hoburg (1664)" (Comenius's Forgotten Propagandists: Redinger and Hoburg [1664]). Lecture delivered at the Dec. 13, 1995 meeting of the Renaissance Research Group of the Institute for Literary Studies.

Oláh, Andor: 1956. "Népi orvoslás, orvostörténet, orvostudomány" (Healing, the history of medicine and medical science. The significance of studying folk medicine from the point of view of medical history). *Communicationes*, vol. 3, pp. 84–105.

Oláh, Andor: 1986. *"Új hold, új király". A magyar népi orvoslás életrajza* ("New moon, new king". The history of Hungarian folk medicine). Budapest.

[Oláh, Miklós] Olahus, Nicolaus: 1938. *Hungaria, Athila,* ed. by Kálmán Eperjessy and László Juhász. Budapest.

Országh, László: 1937. "James Bogdani magyar festő III. Vilmos és Anna királynő udvarában" (James Bogdany, Hungarian painter at the Courts of William III and Queen Anne). In: *Angol Filológiai Tanulmányok*, vol. 2, Budapest.

Orvosok és gyógyításmód a XVII. század első felében (Doctors and therapeutic methods in the first half of the 17th century. Manuscript). Művelődéstörténeti pályamunka. (MS in the Library of the Historical Institute of Loránd Eötvös University).

Őry, Miklós, S. J.: 1970. *Pázmány Péter tanulmányi évei* (Péter Pázmány's student years). Eisenstadt.

Őry, Miklós – Szabó, Ferenc: 1983. "Pázmány Péter (1570–1637)." In: *Pázmány's works.*

Ottlik, Géza: 1966. *School at the Frontier.* Transl. by Kathleen Szász. New York.

Óváry, Lipót: 1879. *III. Pál pápa és Farnese Sándor bíborosnak Magyarországra vonatkozó diplomáciai levelezése 1535–1549* (The diplomatic correspondence of Pope Paul III and Cardinal Alessandro Farnese concerning Hungary [1535–1549]). Publ. by ~. Budapest, MHH Diplomataria, 16.

Óváry, L.: 1901. *A Magyar Tudományos Akadémia Történelmi Bizottságának oklevélmásolatai*, I–II. Budapest.

Pach, Zsigmond Pál: 1968. "A nemzetközi kereskedelmi útvonalak XV–XVII. századi áthelyezésének kérdéséhez" (A contribution to the problem of the shift in international trade routes in the 15th to 17th centuries). *Századok*, vol. 102, pp. 863–896.

Pachner, Eggenstroff v.: 1740. *Vollständige Sammlung aller von Anfang des noch fürwährenden Teutschen Reichstags de Anno 1663 bis anhero abgefassten Reich-Schlüsse*. Regensburg.

Pánek, Jaroslav: 1991. *Comenius. Teacher of Nations*. Prague.

Panofsky, Erwin: 1970. *Meaning in the Visual Arts*. Harmondsworth.

Pápai Páriz, Ferenc: 1690 (1977). "Pax Corporis". In: *Békességet magamnak, másoknak* (Peace for myself and other people). Ed. by Géza Nagy. Bucharest.

Parker, Geoffrey: 1976. "The 'Military Revolution' 1560–1660 – A myth?" *The Journal of Modern History*, vol. 48, no. 2.

Patera, A.: 1892. *Jana Amosa Komenskeho korrespondence*. Prag.

Pázmány Péter művei: 1613, 1636 (1983). *A római anyaszentegyház szokásából minden vasárnapokra és egynéhány innepekre rendelt evangéliomokrul rendelt prédikációk* (Sermons ordered for every Sunday and some holidays by the Roman Church). Pozsony. *Pázmány Péter művei*, ed. by M. Tarnóc, Budapest.

Pepys, Samuel: 1961. *Samuel Pepys naplója* (The Diary of Samuel Pepys). Selected by Tibor Szobotka. Budapest.

Perényi, József: 1956. *II. Rákóczi Ferenc és I. Péter diplomáciai kapcsolatainak kezdetei* (The beginnings of the diplomatic relations of Peter I and Ferenc II Rákóczi). Budapest.

Perényi, József: 1964. "Projets de pacification européenne de F. Rákóczi en 1708–1709". *Annales Universitatis Scientiarum Budapestiensis, Sectio Historica*, VI.

Perjés, Géza: 1965. *Zrínyi Miklós és kora* (Miklós Zrínyi and his times). Budapest.

Perjés, Géza: 1979. *Mohács*. Budapest, Magvető Kiadó.

Perjés, Géza: 1980. "A Rákóczi összeesküvés tervei a háború megvívására" (Plans of Rákóczi's conspiracy to wage the war of independence). In: *Rákóczi-Tanulmányok*.

Perjés, Géza: 1989a. *The Fall of the Medieval Kingdom of Hungary: Mohács 1526 – Buda 1541*. Columbia Univ. Press.

Perjés, Géza: 1989b. "Zrínyi és az 1663–1664-es nagy török háború" (Zrínyi and the great Turkish war of 1663–1664). In: Esterházy.

Perjés, Géza: 1990. "Az oszmán államvezetés racionalitása" (The rationality of Ottoman state management). *Új Erdélyi Múzeum*, vol. 1, pp. 147–162.

Péter, Katalin: 1985. *Esterházy Miklós*. Budapest.

Péter, Katalin: 1986. "A fejedelemség virágkora" (The heyday of the Principality). In: *Erdély története* (The history of Transylvania). Editor-in-chief: Béla Köpeczi. Budapest, vol. 2, pp. 617–783.

Péter, Katalin: 1987. "Zrínyi angol rajongói" (Zrínyi's English fans). In: *Angol életrajz Zrínyi Miklósról*, pp. 27–63.

Pócs, Éva: 1977. "Szöveg – cselekmény – hiedelem összefüggései a nem epikus ráolvasásokban" (The correlation between text, rites and belief in the incantations of non-epic character). *Népi kultúra – népi társadalom*, vol. 9, pp. 51–98.

Pócs, Éva: 1979. "A népi gyógyászat és néphit kutatásának határterületei" (The borderland between the research of folk medicine and folk belief). *Orvostörténeti Közlemények*, Suppl. 11/12, pp. 61–75.

Pócs, Éva: 1983. "Gondolatok a magyarországi boszorkányperek néprajzi vizsgálatához" (Some ideas on the ethnographical examination of Hungarian witch trials). *Ethnographia*, vol. 96, pp. 134–147.

Pócs, Éva: 1984. "Egyházi benedikció – paraszti ráolvasás" (Church benediction – peasant incantation). In: *Történeti antropológia*, pp. 109–137.

Pócs, Éva: 1986. *Szem meglátott, szív megvert. Magyar ráolvasások* (Evil eye looked at you, heart bewitched you. Hungarian incantations). Budapest.

Polgár, László, S. J.: 1987. "Pázmány bibliográfia" (Pázmány bibliography). In: *Pázmány Péter emlékezete*, pp. 449–480.

Polišenský, Josef: 1953. "Komesky a jeho doba." *Historicky Sbornik*.

Polišenský, Josef V.: 1968. *The Frontier in the Economic History of Central Europe.* Bloomington.

Polišenský, Josef V.: 1971. *Der Krieg und die Gesellschaft in Europa 1616–1648. Documenta Bohemica Bellum Tricennale Illustrantia.* Prague.

Polišenský, Josef V.: 1971: *The Thirty Years' War.* London.

Pribram, Alfred Francis: 1901. *Venetianische Depeschen vom Kaiserhofe.* Wien.

R. Kiss, István: 1905. "Történeti adalékok a boszorkányság és ördöngősség hiedelmeihez" (Historical data on the beliefs of witchcraft and sorcery). *Ethnographia,* vol. 16, pp. 210–219.

R. Kiss, István: 1906. *II. Rákóczi Ferenc erdélyi fejedelemmé választása* (The election of Ferenc II Rákóczi as Prince of Transylvania). Budapest.

R. Várkonyi, Ágnes: 1975. *Török világ és magyar külpolitika* (The Turkish world and Hungarian foreign policy). Budapest.

R. Várkonyi, Ágnes: 1980a. "'Ad Pacem Universalem'. (The international antecedents of the Peace of Szatmár)." *Studia Historica Acad. Sci. Hung.,* vol. 145.

R. Várkonyi, Ágnes: 1980b. "'Ad Pacem Universalem' (The international antecendents of the Peace of Szatmár)". In: *Études Historiques.* Budapest, pp. 303–336.

R. Várkonyi, Ágnes: 1981. "A legnagyobb bölcsesség és eszesség ... Bethlen Gábor és az európai béketárgyalások (1648–1714)" (The greatest wisdom and intelligence ... Bethlen and the European peace negotiations [1648–1714]). *Valóság,* vol. 24, no. 1, pp. 1–10.

R. Várkonyi, Ágnes: 1983. "Rákóczi és a hágai békekonferencia" (Rákóczi and the peace conference at The Hague). *Irodalomtörténeti Közlemények,* vol. 87, pp. 202–211.

R. Várkonyi, Ágnes: 1984a. *Erdélyi változások (1660–1711)* (Changes in Transylvania [1660–1711]). Budapest, Magvető Kiadó.

R. Várkonyi, Ágnes: 1984b. "Zrínyi Miklós szövetséglevele Wesselényivel és Nádasdyval a török ellen 1663-ban" (Miklós Zrínyi's contract of allience with Wesselényi and Nádasdy against the Turks). *Történelmi Szemle,* vol. 27, no. 3, pp. 341–368.

R. Várkonyi, Ágnes: 1984c. *Buda visszavívása 1686* (The reconquest of Buda in 1686). Budapest, Kossuth Kiadó.

R. Várkonyi, Ágnes: 1985. "The Principatus Transylvaniae and the Genesis of the anti-Turkish Alliance." In: *Études Historiques.* Budapest.

R. Várkonyi, Á.: 1986. "Hungary and the Europe of the Sacred League". *The New Hungarian Quarterly,* no. 27 (103), pp. 142–155.

R. Várkonyi, Ágnes: 1987a. *A rejtőzködő Murányi Vénus* (The "Hiding Venus of Murány"). Budapest, Magvető Kiadó.

R. Várkonyi, Ágnes: 1987b. "Gábor Bethlen and Transylvania under the Rákóczis at the European Peace Negotiations (1648–1711)." In: *Forschungen über Siebenbürgen und seine Nachbarn. Festschrift für Attila T. Szabó und Zsigmond Jakó.* Ed. by K. Benda, T. Bogyay, H. Glassl, Zs. Lengyel. München.

R. Várkonyi, Ágnes: 1987–1988. "Reformpolitika Zrínyi mozgalmában" (The reform policies of Zrínyi's movement). *Irodalomtörténeti Közlemények,* vols 91–92, pp. 131–141.

R. Várkonyi, Ágnes: 1988a. "Die Belagerung von Ofen im Rahmen der Pläne zur Zurückdrängung der osmanischen Macht." In: Köpeczi, B. – Tarnai, A. (eds), pp. 1–14..

R. Várkonyi, Ágnes: 1988b. "The reconquest of Buda in contemporary Hungarian political thought and public opinion." *Acta Historica Acad. Sci. Hung.,* vol. 34, pp. 3–15.

R. Várkonyi, Ágnes: 1989. "Magyarország művelődése a török kiűzésének korában, 1683–1711" (Hungarian civilization in the period of the expulsion of the Turks). In: Ember,

Győző – Heckenast, Gusztáv (eds): *Magyarország története* (The history of Hungary), vol. IV.

R. Várkonyi, Ágnes: 1992. "A megkésettség anatómiája" (The anatomy of backwardness). In: *Pelikán a fiaival* (A pelican with its young). Budapest, Liget Kiadó, pp. 310–320.

R. Várkonyi, Ágnes: 1993. "Pro quiete regni – for the peace of the realm (The 1568 law on religious tolerance in the Principality of Transylvania)". *The Hungarian Quarterly*, no. 34 (130), pp. 99–122.

R. Várkonyi, Ágnes: 1994a. "Erdély és a vesztfáliai béke" (Transylvania and the Treaty of Westphalia). In: *Scripta manent*. Ed. by István Draskóczy. Budapest, pp. 187–198.

R. Várkonyi, Ágnes: 1994b. "The end of Turkish rule in Transylvania and the reunification of Hungary (1660–1711)". In: *History of Transylvania*. Editor-in chief: Béla Köpeczi. Ed. by Gábor Barta, István Bóna, László Makkai, Zoltán Szász, and Ágnes R. Várkonyi. Budapest, Akadémiai Kiadó.

R. Várkonyi, Ágnes: 1996a. "An undivided Europe?" *Budapest Review of Books* 6, pp. 58–66.

R. Várkonyi, Ágnes: 1996b. "Európa Zrínyije" (Zrínyi through the eyes of Europe). *Irodalomtörténeti Közlemények*, vol. 100, pp. 1–39.

R. Várkonyi, Ágnes: 1997. "Amiről Bethlen Miklós Önéletírása hallgatott" (What Miklós Bethlen's memoirs did not speak of). *Korunk*, vol. 8, no. 7, pp. 55–56.

R. Várkonyi, Ágnes: 1998a. "Magyarország az új kihívások korában (1648–1711)" (Hungary in the period of new challenges [1648–1711]). *Valóság*, vol. 41, No. 6.

R. Várkonyi, Ágnes: 1998b. "Hungarian independence and the balance of power." In: *In the Fabric of Modern Europe. Studies in Social and Diplomatic History*. Ed. by Attila Pók. Nottingham.

Raab, Theodore K.: 1975. *The Struggle for Stability in Early Modern Europe*. Oxford University Press.

Rabe, H.: 1982. "Elemente neuzeitlicher Politik und Staatlichkeit im politischen System Karls V." In: Lutz.

Ráday, Pál: 1866. "Diary of my Journey to Bender in 1709". In: *Rákóczi Tár*, vol. I.

Ráday Iratok: 1955, 1961. *Ráday Pál Iratai 1703–1706*, I–II (Pál Ráday's papers 1703–1706, vols I–II). Ed. by Kálmán Benda, Tamás Esze, Ferenc Maksay, László Papp. Budapest, Akadémiai Kiadó.

(II.) Rákóczi Ferenc fejedelem Emlékiratai : 1739 (1978) see *Archivum Rákóczianum*, 1978.

(II.) Rákóczi Ferenc Önéletrajza. Confessio Peccatoris (1716–1735): 1876. (The autobiography of Ferenc II Rákóczi [1716–1735]). Ed. by Ágost Grisza. Budapest.

(II.) Rákóczi György esküvője (The wedding of György II Rákóczi): 1990. Collected and ed. by Gábor Várkonyi. Budapest.

Rákóczi Tár (Rákóczi repertory): 1866. Vol. I. Pest.

Rákóczi-Tanulmányok (Rákóczi studies): 1980. Ed. by Béla Köpeczi, Lajos Hopp, Ágnes R. Várkonyi, vol. I. Budapest.

Rákóczi-Tükör (Rákóczi mirror): 1973. (Diaries, reports, memoires on the War of Independence. Selected, edited, preface and essays written by Béla Köpeczi and Ágnes R. Várkonyi, vols I–II). Budapest.

Rázsó, Gyula: 1986. "A Habsburg-birodalom politikai és katonai törekvései Magyarországon Mohács időszakában" (Political and military aspirations of the Habsburg Empire in Hungary in the times preceding and following the Battle of Mohács). In: *Mohács tanulmányok*, pp. 127–162.

Régi erdélyi viseletek (Old Transylvanian attires): 1990. (Preface by József Jankovics). Budapest.

Régi és új peregrináció. Magyarok külföldön és külföldiek Magyarországon (Peregrination, old an new. Hungarians abroad and foreigners in Hungary): 1993. Ed. by Imre Kékesi, József Jankovics, and László Kósa. Vol. II, Szeged.

Régi Magyar Költők Tára, 10 (The treasury of old Hungarian poets, Vol. 10. The poetry of the 1660s): 1981. Ed. by Imre Varga. Budapest.

Roberts, Michael: 1956. *The Military Revolution 1560–1660*. Belfast.

Roe, Sir Thomas: 1740. *The Negotiations of Sir Thomas Roe in his Embassy to the Ottoman Porte ... His Correspondence with Bethlen Gábor, Prince of Translyvania, 1621–1628*. Ed. by S. Richardson, and T. Carte. London.

Rómer, Flóris: 1861. "Adalék a boszorkányperekhez (1)" (Contributions to the witch trials). *Győri Történelmi és Régészeti Füzetek* I, pp. 176–185, 219–236, 322–333.

Rómer, Flóris: 1862. "Adalék a boszorkányperekhez (2)" (Contributions to the witch trials). *Győri Történelmi és Régészeti Füzetek* II, pp. 74–81, 158–165, 274–276.

Rómer, Flóris: 1863. "Adalék a boszorkányperekhez (3)" (Contributions to the witch trials). *Győri Történelmi és Régészeti Füzetek* III, pp. 176–182.

Rónay, György: 1974. *Kutatás közben* (In the course of research). Budapest.

Rózsa, György: 1965. "R. de Hooghe és a magyarországi török háború" (R. de Hooghe and the Turkish war in Hungary). *Művészettörténeti Értesítő*, pp. 17–23.

Rózsa, György: 1970. "A Nádasdy-Mausoleum és Nicolaus Avancini" (Nádasdy-Mausoleum and Nicolaus Avancini. The historical material was collected by Ferenc Lancmár [1658], the court chaplain of Nádasdy). *Irodalomtörténeti Közlemények*, pp. 466–478.

Rudolf, H. v. (ed.): 1977. *Der Dreissigjährige Krieg: Perspektiven und Strukturen*. Darmstadt.

Russel, H. R.: 1959. *The Encyclopedia of Witchcraft and Demonology*. London.

Rúzsás, Lajos: 1976. "A magyar közvélemény útkeresése Mohács után a XVI. században" (Seeking ways and means as reflected in Hungarian public opinion in the 16th century after the Battle of Mohács). In: *Mohács tanulmányok*, pp. 323–336.

S. Lauter, Éva: 1989. "Pálffy Pál nádor levelei elé" (Introduction to the letters of Palatine Pál Pálffy). In: "Pálffy Pál nádor levelei, 1644–1653" (Palatine Pál Pálffy's letters, 1644–1653). *Régi Magyar Történelmi Források* (Old Hungarian Historical Sources), vol. I. Ed. by Ildikó Horn, and Andrea Kreutzer. Budapest.

Schauroth, E. Ch. W. von: 1751. *Vollständige Sammlung der Conclusorum, Schreiben und anderen übrigen Verhandlungen des hochpreisslichen corporis evangelicorum*. Regensburg.

Schick, Peter J.: 1987. "Die Hexenverfolgung aus der Sicht des modernen Strafrechts". In: *Hexen und Zauberer*, pp. 397–496.

Schram, Ferenc: 1970–1982. *Magyarországi boszorkányperek 1529–1768*, I–III (Witch trials in Hungary 1529–1768, vols I–III). Budapest.

Schram, Ferenc: 1973. "Népi nőgyógyászati tanácsok a XVII–XVIII. századból" (Some pieces of advice of folk gynaecology from the 17th–18th century). *Orvostörténeti Közlemények*, vols 69–70, pp. 254–277.

Seligmann, Kurt: 1971. *Magic, Supernaturalism and Religion*. New York (In Hung.: *Mágia és okkultizmus az európai gondolkozásban*. Budapest, 1987).

Shaaber, A. Mathias: 1932. "The History of the First English Newspaper." *Studies in Philology*.

Sík, Sándor: 1940. "Pázmány és Erdély" (Pázmány and Transylvania). *Jelenkor*, vol. 2, no. 19, pp. 5–6. – *Vasárnap*, pp. 47–51.

Sinkovics, István: 1986. "Útkeresés Mohács után" (Seeking ways and means after the Battle of Mohács). In: *Magyarország története 1526–1686*, Vol. III/1, pp. 149–222.

Šmerda, Milan: 1989. "'Cseh jobbágyság' – Habsburg abszolutizmus" ("Czech serfs" – Habsburg absolutism). In: *Csehország a Habsburg Monarchiában 1618–1918* (Bohemia in the Habsburg Monarchy 1618–1918). Ed. and transl. by László Szarka. Budapest, Gondolat Kiadó.

Smith, P. L.: 1907. *The Life and Letters of Sir Henry Wotton*, vols I–II. Oxford.

Sörös, Pongrác: 1917. "Frangepán Ferenc, kalocsai érsek, egri püspök" (Ferenc Frangepán, Archbishop of Kalocsa, Bishop of Eger). *Századok*, vol. 51, pp. 429–471, 545–576.

Spielmann, József: 1969. *Der Einfluss von Boerhaves Lehren auf die Medizin in Siebenbürgen.* Halle.

Spielmann, József: 1977. "A közjó szolgálatában" (In the service of the public good). In: *Tudomány- és művelődéstörténeti tanulmányok* (Studies in the history of scholarship and civilization). Bucharest, Kriterion.

Spielmann, József: 1979. "Történelmi reflexiók a népi orvoslás és az orvostudomány viszonyáról" (Thoughts from a historical perspective about the relationship between folk medicine and medical science). *Orvostörténeti Közlemények,* Suppl. 11–12, pp. 35–49.

Spielmann, József–Huttmann, Arnold: 1968. "Blätter aus der Medizingeschichte der Siebenbürger Sachsen." *Die Grünenthal Waage,* vol. 7, no. 2, pp. 61–69.

Srbik, Heinrich von: 1912. *Österreichische Staatsverträge.* Niederlande I. B. (1636–1722). Wien.

Stoll, O.: 1908–1909. *Zur Kenntniss des Zauberglaubens, der Volksmagie in Volksmedicine in der Schweiz.* Jahresbericht der Geogr.-Ethnographischen Gesellschaft in Zürich, Zürich.

Stone, Lawrence: 1984. *The Family, Sex and Marriage in England 1500–1800.* London.

Sz. Jónás, Ilona: 1997. "Pierre Le Moyne, Galerie des femmes fortes." In: *EkvHBÉ,* pp. 113–117.

Szabad, György (1983): *Magyarország állami önállóságának kérdése a polgári átalakulás korában.* Budapest.

Szabó, F.: 1987. "Pázmány hitelemzése a grazi De Fide-traktatusban" (Pázmány's analysis of faith in the 'De Fide' Tract of Graz). In: *Pázmány Péter emlékezete,* pp. 99–180.

Szabó, T. Attila: 1979. "Méliusz Péter és a kolozsvári Herbarium" (Péter Méliusz and the Herbal of Kolozsvár). In: Mélius Juhász, Péter: *Herbárium* (1578).

Szádeczky, Lajos: 1887. "Jelentés a gróf Forgách család levéltárából" (Report from the archives of the Forgách family). *Századok,* vol. 21, pp. 560–572.

Szakály, Ferenc: 1975. *A mohácsi csata* (The Battle of Mohács). Budapest.

Szakály, Ferenc: 1986a. "A török–magyar küzdelem szakaszai a mohácsi csata előtt (1361–1526)" (Stages of the Turkish–Hungarian struggle before the Battle of Mohács [1361–1526]). In: *Mohács tanulmányok,* pp. 11–58.

Szakály, Ferenc: 1986b. *Hungaria Eliberata.* Budapest.

Szakály, Ferenc: 1986c. *Vesztőhely az út porában* (Scaffold in the dust of the road). Budapest.

Szakály, Ferenc: 1990. "Virágkor és hanyatlás 1440–1711" (Heyday and decline, 1440–1711). In: *Magyarok Európában,* II (Hungarians in Europe, vol. 2). Budapest, Háttér Lap- és Könyvkiadó.

Szalay, László: 1859. "János király és az európai hatalmasságok 1526–1528" (King János and the European potentates). In: *Adalékok a magyar nemzet történetéhez a XVI. században* (Contributions to the history of the Hungarian nation in the 16th century). Pest.

Szalay, László: 1864. *II. Rákóczi Ferenc bujdosása* (Ferenc II Rákóczi in exile). Pest.

Szalay, László (ed.): 1865. *Gróf Károlyi Sándor önéletírása és naplójegyzetei,* II (Count Sándor Károlyi's autobiography and diary notes, vol. II). Pest.

Szalay, László: 1870. "Klement János Mihály, II. Rákóczi Ferenc követe Berlinben, Hágában, Londonban" (János Mihály Klement, envoy of Ferenc II Rákóczi to Berlin, The Hague and London). *Századok,* vol. 4.

Szalay, L. (– Salamon, F.): 1863–1870. *Galántai gróf Esterházy Miklós, Magyarország nádora,* I–III (Count Miklós Esterházy of Galánta, Palatine of Hungary, vols I–III). Pest.

Szállási, Árpád: 1975. "A Pax Corporis egyik ismeretlen kiadásáról" (An unknown edition of Pax Corporis). *Orvosi Hetilap,* vol. 116, no. 46, pp. 2730–2731.

Szállási, Árpád: 1985. "Nagykároly helye a magyar orvostörténelemben" (Nagykároly in the history of Hungarian medicine). *Orvosi Hetilap,* vol. 126, no. 16, pp. 977–980.

Szántó, Konrád, OFM: 1987. "Pázmány főpásztori tevékenysége" (The activity of Pázmány as prelate). In: *Pázmány Péter emlékezete,* pp. 269–301.

Széchy, Károly: 1896–1902. *Gróf Zrínyi Miklós*, I–V (Count Miklós Zrínyi, vols I–V). Budapest.

A szécsényi országgyűlés 1705-ben (The Diet of Szécsény in 1705): 1995. Szécsény.

Szekfű, Gyula: 1929 (1983). *Bethlen Gábor* (Gábor Bethlen). Budapest.

Szekfű, Gyula: 1935a. "A tizenhatodik század" (The sixteenth century). In: Hóman – Szekfű, vol. III.

Szekfű, Gyula: 1935b. "A tizenhetedik század" (The seventeenth century). In: Hóman – Szekfű, vol. IV.

Szelestei, N. László: 1980. *Zrínyi Miklós tanácsai a császárnak 1664 tavaszán*. I. k. (Miklós Zrínyi's advice to the Emperor in the spring of 1664).

Szendrey, Ákos: 1986. *A magyar néphit boszorkánya* (The witch of Hungarian folk beliefs). Budapest.

Szerémi, G.: 1545 (1961). *Epistola de perditione regni Hungarorum*. With an introd. and notes by Gy. Székely. Budapest.

Szilágyi, Sándor: 1867. *Bethlen Gábor fejedelem trónfoglalása* (The crowning of Prince Gábor Bethlen). Pest.

Szilágyi, Sándor: 1870. *Rákóczi és Pázmány* (Rákóczi and Pázmány). With the correspondence of the two statesmen and documents. Pest, VIII, 244 pp.

Szilágyi, Sándor: 1873a. *Adalékok Bethlen Gábor szövetkezéseinek történetéhez* (A contribution to the history of G. Bethlen's alliances). Budapest.

Szilágyi, Sándor (ed.): 1873b. *Okmánytár I. Rákóczi György svéd és francia szövetkezéseinek történetéhez 1632–1648* (A repertory of documents concerning the Swedish and French alliances of György I Rákóczi, 1632–1648). (*Monumenta Hungariae Historica Diplomataria*, vol. 21), Pest.

Szilágyi, Sándor (ed.): 1874. *Okmánytár II. Rákóczi György diplomáciai összeköttetéseihez 1648–1657* (A repertory of documents concerning the diplomatic relations of György II Rákóczi, 1648–1657). (*Monumenta Hungariae Historica Diplomataria*, vol. 23), Pest.

Szilágyi, Sándor (ed.): 1875. *A két Rákóczy György fejedelem családi levelezése* (The correspondence of the two Princes György Rákóczi). Budapest.

Szilágyi, Sándor (ed.): 1875–1898. *Erdélyi országgyűlési emlékek*, I–XXI (Monumenta comitialia regni Transylvaniae, 1540–1699, vols I–XXI). Budapest.

Szilágyi, Sándor: 1885. *A linczi béke okirattára* (Documents of the Treaty of Linz). Budapest.

Szilágyi, Sándor: 1893. *I. Rákóczi György, 1593–1648* (György I Rákóczi, 1593–1648). Budapest.

Szimonidesz, Lajos: 1940. *Kermann Dániel evangélikus püspök főbenjáró pere iratai a Magyar Országos Levéltárban* (Documents in the Hungarian National Archives on the case of capital offence committed by Dániel Kermann, Lutheran Bishop). Rózsahegy.

Szlatky, Mária: 1983. *"Minden doktorságot csak ebből késértek." Szemelvények a XVI–XVII. századi orvosi könyvekből* ("I try all doctoring from this." Extracts from medical books of the 16th–17th centuries). Budapest.

Szőnyi, György Endre: 1978. *Titkos tudományok és babonák. A XV–XVII. század művelődéstörténetének kérdéséhez* (Secret sciences and superstitions. Contributions to the cultural history in the 15th–17th centuries). Budapest.

Szőnyi, György Endre: 1981. *Comenius asztronómiai világképe* (Comenius's astronomy). Szeged (*Irodalomtudományi Dolgozatok*, 143).

Szörényi, László: 1993. "A Szigeti Veszedelem és az európai epikus hagyomány" (The Siege of Szigetvár and the European epic tradition, 1979) and "Panegyricus és eposz (Zrínyi és Cortesius)" (Panegyricus and epos (Zrínyi and Cortesius, 1987–1988). In his book: *Hunok és jezsuiták* (Huns and Jesuits). Budapest.

Sztanó, László: 1985. "Olasz beszámoló Zrínyi Miklós 1663. november 27-én vívott Mura menti ütközetéről" (An Italian account of Miklós Zrínyi's battle along the Mura on November 27, 1663). *Hadtörténeti Közlemények*, vol. 32, pp. 676–681.

Sztárai, Mihály: 1985. *Sztárai Mihály historiája Perényi Ferenc kiszabadulásáról – Perényi Péter élete és halála*. Publ. by Imre Téglásy. Budapest.

Szűcs, Jenő: 1988. "Miért szól délben a harang?" (Why the bells ring at noon). In: *Magyarok a Kárpát-medencében* (Magyars in the Carpathian Basin). Compiled and ed. by Ferenc Glatz. Budapest, pp. 57–60.

Tagányi, Károly: 1887. "Adatok megyénk múltjából a XVI. és XVII. századból" (Some data about the past of our county from the 16th and 17th centuries). *Nyitramegyei Közlöny*, 116/117, 2, pp. 35–42.

Takáts, László: 1966. "A magyarországi utolsó török háború egészségügyi ellátásának megszervezése 1788–1789-ben" (The organization of health care in the last Turkish war in Hungary in 1788–1789). *Hadtörténeti Közlemények*, vol. 13, pp. 40–63.

Takáts, László: 1975–1976. "Hazai forrásadatok a katonakórházak XVII–XVIII. századbeli fejlődéséhez" (Some Hungarian data about the development of military hospitals in the 17th–18th centuries). *Honvédorvos*, vol. 27, no. 4, pp. 383–396; vol. 28, no. 3, pp. 251–264.

Takáts, László: 1980. "Az egészségügy szervezése a Rákóczi-szabadságharc idején" (The organization of health care during Rákóczi's war of independence). In: *Rákóczi-Tanulmányok*, pp. 183–204.

Takáts, Sándor: 1915 (1961). *Török és magyar íródeákok* (Turkish and Hungarian scribes). In: *Művelődéstörténeti tanulmányok a XVI–XVII. századból* Ed. by Kálmán Benda. Budapest.

Tappe, E. D.: 1960. "Dr. Benjamin Woodroffe and the Hungarian malcontents". *The Slavonic and East European Review*, vol. 38, no. 91, pp. 534–538.

Tardy, Lajos: 1977. *Rabok, követek, kalmárok az oszmán birodalomról*. Budapest.

Tárkány-Szűcs, Ernő: 1981. *Magyar jogi népszokások* (Hungarian folk customs relating to law). Budapest.

Tarnai, Andor: 1975. "A toposzkutatás kérdéseihez" (On *topoi* as subjects of research). *Literatura*, vol. II, pp. 66–73.

Thaly, Kálmán (ed.): 1866. "Beniczky Gáspár Naplója (1707–1710)" (Gáspár Beniczky's diary [1707–1710]). In: *Rákóczi Tár*, vol. I.

Thaly, Kálmán: 1885. *Társadalmi, művelődési és művészeti viszonyok hazánkban II. Rákóczi Ferenc fejedelemsége alatt* (Social conditions and the state of the arts and civilization in Hungary during the rule of Prince Ferenc II Rákóczi). Budapest.

Thúry, József: 1896. *Török történetírók*, I–II (Turkish historians, vols I–II). Budapest.

Tinódi Cronica: 1554 (1984). Tinódi Sebestyén, *Krónika* (Kolozsvár, 1554) (Chronicle). Ed. by István Sugár. With an introd. by Ferenc Szakály. Budapest.

Tolnai, F. István: [1663]. *Haza békessége* (The peace of our homeland). Szeben, 1664.

Török, Pál: 1930. *I. Ferdinánd konstantinápolyi béketárgyalásai 1527–1547* (The peace negotiations of Ferdinand I in Constantinople, 1527–1547). Budapest.

Történeti antropológia: 1983. *Történeti antropológia. Az 1983. április 18–19-én tartott tudományos ülésszak előadásai* (Historical anthropology. Papers of the scientific session of the Ethnographic Research Center, Budapest, April 18–19, 1983). Ed. Tamás Hofer. Budapest.

Tóth, István: 1980. "Bethlen Gábor korának késő humanista epikája" (The late humanist epic of the age of G. Bethlen). *Confessio*, no. 2.

Tóth, István: 1982. "Bél Mátyás pécs-baranyai kapcsolatai." In: *Bél Mátyás emlékezete Balatonkeresztúron* (Mátyás Bél's connections in Pécs and the country of Baranya). Ed. by I. Marton. Balatonkeresztúr.

Tóth, István György: 1995. "A kisnemesség olvasni tudása a 18. században." In: *EkvBK*, pp. 212–220.

Trencsényi-Waldapfel, Imre: 1941 (1966). *Erasmus és magyar barátai* (Erasmus and his Hungarian friends). Budapest.

Trevor-Roper, Hugh Redwald: 1967. "The European Witch-craze of the Sixteenth and Seventeenth Centuries". In: *Religion, the Reformation and Social Change*. London.

Trócsányi, Berta: 1944. *Magyar református teológusok Angliában a XVI. és XVII. században* (Hungarian Calvinist students of divinity in England in the 16th and 17th centuries). Debrecen.

Turnbull, G. H.: 1947. *Hartlib, Dury and Comenius*, London.

Tusor, Péter: 1998. "Pázmány Péter kísérlete a római állandó követség megalapítására" (Péter Pázmány's attempt to establish a permanent embassy in Rome). In: *Pázmány Péter és kora* (Péter Pázmány and his world). Ed. by Emil Hargittay. Budapest.

Ungarische Drucke und Hungarica 1480–1720: 1993. Katalog der Herzog August Bibliothek, Wolfenbüttel, I–III. Bearbeitet von S. Katalin Németh. München–New York–London–Párizs.

Vajkai, Aurél: 1948. *A magyar népi orvoslás kutatása* (Research on Hungarian folk medicine). Budapest.

Valentinitsch, Helfried: 1987. "Die Verfolgung von Hexen und Zauberern im Herzogtum Steiermark — eine Zwischenbilanz". In: *Hexen und Zauberern*, pp. 297–316.

Van der Wee, Herman: 1995. "La révolution monétaire des Pays-Bas à l'époque moderne", Lecture at the Eötvös Loránd University, Budapest.

Vanyó, Tihamér: 1971. "Orvostörténeti vonatkozások a vatikáni levéltárból" (Some data on medical history from the Vatican archives). *Orvostörténeti Közlemények*, vols 60–61, pp. 241–248.

Váradi Sternberg, János: 1965. *Az 1707-es orosz–magyar tárgyalások előzményei* (The antecedents of the Russian–Hungarian negotiations of 1707). Szeged.

Varga, Endre (ed.): 1958. *Úriszék, XVI–XVII. századi perszövegek* (Feudal Court. Records of trials from the 16th to 18th centuries). Budapest.

Varga, Imre: 1977. *A kuruc küzdelmek költészete* (Poetry of the Kuruc wars). Budapest.

Varga, János: 1982. *A Hungarian Quo Vadis*. Budapest.

Várkonyi, Gábor: 1988. "Batthyány Ádám feljegyzései III. Ferdinánd római királlyá választásáról és megkoronázásáról" (Notes by Ádám Batthyány on Ferdinand III's election as Holy Roman Emperor and his coronation). In: *Memoria Rerum*, vol. I, pp. 148–174.

Vekerdi, László: 1984. *Válság és természettudomány az újkorelőn. Tudománytörténet – technikatörténet* (Crisis and natural history at the beginning of the Modern Age). Budapest.

Veress, András: 1906–1943. *Carillo Alfonz jezsuita atya levelezése és iratai*, I–II (Correspondence and papers of the Jesuit Father Alfonso Carillo, vols I–II). Budapest.

Veress, Andrei: 1929–1933. *Documente privatoare la istoria Ardealului Moldovei şi Tării Romaneşti (1527–1599)*, vols I–IV. Bucureşti.

Veress, Endre: 1944. *Báthory István erdélyi fejedelem és lengyel király levelezése 1556–1580* (Correspondence of Prince István Báthory of Transylvania and King of Poland 1556–1580), 2nd ed. Kolozsvár.

Vida, Tivadar (ed.): 1988. *"Szerelmes Orsikám..." A Nádasdyak és Szegedi Körös Gáspár levelezése.* Afterword by Tamás Grynaeus. ("My beloved Orsi..." The correspondence of the Nádasdys and Gáspár Szegedi Körös). Budapest.

Vita, Zsigmond: 1962. "Pápai Páriz Ferenc Pax Corporisának különböző kiadásai" (The different editions of Pax Corporis by Ferenc Pápai Páriz). *Communicationes*, vol. 25, pp. 147–161.

Vita, Zsigmond: 1965. "A csömör orvosi és népi gyógyítása a XVII. században" (The medical treatment and the healing of nausea in the 17th century). *Communicationes*, vol. 30, pp. 31–35.

Vocelka, Karl: 1981. *Die politische Propaganda Kaiser Rudolfs II. (1576–1612)*. Wien.

329

Wagner, Georg: 1964. *Das Türkenjahr 1664. Eine europäische Bewährung.* Eisenstadt.

Wandruszka, Adam: 1989. *Das Haus Habsburg. Die Geschichte einer europäischen Dynastie.* Wien.

Warburg, Aby M.: 1920. *Heidnisch-antike Weissagung im Wort und Bild zu Luthers Zeiten.* Heidelberg.

Warburg, Aby M.: 1986. *Pogány-antik jóslás Luther korából* (Pagan soothsaying in the age of Luther), translated by Lajos Adamik, afterword by Sándor Radnóti. Budapest.

Weber, Otto: 1891. *Der Friede von Utrecht. Verhandlungen zwischen England, Frankreich, dem Kaiser und den Generalstaaten 1710–1713,* Gotha.

Wéber, Sámuel: 1893. "A boszorkányságról, különös tekintettel a Szepességre" (About witchcraft with a special emphasis on the Szepes area). *Századok* 27, pp. 879–884.

Weensche gezantschapsberichten van 1670 tot 1720 (Reports of Viennese ambassadors from 1670 to 1720): 1934. Ed. by G. van Antal and J. C. H. De Pater, Part II: 1698–1720. 's Gravenhage.

Wellmann, Imre: 1979. "Bél Mátyás (1684–1749)" (Mátyás Bél [1684–1749]). *Történelmi Szemle,* 22, pp. 381–391.

Weszprémi, István: 1781 (1960–1970). *Magyarország és Erdély orvosainak rövid életrajza, I–IV* (Short biographies of Hungarian and Transylvanian doctors, vols I–IV). Budapest.

Wood, Alfred C.: 1925. "The English Embassy at Constantinople 1660–1672". *English Historical Review,* vol. 40, pp. 533–561.

Zalai, Károly – Bánóné Fleischman, Mariann: 1973. "Die Rolle des Staates bei der Entwicklung der Pharmazie in Ungarn". *Orvostörténeti Közlemények,* vols 66–68, pp. 27–37.

Zay, Anna: 1718 (1970). *Herbarium.* With an intr. by Árpád Fazekas. Nyíregyháza.

Zimányi, Vera: 1983. *Lepantó 1571.* Budapest, Móra Ferenc Kiadó.

Zombori, István: 1980. "V. Károly és a magyar trónviszályok (1529–1533)" (Charles V and the struggles of pretenders for the Hungarian throne [1529–1533]). *Történelmi Szemle,* vol. 23, pp. 615–626.

Zoványi, Jenő: 1891. "A sárospataki borbély-céh rendszabályai (Alkottattak 1583-ban, átnézettek 1607-ben)" (The regulations of the barbers' guild of Sárospatak from 1583–1607). *Történelmi Tár,* vol. I, pp. 148–155.

Zrínyi dolgozatok (Papers on Zrínyi): 1983–1989, vols I–VI. Ed. Sándor Iván Kovács. Budapest.

Zrínyi könyvtár (Zrínyi Library): 1985–1991, vols I–IV. Ed.-in-chief: Tibor Klaniczay. Ed. Sándor Iván Kovács. Budapest.

Zrínyi Miklós emlékezete (Remembering Miklós Zrínyi): 1961. Ed. by András Laczkó.

Zrínyi Miklós összes művei (The collected works of Miklós Zrínyi): 1958. Ed. by Tibor Klaniczay, vols I–II. Budapest.

Zrínyi, Miklós: 1651 (1980). *Adriai tengernek Syrenaia* Anno MDCLI Bécs (The Siren of the Adriatic) (Facsimile edition). Afterword by Sándor Iván Kovács. Budapest.

Zsilinszky, Mihály: 1890. *A linczi békekötés és az 1647-i vallásügyi törvények története* (The Treaty of Linz and the history of the religious laws of 1647). Budapest.

Zsilinszky, Mihály: 1898. *Egy forradalmi zsinat története 1707–1715* (The history of a revolutionary synod, 1707–1715). Budapest.

Zsilinszky, Mihály: 1899. *Kermann Dávid evangélikus püspök élete és művei 1663–1740* (The life and works of Dániel Kermann, Lutheran Bishop, 1663–1740). Budapest.

Index of Names

Abafti see Apafi, Mihály
Abbas, Shah 64
Abdurrahman (Abdu-Ráhman) Pasha 151
Acquaviva, P. C. 64
Acsády, Ignác 19, 30, 32, 149, 207, 233, 236, 305
Adamik, Lajos 310, 329
Ahmed Pasha 38
Alexander the Great 308
Alexander VII, King of Poland 113
Ali Pasha 38
Allen, H. M. 310
Allen, P. S. 310
Allendy, René 243, 305
Almási, Benjamin 310
Alsted, Johann Henrik 138
Althaus, F. E. 118, 305
Alvinczi, Péter 68, 253, 262, 305
Alvinczy, see Alvinczi
Ancillon, David 212, 213
András, Mrs. Szabó 249
Angyal, Dávid 94, 108, 110, 210, 216, 305
Ankarloo, Bength 317
Anne, Queen of England 172, 183, 191, 211, 216, 219–221, 321
Antal, G. van 330
Antonio, Juan Sanchez García-Sauco 290
Apáczai Csere, János 91, 257, 300, 305
Apafi, Mihály, Prince of Transylvania 51, 58, 76, 94, 111, 112, 134, 136, 146, 154, 161, 257, 261, 277, 303
Apponyi, Sándor 103, 142, 303, 305
Arany, János 106, 305
Archinto, Count 128
Aretin, Karl Ottomar 212, 306
Artamonov, Vladimir Nikolaevich 190, 193, 222, 306

Atanagi, Dionigi 46
Athila, see Attila
Attila 32, 321
Aubin, Jean 306
Auerbach, B. 109, 306
August, Herzog 313
Augustine, St. 280
Augustus, Christian 222
Augustus II, King of Poland 196, 204
Augustus II, King of Saxony 196
Avancini, Nicolaus 325

Bacon, Sir Francis 207, 253
Bahtyin, Michail 159, 240, 241, 306
Bak, János 311
Bakfark, Bálint 46
Bakos, István 234
Balásfi, Tamás 313
Balázs, Éva, see H. Balázs Éva
Ballagi, Aladár 188, 306
Baló, Mátyás 154
Balogh, Jolán 61, 306
Baluze, Jean Casimir 217
Bán, Imre 139, 141, 306
Bánóné Fleischman, Mariann 330
Baranyai, Pál 215
Barcza, József 90, 306
Bárdos, Kornél 162, 306
Bárdossy, László 12, 13, 16, 19, 20, 23–26, 28, 30, 33, 34, 306
Bariska, István 71, 304, 306, 309
Barlay, Ödön Szabolcs 61, 306, 310
Barta, Gábor 12, 14, 15, 18–22, 30, 36, 38, 306, 324
Barth, Christian 253
Bartha, Mrs. András, née Erzsébet Batári 242

331

Bartók, Béla 296
Basire, Isaac 178
Báthori, András 62
Báthori, Anna 247, 255, 256, 317
Báthori, Gábor, Prince of Transylvania
  247, 255
Báthori, István, Prince of Transylvania,
  King of Poland 17, 46, 59–65, 329
Báthori, Kristóf 258
Báthori, Princess Zsófia 128
Báthory, see Báthori
Batthyány, Ádám 151, 232, 236, 237, 245,
  329
Batthyány, Ferenc 17, 89, 232
Bayer, János 138
Bayle, Pierre 52, 53
Becher, Joachim 167
Beethoven, Ludwig van 296
Bekes, Stephanus 152
Békési, Erzsébet 237
Bél, Mátyás 52, 163, 273–283, 306, 309, 313,
  328, 330
Béldi, Pál 236, 261
Bencsik, Anna 246, 254
Bencze, József 306
Benczédi, László 321
Benda, Kálmán 58, 69, 74, 89, 95, 187, 190,
  191, 198, 199, 210, 214, 220, 304, 306,
  307, 323, 324, 328
Bene, Sándor 105, 112, 113, 117–119, 122,
  128, 131, 137, 138, 140, 147, 307
Beniczky, Gáspár 328
Benna, A. H. 118, 307
Bennet, Henry 129
Bercsényi, Miklós 169, 196–198, 202–204,
  209, 214, 215, 217, 221, 223, 305
Berendorf, see Körtvélyessy, János
Bérenger, Jean 106, 307
Berindei, Mihnea 24, 307
Bessenyei, József 34, 307
Bethlen, Gábor, Prince of Transylvania 50,
  51, 56, 57, 70, 72, 73, 75–77, 79–82, 86,
  89–101, 124, 138, 145, 177, 192, 247, 254,
  256, 261, 306, 307, 309, 312, 314, 321,
  323, 327, 328
Bethlen, István 85
Bethlen, János 7, 76, 166, 213
Bethlen, Kata 232, 238, 271, 319

Bethlen, Miklós 139, 179, 304, 307, 324
Bethlen, Péter 82
Bibó, István 77, 92, 207, 307
Binder, Pál 231, 236, 318
Bíró, Margit 242
Bíró, Péter 307
Bíró, Vencel 56, 57, 76, 113, 130, 307
Bisterfeld, Henrik 138
Bitskey, István 58, 61, 66, 72, 76, 178, 232,
  307, 308
Bittner, Ludwig 191, 308
Blandrata, Giorgio 46
Bleyer, Jakab 118, 308
Bocskai, Erzsébet 97, 258
Bodin, Jean 169
Bodó, Éva Mária 107, 308
Boerhave, Hermann 269, 319, 326
Bogdány, Jakab 191, 321
Bogdany, James, see Bogdány, Jakab
Bogyay, Tamás 89, 323
Bojti, Gáspár Veres 90
Bóka, Éva 67, 308
Bolingbroke, Viscount 184, 220, 221
Bolton, Samuel 105, 135
Bóna, István 324
Bonfini, Antonio 40
Bonnac, Jean-Louis d'Usson, marquis de
  200, 201
Borbély, Demeter 245
Borbély, István 238
Borbély, István, Váradi 246
Borbély, Mátyás 234
Borián, Elréd 147, 308
Bornemisza, Anna 258, 261
Bornemisza, Péter 155, 252, 308
Borosy, András 260, 308
Borsi, Ilona 237
Bory, Mihály 128
Borzsák, István 119, 308
Boskovits, Miklós 160, 308
Botticelli, Sandro 159, 308
Botzi, Klára 229, 241
Boyle, Henry, Baron Carleton 139, 184,
  211, 216, 220, 221
Boyle, Robert 136, 137
Bransetur, Robert 306
Braubach, Max 206, 207, 215, 308
Braudel, Fernand 66, 308

Brechka, Frank T. 268, 308
Brenner, Dominik, see Brenner, Domokos
Brenner, Domokos 184, 191, 196, 198, 208–210, 214, 223, 225
Brodarics, István 13–15, 17, 30, 32, 308
Bucholtz, F. 35, 308
Bucholtz, György 275
Budaházi, Ferenc 260
Bukovszky, Andrea 104, 107, 125, 309
Busbequius (Busbek), Augerius Gislenius 133
Busek, Erhard 288, 309
Byron, Lord George Gordon 296

C(hristian) H(oburg) L(üneburger) P(redigern) J(esu) G(lotte) 134
Calixtus III, Pope 293
Calvin, John 60
Cantacusen (Cantacuzino), Constantin 96
Capistrano, Giovanni da 293
Caraffa, P. A. 128
Cardonnel, Adam de 191
Carillo, Alfonso 62, 63, 64, 329
Carolus, Prince, see Lorraine, Charles
Carte, T. 325
Carter, Charles Howard 66, 118, 309
Casimir, Prince 19
Castaldo, Johann 37
Castriot, George (Scanderbeg) 104, 127, 131, 135, 143
Catherine of Brandenburg 89
Cennerné, Wilhelmb, Gizella 119, 309
Cernovodeanu, Paul 217, 309
Charles, Archduke 172
Charles I, King of England 177
Charles II, King of England 94
Charles III, Emperor, King of Hungary and Bohemia 100, 172, 210
Charles V, Emperor, King of Hungary and Bohemia 9–42, 44, 143, 177, 294, 309, 313, 316–319, 330
Charles XII, King of Sweden 98, 181, 188, 190, 193, 194, 196, 199, 201–203, 306, 315, 320
Charlotte Amelia, Princess of Hessen-Rheinfels 196
Charrière, E. 20, 21, 23, 309
Chastel, André 159, 309

Chiaromanni, Giovanni 122, 123, 128, 129, 140
Churchill, Winston S. 191, 194, 197, 198, 309
Cicero, Marcus Tullius 276
Clarke, Samuel 142
Clement VII, Pope 16, 19, 26
Clement VIII, Pope 62
Clement XI, Pope 208, 217, 306
Clucas, Stephen 138, 309
Codrington, Robert 132, 135, 145, 146
Colbert, Jean-Baptiste, marquis de Torcy 194, 208
Comenius, Johannes Amos 52, 53, 109, 117, 133, 135–143, 146, 148, 275, 276, 297, 298, 306, 309, 314, 320–323, 327, 329
Commager, Henry Steele 309
Cortesius, Alexander 327
Corvinus, Matthias, see Mátyás, King
Cromwell, Oliver 138, 206, 207
Csáky, István 11, 15, 21, 153, 235
Csáky, Mrs. István, née Anna Wesselényi 309
Csáky, László 161
Csáky, Moritz 309
Csapodi, Zoltán 117, 309
Csécsy, János 317
Cseh, Lajos 193, 309
Csepi, András 235, 237
Csepi, Demeter 237
Cserei, Mihály 163
Csernatoni, Márton 158
Csetri, Elek 309
Csonka, Mrs. Lukács 241
Csorba, Győző 158
Csordás, Mrs. 240
Cupid 158
Czobor, Mihály 163

Dallos, Miklós 71
Danhauser, Josef 296
Dániel, István 96
Dániel, Péter 203, 204
Dávid, Ferenc 46
Dávid, Zoltán 266, 309
Deák, András 283, 309
Deák, Farkas 309

Deák, Ferenc 295
Defoe, Daniel 181, 192, 309, 318
Delouche, Frédéric 290, 300
Demény, Lajos 64, 65, 309
Demjén, János 243
Demkó, Kálmán 230, 231, 234, 238, 264, 310
Dercsényi, Dezső 319
Dersffy, Potencia 233
Des Alleurs, Marquis 190, 194, 197, 198, 200, 201, 203, 204, 208, 213
Descartes, René 257, 300
Dezsényi, Béla 276, 310
Dickmann, Fritz 176, 310
Dienst, Heide 265, 310
Djuvara, T. G. 67, 82, 310
Dobó, István 38
Dobozi, István, jr. 205, 199, 205, 212, 213
Dóczy, János 18
Dolezal, Pavel 280
Dolgorukij, Jakov Fjodorovich 196
Dömötör, Tekla 228, 310
Drabicius, Nicholas 132, 133, 136, 137, 140, 141, 146
Draskóczy, István 324
Draskovich, see Draskovics
Draskovics, János 40, 245
Dubček, Alexander 301
Dukkon, Ágnes 137, 310
Duroselle, Jean-Baptiste 289, 292, 294–301, 310
Dury (Dureus), John 138, 329

Eckhardt, Sándor 310
Eckhart, Ferenc 260, 269, 310
Eickhoff, Ekkehard 106, 108, 310
Eisenstein, E. Elisabeth 116, 310
Eleonora Magdolna, Regent 224
Ember, Győző 324
Emmanuel Maximilian 152, 162
Enyedi, Sámuel 257
Eötvös, József 295
Eperjessy, Kálmán 321
Erasmus, Desiderius 11, 12, 21, 25, 28, 29, 39, 41, 43–45, 253, 296, 298, 310, 328
Erdmann, Dietrich Karl 290
Erdődy, Anna 239
Erdődy, Gábor 310

Erdődy, György 230, 234, 243, 281
Erdődy, György jr. 230
Erdődy, Kristóf 234
Erdős, Ildikó 269, 310
Esterházy, Ferenc 240
Esterházy, Miklós 64, 70, 74, 78–80, 83, 85–87, 91, 93, 235, 313, 314, 319, 322, 326
Esterházy, Pál 58, 161, 168, 267, 281, 310, 315
Esze, Tamás 191, 214, 222, 310, 311, 324
Eugene of Savoy (Eugen von Savoyen), see Savoy
Evans, Catherine 107
Evans, Robert John Weston 71, 79, 106, 311

Fabiny, Tibor 191, 311
Fabó, Bertalan 253, 311
Fabriczka, Marijana 260
Farnese, Alessandro 34, 322
Fazekas, Árpád 330
Fèbvre, Lucien 311
Fekete, József 230, 311
Fekete, Sándor 269, 311
Felvinczi, György 233
Ferdinand, Archduke 78
Ferdinand I, Emperor, King of Hungary and Bohemia 11, 12, 14–19, 21–23, 26–32, 34–39, 42, 43, 45, 177, 234, 295, 308, 317, 319, 328
Ferdinand II, Emperor, King of Hungary and Bohemia 69–72, 79, 83, 98, 100, 306
Ferdinand III, Emperor, King of Hungary and Bohemia 329
Ficino, Marsilio 159
Fiedler, Josef 98, 120, 184, 194, 198–203, 210, 212, 213, 217, 219, 311
Fischer, Éva 140, 311
Fischer, Mihály 152
Fodor, Pál 24, 311
Fodor, Veronika 139, 311
Forgách family 230, 303, 326
Forgách, Ádám 121
Forgách, Ferenc 69
Forst, Robert 109, 311
Forstall, Mark 65, 127, 139, 147, 311
Förster, Jenő 267, 311
Fraknói, Vilmos 56, 57, 73, 78, 79, 81, 83, 311

Francis I, King of France 16, 23
Francke, August Hermann 191
Frangepán, Ferenc 7, 19, 30, 34, 35, 128, 129, 325
Frankl, Vilmos, see Fraknói, Vilmos
Frankovith, Gergely 232, 235, 241, 244, 252, 311
Fray, József 203, 204
Frederick I, King of Prussia 191
Frederick V, King of Bohemia 145
Frey, Linda 179, 180, 311
Frey, Marsha 179, 180, 311
Függedi, Erik 307
Fugger, Jacob 17, 19, 20, 314
Fülep, Lajos 319
Fülöp, Lajos 140, 311
Für, Lajos 304
Futaky, István 178, 311

G. Etényi, Nóra 107, 117, 118, 120, 124, 130, 312
Gajzágó, László 206, 207, 312
Gál, István 110, 193, 312
Galavics, Géza 66, 161, 312
Gallas, Johann von, Graf 183, 224
Gángó, Gábor 312
Garas, Klára 156, 312
Garrod, H. W. 310
Gascoigne, Sir Alvary Douglas Frederick 313
Gélis, Jacques 248, 312
Geréb, László 156
Géresi, Kálmán 304
Gergely, Samu 161, 312
Gévay, Anton 15, 19, 20, 24, 28, 30, 312
Géza 291
Giovio, Paolo 315
Glassl, H. 89, 323
Glatz, Ferenc 304, 328
Goes, Johann 111
Göllner, Carl 312
Golovkin, Gavril Ivanovich 195, 196, 203
Gombrich, Ernst H. 159, 160, 286, 312
Gömöri, György 65, 104, 105, 107, 119, 125, 134, 140–142, 145, 178, 179, 312
Gonda, Imre 14, 312
Gondi, Bali 123, 129
Gooss, R. 33, 312

Gorbachev, Michail 301
Gortvay, György 231, 266, 312
Grabner, Elfriede 233, 238, 240, 313
Grass, Günter 288, 313
Gravel, Robert 128
Gregory XIII, Pope 62
Grisza, Ágost 324
Gritti, Lajos 22, 24, 28–30, 318
Gross, Lothar 191, 308
Grotius, Hugo 71, 77, 89, 91, 92, 95, 147, 169, 184, 205–207, 220, 223, 313
Grynaeus, Tamás 228, 231, 238, 313
Guevara, Antonio 40
Gundmann, A. 24, 313
Gunst, Péter 12, 313
Gustavus Adolphus, King of Sweden 82
Gyarmati, Kata 241
Gyöngyösi, István 138, 156, 160, 313, 316
Györffy, György 291
Győri, Tibor 313

H. Balázs, Éva 268, 304, 307, 313
Haan, Lajos 275, 313
Habsburg, Otto von 290
Hagymássy, Kristóf 46
Hajnal, István 57, 67, 313
Haley, K. H. 109, 313
Haller, Peter 46
Hamel-Bruyninx, Jacob Jan 192, 194, 199, 200, 212, 216, 221
Hantsch, H. 29, 313
Hanuy, Ferenc 304
Haraszti, György 309
Haraszti-Taylor, Éva 176, 313
Hargittay, Emil 58, 77, 313, 329
Harley, Robert 172, 175, 182
Harms, W. von 129, 313
Harrach, Leonhard von 19, 21
Hartlib, Samuel 110, 118, 135–140, 305, 309, 329
Hausner, Gábor 310, 313, 320
Havel, Václav 301
Haydn, Joseph 296
Heckenast, Gusztáv 120, 313, 324
Heinsius, Anthonie 197, 210, 216, 217
Heister, Siegbert Count 218
Héjja, Pál 231, 236, 250, 266, 313
Héjjas, Eszter 107, 313

Hengelmüller, Ladislaus Baron 180, 285, 313
Henningsen, Gustav 228, 247, 314, 317
Hercules 162
Herczegh, Géza 90, 314
Herepei, János 139, 314
Hermann, Michael 46
Hermann, Zsuzsa 14, 17, 20, 314
Herner, János 233, 235, 246, 262, 314
Herodotus 285
Hiller, István 58, 74, 78, 111, 120, 123, 314
Hints, Elek 231–233, 248, 314
Hitler, Adolf 298
Hocher, Johann Paul 167
Hodgkinson, Richard 126
Hódi, Sándor 247, 314
Hofer, Tamás 328
Hohenlohe, Wolff Julius Graf zu 114, 115, 127, 128, 130, 131, 139
Hollar, Václav 138, 142
Holorenschaw, H. 110, 314
Hóman, Bálint 314
Honterus, Johannes 46, 47
Hoogh, Romeyn de 325
Hopp, Lajos 20, 35, 199, 306, 310, 314, 324
Hoppál, Mihály 314, 316
Horn, Ildikó 58, 304, 314, 320, 325
Hornyik, János 151, 314
Horsley, R. A. 314
Horváth, Ferenc 96, 187, 217
Horváth, Mihály 21, 26, 81, 308, 314
Hubay, Ilona 108, 314
Hunyadi, János 157, 292
Hunyadi, Mátyás, see Mátyás, King
Huttmann, Arnold 250, 326
Huxelles, Marshal 210

Ibrahim, Grand Vizier 22, 29
Ifjju, Kata 247
Iklódy, András 262–264, 314
Ilgen, Heinrich Rüdiger 191, 212, 213
Illésházy, István 281
Imregh, Monika 106, 315
Imreh, István 315
Inalcik, Halil 108, 315
Incze, Mrs. János 245
Ipolyi, Arnold 228, 241, 315
Isabella, Queen of Hungary 37, 39, 44, 59

István the Saint, King of Hungary 14, 71, 78, 156, 158, 279, 291, 295
Istvánffy, Éva 40
Istvánffy, Miklós 27, 40, 315
Iványi, Emma 150, 310, 315

Jablonsky, Daniel Ernst (Chaplain to the King of Prussia) 212
Jablonszky (Figulus), Daniel Ernst 139 (Comenius' son-in-law)
Jaklin, Balázs 163
Jakó, Zsigmond 90, 315, 323
Jankovics, József 185, 191, 315, 324
Jánoky, Zsigmond 275
János I, King of Hungary 12, 14–16, 18–20, 22, 23, 26–33, 43, 44, 59, 177, 314, 326
János II, see János Zsigmond
János Zsigmond, King of Hungary, Prince of Transylvania 12, 33, 36–38, 44, 45
Janus Pannonius 156, 158, 317
Jászay, Magda 105, 117, 121, 315
Jászay, Pál 15, 16, 18, 80, 315
Jászberényi, Pál 138
Jeucourt 113, 125, 128, 130
Jilek, W. 229, 315
Jó, Pál 235
John George II, Elector 126
Jonah 134
Jonasson, Gustaf 188, 315
Jones, Mervyn D. 103, 315
Joseph I, Emperor, King of Hungary and Bohemia 24, 169, 172, 175, 184, 187, 193, 202, 209, 212–214, 219–222, 306
Jovius, Paulus 29, 315
Juan, Don, de Austria 40
Juhász, István 90, 315
Juhász, László 321
Jupiter 158, 162
Jurisics, Miklós 27

Kakas, István 64
Káldy-Nagy, Gyula 14, 315
Kállay, István 89, 187, 224, 261, 263, 315
Kalmár, János 304
Kamuthy, Farkas 92
Kanizsay, Orsolya 231
Kapronczay, Károly 269, 316
Kapros, Márta 230, 316

Kara, György 65, 316
Kara Mustafa 23, 167
Karkóczi, Mátyás, Mrs. 246
Károlyi, Árpád 24, 25, 31, 35, 36, 97, 149, 152, 218, 224, 235, 304, 316, 319
Károlyi, Mihály 235
Károlyi, Sándor 99, 185, 187, 221–223, 326
Károlyi, Zsuzsanna 256
Kárpáti, E. 12, 29, 316
Kathona, Géza 139, 147, 316
Katzianer, Hans 32
Kecskeméti, Alexis János 253, 260, 316
Keczer, János 153
Kékesi, Imre 324
Keljó, Pál 234
Kellenbenz, Hermann 11, 20, 29, 316
Kemény, János 56, 58, 75, 81, 82, 111, 304, 309
Kempler, Kurt 232, 240, 316
Kenéz, Győző 34
Kermann, Dániel, see Krmann, Daniel
Kéry, János 105, 127, 316
Keserű, Bálint 316
Keserűi Dajka, János 50
Kibédi Varga, Áron 160, 316
Kinizsi, Pál 157
Kinsky, Ferdinand Count 170
Király, Béla 311
Király, Erzsébet 119, 316
Kis, Mrs. Péter 246
Kisielewski, Stefan 288
Kiss, Imre 128
Kistapolcsányi, Benedek 261
Kithonich, János 261
Klaniczay, Gábor 227, 228, 247, 260, 263–265, 268, 316, 317
Klaniczay, Tibor 11, 25, 103, 105, 111, 119, 139, 141, 317, 319, 330
Klement, János Mihály 198–200, 208, 210, 212, 213, 217, 219, 221, 223, 225, 326
Kluch, J. 320
Kodály, Zoltán 163
Kohler, Alfred 11, 12, 24, 25, 38, 317, 319
Kökényesdi, László 190, 194, 198, 200, 209, 210, 213
Kölesséry, Sámuel 238
Kollonits, Lipót 262
Komáromy, Andor (András) 227–229, 234,

236, 237, 241, 242, 244, 245, 249, 260, 261, 263, 269, 317
Komáromy Csipkés, György 222
Komensky, Jan Amos, see Comenius
Kőműves, Mrs. 235
Könczöl, Csaba 306
Köpeczi, Béla 95, 99, 103, 116, 118, 154, 162, 187, 188, 190, 193, 194, 201, 202, 209, 217, 225, 306, 317, 322, 324
Köprülü, Grand Vizier Ahmed 112, 113, 124, 132
Köprülü, Grand Vizier Mohammed 113
Köprülü, Numan 217
Korlátkövi, Osváth 261
Kornis, Gyula 67, 317
Körpüly, Károly 192
Körtvélyessy, János 199, 210, 212, 217
Kósa, László 324
Kosáry, Domokos 12, 16, 17, 21, 22, 103, 113, 228, 231, 276, 317
Kossa, Mrs. Máté 246
Kossuth, Lajos 295, 296
Kosztolányi, Dezső 67, 300, 317
Kotter (Kotterus), Christopher 132, 133, 137, 146
Kovách, Géza 231, 236, 243, 318
Kovachich, Márton György 15, 318
Kovács, Béla 76, 308
Kovács, György 158
Kovács, Ilona 306
Kovács, József László 107, 318
Kovács, Kálmán 193, 314, 318
Kovács, Sándor Iván 106, 318, 330
Kropf, Lajos 193, 318
Kraemer, Heinrich 261
Kraus, Georg 114, 126, 129, 318
Kretschmayr, Heinrich 22, 30, 318
Kreutzer, Andrea 325
Kreuzinger, V. 268, 318
Kristóf, Ildikó 228, 230, 246, 261, 318
Krmann, Daniel 190, 327, 330
Kubinyi, András 12, 318
Kulcsár, Árpád 58, 65
Kulcsár, Péter 84, 314
Kulcsár, Zsuzsanna 318
Küllős, Imola 310
Kvacsala, János 110, 134–137, 139, 191, 318
Kyr, Paulus 250

Laczkó, András 330
Ladivér, Illés 138
Lajos II, King of Hungary and Bohemia 12–14, 16, 18, 33, 38, 43, 177, 288, 294
Lamberg, Franz Count 194
Lancmár, Ferenc 325
Lánczy, Gyula 207, 318
Lányi, Pál 275
Lanz, Karl 26, 28, 318
Lapin, James 107
Laskai, János 315
Laski, Hieronym 19, 22, 23, 34, 316
Laski, Jan 19
László, Emőke 160, 318
László of Macedon 25
László the Saint, King of Hungary 60, 157
Lauter, Éva, see S. Lauter, Éva
Le Geer 138
Le Goff, Jacques 293, 318
Le Moyne, Pierre 326
Le Noble, Eustache 209
Lehoczky, Tivadar 238, 318
Leibniz, Gottfried Wilhelm 206
Leleszi, János 62
Lemaire (Le Maire), Louis 210, 214
Leman, August 83, 318
Lénárt, Ilona, Pörpeni 232
Lencsés, György 258
Lengyel, Zsolt 89, 323
Leonardo da Vinci 296
Leopold I, Emperor, King of Hungary and Bohemia 11, 24, 100, 106, 109–115, 121, 123, 124, 127, 128, 130, 131, 143, 161, 162, 165–167 170, 173, 179, 212, 214, 274, 311, 319
Lesky, Erna 307
Lessenyei Nagy, Ferenc 151
Leszczynski, Stanislaus 196
Levinson, Artúr 124, 130, 319
Lhotsky, Alois 18–21, 319
Lindeboom, Arie Gerrit 232, 319
Linzbauer, Xavér Ferenc 227, 228, 234, 269, 271, 319
Lippay, György 58, 87, 113, 122, 123, 166
Lipsius, Justus 76, 92, 315
Lisola, Franz Paul 124, 128
Listius, Anna 236
Liszt, Ferenc 296

Lobkowitz, Wenzel, Prince 111, 121
Locher, Karl, Graf von Lindenheim 218, 224
Locke, John 53
Lorántffy, Zsuzsanna 51, 233, 235
Lorraine, Charles, Duke of 153, 321
Louis XIII, King of France 82
Louis XIV, King of France 94, 109, 125, 128, 130, 171, 172, 194, 200, 201, 203, 204, 208, 210, 217, 221, 308
Lukács, K. 278, 319
Lukács, László, S. J. 58, 63, 64, 304, 319
Lukács, Zs. Tibor 117, 319
Lukinich, Imre 98, 187, 218, 319
Luther, Martin 296, 297, 329
Luttenberger, A. 24, 319
Lutz, H. 38, 319

Mab, Thomas 126
Machiavelli, Niccolò 169, 296
Maggio, P. L. 64
Magurn, Ruth 159, 319
Magyari, András 271, 319
Magyary-Kossa, Gyula 234, 235, 243, 246, 266–268, 271, 319
Mair, Lucy 264, 319
Majláth, Béla 190, 319
Makkai, László 17, 74, 106, 138, 143, 146, 251, 257, 320, 324
Maksay, Ferenc 307, 324
Mályusz, Elemér 307
Mandrou, Robert 260, 320
Manga, János 320
Mányoki, Ádám 198, 314
Marczali, Henrik 206, 210, 211, 216, 217, 302, 320
Margaret, Archduchess 18, 19
Maria Theresa Empress, Queen of Hungary 227, 256, 257, 260, 261, 268
Márki, Sándor 99, 190, 193, 194, 197, 320
Markó, Árpád 196 320
Marlborough, John Churchill, Duke of 194, 197, 199, 200, 210, 212, 213, 215, 216, 309, 320
Mars 158, 159, 286
Martinuzzi, György (Friar György) 31, 33, 36–38, 45, 47, 304
Marton, I. 328

Márton, Mrs. Szepesi 227
Mary, Queen of England 14, 17, 20, 32, 38
Matar, Nabil I. 110, 136, 320
Matthias, King, see Mátyás, King
Mátyás, King of Hungary 10, 24, 146, 149, 152, 154, 156, 261, 291, 311
Mayer, Theodor 262, 320
Mazowiecki, Tadeusz 301
Meadows, Philip 209
Mednyánszky, Aloysius 83, 320
Mednyánszky, Jónás 138
Megalinus, Joannes 138
Mehmed Bey 25
Meijerfeldt, Augustus John 188, 190, 195, 222
Meillet, Antoine 300, 317
Méliusz (Melius), Péter 232, 251, 253, 320, 326
Melvill, Andrew 139
Mencsik, F. 190, 320
Mentchikov, Alexandr Danilovich 196
Mercury 158
Mészáros, István 275, 320
Michael, Voivode 309
Michelangelo, Buonarroti 46
Mihalik, J. 243
Mike, Sándor 55
Mikes, Kelemen 9
Miklós, Ödön 93, 321
Milton, John 138, 304
Mizauld, Antoine 258
Molin, Alvise 120, 121
Moller, Károly 275
Molnár, Gyula 321
Molnár, Mátyás 311
Molnár, Sándor 113
Moneta, Francesco 315
Monok, István 313
Montecuccoli, Raimund 106, 111, 120, 121, 124, 130, 155
Montesquieu, Charles-Louis de Secondat 288
Moro, István 128
Morone, Giovanni 31
Muchembled, Robert 321
Müller, László 312
Müllern, Heinrich Gustav von 202
Mustafa Pasha 14

Nadányi, János 91, 139, 257, 258, 321
Nádasdy family 111, 313
Nádasdy, Ferenc 122, 123, 155, 157, 161, 323
Nádasdy, Tamás 17, 157, 161, 231, 233
Nagy, Géza 92, 321, 322
Nagy, Imre 301
Nagy, János, Gyöngyössi 156
Nagy, László 64, 84, 149, 247, 256, 321
Nedeczky, Gábor 190, 211, 321
Nedeczky, Sándor 190, 195, 196, 202–204, 210, 211, 215
Negri, Antonio 128, 140
Nehring, Karl 66, 111, 321
Német, Erzsébet (Örzse) 244, 245
Németh, S. Katalin 107, 134, 135, 321, 329
Niederhauser, Emil 14, 312
Nógrádi, Mátyás 257
Notter, Antal 312

Okolicsányi, Mihály 214
Oláh, Andor 229, 230, 232, 238, 240, 271, 321
Oláh, Miklós 17, 25, 32, 38, 158, 287, 321
Oppenheimer, Samuel 168
Orlovszky, Géza 313
Orosz, István 304
Orosz, Pál 263
Országh, László 191, 321
Ortelius, Abraham 177
Ortutay, Gyula 310
Őry, Miklós, S. J. 57, 59, 61–66, 71, 304, 321
Ottlik, Géza 288, 321
Ottlyk, György 214
Óváry, Lipót 20, 26, 31, 34, 35, 321, 322
Ovid, Ovidius, Publius Naso 253

Pach, Zsigmond Pál 205, 319, 322
Pachner, Eggenstroff v. 130, 322
Paganini, Niccolo 296
Paget, William Lord 165, 170, 179, 191, 312
Pálffy Archivum 156, 260
Pálffy, István 85, 86, 156, 234, 235, 259
Pálffy, János 99, 173, 185, 187, 218, 222–224, 281, 282
Pálffy, Pál 65, 325
Pallas 158
Palmes, Francis 184, 220, 221

Pánek, Jaroslav 137, 138, 298, 322
Panofsky, Erwin 159, 322
Pápai, János 95, 96, 187, 202, 205, 217
Pápai, Mrs. János 246
Pápai Páriz, Ferenc 257–259, 267, 271, 322, 329
Pápai Páriz, Ferenc, jr. 315
Pápay, Gáspár 195
Papp, Mrs. Gábor 315
Papp, László 324
Parker, Geoffrey 205, 322
Pater, J. C. H. de 330
Patera, A. 140, 322
Paul III, Pope 31, 32, 321
Pázmány, Miklós 158
Pázmány, Péter 51, 55–87, 91, 232, 252, 304, 307, 311–313, 317–323, 325–327, 329
Pécsi, Lukács 252
Pell, John 137, 140
Pepys, Samuel 119, 322
Perényi, J. 190, 196, 322
Perényi, Péter 18, 31
Perjés, Géza 12, 13, 21, 22, 24, 28, 36, 95, 105, 106, 111, 112, 114, 322
Perliczy, János Dániel 267, 268
Perseus 162
Peter the Great, Czar 187, 190, 191, 193, 195, 196, 198–200, 202–204, 212, 214, 216, 217, 219, 221–223, 320, 322
Péter, Katalin 80, 86, 104, 120, 124, 125, 132, 138, 140, 146, 322
Péter, László 107
Peterborough, Charles Mordaunt, 3rd Earl of 184, 221, 223, 224
Petkó, Zsigmond 158
Petneházy 152, 153
Philip II, King of Spain 295
Philipp, Johann 124, 127, 131
Pirka, Kata 246
Pisa, Alfonso 62
Piscator, Ludovicus 138
Pius II, Pope 294
Plato 21
Pócs, Éva 239, 322, 323
Pók, Attila 324
Polgár, László, S. J. 56, 58, 323
Polišenský, Josef V. 67, 78, 143, 323

Polignac, Melchior de 210
Pollardt, P. M. 64
Pölöskei, Ferenc 304
Poniatovska (Poniatovia), Christiana 132, 137, 146
Poór, János 316
Poppel, Éva 232, 236, 237, 245
Porcia, Johannes Ferdinand, Duke 111, 121, 123, 127
Possevino, Antonio 61
Potocki, József, Palatine of Kiev 202
Prágai, András 41
Pribram, Alfred Francis 123, 323
Pucheim, Hans Christoph 114, 115, 131
Pufendorf, Samuel 169
Pulay, János 224

Questenberg, Gerard 79

R. Kiss, István 190, 242, 323
R. Várkonyi, Ágnes 23, 58, 66, 73, 77, 82, 84, 91, 95, 97, 98, 105, 106, 109, 112, 127, 128, 142, 149, 155, 176–180, 184, 228, 230, 236, 238, 246, 293, 304, 306, 317, 320, 321, 323, 324
Raab, Theodore K. 109, 176, 324
Rabe, H. 12, 19, 324
Rabelais, François 240, 306
Raby, Wentworth Thomas, 3rd Earl of Srafford 221
Ráday, Pál 94–98, 181, 188, 190, 191, 195, 197–199, 202–205, 207, 208, 212, 213, 223–225, 263, 275, 276, 306, 324
Radnóti, Sándor 329
Ragotski, see Rákóczi, Ferenc
Rákóczi, Erzsébet 234
Rákóczi, Ferenc I, Prince Elect of Transylvania 58, 305
Rákóczi, Ferenc II, Prince of Transylvania 51, 71, 77, 85, 86, 94–101, 134, 163, 168, 170–172, 175, 179–181, 183, 184, 187–225, 263, 265, 267, 274, 276, 277, 293, 303, 305, 309, 311, 314, 315, 317, 318, 320, 322–324, 326–328
Rákóczi, György I, Prince of Transylvania 41, 51, 55, 56, 67, 72, 84–87, 91, 93, 94, 100, 177, 188, 233, 319, 327

Rákóczi, György II, Prince of Transylvania 51, 110, 128, 132–134, 138, 141, 188, 206, 207, 319, 324, 327
Rákóczi, László 235, 314
Rassow, P. 316
Rázsó, Gyula 12, 24, 324
Rebek, Laurencius 147
Redinger, Jacob 135, 136, 321
Reninger, Simon 111, 112
Resgen, Karl B. 207, 308
Réz, Pál 318
Richardson, Samuel 325
Richelieu, Armand Jean du Plessis 82, 83
Ridolfini, Domenico 60
Rigó, Péter 247
Rihmer, Zoltán 304
Rinck, Gottlieb 166
Ring, Éva 316
Robbins, Kieth 290
Robert, Sir Sutton 180
Roberts, Michael 205, 325
Roe, Sir Thomas 78, 110, 325
Roggendorf, Wilhelm 26
Rojkó, Mrs. 248
Romano, Sergio 290
Rómer, Flóris 228, 235, 237, 246, 325
Rónay, György 71, 325
Roosevelt, Theodore 8, 285, 314
Rorario, Girolammeo 34
Rossini, Gioacchino Antonio 296
Rottal, János 111, 112
Rózsa, György 156, 162, 325
Rozsnyai, Mrs. Borbála 260
Rubens, Peter Paul 159, 160, 286, 319
Rudolf I 62, 78
Rudolf II, Emperor, King of Hungary and Bohemia 277, 329
Rudolf, H. v. 325
Rupert, Prince 145
Russel, H. R. 325
Rúzsás, Lajos 12, 19, 304, 325
Rycaut, Paul 110

S. Lauter, Éva 58, 65, 325
Safirov, Pjotr Pavlovich 196
Sagredo, Giovanni 113, 121
Salamon, Ferenc 78, 80, 326

Samu, János, Mrs. 246
Sárkány, Antal 231
Savoy, Prince Eugene of 98, 109, 165, 168, 170, 172, 173, 182, 184, 198, 215, 223, 308
Sbrik, Heinrich von 113, 325
Scanderbeg, see Castriot, George
Schalk, F. 316
Schauroth, E. Ch. W. von 130, 325
Schick, Peter J. 325
Schmettau, Wolfgang von 191, 210
Schönborn, Johann Philipp von 110, 123, 127
Schram, Ferenc 228–230, 235, 237, 238, 240–242, 244–248, 253, 260, 261, 325
Seligmann, Kurt 228, 325
Sennyey, István Chancellor 70
Sennyey, István Senator 222
Serédy, Gáspár 278
Serini, Nicholas, see Zrínyi, Miklós
Serveto, Miguel 46
Seular, Lucas 233
Shaaber, A. Mathias 116, 325
Sieniawska, Helen Elisabeth, née Lubomirski 196, 197, 203, 204
Sigismund I, King of Poland 14, 19
Sigismund III, King of Poland 84
Sigismund, Polish King 22, 44
Sík, Sándor 57, 84, 325
Silvius, Aeneas Piccolomini 294
Simonyi, Ernő 305
Sinan, Vizier 63
Sinkovics, István 19, 36, 325
Sinor, Denis 302
Sinzendorf, Philipp Ludwig 215
Sinzendorf, Rudolf 113, 121, 144
Sipos, Mrs. János, née Orsolya Gombos 245
Sixtus V, Pope 62
Sloane, Sir Hans 132
Šmerda, Milan 67, 69, 74, 325
Smith, P. L. 110, 325
Sobrák, Mrs. István 238
Sörös, Pongrác 31, 33–35, 325
Sós, Mihály 237
Spanheim, Ezechiel von 191, 211, 216
Spielmann, József 227, 231, 238, 250, 257–261, 269, 326

341

Spinola, Mario 167, 206
Sprenger, James 261
St. John, Henry, see Bolingbroke, Viscount
Statileo, John 19, 23
Stepney, George 7, 172, 175, 180–183, 186,
 192, 193
Stoll, O. 228, 326
Stone, Lawrence 229, 233, 238, 326
Strada, Framianus 10
Strozzi, Peter 113, 130
Sugár, István 328
Suleiman I 10, 13, 14, 16, 18, 22–24, 26, 28–
 30, 33, 36–39, 43–45, 108, 122, 143, 157,
 294, 297, 308, 315
Sully, Maximilien de Béthune 82, 83
Sustermans, Justus 286
Swann, William 128, 129
Sylvester II, Pope 291
Sylvester, János 158
Sz. Jónás, Ilona 108, 326
Szabad, György 304, 326
Szabó, Attila 320
Szabó, Ferenc, S. J. 58, 71, 304, 321, 326
Szabó, T. Attila 232, 251, 310, 323, 326
Szádeczky, Lajos 326
Szakály, Ferenc 13, 15, 22, 30, 105, 304,
 326, 328
Száki, Ferenc 138
Szalay, László 14, 20–22, 78, 80, 86, 98, 191,
 198, 221, 224, 301, 326
Szállási, Árpád 259, 326
Szamosközy, István 156
Szánthay, Mrs. Mihály 243
Szántó, István 61, 62
Szántó, Konrád, OFM 326
Szántó, Sz. 64
Szapolyai, János, see János I, King of
 Hungary
Szász, Kathleen 321
Szász, Zoltán 320, 324
Széchenyi, György 170
Széchenyi, István 295
Széchenyi, Pál 318
Széchy, Károly 105, 111, 326
Széchy, Mária 236, 305
Szedrei, Ferenc 138
Szegedi Körös, Gáspár 231, 313, 329

Székely, András 309
Székely, Éva 247
Székely, György 315, 327
Szekfű, Gyula 9, 16, 24, 57, 67–69, 71, 73,
 77–81, 86, 177, 193, 314, 327
Szelepcsényi, György 128
Szelestei, N. László 131, 144, 145, 327
Szenczi Fekete, István 318
Szenczi, Miklós 304
Szenczy, György 152, 153
Szenczy, Zsuzsa 260
Szendrey, Ákos 228, 327
Szerémi, György 27, 327
Szigeti, József 305
Szilágyi, Sándor 56, 57, 81, 84, 85, 87, 90,
 92–94, 188, 235, 310, 319, 327
Szimonidesz, Lajos 190, 327
Szirmay, András 169
Szlatky, Mária 230, 232, 233, 235, 242, 244,
 251, 252, 327
Szobotka, Tibor 322
Szöllősy, Sára, Mrs. István Szabó 237
Szőnyi, György Endre 137, 327
Szörényi, László 106, 327
Sztanó, László 106, 327
Sztárai, Mihály 31, 327
Szűcs, Jenő 293, 328
Szydlowiecki, Krzysztof 19

Tacitus, Cornelius 121
Tagányi, Károly 228, 237, 261, 328
Takáts, László 230, 231, 266, 328
Takáts, Sándor 246, 328
Tamerlane (Tamberlain) 104, 135, 143
Tappe, E. D. 191, 328
Tardy, Lajos 34, 328
Tárkány-Szűcs, Ernő 230, 328
Tarnai, Andor 119, 306, 317, 328
Tarnóc, Márton 315
Tassi, Ferenc 152–154
Tasso, Torquato 305
Téglásy, Imre 327
Telegdi, Borbála 61
Teleki, Mihály 65, 236
Terts, István 300
Teutsch, Andreas 227, 267
Thaly, Kálmán 196, 240, 305, 328

Thököly, Imre 51, 96, 97, 161, 167, 245, 309, 317
Tholnai Szabó Kis, András 235
Thoroczkay, Gábor 304
Thúry, József 36, 328
Thurzó, Elek 17, 25, 31
Thurzó, György 67, 69
Thurzó, Szaniszló 69, 75
Tiepolo, Paolo 45
Tilly, Johann Tserclaes 82
Tinódi (Lantos), Sebestyén 39, 40, 328
Tofeus, Mihály 136
Tolnai, F. István 90, 328
Tomasetig, Cesare 288
Torcy, see Colbert, Jean-Baptiste
Törő, László 314
Török, Kata 247
Török, Pál 12, 15, 26, 30, 328
Tóth, István 90, 281, 328
Tóth, István György 328
Tóth, Katalin 58
Tóth, Réka 113, 320
Tournon, Henrik János 198, 201
Townshend, Charles, 2nd viscount 210
Trauttmannsdorf, Maximilian 79
Trencsényi-Waldapfel, Imre 21, 25, 328
Trevor-Roper, Hugh Redwald 228, 328
Trócsányi, Berta 191, 329
Turenne, Henri de la Tour d'Auvergne 130
Turnbull, G. H. 138, 329
Tusor, Péter 304, 329

Ulászló I 68
Urban VIII, Pope 78, 79, 82, 318
Urbich, Johann Christoph 214, 219, 221, 222

V. Windisch, Éva 304, 307
Vajk, see István the Saint
Vajkai, Aurél 238, 329
Valentinitsch, Helfried 228, 265, 314, 329
Van der Wee, Herman 118, 329
Van Swieten, (Gerard) Gerhard 227, 259, 268–270, 307, 308, 313, 316, 318
Vanyó, Tihamér 329
Váradi Sternberg, János 190, 329

Várady, Pál 18
Varga, Endre 230, 329
Varga, Ilona 260
Varga, Imre 72, 325, 329
Varga, J. János 309
Varga, János 329
Varga, Katalin 236
Várkonyi, Gábor 58, 69, 324, 329
Vass, Péter 304
Vay, Ádám 96
Veinstein, Gilles 24, 307
Vekerdi, László 232, 329
Venus 158, 159, 286
Vér, Judit 236
Veress, András, see Veress, Endre
Veress, Andrei, see Veress, Endre
Veress, Endre 64, 65, 329
Vida, Mrs. István, née Borbála Szabó 235, 241, 245
Vida, Tivadar 231, 329
Villars, Claude Louis Hector 100
Viller, P. B. 64
Virgil, Vergilius Publius Maro 281
Vita, Zsigmond 329
Vitéz, Zsuzsanna 236, 261
Vittnyédy, István 122, 138, 139
Vocelka, Karl 118, 329
Vogel, Sándor 318
Voigt, Vilmos 310
Vörösmarty, Mihály 295

Wagner, Georg 106, 155, 329
Waldeck, Georg Friedrich 139
Waldendorf, Wilderich von 124
Walesa, Lech 301
Wallenstein, Albrecht Eusebius Wenzel 79, 80, 84
Wandruszka, Adam 15, 307, 329
Warburg, Aby M. 137, 159, 160, 329
Warner 139
Warre, Richard 183
Wasenhofen 128, 129
Weber, Otto 225, 330
Wéber, Sámuel 330
Wellmann, Imre 273, 275, 316, 330
Wenzel, Johann, see Wratislaw, Johann Wenzel

Werbőczy, István 18, 19, 21, 22, 59, 306
Weres, Balázs 59
Wese, Johann 31
Wesselényi, Anna 235
Wesselényi, Ferenc 58, 76, 112–114, 121–124, 128, 138, 156, 157, 167, 233, 236
Weszprémi, István 243, 252, 270, 330
William III 321
William Frederick 130, 131
Williams, John 105, 135
Williamson, Thomas Woodrow 128, 129
Wilson, Sir Joseph 298
Winchilsea, Lord, Heneage Finch 94, 110, 112, 128, 129
Windisch, János 139
Windischgrätz, Baron 113
Wood, Alfred C. 118, 330
Woodroffe, Benjamin 328
Wotton, Sir Henry 325
Wrangel 130
Wratislaw, Johann Wenzel, Graf von 172, 182

Yeltsin, Boris 301

Zádor, Anna 319
Zajkás, Gábor 104
Zalai, Károly 330
Zalán, Péter 310
Zay, Anna 330
Zerdahelyi, Mrs. Mihály 261
Zeus 285
Zimányi, Vera 59, 66, 321, 330
Zombori, István 12, 27, 330
Zoványi, Jenő 246, 330
Zrényi, Nicolao, see Zrínyi, Miklós
Zrínyi, István 71
Zrínyi, Miklós 9–11, 42, 51, 58, 65, 68, 76, 78, 84, 103–148, 155–158, 160–163, 165–169, 278, 294, 305, 307–309, 311, 312, 315–318, 320, 322–324, 326, 327, 330
Zrínyi, Péter 122, 124, 128, 129
Zsámboki, János 40
Zsilinszky, Mihály 94, 190, 330

Index of Place Names

Adriatic 155
Albania 104
Algiers 10
Amsterdam 53, 116, 117, 136, 139–141, 314
Anatolia 64
Antwerpen 40
Aragon 12
Asia 146
Atlantic 116
Augsburg 9, 24, 25, 35, 47, 116, 287, 297
Austria 18, 26, 43, 76, 78, 104, 106, 120, 125, 129, 132, 134, 142, 166–168, 171, 173, 264, 281, 290, 291, 300, 318

Babócsa 130
Bács, county 313
Balaton, Lake and region 282, 319
(the) Balkans 15, 144, 165, 177–179, 286
Baranya, county 328
Barcelona 26, 172
Barkó (Brekov) 204, 215
Bártfa (Bardejov) 41
Basel 231, 258
Bátor 152
Békés, county 230, 271
Belgium 82
Belgrade 293
Bender 188, 190, 199, 201–203, 214
Bereg, county 318
Berlin 191, 198, 201, 205, 213, 221, 299, 301, 326
Berzence 130, 140
Bessarabia 188
Beszterce (Bistriţa; Bistritz) 46
Besztercebánya (Neosolium, Neusohl, Banská Bystrica) 90, 92, 273, 279, 282

Bihar, county 56, 59–61, 222
Bohemia 7, 12–15, 17, 29, 43, 52, 53, 67, 104, 109, 110, 113, 120, 125, 129, 132, 134, 137, 142, 145–148, 168, 176, 274, 288, 291, 292, 297, 326
Bosporus 108, 116
Brandenburg 130, 131
Brassó (Braşov; Kronstadt) 46, 49, 233
Bratislava, see Pozsony
British Isles 107, 139
Brussels 294, 308
Buda 7, 9, 12, 14, 21, 22, 24, 26, 31, 34–36, 39, 44, 59, 79, 80, 112, 113, 149–157, 161–163, 168, 169, 173, 294, 305, 316, 321–323
Buda Castle 152, 153, 155, 156
Budapest 287, 296, 303
Burgundy 308

Cambrai 24
Camerino 60
Candia 111, 145, 154
Carinthia 111, 129, 166, 265
Carlowitz, see Karlóca
Carpathian Basin 296, 328
(the) Carpathians 292
Castile 12
Caucasus 316
Central Europe 7, 8, 13, 19, 24, 52, 60, 108, 110, 116, 125, 132, 137, 142, 143, 145, 148, 176, 177, 180, 181, 185, 186, 193, 227, 273–275, 280, 283, 287, 290, 291, 293, 297–300, 309, 316, 323
Central Hungary 35
Cisdanubia 114
Cluj, see Kolozsvár
Cognac 16, 20, 22–24, 177

Comorn 114

Constantinople 26, 28, 64, 75, 78–80, 84,
85, 108–110, 116, 117, 122, 128, 139, 165–
167, 179, 180, 187, 190, 191, 195, 197,
201, 202, 286, 294, 328, 330

Cracovia 308

Cracow 117, 142

Craina 111

Crépy 36

Crete 108, 109, 111, 122

Croatia 10, 17, 36, 40, 51, 99, 103, 105, 108,
121, 123, 141, 142, 155, 165, 171, 173,
176, 229, 274, 294

Csabar (Čabar) 168

Csáktornya (Čakovec) 104, 121, 122, 127,
129, 139, 169

Csallóköz 281

Csesznek 240

Cumberland 146

Czakenthurn, see Csáktornya

Czech Estates 74

Czechoslovakia 300

Dacia 96

Dada 240

Dalmatia 114, 142, 145

Danube 14, 129, 141, 142, 151, 153, 167,
173, 281, 282, 286, 288, 292, 295, 316

Danube region 16, 274, 286

Danzig 139, 196, 210, 214

Debrecen 59, 222, 234, 257, 259, 260

Denmark 113, 128

Dés (Dej) 87, 245

Deutschland 311

Drava 14, 32, 129, 140, 141

Drégely 38

Dresden 196

Dubrovnik 301

Durham 178

East Berlin 301

East Central Europe 290

Eastern Europe 8, 193, 196, 201, 288, 292,
298, 299

Eger 18, 38, 151, 208, 297

Elblag 137

England 64, 65, 78, 98, 104, 105, 108, 109,

113, 117, 128, 136, 139, 142–147, 167, 172,
175–177, 180–183, 185, 187, 191, 192,
197–200, 202, 209, 212, 215, 216, 219,
221, 224, 225, 231, 257, 305, 312, 315,
320, 326, 329, 330

Enyed, see Nagyenyed 91

Eperjes (Prešov) 136, 138, 235, 250

Éradony 235

Érsekújvár (Nové Zámky) 72, 86, 113, 120,
121, 136, 141, 167, 218, 234, 235, 312

Eszék (Osijek) 23, 32, 112, 115, 142, 151,
154

Esztergom 26, 29, 51, 63, 91, 113, 115, 158,
166, 170, 173, 222, 232, 260, 262, 294

Eurasia 316

Europe 9–13, 16–18, 20, 21, 23–25, 27, 28,
32, 34–36, 38, 40–44, 46, 47, 58, 59, 62,
64–67, 73, 75–77, 79–84, 86, 89–100, 103–
105, 107, 109, 110, 112, 113, 116–122, 124,
125, 127, 129, 131, 136–139, 143, 144,
146–150, 154, 155, 157, 158, 160–163,
165, 166, 168, 170–173, 175–178, 181–
185, 187, 188, 190, 192–195, 197–200,
204–208, 211, 212, 215, 216, 225, 228,
231, 250, 273–276, 282, 285–302

Fehérhegy (Bila Hová; Whitehall) 67, 82,
182–184, 221

Fejér, county 240

Fertőd 296

Firenze (Florence) 116, 293, 303, 315

Fogaras (Făgăraş; Fogarasch) 51

Fontainebleau 177

Foxin (Focşani) 222

France 16, 20, 22, 28, 32, 36, 44, 67, 74, 82–
84, 105, 109, 139, 144, 147, 170, 177, 180,
185, 197, 198, 200, 201, 204, 208–210,
214, 215, 217, 223, 228, 231, 248, 317–
320, 330

Frankfurt an der Oder 198

Fünfkirchen 130

Gecse 277

Geneva 228

Gent 26

German Democratic Republic (GDR) 299

German Empire 79, 316

German Principalities 32, 83, 231
Germany 15, 105, 109, 129, 139, 144, 147,
    167, 168, 298, 312
Gernyszegh 260
Gertruydenberg 98, 187, 204, 205, 208–211,
    214–217, 220, 222
Giurgevo 63
Glasgow 290
Granada 16
Graz 11, 32, 85, 123, 128, 130
Great Britain 220
Győr 12, 63, 67, 70, 71, 115, 259
Gyula 246
Gyulafehérvár (Alba Iulia; Karlsburg) 31,
    46, 66, 87, 178, 181

Habsburg Empire 7, 55, 61, 66, 71, 73, 74,
    82, 83, 225, 307
Habsburg Monarchy 311, 316
Habsburg provinces 264
Hague, The 80, 98, 100, 177, 183, 191, 194,
    195, 198, 201, 204, 205, 208, 210, 212,
    215, 224, 323, 326
Hainburg 15
Halle 191, 198, 273
Hamburg 128
Harlem 140
Heidelberg 135
Heilsberg 181
Hernádnémeti 204
Höchstädt-Blenheim 181
Holland, see the Netherlands
Homonna (Humenné) 214
Huszt 97, 197–201

Ilyvó (Lwow, Lviv, Lemberg) 223
Ingolstadt 35
Ipoly river 316
Ireland 139
Iron Gate 143
Istanbul 22, 29, 33, 34, 306
Italy 16, 82, 168

Jassy 203, 204
Jászberény 203, 208, 209
Jenő (Ineu) 63

Kalocsa 7, 30
Kamenicze 203
Kanizsa 122, 141, 157
Karlóca 94, 170, 179, 305
Kassa (Kassau; Košsice) 37, 38, 68, 89, 152,
    202, 203, 214, 227, 234, 243, 271
Kecskemét 151, 314
Kensington 221
Késmárk (Kežmarok) 235
Kiel 290
Kiev 202
Királyfalva (Königsdorf) 282
Királyföld 243
Kisír 205, 208
Kiskunság 310
Köln 131
Kolozs county 235, 260
Kolozsvár (Cluj-Napoca) 46, 47, 61, 64, 89,
    229, 233, 234, 245, 246, 249, 254, 293, 326
Komárom (Komárno) 114, 115, 246, 261
Koppan, see Koppány
Koppány 130, 140
Körmöcbánya (Kremnica) 31
Köröm 218
Koron 27, 30
Kőrös (Nagykörös) 151, 237
Körös river 60
Kőszeg 27, 70, 71, 236, 306
Krajna 168
Kukizov 223, 224

La Goleta 31
Laibach 147
Légrád (Legrad) 111
Leipzig 126
Lepanto 40, 58, 62, 66
Leuven 65
Léva (Levice) 141
Levante 309
Leyden 257
Liège 42
Linz 27, 95, 113, 327, 330
Lippa 63
Lithuania 311
Lőcse (Levoča) 151, 233, 235
London 104, 112, 116, 118–120, 125, 126,
    128, 129, 132, 137–139, 146, 171, 180,

183, 191, 198, 201, 207, 211, 216, 221, 224, 286, 293, 294, 303, 307, 309, 315, 316, 326
Lower Austria 70, 265
Lower Hungary 151, 156
Lower Saxony 126
Lübeck 129
Lublin 196
Lund 31

Maastricht 300
Madaras 85
Madrid 113, 290
Mähren 114
Mainz 123, 127, 131
Malplaquet 201
Mapagelo Brokowisto 126
Máramaros (Marmaţici) county 243
Marien-Veder 191
Marosvásárhely (Tîrgu Mureş) 231
Marót 14
Medgyes (Mediaş) 255
(the) Mediterranean 23, 104, 108, 110, 144, 167, 295
Mediterranean Sea 15
Miskolc 97
Modena 31
Mohács 11–14, 16–18, 24, 32, 36, 42, 43, 46, 59, 60, 156, 160, 168, 177, 287, 288, 294, 306, 308, 315, 317, 318, 322, 325, 326
Moldavia 63, 85, 96, 98, 202, 203, 222, 272
Monostor 64
Moravia 15, 50, 53, 104, 109, 113, 114, 120, 125, 126, 129, 132, 134, 136–138, 141–143, 145, 147, 148, 166, 178, 274, 297
Morena 27
Moscow 114, 201, 203
Munkács (Mukačevo) 86, 191, 195–197, 199, 200, 214, 219, 223, 225, 237
Münster 287
Mura river 111, 124, 327
Muraköz 104
Murány (Muráň) 156, 313, 323

Nagyenyed (Aiud) 90, 91, 180, 258, 315
Nagykároly (Carei) 326
Nagymihály (Mihalovce) 214
Nagyszalonta (Salonta) 85

Nagyszombat (Tyrnavia; Trnava; Tirnau) 68, 81, 84, 87, 93, 172, 175, 182, 183, 234, 252, 259, 269, 277, 278, 296, 316
Nagyvárad, see Várad (Oradea)
Nándorfehérvár (Belgrád) 25, 33, 112, 292, 293
Nantes 297
Naples 9, 30
Németújvár (Güssing) 259
Nemti 151
(the) Netherlands 53, 98, 105, 113, 116, 128, 136, 139, 143, 144, 167, 171, 182, 183, 187, 191, 192, 197–200, 207, 209, 212, 216, 220, 228, 231, 267, 288, 291, 329
Neu-Serinwar, see Zrínyiújvár
Nieder-Hungarn 130
Nijmegen 94, 100
Nikolsburg 76
Nógrád 141, 248, 267
Nordrhein-Westfalen 308
North-East-Hungary 195
North-West Hungary 175, 193
Nürnberg 129, 156
Nyitra (Nitra) county 328

Oklád 272
Olmütz (Olomouc) 14, 18, 19, 21, 126
Ónod 209
Osnabrück 287
Österreich 311, 312, 319
Ostrowa 126
Ottoman Empire 7, 11 13, 15, 20, 23–25, 29, 34, 39, 42, 65, 66, 85, 104, 108, 110, 117, 121, 122, 143, 148, 165, 167, 176, 286–288, 292, 294
Oxford 107, 141, 142, 303

Padova 231
Pannonia 121
Pápa 232, 245
Papal State 105
Paris 21, 113, 116, 117, 130, 144, 147, 190, 194, 258, 294
Passau 38
Pavia 10, 16
Pécs 130, 139, 281, 297
Pera 117, 129
Persia 30, 64

Pest 150, 151, 260, 268, 316
Pest county 308
Pilis county 308
Poland 7, 14, 16, 18–22, 37, 38, 44, 46, 50,
    53, 60–62, 84–86, 96, 109, 113, 155, 167,
    176, 177, 180, 184, 185, 188, 191, 196,
    200, 217, 219, 221–223, 225, 228, 290–
    292, 301, 311
Poltava 188, 190, 194, 195, 197, 200
Poroszló 217, 247
Porte 20, 22, 29, 34, 38, 62, 78, 111, 117,
    122, 128, 312
Portugal 209, 212
Potsdam 297
Pozsony (Pressburg; Bratislava) 17, 18, 27,
    55, 67, 69, 71–73, 76, 79, 83, 86, 115, 122–
    124, 140, 166, 169, 234, 243, 246, 267,
    273, 278, 279, 281, 282, 303, 308
Pozsony county 276, 279
Prague 19, 67, 68, 126, 293
Prussia 76, 95, 170, 180, 191–193, 197–200,
    210, 212, 228, 318

Rába river 114, 173
Radkersburg 129
Ragusa 142
Rahó 196
Rastatt 96, 100, 187
Ratisbon 44
Regensburg 7, 35, 36, 65, 105, 113, 114, 116,
    126–134, 139, 140, 142–144
Rhine 7, 82, 105, 106, 109, 110, 113, 130,
    131, 146, 166, 294, 306
Romania 49, 217, 290
Romanian Voivodeships 177, 309
Rome 38, 46, 57, 62–64, 67, 73, 83, 86, 109,
    116, 290, 294, 307, 311, 315, 329
Rotterdam 53
Royal Hungary 39, 41, 112, 114, 121–123,
    138, 141
Rozgony 31
Russia 113, 155, 167, 180, 187, 188, 191,
    195, 196, 198–200, 202, 203, 209, 217,
    221, 329
Ryswick 170

Salánk (Salanki) 222
Salzburg 142, 147, 310

Sárospatak 31, 52, 138, 191, 330
Sarud 187, 217
Sárvár 156, 231
Save 295, 297
Savoy 198, 215, 220, 221, 225
Saxonia 22, 40
Schleissheim 162
Scotland 291
Seges, see Segesd
Segesd 116, 129, 130
Sellye 68
Selmecbánya (Banská Štavnica) 126, 234
Sempte (Šintova) 25
Silesia 104, 113, 120, 125, 126, 129, 134,
    137, 142, 143, 147, 274
Slavonia 36
Solt county 70, 308
Somogy county 70, 306
Sopron 51, 78, 103, 138, 162, 235, 246, 306
Spain 12, 23, 66, 74, 78, 82, 83, 112, 128,
    309
Strassburg 116, 127
Styria 29, 129, 264, 265
Suchova 202
Sweden 82, 83, 95, 100, 109, 113, 139, 143,
    167, 177, 180, 193, 196, 197, 199, 217,
    228, 231, 319, 320
Switzerland 139, 147, 177, 207
Szabolcs 240
Szamosújvár (Gherla) 64
Szatmár (Satu-Mare) 98, 99, 185, 187, 220,
    224, 235, 307, 311, 319
Szeben (Sibiu; Hermannstadt) 45, 46, 49
Szécsény 51, 95, 212, 326
Szeged 129, 151, 214, 231, 234, 237
Székesfehérvár 15, 113, 297
Szentgotthárd 166
Szentgyörgy (Jur pri Bratislave) 282
Szentmártonkáta 202
Szepes county 15, 31, 267, 330
Szerémség 14
Szerencs 219
Sziget 108, 130, 157
Szigetvár 10, 11, 103, 108, 124, 139, 155,
    157, 294, 327
Szögyén 156
Szolnok 38, 152–154
Szőny 80, 315

Targoviste 63
Temesvár (Timişoara) 31, 38, 64, 112, 297
Tirnau, see Nagyszombat
Tirol 310
Tisza 37, 151, 152
Tokaj 79, 152, 153, 282
Toledo 9, 30, 33
Torda (Turda; Thorenburg) 45–47, 49–53, 297
Transdanubia 44, 114, 232, 236
Transylvania 7, 15, 22, 23, 33, 36–38, 41, 43–46, 48–53, 55–67, 69, 70, 72, 73, 75–77, 79–82, 84–86, 89–101, 109–111, 121, 123, 132–134, 136, 138, 142, 143, 145–148, 151, 154–156, 161, 165–167, 169–173, 175–188, 190–193, 197–200, 202, 204, 207–214, 216–220, 222–225, 227, 229, 230, 232, 233, 236, 238, 247, 254, 257–261, 264, 266, 271, 272, 274, 277, 286, 291, 293, 294, 297, 299, 305, 309, 312, 314, 318, 320, 321, 323–330
Trent 71
Tunis 10, 31
Turkey 23, 205, 310
Turkish Empire 59
Tyrnavia, see Nagyszombat

Udvarhelyszék (Odorhei) 47, 90
Ugocsa county 260
Újvár, see Érsekújvár
Ukraine 108
Ungvár (Uzsgorod) 202
Upper Austria 265
Upper Hungary 37, 72, 76, 114, 167, 169, 229, 256, 264, 297
Urals 290
Utrecht 89, 95, 96, 99, 100, 185–187, 207, 225, 257, 330

Vág river 151
Várad (Oradea; Grosswardein) 25, 30–34, 36–38, 45, 46, 58–61, 69, 76, 91, 111, 167, 306, 316
Várna 68
Vásárhely (Hódmezővásárhely) 242
Vasvár 161, 166, 167

Vat 113
Vatican 306, 329
Venice 14, 16, 20–23, 26, 32, 36, 45, 80, 82, 83, 105, 111, 113, 114, 117, 120–122, 139, 144, 147, 166, 198, 310, 315
Verecke 198
Versailles 190, 201, 296, 298
Veszprém 30
Veszprém county 277
Vienna 7, 10, 11, 14, 17–19, 21, 23, 24, 26, 28, 29, 31, 33, 38, 40, 41, 49, 62, 64, 67, 71, 74–76, 79, 80, 82, 85, 86, 90, 112, 113, 115–117, 120–123, 125, 126, 128–130, 144, 152, 161, 166–169, 171, 172, 175, 176, 179, 181, 182, 184, 192–194, 201, 202, 209, 214, 218–224, 229, 234, 235, 245, 246, 265, 268, 269, 273, 303, 308, 310, 312, 313
Villach 34
Vízvár 124
Vorarlberg 310

Wallachia 49, 50, 63, 96, 98, 222
Warsaw 190, 193, 195, 198, 199, 201, 203
Western Europe 108, 122, 207, 274, 275, 288, 293, 294, 297
Westminster 80, 110, 177
Westphalia 23, 52, 89, 93–95, 100, 108, 109, 154, 165, 166, 170, 173, 175–177, 186, 206, 207, 212, 274, 287, 297, 308, 310, 324
Whitehall, see Fehérhegy
Wien, see Vienna
Wienerneustadt 9, 27, 29, 35
Wittenberg 35, 46, 124
Wolfenbüttel 313, 329

Zagreb 260
Zala county 245
Zemplén 169
Zenta (Senta) 165, 169, 173
Zigeth 116
Zrínyiújvár 111, 112, 122–124, 129, 142, 308, 321
Zsitvatorok 66, 78, 80, 321
Zvadka (Zavadka) 197

Typesetting by PP Editors, Ltd., Budapest
Printed in Hungary by Akaprint, Budapest

HUNGARY IN 1663–1664

The frontier of the country before 1526

The frontiers of the three parts
of Hungary after the division of the country

KINGDOM OF BOHEMIA

MORAVIA

THE KINGDOM OF HU...

THE HOLY ROMAN EMPIRE

THE HABSBURG EMPIRE

THE ARCHDUCHY OF AUSTRIA

BESZTERCE...
KÖRM...

SELMECBÁNYA

NAGYSZOMBAT

VIENNA

POZSONY

ÉRSEKÚJVÁR

GYŐR

ESZTERGOM

SOPRON

THE KINGDOM OF HUNGARY

BUDA

VASVÁR

GRAZ

SZENTGOTTHÁRD

The territory annexed to the O...

NAG...
KECSK...

CARINTHIA

STYRIA

ZRÍNYIÚJVÁR
CSÁKTORNYA

KANIZSA

Danube

FRIULI

PÉCS

CARNIOLA

SLAVONIA

SZIGETVÁR

ZAGREB

MOHÁCS

THE VENETIAN REPUBLIC

FIUME

BUCCARI

CROATIA

ESZÉK

THE OTTOMAN EMPIRE

The territo...

K...